Normativity and the Problem of Representation

This book tackles questions which revolve around the representational purport (or lack thereof) of evaluative and normative claims.

Claims about what we ought to do, what is best, what is justified, or simply what counts as a good reason for action—in other words, evaluative or normative claims—are familiar. But when we pause to ask what these claims mean and what we are doing when we use them, puzzles arise. Are there facts of the matter about what ought to be done, much like there are facts of the matter about mathematics or the natural world? If so, claims about what ought to be done are probably trying to represent the ought facts. Alternatively, perhaps there are no evaluative facts, in which case either evaluative claims are trying to represent facts which do not exist, or evaluative claims are not in the representation business to begin with. The latter option is intriguing, and it is the subject of much recent work in expressivism, pragmatism, and semantic relativism. But if ought claims are not representing anything as factual, why do we think such claims are true or false, and what are we doing when we disagree with one another about them? This book sheds light on this important area of philosophy.

This book was originally published as a special issue of the *Canadian Journal of Philosophy*.

Matthew S. Bedke is a Professor of Philosophy at the University of British Columbia, Canada. He specializes in meta-ethics and meta-normativity, and his work addresses topics such as the nature and psychology of normativity, debunking arguments in ethics, and motivational internalism.

Stefan Sciaraffa is an Associate Professor of Philosophy at McMaster University, Hamilton, Canada. He specializes in political philosophy, the philosophy of law, and meta-ethics. His work addresses the institutional structures, attitudes, behaviours, practical reasoning, and discourse that constitute relationships of political community.

Normativity and the Problem of Representation

Edited by
Matthew S. Bedke and Stefan Sciaraffa

LONDON AND NEW YORK

First published 2020
by Routledge
2 Park Square, Milton Park, Abingdon, Oxon, OX14 4RN

and by Routledge
52 Vanderbilt Avenue, New York, NY 10017

Routledge is an imprint of the Taylor & Francis Group, an informa business

First issued in paperback 2021

Chapters 1–3, 5–9, 11–13, 15 © 2020 Canadian Journal of Philosophy
Chapter 4 © 2018 Max Kölbel. Originally published as Open Access.
Chapter 10 © 2017 Matthew Simpson. Originally published as Open Access.
Chapter 14 © 2018 Anandi Hattiangadi. Originally published as Open Access.

With the exception of Chapters 4, 10 and 14, no part of this book may be reprinted or reproduced or utilised in any form or by any electronic, mechanical, or other means, now known or hereafter invented, including photocopying and recording, or in any information storage or retrieval system, without permission in writing from the publishers. For details on the rights for Chapters 4, 10 and 14, please see the chapters' Open Access footnotes.

Trademark notice: Product or corporate names may be trademarks or registered trademarks, and are used only for identification and explanation without intent to infringe.

British Library Cataloguing-in-Publication Data
A catalogue record for this book is available from the British Library

ISBN13: 978-0-367-35392-6 (hbk)
ISBN13: 978-1-03-209126-6 (pbk)

Typeset in Myriad Pro
by codeMantra

Publisher's Note
The publisher accepts responsibility for any inconsistencies that may have arisen during the conversion of this book from journal articles to book chapters, namely the inclusion of journal terminology.

Disclaimer
Every effort has been made to contact copyright holders for their permission to reprint material in this book. The publishers would be grateful to hear from any copyright holder who is not here acknowledged and will undertake to rectify any errors or omissions in future editions of this book.

Contents

Citation Information vii
Notes on Contributors x

1 Gripped by authority 1
  Terry Horgan and Mark Timmons

2 Expressivism, meaning, and all *that* 25
  Sebastian Köhler

3 Relativism and the expressivist bifurcation 45
  Javier González de Prado Salas

4 Perspectival representation and fallacies in metaethics 67
  Max Kölbel

5 Two nondescriptivist views of normative and evaluative statements 93
  Matthew Chrisman

6 The unity of moral attitudes: recipe semantics and credal exaptation 113
  Derek Shiller

7 Neo-pragmatism, morality, and the specification problem 135
  Joshua Gert

8 Building bridges with words: an inferential account of ethical univocity 156
  Mark Douglas Warren

9 Keeping track of what's right 177
  Laura Schroeter and François Schroeter

10	Solving the problem of creeping minimalism *Matthew Simpson*	198
11	The real and the quasi-real: problems of distinction *Jamie Dreier*	220
12	Representing ethical reality: a guide for worldly non-naturalists *William J. FitzPatrick*	236
13	A semantic challenge to non-realist cognitivism *David Copp*	257
14	Moral supervenience *Anandi Hattiangadi*	280
15	Why conceptual competence won't help the non-naturalist epistemologist *Preston J. Werner*	304
	Index	327

Citation Information

The chapters in this book were originally published in the *Canadian Journal of Philosophy*, volume 48, issues 3–4 (August 2018). When citing this material, please use the original page numbering for each article, as follows:

Chapter 1
Gripped by authority
Terry Horgan and Mark Timmons
Canadian Journal of Philosophy, volume 48, issues 3–4 (August 2018) pp. 313–336

Chapter 2
Expressivism, meaning, and all that
Sebastian Köhler
Canadian Journal of Philosophy, volume 48, issues 3–4 (August 2018) pp. 337–356

Chapter 3
Relativism and the expressivist bifurcation
Javier González de Prado Salas
Canadian Journal of Philosophy, volume 48, issues 3–4 (August 2018) pp. 357–378

Chapter 4
Perspectival representation and fallacies in metaethics
Max Kölbel
Canadian Journal of Philosophy, volume 48, issues 3–4 (August 2018) pp. 379–404

Chapter 5
Two nondescriptivist views of normative and evaluative statements
Matthew Chrisman
Canadian Journal of Philosophy, volume 48, issues 3–4 (August 2018) pp. 405–424

Chapter 6
The unity of moral attitudes: recipe semantics and credal exaptation
Derek Shiller

Chapter 7
Neo-pragmatism, morality, and the specification problem
Joshua Gert

Chapter 8
Building bridges with words: an inferential account of ethical univocity
Mark Douglas Warren

Chapter 9
Keeping track of what's right
Laura Schroeter and François Schroeter

Chapter 10
Solving the problem of creeping minimalism
Matthew Simpson

Chapter 11
The real and the quasi-real: problems of distinction
Jamie Dreier

Chapter 12
Representing ethical reality: a guide for worldly non-naturalists
William J. FitzPatrick

Chapter 13
A semantic challenge to non-realist cognitivism
David Copp

Chapter 14
Moral supervenience
Anandi Hattiangadi
Canadian Journal of Philosophy, volume 48, issues 3-4 (August 2018) pp. 592–615

Chapter 15
Why conceptual competence won't help the non-naturalist epistemologist
Preston J. Werner
Canadian Journal of Philosophy, volume 48, issues 3-4 (August 2018) pp. 616–637

For any permission-related enquiries please visit:
http://www.tandfonline.com/page/help/permissions

Notes on Contributors

Matthew Chrisman is a Professor in Philosophy at the University of Edinburgh, UK. His research is focused on ethical theory, political philosophy, the philosophy of language, and epistemology.

David Copp is a Distinguished Professor of Philosophy, emeritus, at the University of California, Davis, USA. He has published and lectured widely on topics in moral and political philosophy.

Jamie Dreier is Judy C. Lewent and Mark L. Shapiro Professor of Philosophy at Brown University, Providence, USA, where he has been teaching since 1988. He works on meta-ethics, meta-metaethics, and the theory of rational choice.

William J. FitzPatrick is the Gideon Webster Burbank Professor of Intellectual and Moral Philosophy at the University of Rochester, USA. His work focuses on meta-ethics, and he serves as an associate editor for *Ethics*.

Joshua Gert is Leslie and Naomi Legum Distinguished Professor of Philosophy and Department Chair at the College of William and Mary, USA. His primary research interests include neo-pragmatism, meta-ethics, and colour.

Javier González de Prado Salas is an Assistant Professor at UNED, Spain. His main area of research lies in the intersection of normativity theory, philosophy of language, and epistemology.

Anandi Hattiangadi is a Professor of Philosophy at Stockholm University, Sweden, and Pro Futura Scientia Fellow at the Swedish Collegium of Advanced Studies. She has research interests in epistemology, metaphysics, philosophy of language, philosophy of mind, and meta-ethics.

Terry Horgan is a Professor of Philosophy at the University of Arizona, Tuscon, USA. He publishes in various areas of philosophy, including philosophy of mind, epistemology, metaphysics, and meta-ethics.

Sebastian Köhler is an Assistant Professor of Philosophy at the Frankfurt School of Finance & Management, Germany. He works on meta-ethics, personal identity, and responsibility.

Max Kölbel is a Professor of Analytic Philosophy and Philosophy of Language at the University of Vienna, Austria. He works in the philosophy of language, epistemology, metaphysics, and meta-ethics.

François Schroeter is a Senior Lecturer in Philosophy at the University of Melbourne, Australia. His work focuses on meta-ethics and moral psychology.

Laura Schroeter is a Senior Lecturer at the University of Melbourne, Australia. Her research focuses primarily on concepts, reference, two-dimensional semantics, and meta-ethics.

Derek Shiller is a software engineer in New York City, USA. He writes on issues relating to consciousness, ethics, and normative attitudes.

Matthew Simpson is a Teaching Fellow in Philosophy at University College London, UK.

Mark Timmons is a Professor of Philosophy at the University of Arizona, Tuscon, USA. He publishes in the areas of meta-ethics and Kant's ethics.

Mark Douglas Warren is an Assistant Professor of Philosophy at Daemen College, USA. His research is in meta-ethics with a focus on inferentialism.

Preston J. Werner is a Lecturer in Philosophy in the Department of Philosophy and at the Centre for Moral and Political Philosophy at the Hebrew University of Jerusalem, Israel. He works mainly in meta-ethics and philosophy of mind.

Gripped by authority

Terry Horgan and Mark Timmons

ABSTRACT
Moral judgments are typically experienced as being *categorically authoritative* – i.e. as having a prescriptive force that (i) is motivationally gripping independently of both conventional norms and one's pre-existing desires, and (ii) justificationally trumps both conventional norms and one's pre-existing desires. We argue that this key feature is best accommodated by the meta-ethical position we call 'cognitivist expressivism', which construes moral judgments as sui generis psychological states whose distinctive phenomenological character includes categorical authoritativeness. Traditional versions of expressivism cannot easily accommodate the justificationally trumping aspect of categorical authoritativeness, because they construe moral judgments as fundamentally desire-like. Moral realism cannot easily accommodate the aspect of inherent motivational grip, because realism construes moral judgments as a species of factual belief.

Metaethical expressivism has its challenges, including those that concern embedding, negation, and making sense of contexts in which one makes a moral judgment but thinks, 'I might be wrong.' In some of our previous work we have had something to say in response to these challenges and in defense of our own non-reductive brand of expressivism, 'cognitivist expressivism'.[1] However, another serious challenge to irrealist versions of expressivism like ours concerns the *authority* of moral reasons and the moral judgments they ground.[2] We have begun to address this challenge, too, in some of our most recent work,[3] but there is more to do. In particular, there is the phenomenon that we like to refer to as the *experienced authority* of moral reasons and associated moral judgments. Some philosophers argue that the experienced authority of moral reasons provides pro tanto reason to favor either some robust form of moral realism or moral error theory (the latter type of view perhaps accompanied by a fictionalist story about moral judgment). The argument we have in mind is overtly phenomenological, and in this chapter we argue that careful attention to the phenomenology of the experienced authority of moral reasons makes trouble for competing metaethical views, but is fully compatible with our brand of non-reductive irrealist expressivism.[4]

Here is our game plan. Because we are concerned with a phenomenologically grounded challenge to expressivism, we begin in Section 1 with a specific scenario involving an agent's morally tinged decision and its psychological aftermath that will be put to use later in the paper when we respond to the challenge. Then, in Section 2, we turn to some of the work by Jean Hampton who provides a detailed phenomenological description of what it is like to experience the authority of reasons, a description nicely complemented by remarks from J. L. Mackie.[5] What we point out is that the experienced authority of moral reasons is Janus-faced: it has a motivational dimension and a normative justificatory dimension, which we use the work of Hampton and Mackie to highlight. Properly accommodating these dimensions of concrete moral experience, we claim, sets a challenge for metaethical theories, including our own brand of expressivism. With our concrete scenario, a phenomenological description of reasons experiences, and the challenge on the table, we turn in Section 3 to select metaethical theories (including versions of 'reductive' expressivism), arguing that each of them has trouble in the face of the phenomenological challenge. Either they do not acknowledge the phenomenology, or they do but must pay a high price for doing so. In Section 4, we articulate a *non-reductive* form of expressivism that we call 'cognitivist expressivism,' and then in Section 5, we return to our concrete scenario and explain how cognitivist expressivism can meet the challenge we set for metaethical theories, and do so without tears. Section 6 is our conclusion.

1. A concrete scenario: Clive's cowardice

The (fictional) scenario is from Ian McEwan's 1998 novel *Amsterdam*, in which the character Clive Linley, a Londoner and a composer of some notoriety, is struggling to complete a symphony, celebrating the new millennium, for an upcoming concert in Amsterdam. His aim is to compose a masterpiece that will become the crowning achievement of his already illustrious career. Frustrated with a succession of failed attempts to compose the finale, Linley decides to seek inspiration by spending time away from the city, hiking in the Lake District located in a mountainous region of northwest England. While hiking, Linley is suddenly struck with an idea for the finale, and stops to scribble notes, attempting to work out the melody. His concentration is interrupted when he hears the nearby voices of a man and a woman quarreling. Clive climbs to the top of a large rock where he can see the quarreling couple standing face to face in a small clearing about thirty yards away. As the confrontation continues, loud talking soon gives way to shouting. The man grabs the woman's elbow, violently pulling her in his direction. Witnessing all this, Clive, with pencil and notebook in hand, sighs and ponders what to do:

Was he really going to intervene? He imagined running down there. The point at which he reached them was when the possibilities would branch: the man might run off; the woman would be grateful .... Even this least probable of outcomes would destroy his fragile inspiration. The man was more likely to redirect his aggression at Clive while the woman looked on, helpless. Or gratified, for that was possible too; they might be closely bound, they might both turn on him for presuming to interfere .... What was clear now was the pressure of choice: he should either go down and protect the woman, if she needed protection, or he should creep away ... He could not remain here doing nothing. (93)

Clive closes his eyes and tries to concentrate on the elusive melody he is after. But at the sound of angry voices he takes another look. The woman breaks loose of the man's hold with a sharp downward jerk of her arm, and turns to run, but the man tackles her from behind. They fall to the ground, the woman trying to crawl away, the man holding onto her ankles. The man, having gotten up, is now dragging the woman, both hands on her left ankle; she screams. Clive now understands the seriousness of the unfolding event; he thinks for a moment that he absolutely *must* intervene, come to the woman's aid. But the significance, the importance of his work! Clive hurries away from the scene, trying hard to recall those few notes of the melody he was so desperately trying to work out. 'He was trying to call it back, but his concentration was being broken by another voice, the insistent, interior voice of self-justification:... if he had approached the couple, a pivotal moment in his career would have been destroyed' (95). Back from his hike, Clive decides to leave immediately for London, certain that he can work out the entire finale on the train. As he excitedly waits for his taxi ride to the train station, he reflects: 'He wanted the anonymity of the city again, and the confinement of his studio, and – he had been thinking about this scrupulously – surely it was excitement that made him feel this way, not shame' (96).

For our purposes here, let us construe this scenario – by stipulation – as conforming to the following interpretation, which is suggested implicitly by McEwan's own characterization. Clive experiences a specific consideration – viz., that the woman is being assaulted and needs help – as an authoritative moral reason to intervene, despite deciding not to do so. The envisioned possibility of the man redirecting his aggression toward Clive, perhaps with the woman joining in, enters his mind primarily as a potential excuse for not intervening whose flimsiness he already appreciates (he would be in no serious danger of significant bodily harm) – and which in any case, he realizes, is clearly outweighed by a compelling moral reason once he sees the woman try to escape and the man then dragging her by the ankle. And the subsequent feeling that keeps him scrupulously thinking about what happened, rather than being able to concentrate on working out the finale of his symphony, really is shame rather than excitement.

We offer this story as a fictional, but reasonably concrete, case involving what we go on to characterize as someone who is gripped by the experienced authority of moral reasons.[6] We shall return to this story in Section 5 when we explain how our irrealist version of metaethical expressivism is able to accommodate the experience of the normative authority of moral reasons as featured in our story. In the meantime, our next order of business is to dwell on the phenomenology of moral-reasons experiences, guided primarily by the pertinent phenomenological observations we find in some of Jean Hampton's work.[7]

2. The authority of moral reasons

We turn now to a characterization, in general terms, of the phenomenology of moral-reasons experience, leaning heavily on a chapter from Jean Hampton's posthumously published book, *The Authority of Reason*, from which we quote liberally. Her chapter is particularly nice for our purposes, because in addition to offering a fairly detailed characterization of the phenomenology in question, she also explains why she thinks only a robust form of non-naturalist moral realism is consistent with this phenomenology. We also quote from Mackie, whose phenomenological observations complement Hampton's. Our aim, then, in consulting these authors is to assemble a collection of phenomenological observations about moral-reasons experience that we think any plausible metaethical theory ought to 'accommodate,' in a sense to be explained in the following section.

In the third chapter of her book, entitled 'Reason's Authority,' Hampton's stated goal is to argue that there is something about ethics 'that appears to make it scientifically problematic,' viz., 'a certain thesis held by moral objectivists about moral norms and the reasons they generate that fails to pass scientific muster' (83). Her argument is phenomenological, focusing on introspectively salient aspects of moral experience (Note well: that such aspects are available to introspection will be crucial when we eventually address the phenomenological challenge, appealing to our version of expressivism). Hampton's argument proceeds in two stages. In the first stage she offers what she says is a 'minimalist and metaphysically neutral' initial characterization of how the normativity of moral reasons is experienced (83). In the second stage, she describes two metaphysically different ways of 'embellishing' the initial characterization (83), and she argues that only the second way – a version of non-naturalist moral realism – comports with the phenomenology of moral-reasons experience. In this section we briefly summarize her argument, in a way that closely follows her own text.

1.1. The first stage

Hampton begins by saying that the notion of authority in question is not decisiveness, because the reasons in support of a particular act can carry authority even if they are outweighed by reasons in support of some other act; and that the pertinent notion is not strength of motivational commitment either, because the reasons in support of a particular act can be experienced as stronger, qua reasons, than considerations upon which one chooses to act. Rather, she says,

> a theory of the authority of norms tries to explain *what it means* for a norm to be 'applicable' to us. The word 'applicable' is a poor one, because norms don't merely 'apply' to us, they *direct* us. Indeed, we use all sorts of words to elaborate on this applicability: besides 'authority,' we speak of a norm's 'prescriptivity' or its 'obligatory force' over us, its 'compelling nature' or its 'pull,' its status as an 'order' or a 'command' (and not a mere 'suggestion').... That is, normative authority presupposes ... that it is correct to say that it specifies a reason for x-ing for an agent. (88)

Here, she does not say explicitly what she takes a 'norm' to be, and for present purposes this does not much matter.[8] The crucial thing presently, we take it, is this: to *experience* a norm 'as specifying a reason for x-ing for an agent,' where consideration C is the specified reason, is to experientially *regard* consideration C as a reason for x-ing for an agent (Presumably, the agent in question might or might not be oneself. Often enough, one experiences a moral reason as universalizable: a reason for x-ing for *anyone* who might be in the pertinent circumstantial situation).

She points out that 'this compelling quality of reasons is not ... the same as the feeling of liking or approving the directive of a reason. It is easy to give examples of people who know they have a reason to x, and who not only do not like the action that the reason directs, but even despise it' (89).

She also points out that not all reasons have the same kind of directive force. 'In particular, some reasons command us, and thereby give us mandates, and others direct us in ways that indicate permissions, rather than commands' (90). Nonetheless, 'what permissive and mandatory reasons have in common, such that they are all *reasons*, is their authority – the sense in which they have for us a "compelling rightness"' (91).

She takes all this to be phenomenological description, a matter of isolating 'the distinctive "feel" of reasons' (93). She also takes it to be so far metaphysically neutral; she denies that she has meant 'to suggest that this compelling quality must be understood as somehow "in the world," and thus a part of our reality' (93). But next comes stage 2 of her argument, in which she articulates and compares two competing theses about normative authority – specifically, about moral normative authority – each of which she considers metaphysical.

1.2. *The second stage*

The first thesis she considers might naturally be regarded as compatible with a broadly naturalistic metaphysical worldview, and as not being 'scientifically problematic.' As a prelude to introducing it, she begins with the following observations:

> Consider a norm in the sport of dressage, requiring owners of horses performing dressage tests in a competition to present the horse in the show ring with its mane braded. It purports to give those who recognize it a reason to act in a certain way .... [T]o explain the authority of this or any similar norm, such as rule in baseball, or a norm of etiquette, or a norm about taste in foods, we would tell a story locating

the social forces that generated the norm, and the psychological responses to those forces by certain people that give these norms their power. In this view, the norm is the (mere) invention of particular human beings by virtue of their interests, and the sense such people have that a norm authoritatively applies to them ... is entirely a matter of social and psychological contingencies .... This sort of norm, which I will call culture-dependent, is ubiquitous, and includes norms of etiquette, rules of various sports, and ideals of physical beauty. (94)

She now introduces the first thesis as follows, by way of contrast with norms that are obviously and unproblematically culture-dependent:

> [S]ome theorists believe that *all* norms, including all moral norms, are culture-dependent. Those who believe this explain the authority of all norms as (what I will call) a 'psycho-social' phenomenon. (94)

(She is here using the expression 'culture-dependent' broadly enough to encompass psychological factors that might be innate or otherwise deeply ingrained in human nature, as well as factors resulting from socialization.)

After explaining why she takes Gibbard's expressivism, Mackie's error theory, and Boyd-style naturalist realism to be versions of the psycho-social thesis, she summarizes as follows what she takes to be the common thread that runs through the various respective versions of the psycho-social metaphysical approach:

> All these versions of the psycho-social thesis accept the same basic strategy for explaining the authority of reasons – that authority is understood to be merely in the head (explicated as a feeling, or a cognitive state, or a theoretical belief), and its origins are explicable by virtue of human psychology, human biology, and/or human sociology. (96)

She turns next to a second metaphysical 'elaboration' of the features of moral-authority experience that she described in the first stage of her argument – an alternative elaboration that she takes to be incompatible with the psycho-social thesis. She calls it the 'objectivist' thesis, which she characterizes as follows (we insert numbered brackets into this quoted passage, and ones following it, in order to flag the various key phenomenological observations).

> Those who are normative objectivists maintain that some norms (but not all norms – for example, not norms of dressage) are examples of what I will call culture-independent or objective norms. The authority of these norms is supposed to be [1] independent of social and psychological contingencies .... [O]bjectivists argue that such (independent) authority is the reason society has (or ought to have) such norms as part of its culture, and they insist that no matter the facts of our society or our psychology, we ought to recognize, accept, and obey them. (96)

The notion of objectivist authority, she says, figures in the objectivist view in a number of ways:

> First, and most importantly, it appears in the theory's explanation of how it is that moral norms 'apply' to us .... [T]hese reasons, no matter what we may think or how we have been raised, have authority over us. [2] Such authority is 'outside' the agent, and that to which she is responding when she says that she understands that she ought to act from them .... [T]he authority is not the invention of the

agent, nor of human communities, but something to which agents and human communities respond.

Second, the moral objectivist assumes that the notion of authority is one that human beings can 'see' or (in some way) discover .... [W]e usually 'feel' or 'comprehend' its (objective) authority, which means [3] experiencing a sense of its pull, such that we take it to be something that we are in certain circumstances bound to act upon.

Third, the moral objectivist claims that having felt this authority, it is – at least sometimes – an authority for the sake of which we can act, so that it is [4] motivationally efficacious. (98–99)

She further elaborates the aspect of 'outsideness' as involving a distinctive kind of necessity, about which she says:

Let us say that moral reasons generated by objectively authoritative moral norms are necessary in the sense that [5] their *governance* over us is inescapable. And by 'inescapable' here I mean that these reasons 'apply' to us 'no matter what.' According to this way of thinking about objective authority, no matter what we may do or think, we are directed by these reasons – either in the form of permissions or in the form of mandates. And the governance is inescapable or necessary because there is no way that we can throw it off, or change it by our actions, beliefs, or social systems .... So understood, normative necessity is still a metaphysical concept because it is supposed to hold regardless of whether or not we know about it or are aware of it. It is just not the metaphysical concept that is usually referred to by the term 'necessity.' (105–106)

And she urges that the 'outsideness' of moral normative authority, with its aspect of necessity or inescapability, is central to the actual phenomenology of moral-reasons experience:

This way of thinking about authority is, I think, closest to the way that the authority of reasons *feels* to us – that is, it approximates what the experience of 'having a reason' is like for those who understand and act from reasons .... [R]easons feel like orders – strong in the case of mandates, weak in the case of permissions, but directives nonetheless, with an [6] inescapable rightness about them. (106)

Although she does not say so explicitly, her overall discussion of moral authority clearly implicates – especially in light of the just-quoted passage – that the objectivist thesis fits people's actual moral-authority phenomenology better than does the psycho-social thesis.

This feeling that reasons have an inescapable rightness about them and, moreover, one that is irreducible, is captured nicely by Mackie's well-known characterization. Mackie famously observed that were it true that there are instantiated objective values they would be experienced as [6] having 'to-be-pursuedness somehow built into them.' He adds that 'if there were objective principles of right and wrong any wrong (possible) course of action would have not-to-be-doneness somehow built into it' (1977, 40). This sense of to-be-pursuedness and not-to-be-doneness as reflected in one's moral experiences captures both the categorical authoritativeness and independence of those reasons that are experienced as mandating the actions they favor, and it also reflects [7] the seeming irreducibility of the pertinent categorical authoritativeness of such reasons.[9]

Let us now itemize, for purposes of subsequent citation, various interconnected features that Hampton (with some help from Mackie) has identified as elements of the phenomenology of being gripped by the authority of moral reasons. For simplicity, we restrict attention to reasons that one experiences as morally *requiring* a certain action, and as requiring such an action *by oneself*. (Her discussion can be generalized to cover reasons that one experiences as favoring a certain action without requiring it, and to cover reasons that one experiences as pertaining to other persons – or to anyone who might find oneself in certain circumstances.) And we focus, as does Hampton, upon experiences of *non-normative* considerations as being reasons for a certain kind of action – non-normative considerations in virtue of which such an action is experienced as being inescapably, authoritatively required. Such experiences, we suggested at the outset of this paper, have a Janus-faced character, involving a blend of the normative and the motivational. The key phenomenological elements of such fittingness-experience are these[10]:

- *Pull*: Such reasons are experienced as pulling one toward a certain specific moral judgment and corresponding action (perhaps a refraining). [3]
- *Independence*: The pull of such reasons is experienced as being independent of pre-existing desires or human conventions. [1]
- *External source*: The source of the independence is thus experienced as 'outside' oneself. [2]
- *Inescapable necessity*: Such reasons are experienced as inescapable in the sense that they necessarily apply to one; their conditions of application are not contingent. [4]
- *Grip*: Such reasons, when not experienced as being outweighed by other reasons of the same kind that pull toward some incompatible moral judgment and corresponding action, normally exert an involuntary phenomenological grip upon oneself that is experienced as binding – where becoming thus experientially bound toward performing the particular action constitutes a moral judgment that one ought to perform that action, an action that is experienced as something to-be-done (or in the case of wrong actions, not-to-be-done). [7]
- *Compelling rightness*: In cases where one is gripped by a reason for performing a certain action, thereby judging that one ought to perform it, one experiences the envisioned action as compellingly demanded, something one *must* judge and something one feels *ordered* to do. [6]
- *Motivation*: Experiencing the authority of moral reasons is *inherently motivational*; one is typically motivated to judge and act accordingly (although

their motivational strength can be outweighed by other psychological states such as pre-existing desires). [5]

This collection of phenomenological observations about experiencing moral reasons, then, is supposed to capture the experienced authority of moral reasons (If the moral authority of a reason is experienced as a pull without (yet) being experienced as binding, then it is a pull toward both making a moral judgment and performing a corresponding action. But if and when the authority gets experienced as binding – i.e. as exerting a grip upon oneself – this experience constitutes *making* the moral judgment (for that reason).) Thus, as noted at the outset, the experienced authority of a moral reason for some doing or refraining is Janus-faced: it has both normative elements and motivational elements that combine to give the experience the rich phenomenological character it has. So, although *Motivation* has mainly to do with the motivational dimension of the experienced authority of moral reasons, the remaining features either have to do with the normative dimension (*Independence, External source, Inescapable necessity*), or they feature a fusion of the motivational and the normative (*Pull, Grip, Compelling Rightness*). With these phenomenological observations in view, we turn next to a particular challenge facing any metaethical theory, based on these observations.

3. The challenge: a looming trilemma

The challenge associated with the rich phenomenal character of the experienced authority of moral reasons, as we have described such experience, can be explained as figuring in a seeming trilemma for metaethical views that involves three metaethical desiderata. *First*, it counts in favor of a metaethical theory that it be able to acknowledge the phenomenology of moral experience, including experiencing the authority of moral reasons as they bear on an individual's choice and action. *Second*, it counts in favor of a metaethical view is that it avoids problematic metaphysical and associated epistemological commitments. *Third*, in light of the fact that moral experience, thought, and discourse seem humanly unavoidable, it counts in favor of a metaethical view that its commitments are not in tension with preserving morality. So, ideally, one wants a metaethical theory that meets these desiderata:

Acknowledgement: acknowledges the Janus-faced phenomenology of moral-reasons experience,

Metaphysics: avoids troublesome metaphysical views, and

Preservation: is not in tension with the preservation of the practices of morality.[11]

The clearest way to satisfy the first and third desiderata simultaneously – and arguably the only adequate way – is to *accommodate* the phenomenology, in this sense: (i) acknowledge its various aspects as summarized at the close of

Section 2 above, and (ii) treat those features as not ubiquitously misrepresenting the world – rather than treating them as ubiquitously non-veridical.

The looming trilemma is that these three desiderata seem hard to satisfy simultaneously. And insofar as a metaethical view fails to satisfy one or another desideratum it loses what David Enoch (2011, 14) aptly refers to as 'plausibility points.' We now want to press this looming trilemma by briefly considering a handful of familiar metaethical views, namely: two types of reductive view, reductive ethical naturalism and reductive expressivism, and two types of non-reductive view, ethical non-naturalism and moral error theory. We refer to the trilemma as 'looming' because we acknowledge that creative advocates of these views might think that they can find ways to avoid it. Nevertheless, the challenge to do so remains. We begin with reductive versions of ethical naturalism and ethical expressivism.

According to reductive ethical naturalism – a version of moral realism – there are metaphysically robust moral properties (including relations) that are a species of some type of metaphysically robust, objective (i.e. 'stance-independent') natural properties and facts.[12] This sort of view is partly motivated by wanting to avoid troublesome metaphysical commitments, and seems compatible with preserving morality. However, from what we can tell, this view succumbs to the first horn of the looming trilemma: it ultimately fails to adequately accommodate both aspects of the Janus-faced moral phenomenology we described in the previous section. In her book, Jean Hampton remarks in a number of places that all such versions of ethical naturalism 'leave out the guts of morality' (1998, 47, 120 n.9), by which she means the kind of inescapable necessity that she thinks is an aspect of much moral experience, including experiencing the authority of moral reasons. The problem is that such views end up not acknowledging that moral reasons (and the obligations they ground) have the kind of inescapable necessity that people experience them as having. That is, Hampton claims (and we agree) that versions of ethical naturalism end up treating the authority of moral reasons as a contingent matter, and so fail to acknowledge the phenomenological character of moral-reasons experiences. (See the quotation in Section 2 about Boyd-style ethical naturalism.) Moreover, such views typically embrace some form of motivational externalism, thus denying the phenomenological aspect of reasons-experiences that seems inherently motivational. The result is that reductive ethical naturalism has trouble with *Acknowledgement*, at least with respect to the phenomenology of the authority of moral reasons.

Another type of reductive view includes certain versions of expressivism (including old-time non-cognitivism). Both advocates and opponents of expressivism often characterize moral experiences and moral judgments by reference to states of mind which quite clearly do not purport to represent metaphysically robust, instantiated, properties or relations or metaphysically robust facts. Sometimes the reference to such states of mind is put forth merely as an instructive analogy; sometimes the suggestion is that although prototypical such states of mind are not moral experiences, nevertheless the pertinent mental category includes moral experiences or moral judgments as a sub-species; and sometimes it is not made fully clear whether the first or the second construal is being suggested. At one time or another, expressivists have compared moral experiences and moral judgments to prototypical non-moral mental states of the following kinds, among others: desires, commands, universalized commands, attitudes of approval or disapproval, states of norm-acceptance, states of planning what to do. (Such comparisons are *strongly* reductive insofar as they treat moral experiences and moral judgments as a species of one or another of these kinds of mental state; and they are least *weakly* reductive insofar as they treat moral experiences as *not pertinently different* from prototypical instances of some such mental state.[13]) Like reductive ethical naturalism, expressivist views advertise that they satisfy *Metaphysics* and *Preservation*.

However, when it comes to meeting *Acknowledgement*, no such comparison – and no combination of such comparisons – seems theoretically satisfying. The problem is this: for each such comparison-category, prototypical instances of that category are mental states that simply do not seem to have the phenomenological aspect of inescapable authoritativeness. Ordinary desires don't seem to have it, because categorical authoritativeness is experienced as being independent of one's pre-existing desires. The mental states expressible as ordinary commands don't seem to have it, because their phenomenology is not as-of a state of mind expressible by uttering a command, but rather (a) as-of being 'commanded' oneself, and (b) as of this command's having 'compelling rightness.' Ordinary states of norm-acceptance or action-planning don't seem to have it, because typically they are experienced either as straightforwardly voluntary (as in voluntarily playing a game and thereby subjecting oneself to its rules), or at any rate as states one is in by virtue of one's contingent social circumstances (as in the case of the fictional character Ivan Denisovich [Solzhenitsyn 1962], who accepts the norms of bricklaying upon having been sentenced, in Stalin's post-war Soviet Union, to 25 years of bricklaying in Siberia).[14]

So, reductive versions of both ethical naturalism and ethical expressivism arguably fail to acknowledge one or both aspects of the Janus-faced experience of being gripped by the authority of moral reasons.

We turn now (and again, very briefly) to non-reductive metaethical views we have identified: ethical non-naturalism and error theory. Both views take seriously the irreducible character of concrete moral experience, and so they eschew any attempt to reduce putative moral properties and facts to properties and facts of some other kind, whether natural or supernatural. The difference, of course, is that the non-naturalists (of the sort we are concerned with)[15] attempt to fully accommodate the phenomenology of the authority of reasons, whereas error theorists do not. Let us take a closer look at both types of theory.

Consider, first, non-naturalism. In light of the phenomenological character of moral-reasons experience, a non-naturalist like Hampton will hold that there are metaphysically robust properties and facts that are inherently normative – they provide categorically authoritative normative reasons for choice and action that do not depend on one's desires, valuings, or intentions, and do not depend on human conventions – which nevertheless are part of the fabric of the world, to which we have access. Of course, the non-naturalist who wants to fully accommodate moral-authority phenomenology must also claim that the non-normative properties and facts that possess categorically authoritative normativity also are intrinsically motivating; otherwise she won't fully accommodate the motivational dimension of such experiences. This makes the view look doubly queer, which is certainly a theoretical cost for the theory (and explains why Mackie's queerness objection combines the normative with the motivational dimensions of moral experience). In short, although non-naturalist realism thoroughly accommodates the phenomenology of moral-reasons experience, thereby simultaneously satisfying both *Acknowledge* and *Preservation*, it fares quite badly with respect to *Metaphysics*.

According to moral error theory, the phenomenology of ordinary moral experience purports to represent as instantiated the sorts of metaphysically robust properties and facts posited by non-naturalism; likewise for ordinary moral thought and moral discourse. In view of this presumed ontological commitment, moral error theorists are ontological skeptics, charging ordinary moral experience, moral thought, and moral discourse with systematic error. Focusing just on moral-authority phenomenology, the error theory characterizes itself as not accommodating (in the sense stipulated above) this phenomenology. This poses a serious *prima facie* problem with respect to satisfying *Preservation*. Of course, an error theorist might nevertheless aim to preserve morality – as did Mackie, and as do some contemporary error theorists like Jonas Olson (2014). But one theoretical cost for such a view is its apparent 'bad faith' problem – viz., (on one hand) recommending that people continue to use moral concepts, to make moral judgments, and to take moral experience seriously, all the while (on the other hand) believing that it is all deeply error ridden. In other words, the tension referred to in *Preservation* remains, because error theory only *acknowledges* the phenomenology of moral-reasons experience but explicitly disavows *accommodating* this phenomenology.

The upshot of the preceding discussion is that the looming trilemma arising in light of the phenomenology of moral authority causes serious problems for each of the standard metaethical positions. Reductive moral realism apparently fails to satisfy the desideratum *Acknowledgement*, as do standard, reductive, versions of expressivism. Nonreductive moral realism apparently fails to satisfy the desideratum *Metaphysics*. And moral error theory apparently fails to satisfy the desideratum *Preservation*.

4. The neutrality thesis

In our view, each of the positions in the familiar menu of theoretical options in metaethics really does fail to satisfy at least one of those three desiderata. The way forward, we maintain, is to embrace a non-standard version of expressivism – a *non-reductive* version that not only acknowledges the phenomenology of moral authority but also (unlike error theory) claims to accommodate it too.

The possibility of such a position in the space of theoretical options in metaethics has thus far been largely obscured from view because of a widespread presupposition among those who have acknowledged the phenomenology of moral authority, viz., non-reductive moral realists like Hampton and error theorists like Mackie and Olson. Both non-naturalism and error theory take seriously the irreducible character of concrete moral experience, and so they eschew any attempt to reduce putative moral properties and facts to properties and facts of some other kind, whether natural or supernatural. (The difference, of course, is that the non-naturalists [of the sort we are concerned with] attempt to fully accommodate the phenomenology of the authority of reasons, whereas error theorists do not.) The presupposition can be formulated this way, as an entailment claim:

(1) *Experiencing the authority of moral reasons*: Ordinary moral experiences of moral reasons have an inherent aspect of authoritative compelling rightness.

entails:

(2) *Ontological purport*: This aspect of authoritative compelling rightness of moral reasons purports to represent a metaphysically robust, objective, relation of *being a reason for* as instantiated in the world.

Two features of the allegedly entailed proposition (2) are crucially important. First (as emphasized earlier), the modifier 'metaphysically robust' is intended to signal that the notion of 'a relation instantiated in the world' is to be understood *non-minimalistically*, as carrying ontological commitment to such a putative relation.[16] Second, the label 'objective' is intended to entail that this putative relation is not a psychological one – and in particular, is not the in-the-world psychological relation *being regarded as a reason*, which obtains between a non-normative consideration and an experiencing agent.

Both non-naturalists and error theorists accept this (purported) entailment by simply not noticing that (1) and (2) make distinct claims, and by thus supposing that one can determine on the basis of introspection alone that (2) is true. We ourselves maintain, however, that (2) is not something one can reliably determine to be true on the sole basis of introspection; nor is (2) a claim that provides the only viable potential explanation of those elements of the phenomenology of being gripped by moral reasons that themselves are reliably discernable by direct introspection. So in our view, the inference from (1) to (2) is fallacious; we call it *the non-naturalist fallacy* (see also Horgan and Timmons forthcoming).

By calling it a fallacy we are not claiming that the pertinent phenomenology does not have ontological purport. This is because we are not claiming that one can determine whether or not (2) is true on the sole basis of introspection. That one cannot tell either way is what we are calling our *neutrality* thesis regarding introspection directed toward one's experiencing the authority of moral reasons.[17]

Nor will we be claiming that our expressivist treatment qualifies, abductively via 'inference to the best explanation,' as the clearly best hypothesis about the nature of the inescapable-authoritativeness phenomenology in experiencing moral reasons. We grant, therefore, that non-naturalist moral realism and error theory provide alternative prima facie viable, potential explanations of the pertinent phenomenology. Insofar as one restricts oneself to phenomenological considerations – either direct deliverances of introspection, or abductive considerations concerning the potential explanation of introspective phenomenological data – we contend only that the expressivist approach we will describe below constitutes *one* prima facie viable way to theoretically embrace and explain the categorical-authoritativeness phenomenology that figures in moral deliberation, alongside of the non-naturalist way (and the error-theoretic way). This will suffice to undermine the move from (1) to (2) on the basis of an appeal to phenomenology, leaving our version of expressivism in the running as a viable option for coming to terms with the phenomenology in question. Wider, largely non-phenomenological, considerations – including how the competing theories fare with respect to the three desiderata *Acknowledgement*, *Metaphysics*, and *Preservation* – thereafter can be brought to bear in doing comparative cost-benefit evaluation of non-naturalist moral realism, error theory, and our non-reductive version of expressivism.[18]

We emphasize that we are not presupposing the neutrality thesis at the outset of the discussion below. Rather – and granting as we do, that non-naturalism (and moral error theory) can also acknowledge the pertinent phenomenology – the case for neutrality will emerge as the discussion unfolds.

5. Nonreductive expressivism

Expressivists focus their metaethical theorizing, first and foremost, on the pertinent *states of mind* associated with matters ethical: moral experiences and moral judgments. Moral assertions are then treated as *expressing* moral judgments but not as *describing them*. A key tenet of any version of expressivism is that moral experiences and moral judgments do not purport to attribute metaphysically robust, instantiated, moral properties or relations, or to describe metaphysically robust moral facts. (This does not preclude the use of property-talk or relation-talk or fact-talk or truth-talk in moral discourse, but it does construe such talk as operating minimalistically rather than carrying ontological purport.)

Typically when one forms a moral judgment, one experiences certain considerations as *reasons* for that judgment – and indeed, as categorically authoritative reasons. Such reasons-experiences should be construed by expressivists in the same kind of way that moral judgments themselves are construed – viz., as states of mind that do not purport to attribute metaphysically robust relations (say, *being fitting in light of*, *being a reason for*, or *being required by*, or the like). This point was emphasized by Charles Stevenson (1961), and we ourselves heartily concur.

So the task we face has three intertwined aspects. First is the need to articulate, at least in broad outline, a version of expressivism that differs from standard versions in being clearly non-reductive. Second is the need to provide, within this wider expressivist theoretical framework, an intelligible and plausible expressivist construal of moral reasons-experiences themselves, over and above the moral judgments to which they give rise. Third is the need to do so in a way that also accommodates the phenomenological aspect of categorically authoritative moral normativity that non-naturalists like Hampton so rightly emphasize is central to moral experience. We address the first item in the remainder of the present section, and the second and third items in Section 6.

In a number of our past writings we have articulated and defended a non-reductive and metaphysically irrealist metaethical position that we call 'cognitivist expressivism.' It is so labeled because on our view, moral judgments are a species of genuine *belief* – although not a species of belief that purports to represent metaphysically robust moral properties or moral facts. For present purposes, however, what matters is not our claim that moral judgments are beliefs – a claim that one might question even if one accepts our position otherwise – but rather our contention that moral judgments are, in important respects, states of mind that cannot be reductively analyzed (Although we do claim that they are beliefs, we also claim that they are a distinctive and irreducible *species* of belief, significantly different from the states of mind ordinarily classified as beliefs.) We will now briefly characterize the position, in a way that emphasizes the irreducible character of moral judgments but leaves aside the question of whether or not they are a species of belief.

An ordinary belief is a certain kind of psychological commitment state with respect to a potential way the world might be – viz., a commitment to the world's actually *being* that way. We therefore call ordinary beliefs *is-commitments*. According to our non-reductive metaethical expressivism, a moral judgment too is a psychological commitment-state with respect to a potential way the world might be – an *ought-commitment*, as we call it. On this picture, to believe that Bertie will apologize to Madeline is to be is-committed with respect to the (non-moral, descriptive) way-the-world-might-be *that Bertie apologizes to Madeline*. Similarly, to judge morally that Bertie ought to apologize to Madeline is to be ought-committed with respect to that same way-the-world-might-be, viz., *that Bertie apologizes to Madeline*. (As metaethical irrealists, we maintain that there is no such way-the-world-might-be as the putative belief-content *that Bertie ought to apologize to Madeline*. Likewise, there is no such metaphysically robust relational fact as the putative fact *Bertie's having failed to keep his promise **being an objective moral reason for** Bertie to apologize to Madeline*; and there is no such metaphysically robust relation as *moral fittingness* between Bertie's apologizing and his having failed to keep his promise.)

Further delineating ought-commitments as distinctive, irreducible, psychological states is not a matter of trying to analogize them to, or to subsume them under, states such as desires, commands, universalized commands, plans, norm-acceptances, or the like.[19] This reductive approach, as already emphasized, looks incapable of accommodating the authoritativeness aspect of moral phenomenology. How then should one go about giving an illuminating expressivist characterization of these mental states? Well, largely by 'triangulating' them *vis-à-vis* other kinds of mental states, both with respect to phenomenology and with respect to functional roles in thought and action-guidance: for instance, underscoring their phenomenological and functional-role similarities to ordinary non-descriptive beliefs, while also emphasizing important phenomenological and functional-role differences too; underscoring their phenomenological and functional-role similarities to ordinary desires, while again also emphasizing important differences too; etc. This we have done at some length in prior writings.

We will not rehearse here our prior discussions of such matters. Instead we will proceed directly to the task at hand: extending our non-reductive expressivism to incorporate moral-reasons experiences, and arguing that the resulting position smoothly accommodates the phenomenology of moral authority.

6. Addressing the challenge

We are now prepared to defend our neutrality thesis, making our case for claiming that careful attention to moral-authority phenomenology does not reveal whether or not such experiences carry, as an aspect of their content, commitment to metaphysically robust, non-natural, properties, relations, and facts. Focusing largely on the Clive example from Section 1, we aim to make clear why moral-reasons experiences can possess all the elements of moral-authority phenomenology that Hampton (together with Mackie) correctly attributes to them (and more besides) without purporting to represent metaphysically robust, categorically authoritative, fittingness-relations or fittingness-facts. The methodology will be *the phenomenological method of similarity and contrast* (as we will call it) – viz., comparing moral-reasons experiences to various other kinds of mental states, noting both important phenomenological similarities and important phenomenological differences.

Consider the onset of Clive's non-normative belief that the woman is in serious danger of being harmed. He experiences what he sees happening – including, in particular, the woman's screaming while the man drags her by the ankles – as pulling him toward believing this, i.e., pulling toward an is-commitment vis-à-vis that content (This is the aspect of *Pull*.) He experiences this as an 'external' pull, emanating from what he sees happening outside of himself. (This is the aspect of *External Source*.) He finds himself involuntarily gripped, in virtue of the strength of this pull, by an is-commitment vis-à-vis the likelihood of her being harmed. (This is the aspect of *Grip*.) This is-commitment arises independently of any pre-existing desires he has, and independently of human conventions – indeed, in this case it occurs despite his pre-existing desire *not* to believe that she is in serious danger. (This is the aspect of *Independence*.) Since his becoming thus is-committed is both involuntary and independent of his pre-existing desires, it is experienced as inescapable, given his current evidential situation. (This is the aspect of *Inescapability*.)

Consider now the onset of Clive's judgment that he is morally obligated to intervene on the woman's behalf – with this judgment being construed as an ought-commitment vis-à-vis the non-normative content *that I intervene on the woman's behalf*. This experience is phenomenologically similar, in each of the ways lately noted, to the onset of an is-commitment. He experiences her being in serious danger of being harmed (something about which he now has an is-commitment) as pulling him toward an ought-commitment with respect to his intervening. (This is the aspect of *Pull*.) He experiences this as an 'external' pull, since her being in danger of harm is something outside of himself. (This is the aspect of *External Source*.) He finds himself involuntarily gripped, in virtue of the strength of this pull, by an ought-commitment vis-à-vis intervening on her behalf. (This is the aspect of *Grip*.)[20] The onset of this ought-commitment occurs independently of any pre-existing desires he has, and independently of human conventions – indeed, in this case it occurs despite his pre-existing desire *not* to intervene. (This is the aspect of *Independence*.) Since his becoming thus ought-committed is both involuntary and independent of his pre-existing desires, it is experienced as *inescapable*, given his current evidential situation. (This is the aspect of *Inescapability*.) Finally, he experiences the contemplated action of intervening as compellingly right – something he must do. (This is the aspect of *Compelling rightness*).

The onset of Clive's is-commitment to the woman's being in danger of harm and the onset of his ought-commitment to intervening on her behalf are thus similar to one another in all the ways lately noted. (These similarities, we contend, are strong enough and broad enough to render the ought-commitment a species of the genus *belief* alongside the is-commitment – although our argumentation in this paper does not require agreement on this point.) In each case, the non-normative consideration experienced as *reason* for the commitment exhibits the same set of elements that Hampton identifies as figuring in the phenomenology of categorical authoritativeness – viz., *Pull*, *Source*, *Grip*, *Independence*, and *Inescapability*. And this is so even if – as we ourselves maintain – Clive's experiencing the woman's danger of harm as reason for his intervening does not purport to represent a metaphysically robust relation of 'fittingness.'

On the other hand, the onset of Clive's ought-commitment also differs in an important respect from the onset of his is-commitment regarding the woman's being in danger of harm – viz., the ought-commitment has a motivationally 'hot' role within Clive's psychology, all by itself.[21] The is-commitment, by contrast – like other is-commitments *vis-à-vis* non-normative contents – plays no motivational role by itself apart from other pertinent psychological states with which it might combine, such as pre-existing desires. Thus, one's reason-experience in the case of the ought-commitment also has the final phenomenological element on the list at the end of Section 3, viz., *Motivation*. (This element can be present and operative without being motivationally dominant – as in Clive's case, since he does not act in accordance with his experienced moral obligation.)

The phenomenological element *Motivation* is also present, of course, in prototypical experiences of desire. In that respect at least, moral experiences are similar to ordinary desires – a point often emphasized by metaethical expressivists. Yet the differences from desire are palpable too. For one thing, desires are not commitment-states, whereas moral judgments are. And although a desire often is experienced as a reason for a specific action (given the belief that the action will lead to desire-satisfying consequences) – and thus exhibits *Pull* toward the action – the source of this pull is the desire itself, and so is not experientially external; thus, *Source* is not present. Also, acting on the basis of a desire, or forming an intention to act on the basis of a desire, typically is a voluntary matter, and thus does not exhibit *Inescapability*. And since desires themselves are the sources of the actions or intentions to which they sometimes give rise as reasons, such desire-based reasons do not exhibit *Independence*.

Yet further elements of the categorically-authoritative-fittingness aspect of moral phenomenology, beyond those explicitly mentioned by Hampton, can be brought into view by considering self-directed reactive attitudes that typically arise when one fails to act in a way that one experiences as morally obligatory – and by comparing these with self-directed reactive attitudes that typically arise when one violates an ongoing intention of a non-moral kind, such as an intention to stick to one's diet until one has lost ten pounds. In both kinds of case, one is apt to experience a sentiment of guilt or of shame, which in turn is apt to motivate one to take compensatory remedial action as best one can. And in both cases, such a sentiment is apt to arise because the pertinent state is experienced as exerting a governing authority over oneself – an authority that one has contravened. But there is a crucial difference. Although a voluntarily formed intention, such as the intention to follow a specific diet because of one's desire to lose ten pounds, is apt to exert an experienced authority over oneself that will induce guilt and/or shame in circumstances where one has violated that intention, this authority and resultant sentiment(s) are experienced as *contingent and desire-dependent*: the authority one has contravened is experienced as operative upon oneself only in virtue of one's voluntarily-formed intention, and thereby only in virtue of the pre-existing desire that motivated that intention in the first place. By contrast, the phenomenological authority of moral reasons, and the resultant self-directed reactive sentiment(s), are experienced as *inescapable and desire-independent*: the authority one has contravened is experienced as operative upon oneself independently of any medium-term or long-term intentions one might have voluntarily formed, and independently of one's pre-existing desires.

We submit that everything we have said in the present sub-section about the inherent aspect of the-authority-of-moral-reasons phenomenology is compatible with the contention that moral experience does not purport to represent a metaphysically robust, instantiated, moral-reasons relation.[22] We are claiming no more than that, because as we emphasized earlier, the pertinent phenomenology also is compatible with the contention that moral experience *does* purport to represent metaphysically robust, instantiated, moral-reasons relations. (We claim that direct introspection cannot reliably settle this issue either way, and that the phenomenology can be acknowledged by each of three competing metaethical positions: Hampton-style non-naturalist realism, Olson-style error theory, and our own non-reductive version of expressivism.) But the fact that our own expressivism can acknowledge and accommodate the phenomenology of moral authority is all we need, for our dialectical purposes.

Note finally, that if we are correct in arguing that cognitivist expressivism satisfies *Accommodation* (at least as far as the phenomenological character of moral-authority experience is concerned), then since it also satisfies *Metaphysics* and *Preservation*, it piles up serious plausibility points.

7. Conclusion

Careful examination of the rich phenomenology of experiencing moral reasons reveals that such experiences include an inherent aspect of categorical authority that has both motivational and normative elements. Accommodating this phenomenology sets a challenge for both standard reductive and non-reductive metaethical theories, which makes trouble for such theories. Reductive naturalism and reductive expressivism have trouble accommodating the pertinent phenomenology. Non-naturalism and error theory – both of which are non-reductive in what they attribute to ordinary moral experience, thought and discourse – nevertheless commit what we call the 'non-naturalistic' fallacy insofar as they take for granted that one can reliably determine on the basis of introspection alone that the phenomenology in question has non-naturalist, moral realist, ontological purport. That one cannot reliably determine this matter about ontological purport on the sole basis of introspection is our neutrality thesis. Our preferred non-reductive version of expressivism – cognitivist expressivism – can smoothly and without distortion accommodate the aspects of the phenomenology of moral-authority experience, as illustrated by our story of Clive.

We also advocate a wider claim: our non-reductive version of expressivism can accommodate moral authority as a characteristic of a broad range of moral experiences (including, but not restricted to, experiencing the authority of moral reasons) that can be reliably detected on the sole basis of introspection. But a full defense of this claim requires careful examination of other species of moral experience, which we have begun to do in some of our other work (Horgan and Timmons 2008, 2015, 2017, 2018, forthcoming).[24]

Notes

1. We address embedding in Horgan and Timmons (2006); negation in Horgan and Timmons 2009; and the possibility of deep moral error in Horgan and Timmons 2015.
2. We are using 'moral reasons' in a broad sense to refer not only to reasons whose characterization involves moral terms (e.g. that such and so action is wrong), but also to non-normative reasons (e.g. that such and so action would cause much harm) of the sort that purport to explain why actions, attitudes, and other objects of moral evaluation have the moral status they have, and which one appeals to in supporting a moral judgment.
3. Horgan and Timmons 2018 (forthcoming).
4. We understand phenomenology to be a largely descriptive field of study whose methodology is introspection and whose subject matter is the concrete 'what-it-is-likeness' of experience. So, we do *not* include (as some do) within the scope of phenomenological inquiry all of the deeply embedded aspects of ordinary moral thought and discourse.
5. Hampton's discussion is actually broader in scope than morality; her description also is meant to capture the authoritative grip of epistemic reasons.
6. As we use the germ 'grip' here and throughout, being 'gripped' by the experienced authority of a certain consideration C, as a reason for (or against) performing act Φ, constitutes being in a state of *judging*, on the basis of C, that one ought to (or ought not to) perform Φ. When one is thus gripped, one experiences the reason as moral-normatively decisive; but it need not be also motivationally decisive (and in Clive's case, is not). The judgment need not be consciously explicit; instead, its content might be implicit in the specific phenomenological character of one's current experience – in much the same way that appreciation of pertinent background information often is implicit in the specific phenomenological character of the experience of understanding a culturally topical joke, even though that information is not being explicitly consciously rehearsed. 'Chromatic illumination' is our expression for such implicit conscious appreciation of content that is not being explicitly represented in consciousness. In Horgan and Timmons (forthcoming) we discuss chromatic illumination at length, with specific attention to its operation in moral experience. The notion of chromatic illumination was originally introduced, in connection with the contention that the justification-

7. Moral-reasons experiences need not include an explicit *judgment* that such-and-such considerations constitute moral reasons for thus-and-such action. Often enough, it seems, one experiences certain considerations as moral reasons for a certain action Φ – one experiences those considerations 'moral-reasonishly *vis-à-vis* Φ,' so to speak – without forming such an explicit conscious judgment whose content is that considerations C constitute moral reasons for action Φ. Indeed, much might be operative in consciousness only implicitly, by way of chromatic illumination (cf. note 6): perhaps certain considerations that are figuring as authoritative moral reasons, perhaps one's appreciation of those considerations *as* authoritative moral reasons, and perhaps even one's being *gripped* by that appreciated authority. The phenomenology to be described below comports with these observations.
8. Hampton does provide a conception of norms on pp. 49–53 of her book.
9. The irreducibility of such experience is nicely put by David Enoch when he observes that with regard to normative facts generally, 'Normative facts are just too different from natural ones to be a subset thereof' (2011, 4), moral reasons being a special case.
10. One can easily add to this list. In our Forthcoming, we discuss the phenomenology of moral deliberation which, as Nagel (1986, 49) rightly observes, often includes the thought that whatever decision one comes to on the basis of such deliberation, *one might still be mistaken*.
11. We acknowledge that an advocate of metaethical error theory might challenge the contention that *Preservation* is a legitimate theoretical desideratum – perhaps by claiming that the goal of preserving the practice of morality is the 'wrong kind of reason' for accepting a metaethical theory. But at the very least, this goal constitutes a legitimate and important reason to *seek* a credible metaethical theory that preserves morality while also satisfying the desiderata *Acknowledgement* and *Metaphysics*. And of course if such a theory can be found, then its availability will undermine the principal motivation for error theory – viz., the contention that moral-authority experience purports to represent putative 'do-be-done-ness' facts and properties that are metaphysically queer.
12. Here and throughout, we use the modifier 'metaphysically robust' to signal that the contextually operative use of the terms 'property' and 'fact' is not a minimalistic use. Although we recognize that these terms are sometimes used minimalistically – in which case, for instance, asserting 'Abortion is morally wrong' is essentially equivalent to asserting 'That abortion is morally wrong is a fact,' or to asserting 'Abortion has the property of moral wrongness' – we deny that such minimalistic uses are the *only* ones that are ever contextually operative. We also deny that they have any privileged 'default' status.
13. We say 'not pertinently different from', rather than 'pertinently similar to', because our own non-reductive version of expressivism, as described in Sections 5 and 6 below, does emphasize certain pertinent similarities between moral-authority experiences and various kinds of mental state not involving morality. Even so, our brand of expressivism is neither strongly reductive nor weakly reductive, because it also emphasizes pertinent *differences* between moral-authority experiences and each of those other kinds of mental state.
14. Experiencing a state of mind like norm-acceptance or action-planning as voluntary, or as contingent upon one's social circumstances, need not be a matter of an explicit higher-order judgment that attributes voluntariness or contingency

to one's first-order state of norm-acceptance or action-planning. Instead, it can be a matter of how the first-order mental state is chromatically illuminated; cf. notes 6 and 7 above.

15. Recently Cuneo and Shafer-Landau (2014); have proposed what they call 'conceptual non-naturalism' one aim of which is to avoid troublesome metaphysical and epistemological difficulties that arise for robustly metaphysical versions of the sort we are considering. For a trenchant critique of this view, see Copp 2018a. See also Copp (2018b), for a critique of the metaethical views of Parfit and Scanlon, whose versions of non-naturalism are also supposed to avoid these same troublesome commitments.

16. Words like 'relation', 'property', 'fact', and 'true' all have minimalistic, disquotational uses in ordinary discourse that need not be ontologically committal – a point rightly emphasized, for instance, by metaethical expressivists like Simon Blackburn who embrace 'quasi-realism' about ordinary moral thought and discourse. But it is a serious mistake, we maintain, to infer from this that the *only* actual or legitimate uses of such words are minimalistic. That mistake is a dangerous first step down a looming garden path to metaethical quietism (cf. Horgan and Timmons 2015) (As we say in that paper, Beware of becoming beHorwiched!).

17. Note that ironically, if we are right, then when it comes to the introspectible aspects of experiencing the grip of moral reasons, the moral error theory remains unmotivated. It must therefore rely on appealing to other features of moral thought and discourse in order to claim that such thought and discourse is error-ridden.

18. We acknowledge that a hybrid theory that combines aspects of naturalist moral realism with aspects of expressivism might be dialectically in the running too, insofar as it embraces a construal of moral-authority phenomenology like the one we propose below. But an advocate of such a position would bear the dialectical burden of providing an adequate theoretical motivation for the two claims (1) that moral experience and moral judgment purport to represent metaphysically robust moral properties and moral facts, and (2) that these are identical to certain *natural* properties and facts whose essence is non-normative (Discussion with David Copp during the 'Representation and Evaluation' conference prompted the present note.)

19. Nor, of course, is it a matter of construing an ought-commitment as a higher-order belief that attributes a first-order state to oneself, e.g. the psychological state *regarding non-normative consideration C as a moral reason for action A*.

20. The following objection arises, which was pressed upon us at the 'Representation and Evaluation' conference by our commentator Bruno Guindon and also by several audience members including Paul Bloomfield and Bill FitzPatrick:

> Although cognitivist expressivism recognizes and accommodates the externality of the non-normative considerations that one experiences as authoritative reasons, it does not recognize and accommodate the externality of the experienced status of those considerations *as authoritative reasons*; and in this respect, cognitivist expressivism is really a version of metaethical error theory.

> Our response is to urge that introspection alone cannot reliably ascertain whether or not the experiential externality of moral reasons, *qua* authoritative moral reasons, involves anything more than the further phenomenological features that we describe just below – in particular, involuntariness and independence of pre-existing desires. Our own view is that the phenomenology

as we describe it already *constitutes* experiencing the pertinent non-moral considerations as morally authoritative.
21. This motivational role might be direct, or might be a matter of generating a new desire with the same content as the ought-commitment. We ourselves find the former possibility more plausible, phenomenologically and psychologically.
22. Concerning the phenomenological aspect *External Source*, the following remarks bear emphasis. Hampton's own formulation, as expressed in the pertinent bullet point at the end of Section 2, is ambiguous. On one hand, it can be construed as including both (i) that the non-normative factual consideration which one experiences as a reason is external to oneself, and (ii) that this fact is experienced as authoritative over oneself in a categorical way, independently of one's pre-existing desires, one's contingent social roles, etc. On the other hand, it can be construed as including not only features (i) and (ii) but also this feature: representing a putative, external, independent, metaphysically robust, *moral-reasons relation*. We, of course, are construing *External Source* the former way in claiming that our non-reductive expressivism is compatible with what is *reliably introspectible* about this aspect of moral phenomenology. To contend that introspection reliably reveals that moral phenomenology satisfies the stronger construal of *External Source*, we contend, is to commit the non-naturalist fallacy.
24. For helpful comments and discussion, we thank the participants at the 2017 conference 'Representation and Evaluation' at the University of British Columbia, especially Bruno Guidion (our commentator), Paul Bloomfield, David Copp, Bill FitzPatrick, and the two conference organizers Matt Bedke and Stefan Scriaraffa.

References

Copp, D. 2018a. "Are There Substantive Moral Conceptual Truths?" In *Moral Skepticism: New Essays*, edited by D. E. Muchaca, 91–114. London and New York: Routledge.

Copp, D. 2018b. "A Semantic Challenge to Non-Realist Cognitivism." *Canadian Journal of Philosophy* 48: 554–575.
Cuneo, T., and R. Shafer-Landau. 2014. "The Moral Fixed Points." *Philosophical Studies* 171: 399–443.
Enoch, D. 2011. *Taking Morality Seriously: A Defense of Robust Realism*. Oxford and New York: Oxford University Press.
Hampton, J. 1998. *The Authority of Reason*. Cambridge: Cambridge University Press.
Horgan, T., and M. Potrč. 2010. "The Epistemic Relevance of Morphological Content." *Acta Analytica* 25: 155–173.
Horgan, T., and M. Timmons. 2006. "Cognitivist Expressivism." In *Metaethics after Moore*, edited by T. Horgan and M. Timmons, 255–298. Oxford and New York: Oxford University Press.
Horgan, T., and M. Timmons. 2008. "What Can Moral Phenomenology Tell Us about Moral Objectivity?" *Social Philosophy & Policy* 25: 267–300.
Horgan, T., and M. Timmons. 2009. "Expressivism and Contrary-Forming Negation." *Philosophical Issues* 19: 92–112.
Horgan, T., and M. Timmons. 2015. "Modest Quasi-Realism and the Problem of Deep Moral Error." In *Passions and Projections: Themes from the Philosophy of Simon Blackburn*, edited by R. N. Johnson and M. Smith, 190–209. Oxford and New York: Oxford University Press.
Horgan, T., and M. Timmons. 2017. "Sentimentalist Moral-Perceptual Experience and Realist Pretensions: A Phenomenological Inquiry." In *Ethical Sentimentalism*, edited by K. R. Stueber and R. Debes, 86–106. Cambridge: Cambridge University Press.
Horgan, T., and M. Timmons. 2018. "The Phenomenology of Moral Authority." In *Moral Skepticism: New Essays*, edited by D. E. Muchaca, 115–140. London and New York: Routledge.
Horgan, T., and M. Timmons. Forthcoming. "The Phenomenology of Deliberation and the Non-Naturalistic Fallacy." In *The Naturalistic Fallacy*, edited by N. Sinclair. Cambridge: Cambridge University Press.
Horgan, T., and M. Timmons. Forthcoming. *Illuminating Reasons: An Essay in Moral Phenomenology*. Oxford: Oxford University Press.
McEwan, I. 1998. *Amsterdam*. New York: Anchor Books.
Mackie, J. L. 1977. *Ethics: Inventing Right and Wrong*. Harmondsworth: Penguin Books.
Nagel, T. 1986. *The View from Nowhere*. Oxford and New York: Oxford University Press.
Olson, J. 2014. *Moral Error Theory: History, Critique, Defense*. Oxford and New York: Oxford University Press.
Solzhenitsyn, A. 1962. *One Day in the Life of Ivan Denisovich*. Rutherford, NJ: Signet Classics.
Stevenson, C. L. 1961. "Relativism and Non-Relativism in the Theory of Value." *Proceedings and Addresses of the American Philosophical Association* 35: 25–44 (reprinted as Chapter 5 of his *Fact and Value*. New Haven: Yale University Press, 1963).

Expressivism, meaning, and all *that*

Sebastian Köhler

ABSTRACT
It has recently been suggested that meta-normative expressivism is best seen as a meta-semantic, rather than a semantic view. One strong motivation for this is that expressivism becomes, thereby, compatible with truth-conditional semantics. While this approach is promising, however, many of its details are still unexplored. One issue that still needs to be explored in particular, is what accounts of propositional contents are open to meta-semantic expressivists. This paper makes progress on this issue by developing an expressivist-friendly deflationary account of such contents.

1. Introduction

Meta-normative expressivism is commonly seen as proposing an alternative to truth-conditional semantics. Recently, however, it has been suggested that expressivism is a meta-semantic, rather than a semantic view and as such compatible with truth-conditional semantics. While this approach has significant potential, many relevant issues surrounding it are underexplored. One such issue is what approaches regarding propositional contents – to which semantics explicitly appeals – are compatible with meta-semantic expressivism. This paper expands expressivists' options with a deflationary account to the contents of sentences, which allows expressivists to say that normative sentences have propositional contents as their meanings.

The paper proceeds as follows: Section 2 motivates meta-semantic expressivism and argues that it needs an account of propositional contents. Section 3 develops a deflationary account of such contents. It does so, by first identifying the role that attributions of such contents play and then giving a deflationary account of how they play that role using Wilfrid Sellars' work. It then demonstrates how this view fits with expressivism and also suggests a novel understanding of expressivism, which cashes out expressivism's commitments in the philosophy of mind using conceptual role semantics.

2. Expressivism: meta-semantic, not semantic

Expressivism consists of two theses.[1] First, that the meaning of declarative sentences is to be explained in terms of the judgements their assertoric uses conventionally express. Second, that there is a distinctive difference between ordinary descriptive and normative judgements: while the former are motivationally inert representational states, the latter are non-representational states that play a motivating role in the production of action. This paper focuses mostly on the first thesis. Let me first clarify the second, though.

In particular, note that 'representational' in this thesis must be understood in a particular fashion. At the end of the day, most expressivists will not deny that normative judgements are representational states in some minimal sense, e.g. in the sense of being beliefs or truth-apt. What they deny is that normative judgements are representational in the robust theoretical sense employed by representationalist accounts of domains of thought and discourse.

Representationalist accounts, roughly, hold that the distinctive nature of a relevant domain is to be explained in terms of the things it is *about* or *represents*. For example, representationalists about 'truth' or 'wrong,' would *start* by assuming that the domains invoking these terms are about or represent something, namely *truth* or *wrongness* and would then try to account for these domains in terms of the nature of these things, i.e. by investigating the nature of truth or wrongness. Representationalism, hence, gives *metaphysical* questions about what domains are about or represent explanatory primacy in accounting for those domains. Note, however, that the notions of 'being about' or 'representation' play real theoretical and explanatory work on such accounts, which could not, for example, be played by 'minimalist' or 'deflationist' accounts of these notions. Hence, representationalists need a theoretically robust notion of 'representation.' This notion is, of course, hard to specify. Whatever it ends up being, though, expressivists hold that ordinary descriptive, but not normative judgements are representational in *that* sense. With these remarks in place, let's turn to expressivism's first thesis.

This thesis has commonly been read as a *semantic* claim. *Semantics* aims at giving an account of the literal meanings of sentences in natural languages with the central aim of systematically explaining the compositionality of such languages. Part of any semantic approach is a theory of interpretation. Given that natural languages are messy, clearer meanings need to be assigned to the sentences of the language for which one is developing a semantics. To do this, one has to interpret the relevant language, the 'object-language,' in a way that eliminates ambiguities, unpacks context-sensitivity, etc. to derive a version of it that wears its literal meanings on its sleeve. One then uses another language, the 'meta-language,' competence with which is presupposed, to specify the *semantic contents* of singular terms, predicates, and logical and sentential connectives in a way that allows us to compute the semantic contents for any arbitrary sentence from the semantic contents of its parts and their arrangement. 'Semantic contents' can be seen as the literal meanings of the linguistic items in questions, as assigned by semantics.

Located within semantics, expressivists' first thesis has been understood as the claim that the semantic contents of declarative sentences are the judgements they express. Gideon Rosen (1998, 387), for example, characterizes it thus:

> The centerpiece of any [expressivist] 'account' is what I shall call a psychologistic semantics for the region: a mapping from statements in the area to the mental states they 'express' when uttered sincerely.

Ralph Wedgwood (2008, 35–36) characterizes expressivism similarly:

> According to an expressivist account [...] the fundamental explanation of the meaning of [normative] statements and sentences is given by a *psychologistic semantics*. According to a plausible version of the principle of *compositionality*, the meaning of a sentence is determined by the meaning of the terms that it is composed out of, together with the compositional structure of the sentence (perhaps together with certain features of the context in which that sentence is used). So assuming this version of the compositionality principle, this expressivist approach will also give an account of the particular terms involved in these sentences in terms of the contribution that these terms make to determining what type of mental state is expressed by sentences involving them.

And Mark Schroeder (2008, 33) proposes a similar understanding of expressivism:

> On the picture to which expressivists are committed [...] [t]he primary job of the semantics is to assign to each atomic sentence a mental state – the state that you have to be in, in order for it to be permissible for you to assert that sentence. [...] [The] primary semantic values of the sentences are the states that are *expressed* by the sentences, in the minimal sense advocated by the interpretation of expressivism as assertability semantics [...].

Call this reading of expressivism's first thesis 'Psychologized Semantics.' This reading is common, but also deeply problematic, because Psychologized Semantics is incompatible with a common, almost orthodox, way to pursue semantics: *truth-conditional semantics*.[2] Truth-conditional semantics approaches the task of semantics through the *truth-conditions* of sentences – the conditions under which those sentences would be true. One powerful and familiar – almost orthodox – view approaches this task in terms of *propositional contents*, on which a sentence's semantic content is a *proposition* that either is or determines the sentence's truth-conditions. The semantic values of singular terms, predicates, and the logical and sentential connectives are then understood in terms their contributions to those propositional contents. While this is not the only way of doing truth-conditional semantics, I take it that it is the most powerful research programme within truth-conditional semantics.

The problem for expressivists is that Psychologized Semantics seems *incompatible* with this way (or even any way) of doing truth-conditional semantics. After all, Psychologized Semantics assigns mental states, rather than propositions, as the contents of sentences. Furthermore, expressivists seem to be blocked from allowing propositions to be assigned to sentences derivatively – and so making use of truth-conditional semantics in that way – by pairing the sentences with the content of the assigned mental states. Very roughly, this is so, because the contents of the kinds of attitudes expressivists take to constitute normative judgements are not of the right kind to interact in the required way with both the sentential connectives and the contents of the thoughts expressed by e.g. descriptive language.[3] In the normative case, this suggests that expressivists have to claim that the attitude *is* the content of the sentence. If expressivists accept this, however, they have to accept Psychologized Semantics, which applies to all declarative sentences. This is because expressivists need a unified account of the contents of normative and non-normative sentences, to account for their contribution to the semantic contents of complex sentences with both normative and non-normative parts. This, however, forces expressivists to abandon truth-conditional semantics.

This is troublesome for at least two reasons: First, one should not have to call truth-conditional semantics into question just in virtue of accepting expressivism, a *meta-normative* view. Truth-conditional semantics is a powerful, highly fruitful, and widely accepted research program in philosophy *and* linguistics. Having to reject this program would be a significant theoretical cost and so it would be preferable if expressivists were not *committed* to doing so. This is not to deny, of course, that calling truth-conditional semantics into question *can* be fruitful. This should happen, though, on the basis of independent *linguistic* evidence for a failure of truth-conditional semantics, not on the basis of the kinds of *meta-normative* commitments that motivate expressivism (such as, for example, ontological parsimony).[4]

Having to abandon truth-conditional semantics is problematic, secondly, because it is unclear whether expressivists have a workable alternative. As the discussions surrounding the Frege-Geach Problem indicate, developing a compelling compositional semantics for normative language that does not proceed along truth-conditional lines – or at least proceeds along the lines required by meta-normative expressivism combined with Psychologized Semantics – is hard.[5]

Recently, however, some authors have suggested that expressivism is not actually committed to Psychologized Semantics.[6] Their starting point is to distinguish semantics from another project in the philosophy of language: meta-semantics. Recall that semantics proceeds to give the literal meanings of sentences in terms of *another language*, which is *presupposed* as meaningful (namely, the meta-language). In doing so it employs semantic notions such as 'content,' 'truth,' 'extension,' etc. at least some of which are taken as theoretical primitives for the sake of investigation.

Meta-semantics, in contrast, attempts to give a deeper explanation of the phenomenon 'literal meaning,' preferably in terms not mentioning such meanings. This involves two projects. First, cashing out the semantic notions in non-semantic terms as far as possible. Here meta-semantic accounts explain what is attributed when literal meanings are assigned, when truth-conditions are specified, extension fixed, etc.[7] Second, it gives an account of those properties – the 'meaning-constituting properties'[8] – *in virtue of which* linguistic items have their literal meanings.

With this distinction in view, the crucial question is whether Psychologized Semantics is the best interpretation of expressivism's first thesis. After all, we could also locate it within meta-semantics, as the view that declarative sentences have their meaning in virtue of the judgements those sentences express. Expressivists who accept this would hold that the difference between normative and ordinary descriptive sentences lies in their meaning-constituting properties. On this account, normative sentences have their meaning in virtue of expressing non-representational, motivational states, while descriptive sentences have their meaning in virtue of expressing representational states. Note that on this interpretation, expressivism *itself* seems to have no *positive* commitment how to cash out 'literal meaning.' The same goes for all other semantic notions. Expressivism only comes with a negative commitment: the semantic notions cannot be cashed out such that normative thought and discourse become representational.

One might worry, of course, that this is *still* incompatible with truth-conditional semantics. This worry, however, is based on the false assumption that truth-conditional semantics is *committed* to an understanding of its core concepts, such as 'truth,' 'extension,' 'reference,' etc. on which those concepts concern what sentences represent or are about *in the representationalist's sense*. Only on such a reading would e.g. an assignment of a proposition to a normative sentence make that sentence representational. Such a reading, however, is a *meta-semantic* assumption about truth-conditional semantics, which is not forced on us if we accept this theoretical approach in semantics. In fact, we should assume for semantics what we assume about any of the other sciences, namely that their core concepts do not have any particular philosophical underpinning build into them, but are used *within* the relevant sciences as theoretical primitives. Of course, the success of scientific theories might only be explainable via certain philosophical underpinnings. Whether this is true for truth-conditional semantics and representationalists' approach to it, though, is an open question. After all, there seem to be legitimate ways of reading the relevant concepts that leave the legitimacy of truth-conditional semantics as an explanatory project intact, but do not require that we understand them as the representationalist does.[9] If all of this is correct, however, there is no *in principle* reason to assume that meta-semantic expressivism rules out truth-conditional semantics.

Of course, whether meta-semantic expressivism *is* compatible with truth-conditional semantics depends on whether the semantic notions *can* be understood in expressivist-friendly ways. While some work has been done in this area – especially on the notion of 'truth' –, there is one semantic notion, namely 'propositional content' that is still under-explored. Significantly, what is unexplored is a deflationist option for the expressivist.[10]

As I understand it, *deflationism* regarding some phrase provides a *non-representationalist* account of it.[11] According to such accounts we should not proceed in terms of invoking entities the phrase represents. Instead, we give a two-part account. First, the account must specify the patterns of use that characterize the phrase, in a way that does not mention any entity it represents. Second, an account of why our vocabulary includes this phrase, which proceeds in terms of some *non-representational function*. According to accounts of this kind, we can completely explain the phrase's function in our linguistic practice *without* invoking any entity it represents. This way the second part explains why we use the phrase in question and vindicates that it is exhaustively characterized by the patterns of its use. This leads such accounts to be ontologically conservative regarding the relevant phrase.

I think a deflationist account of propositional content should be quite attractive for expressivists. First, it shares expressivism's central commitment to deflating notions that tempt representationalist inclined philosophers to expand our ontology in often problematic ways. Second, deflationary approaches to notions that seem to bar expressivism from preserving the 'realist sounding' surface features of normative discourse open the door for what Huw Price (2013) has called 'functional pluralism.' *Functional pluralism* is the view that for many different kinds of declarative sentences we should not *start* our account of those by assuming that the domain in which they figure represents something. Rather, we should account for them via some distinctive non-representational function that they play. Deflationary approaches make room for functional pluralism, by removing any representationalist commitment from exactly those notions characteristic for declarative sentences. But, expressivists should be sympathetic to functional pluralism, given that they will probably accept non-representational accounts for domains other than the normative. After all, they are *expressivists* because they think that representationalism encounters significant problems in the normative domain. But, the same likely holds for other domains as well.

For these reasons, I think it is attractive for expressivists to have a deflationary account of propositional contents as the meanings of declarative sentences in their theoretical repertoire.[12] However, even though expressivists often suggest sympathies for a deflationary account, no work has, so far, been done of fleshing such an account out in an expressivist-friendly way or of demonstrating how it would actually fit with expressivism.[13] This is what I will do here.

Specifically, I will provide an expressivist-friendly, deflationary account of the use of *that*-clauses in *meaning-attributions*. These are sentences of the form

(M) 'S' (in language L, at time t) means that p.

This focus on the use of *that*-clauses in meaning-attributions, rather than on propositions is important, given that a deflationary account is a *non-representational* account. Hence it will, primarily, focus on *attributions* of propositional contents and explain (at most) what propositional contents are in a way that is derivative of that explanation and metaphysically harmless. Propositional contents, though, are attributed by certain uses of *that*-clauses. Specifically, if we are interested in propositional contents as they figure in the theory of meaning, the relevant uses are those of *that*-clauses in *meaning-attributions*. Hence, to develop a deflationary account of such contents, these are the uses that require accounting for. This is what I will do in what follows.

3. Deflationism about *that*-clauses

To structure the investigation, let me note three desiderata the account has to satisfy. First, it needs to identify and account for the role of *that*-clauses in meaning-attributions. Second, it must be compatible with *that*-clauses playing their role in some non-representational fashion. So, the account should not make reference to *that*-clauses representing certain entities. Third, the account must be compatible with expressivism. Hence, it should allow the legitimacy of meaning-attributions to declarative sentences, even if the meta-semantic account for those is non-representationalist. I will develop the account by satisfying these desiderata in turn.

3.1. The role of that-clauses in attributions of meaning

The first step is to *identify* what role *that*-clauses play in meaning-attributions. To do so, we should consider paradigmatic uses of *that*-clauses in meaning-attributions. One is the use of *that*-clauses in the context of translation. *Translation* is a situation in which one faces a sentence in a foreign language and tries to assign meaning to it: one tries to determine whether two sentences in two different languages *mean the same thing*. In such contexts *that*-clauses are used as follows:

(1) 'Heinrich ist ein Imker' (in German) means *that* Heinrich is a bee-keeper.[14]

What is going on in (1) is that we mention a German sentence and then give its meaning by introducing a *that*-clause. Specifically, we consider a sentence in a language to be assigned meaning to – the *object language* –, and then assign meaning to that sentence by pairing it with a sentence in the language in which meaning is to be assigned – the *meta-language*. But, we do not pair those sentences in just *any* way. Rather, we *modify* the meta-language sentence *using a that-clause* and *then* assign it to the object language sentence. And, it seems exactly *this modification* that allows the meta-language sentence to play its *meaning-giving* role in (1). Neither merely mentioning nor using the sentence would straightforwardly do the job. Consequently, in this kind of situation *that*-clauses play purely intra-linguistic roles, as a tool for semantic ascent: they allow assignment of meta-language sentences to object language sentences in a *meaning-giving* way.

What goes for translation goes for *interpretation* generally. When interpreting what certain sentences mean in the mouth of other speakers of English, we can assign meaning in the same way. For example, when we interpret another speaker of English, call her 'Helene,' we can employ *that*-clauses as follows:

(2) 'Heinrich is a bee-keeper' (in Helene's idiolect) means *that* Heinrich is a bee-keeper.

Again, in (2) we consider sentences in an object language and then assign meaning to them by pairing them with a sentence modified by a *that*-clause in a meta-language. And, once more it is *this modification* that allows the meta-language sentence to play its *meaning-giving* role. So, in the case of interpretation *that*-clauses play a purely *intra-linguistic* role as well.

Hence, we've identified the role *that*-clauses play in meaning-attributions: they play an intra-linguistic role in translation and interpretation. We now need an account that explains *how that*-clauses (and meaning-attributions generally) play this role, and one on which *that*-clauses can play this role in some non-representational fashion.

A first important thing to note is a constraint on such accounts. Accounting for the role of *that*-clauses in meaning-attributions is part of meta-semantics. Specifically, it is part of an attempt to cash out the notion of 'literal meaning.' This notion, however, is already associated with certain properties of sentences. A suitably theory-neutral description of these properties can be given in terms of the role meaning-attributions play. Specifically, they are that sub-set M of the properties of a sentence S_1, for which it holds that some sentence S_2 is a good translation or interpretation of S_1 if and only if S_2 has M. I will call these properties the 'meaning-explananda.' The constraint on satisfactory accounts of meaning-attributions is that they need to say something about what accounts for the meaning-explananda.

Of course, deflationary views of *that*-clauses reject the common and straightforward way of doing so: introducing an entity (e.g. a proposition) into our ontology that is the *meaning* of the relevant kinds of sentences (and, hence, represented by the *that*-clause) and whose various distinctive features account for the meaning-explananda and, hence, the role of *that*-clauses in translation and interpretation. This would be representationalism about *that*-clauses, and so is an explanation that is closed to deflationary views of meaning-attributions. Still, even on deflationary accounts there should be some properties of sentences that account for the meaning-explananda, properties fully describable in terms not mentioning meanings. I will call these the 'basic properties.' An example for a basic property might, for example, be the property of being used in a certain way by competent speakers.

It is important to note that commitment to a view on which the meaning-explananda are fully accounted for in terms of basic properties is in principle perfectly compatible with the following commitments: First, that explanations of the meaning-explananda that mention meaning (e.g. semantics) are perfectly legitimate. Second, that such explanations are the best explanations (currently or ever) available to us (given our cognitive and other epistemic limitations, time constraints, etc.), so that it is completely legitimate to carry out semantics employing the semantic notions, and to assume such an enterprise to be the best project available to us to account for the compositionality of natural languages. Third, that we could never engage in interpretation or translation solely in terms mentioning only basic properties instead of using terms mentioning meaning. Fourth, that ordinary speakers could never fully spell out what those properties are. All that this view amounts to is that what accounts for the meaning-explananda *fundamentally* are facts fully describable in terms not mentioning meaning. What would a view of this kind say about meaning-attributions, though? I think a plausible approach – which can be fleshed out along deflationary lines – is Wilfrid Sellars (1954) account of meaning-attributions.

It is plausible to read Sellars (e.g. 1954, 1969) as adopting a view on which the meaning-explananda can be fully accounted for in terms not mentioning meanings, namely, in terms of rules about and patterns of linguistic behaviour. However, Sellars did not doubt the legitimacy of meaning-attributions. Instead, he thought that their legitimacy could be accounted for *without* expanding the metaphysical commitments of his explanatory account.

On his account, meaning-attributions are *illustrating sortals*: 'Means that p' is a sortal phrase, which illustrates particular basic properties, and in this way, allows classifying sentences in accordance with those properties. What does this mean? According to this account, meaning-attributions are a tool for semantic ascent: by use of a meaning-attribution we introduce a meta-linguistic phrase ('means that *p*') that allows us to classify sentences in the object language as having certain basic properties. These are those (or relevantly similar) basic properties as possessed by the sentence in the meta-language we have transformed into a *that*-clause. However, meaning-attributions play this role *not* by explicitly telling us what the relevant basic properties are. Rather they do this by *illustrating* these basic properties using the meta-language sentence that has these basic properties *as an example*. It is the role of *that*-clauses in this context to *pick out* the basic properties of *sentences*. To transform a declarative sentence *S* into a *that*-clause is to transform it into a *meta-linguistic* predicate that picks out the basic properties that *S* has in our language, where *S* serves as an *illustration* for the basic properties relevant in that context. The word 'means' in a meaning-attribution, according to Sellars, is merely a special copula telling us *that* the object language sentence has the basic properties picked out by the *that*-clause.

Let me make this clear with an example. Take,

(1) 'Heinrich ist ein Imker' (in German) means *that* Heinrich is a bee-keeper.

On Sellars' account, (1) attributes certain basic properties to the German sentence 'Heinrich ist ein Imker'. (1) does this by using the English sentence 'Heinrich is a bee-keeper' as an example to *illustrate* the basic properties in question. Indicating that this is what the sentence is used for is the job of transforming the sentence into a *that*-clause. More specifically, by transforming 'Heinrich is a bee-keeper,' we are introducing a predicate that serves to pick out the relevant basic properties, by using the sentence as an illustrative example for something with those properties. 'Means,' then, merely attributes those properties to the German sentence.

Sellars' account satisfies the first desideratum, as it accounts for the role of *that*-clauses in translation and interpretation. Whether it can also offer a deflationary account of *that*-clauses, though, depends on whether it can also satisfy the second desideratum, i.e. whether it is compatible with *that*-clauses playing their role in some non-representational fashion. So, let's investigate that issue.

3.2. Non-representationalism about that-clauses

I should start by noting that Sellars' account is compatible with a *reductionist* approach, on which facts about literal meanings are nothing but facts about basic properties. Such an approach would *not* fit the second desideratum, as it *would* postulate that there are literal meanings represented by *that*-clauses, which it identifies with basic properties. Endorsing such a reductionist view would also not help meta-semantic expressivism's quest toward compatibility with truth-conditional semantics, because a combination of those views would imply Psychologized Semantics. After all, on an expressivist account, the most likely candidate for the basic property of a sentence is the property of expressing a certain mental state, and so if literal meanings and basic properties are the same, we are back to Psychologized Semantics.

While the Sellarsian account is compatible with reductionism, though, it *also* does *not* entail such a reduction, i.e. it does not entail that facts about literal meanings are nothing but facts about basic properties and so does, hence, not entail that the relation in which *that*-clauses stand to basic properties is the one that would be employed by representationalists.[15] So, the account is compatible with a non-reductionist treatment, which is not, at least on first sight, incompatible with the second desideratum. Consequently, I will here only consider the non-reductionist version of Sellars' account, which I will call the 'Sellarsian account.'

Before I show that the Sellarsian account satisfies the second desideratum, let me note, though, that there are actually good reasons independently of my project to not understand the account reductionistically. This is so, because of the particular relation in which *that*-clauses stand to basic properties, which does not seem to me well understood in terms of representation. On Sellars' account, meaning-attributions assign basic properties to sentence S_1, by using another sentence S_2 *as an illustrating example*. So, the way in which talking about S_2 picks out properties should be akin to the way in which *taking as an example of* generally picks out properties. Taking as an example, though, has peculiar features.

To take some *x* as an example of some *F* is to be in a state where certain aspects of *x* are *salient* to oneself *as* those features something has in virtue of being an instance of *F*. Assume one takes David Lewis' papers as an example of papers with a high chance of getting published in high quality philosophy journals. In this case, certain aspects of David Lewis' papers will be salient to one *as* those features that papers have in virtue of having a high chance of getting published in high quality philosophy journals.

Certain aspects of an object being 'salient' in this way just means that one is disposed to give a special role to *those* aspects in determining whether *other* objects are members of the same general kind (the kind the first object is being taken as an example of). This special role is to treat those aspects as a *reference-point* in determining whether other objects fall within that general kind. This means that one's judgements about objects being identical (or relevantly similar) to *x* in these aspects will have some weight in settling one's judgements with regards to whether some object falls within the relevant kind. Of course, what weight one gives to these judgements can vary across cases: sometimes, one might already have extensive and explicit knowledge of the properties that instances of a general kind have and so needs to consider examples as reference-points only to confirm one's judgements about particular cases. In other cases, however, the *only way* one can explicitly think about a certain general kind is via such reference-points.

What *taking as an example of* does, is to feed on our ability to pick up on features and aspects of objects in ways that are certainly far more extensive than our ability to make explicit, both in language and in thought, to provide resources for new and often quite economical ways of thinking and talking about those features. For example, *taking as an example* actually makes it *easier* for us to deliberate about and determine whether some object *x* belongs to some general kind *F*. As long as we can rely on certain reference-points with regards to that general kind, we can determine whether *x* is an *F* by determining whether *x* is identical or sufficiently *similar* to the reference-points in relevant respects. Second, it makes it possible (via its expression or the invitation to others to come to be in that state) to *communicate* to others that some *x* belongs to a general kind *F*, even when we cannot spell out the features shared by instances of *F* or the features of *x* in virtue of which it is an instance of *F*. The only thing required is that one can presuppose a common reference-point, or give others a common reference-point by pointing out an object in which, for example, the relevant features are easier to pick out than in *x*. Proceeding from there one can then rely on one's audience's abilities to pick out similarities to lead them to the conclusion that *x* is indeed an *F*.

However, if *taking as an example of* functions in the ways presented here, it will not be appropriate to think that it represents the properties that it picks out. The relationship that holds between instances of *taking as an example of* and the properties picked out by its instances is importantly different from the relationship between ordinary descriptive beliefs and the properties they pick out. If this is correct, this provides a very good reason to read Sellars' account in a non-reductive way. After all, on this account uses of *that*-clauses are just a particular instance of *taking as an example of*. With these remarks out of the way, let me now turn to the question whether the Sellarsian account satisfies the second desideratum.

It turns out that it does: the account mentions nowhere entities in a way that would play into a representationalist's hand. The only entities mentioned on the Sellarsian account are basic properties. However, the relation in which *that*-clauses stand to these properties forecloses a reduction of *that*-clauses in terms of those properties. So, *that*-clauses do not represent basic properties. But, the Sellarsian account makes no mention of any other entities either! Consequently, while we can give an account of *that*-clauses in terms of their function, it will not be the function a representationalist about *that*-clauses would appeal to. According to the Sellarsian account, the best explanation of *that*-clauses makes no reference to *that*-clauses functioning to represent entities.

Note also, that on the Sellarsian account, there will be no informative analysis of *that*-clauses. We can only characterize *that*-clauses in a relatively platitudinous way. The same goes for the verb 'means' in the context of meaning-attributions. While 'means' functions in particular ways in a meaning-attribution, 'means' will not be *analysable* in terms of this function. So, according to the Sellarsian account, there will not be much of an informative answer to the question what it is that is assigned to 'Heinrich ist ein Imker' in

(1) 'Heinrich ist ein Imker,' means *that* Heinrich is a beekeeper.

except for the answer that *that Heinrich is a beekeeper* is assigned to 'Heinrich ist ein Imker' *as its meaning*.

This means, of course, that the Sellarsian account of *that*-clauses *is* a deflationary view about *that*-clauses. What does the view say about propositional contents, though? Note first, that the Sellarsian view is compatible with *that*-clauses legitimately functioning *syntactically* as referential terms. On this account, *that*-clauses pick out basic properties by using some sentence *as an example* for something with those (or relevantly similar) properties. What will be most salient in the context of using a *that*-clause, consequently, are those features of sentences relevant for its having particular basic properties. Thus, *that-clauses* will behave in a way that is structurally isomorphic to the basic properties of the sentence following the 'that.' This means, though, that *that*-clauses will behave, linguistically, like referential singular terms that refer to something that supervenes on, but does not reduce to, basic properties. Consequently, the Sellarsian account offers an explanation of why *that*-clauses function syntactically this way, even though the explanation of why *that*-clauses are in our vocabulary makes no reference to such entities.

If *that*-clauses behave in this way, though, we can introduce other ways of talking about what *that*-clauses refer to.[16] In particular, we can use the label 'propositional contents' to refer to what is attributed by *that*-clauses. So, for example, rather than saying

(M) 'S' (in a language *L*, at time *t*) means *that p*.

we might now, at least in some contexts, say

(P) 'S' (in a language *L*, at time *t*) expresses the proposition *that p*.

It is important to note, however, that the *metaphysical commitments* of claims made by sentences such as (P) will not go beyond those undertaken by claims invoking sentences such as (M). For example, the way in which sentences like (P) figure in giving the meaning of sentences must be derivative from the way sentences such as (M) do so. In fact, it does not seem too far-fetched to say that in contexts in which it is appropriate to use (P), it simply provides alternative ways of providing information already provided by (M). Of course, this is compatible with sentences such as (P) being more precise or expressively more powerful than simple meaning-attributions. This is especially the case when they employ formal machinery such as sets of possible worlds to make the notion of a proposition more precise. However, even if such sentences do the work of ordinary meaning-attributions much better, they do not convey information that is of a different type to the information already conveyed by meaning-attributions.

What should we say about the status of these 'propositions'? I think the following stance is most reasonable: talk of such contents is extremely useful and harmless in many cases, but we should be cautious not to read *any* metaphysical implications into it. This view fits nicely with viewing semantics and the invocation of propositional contents in that context as a *theoretical modelling exercise* set up specifically to capture very specific features of sentences in natural languages. Models can, in many cases, plausibly be thought of as useful fictions and the approach to propositional contents suggested here fits this approach nicely.

With the Sellarsian account of *that*-clauses, we now have a deflationary account of *that*-clauses that allows talk of propositional contents.[17] Furthermore, this account has no particular commitments that would rule out that *that*-clauses or propositional contents could be attributed in a meaning-giving way to normative sentences even if expressivism was true. Hence, it seems to fit our third requirement as well. Whether it does, however, still needs to be investigated more explicitly. After all, the Sellarsian account has particular commitments about meaning, and it is unclear how these relate to expressivism's commitments about meaning-constituting properties.

3.3. The fit with meta-semantic expressivism

On the Sellarsian account, meaning-attributions are a tool to pick out basic properties and assign them to sentences without needing to be able to specify them. If we accept this account of meaning-attributions, though, what is the relation between sentences' meaning, their basic properties, and their meaning-constituting properties?

On the Sellarsian account, a sentence's meaning does not reduce to its basic properties. Nor does it reduce to *anything* fully describable in terms not mentioning meaning. However, the sentence's meaning *supervenes on* its basic properties. This makes these properties the most plausible candidate for those properties *in virtue of which* sentences have their meaning. Consequently, the relationship between sentences' meaning, their basic properties, and their meaning-constituting properties is that sentences' basic properties just are their meaning-constituting properties. In what follows, I will, consequently, use 'basic properties' and 'meaning-constituting properties' interchangeably.

This identity between the basic and the meaning-constituting properties is good news, as it makes clear how the Sellarsian account combines with meta-semantic expressivism. On the combination of those two, the meaning-explananda of declarative sentences would be fully accounted for in terms of the mental states that uses of those sentences express. *That*-clauses in meaning-attributions would then have the function of picking out the mental states expressed by the use of those sentences followed by the *that*-. And, meaning-attributions would serve to use *that*-clauses to assign the property of expressing a mental state to sentences. However, the *meaning* of a declarative sentence, on this account, would consist in a propositional content, where this is to be understood along deflationary lines presented here. Furthermore, the sentence will have this propositional content *in virtue of* expressing a mental state, so that the property of expressing a mental state will be the meaning-constituting property of that sentence. Of course, this raises a couple of further issues, which I will address for a clearer view of the picture on the table.

According to expressivism, the meaning-constituting properties involve mental states. On the traditional understanding of expressivism, these will themselves have propositional contents, but not necessarily the same propositional contents as the sentences expressing them. For example, if expressivists held – the toy-view – that

(3) Abortion is morally wrong

expresses a desire that no one commit an abortion, (3) would have the content *that abortion is morally wrong*, but this content would supervene on a desire with the content *that no one commit an abortion*. Even though this kind of structure might appear strange, let me note that it is not necessarily so. Michael Ridge (2014, 125–131), for example, has argued that normative sentences express beliefs that share the content of the sentence, but that these beliefs are constituted by a non-normative belief and desire pair that have different contents from the normative belief and the sentence.

On Ridge's account, however, the same notion of content figures in all of these cases, which is made possible by his particular account of propositions. One might ask, though, whether expressivists who use the Sellarsian approach instead are not committed to using two different notions of content: one for linguistic items and one for mental states. After all, on the above picture, the *mental* content does significant theoretical work that seems foreclosed by the deflationary approach to content suggested here. This indicates that expressivists cannot use the Sellarian account to account for both linguistic and mental content.

It is unclear how devastating this would actually be. After all, the best accounts of mental and linguistic content might not converge. It seems to me, however, that there is actually a feasible alternative to biting the bullet on this. This is to reject the assumption that for expressivists' theoretical purposes their commitments in the philosophy of mind require invoking mental content. This is a common way to understand expressivism – after all, expressivism has traditionally been understood as the view that normative judgements are *conative attitudes* –, but it is not forced on expressivists. Indeed, it seems that what should do the work of the meaning-constituting properties should be the same as that which explains in virtue of what *normative judgements* have their contents. After all, most contemporary expressivists *agree* that normative judgements are *beliefs* and so they will need an account that explains in virtue of what these beliefs have their contents. While they *can* invoke other propositional attitudes here, I see no reason why they need to. Most fundamentally, what accounts for the content of all mental states should not be something that would itself be described in terms of contents anyway, so why not invoke it to account for the contents of normative beliefs directly, if this is possible?

In fact, there is a perfectly viable approach in the philosophy of mind for accounting for mental content that would allow cashing out expressivism's second thesis, without using a notion of content that is separate from the Sellarsian account. Before I present the view, I should highlight that the approach departs in some significant ways from traditional conceptions of expressivism. In particular, it undergoes *no* commitment to the view that normative judgements are partially constituted by familiar conative attitudes such as desires, emotions, or intentions. Rather, the view suggests a different way of cashing out expressivism's commitments about normative judgements, though one fully in line with the motivations for expressivism.

The approach I have in mind uses a certain school within functionalism about the mind. According to *functionalism about the mind*, mental states are dispositional states fundamentally characterized by their causal role within a mental economy. Functionalism itself is compatible with a notion of content figuring irreducibly in the functional characterization of mental states. However, there is a school within functionalism according to which, on the most fundamental level, propositional attitudes can be fully characterized *without* making reference to propositional content. This is *conceptual role semantics*.[18] According to *conceptual role semantics*, mental states can be *fully* characterized by their role within a mental economy. On this view, the features of mental states we would normally account for by invoking mental content can be fully integrated into that state's functional role (which then *explains* in virtue of what the state has its content).

Using conceptual role semantics, expressivists can plausibly cash out their second thesis purely in terms of functional roles.[19] For these purposes, we can first notice that the functional role of a state can be helpfully distinguished into three parts. First, 'mind-entry' conditions, which specify the state's role in the procession of sensory stimuli. Second, 'mind-to-mind' conditions, which specify the state's role in the processes of deliberation, reasoning, and inference. Third, 'mind-exit' conditions, which specify the state's role in the production of bodily behaviour.

Using this distinction, expressivists can suggest that normative judgements are characterized by very minimal mind-entry conditions, mind-to-mind conditions just sufficiently robust to account for the role normative judgements play in reasoning and deliberation, and very robust mind-exit conditions. She might then contrast this with the role that characterizes paradigmatically representational mental states, which would involve significantly robust mind-entry conditions, mind-to-mind conditions sufficiently robust to account for the role these judgements play in reasoning and deliberation, but very limited mind-exit conditions.

If expressivists endorse this view, their commitments in the philosophy of mind and, hence, their view of the meaning-constituting properties, would *not* require them to invoke a separate notion of content from that provided by the Sellarsian account. On this view, it is the *functional role* of the mental state (or at least a part of it) expressed by a sentence that figures in its meaning-constituting properties. Combined with the Sellarsian view, we get the result that it is this *functional role* that is illustrated and attributed by *that*-clauses and on which the content of that sentence supervenes. No additional notion of content is required. Of course, this does not tell us how the account can be generalized to mental content and so does not tell us whether expressivists *can* use the same account for both semantic and mental content.[20] The suggestions here suffice to show, however, that such an approach cannot be ruled out solely based on expressivism's meta-ethical commitments. The worry that expressivists need two separate notions of content, if they endorse the Sellarsian account does not, consequently, hold water.

Notes

1. Forms of expressivism so characterized are developed by Simon Blackburn (1998), Allan Gibbard (2003), Horgan and Timmons (2006), Michael Ridge (2014), and Mark Schroeder ([2008], though he does not accept it).
2. This way of arguing against expressivism and highlighting the cost of abandoning truth-conditional semantics is prominently championed by Mark Schroeder (2008, 2010).
3. Using Psychologized Semantics, Schroeder (2008) develops a view that ends up allowing expressivists to assign contents derivatively in a way that provides a unified semantics operating on those contents. He argues, though, that this requires too many problematic commitments, without being attractive enough to be a feasible alternative to truth-conditional semantics.
4. Of course, such independent linguistic evidence could then help semantic expressivism. Nate Charlow (2014, 2015), for example, argues that the semantics of imperatives already requires a different semantic approach, which helps semantic expressivism as well.
5. Of course, philosophers have worked hard to develop such alternatives (see e.g. [Blackburn 1993; Gibbard 2003; Horgan and Timmons 2006; Schroeder 2008; Baker & Woods 2015; Charlow 2015]). I will stay neutral on whether such an account works, as surely it is better if expressivism is not hostage to fortune to one.
6. These are e.g. Matthew Chrisman (2016), Michael Ridge (2014) and Alex Silk (2013).
7. In some sense, of course, semantics is *also* concerned with an enterprise like this. So, for example, when a semanticist spells out the notion of a truth-condition in terms of a set of possible world, she *is* trying to cash out a semantic notion in non-semantic terms. This is different, though, from the enterprise that concerns meta-semantics. After all, even if we concede that a truth-condition is a set of possible worlds, there are many different *interpretations* of what we could be saying when we concede this. If we are instrumentalists about semantics, for example, we might think that all we are doing is to introduce a useful, but strictly speaking false, fiction. On the other hand, we might be *realists* and hold that we are talking about what meaning *really* consists in. It is in this sense, in which meta-semantics is concerned with the named enterprise (compare: in one sense normative ethics tries to 'cash out' the moral notions in non-moral terms as far as possible. But, there are many different *meta-ethical* interpretations of what is going on when we do this).
8. I borrow this phrase from Paul Horwich (1998a: 5).
9. See e.g. (Sellars 1974; Davidson 1990; Field 1994, 2001; Shiffer 1996, 2003; Horwich 1998b; Williams 1999).
10. Ridge (2014) and Schroeder (2013) have explored views that allow expressivists to be *realists* about propositions (Ridge's preferred account is a version of Scott Soames' view [2010]). My aim is not to argue against these views, but to put another option on the table.

11. Of course, the label 'deflationism' is used in a variety of ways in the philosophical debate and my use of this label might cut across the use of other people. What I have in mind are views committed to a particular way of *deflating* certain kinds of linguistic phrases that it is tempting to read in very theoretically committing ways. Specifically, these views do *not* deflate such notions via an representationalist order of explanation (which is also provides a possible way for 'deflation,' if one argues that the phrase is to be explained in terms of what it represents, but that theoretical requirements for the thing to be instantiated are minimal). Instead, they *start* with a non-representational explanation. Views that are deflationary in this sense are to be found e.g. in (Ramsey 1927; Grover, Camp, and Belnap 1975; Price 1988; Brandom 1994; Field 1994; Horwich 1998b). Note that such views can, but need not deny that, for example, truth is a property (or reference a relation, etc.). However, they will use *their non-representational account* to explain what it means to talk about that property (relation, etc.) in a way that doesn't increase the metaphysical commitments of the account.
12. I explain how the account offered here also covers mental content in Köhler (2017). There I argue that the account covers the content of all propositional attitudes and not only allows expressivists to hold that normative judgements are beliefs in normative propositions, but also that there are other propositional attitudes with normative propositions as their contents, such as e.g. desires.
13. Blackburn (1998, 77–83) and Gibbard (2003, 180–196) have suggested sympathies towards deflationary accounts of propositions, but neither has provided the details of such an account or how it would fit with expressivism.
14. For reasons of simplicity I omit the time parameter here and in what follows.
15. Compare: a pro-sententialist theory of truth (e.g. [Grover, Camp, and Belnap 1975]) holds that there is a relation between the truth-predicate and some entity, but it does not hold that this entity *is* truth and so invokes a different relation to the one that would be employed by a representationalist about truth.
16. Note that this further step requires us to endorse a deflationary account of *reference* for the account not to collapse into a form of *fictionalism*. Note also, that this step is not *required* by the Sellarsian account. What I've said before only shows that on the Sellarsian account, *that*-clauses legitimately behave in a *syntactic* manner like referential terms. This view is compatible with holding that *that*-clauses do not in fact refer to anything – that the surface features of language are deceiving in this case. This would be a deflationary account of *that*-clauses, but not, strictly speaking, of propositional contents.
17. Some readers might wonder what kind of compositional semantics for 'means that' fits with the Sellarsian account. First of all I should highlight that the Sellarsian account itself should be understood as a *meta*-semantic account of *that*-clauses, as well as of 'means.' Even so, the Sellarsian account might itself have certain implications for semantics, depending on how we spell it out. For example, on Sellars' original account of meaning-attributions, the *that*-clauses would be an indexical predicate and 'means' a specialized form of the copula. In this case *that*-clauses would have to be accounted for *in semantics* via extensions. However, if we follow some of my suggestions here as to how *that*-clauses function syntactically and how propositions might fit into the Sellarsian account, *that*-clauses would be singular terms and 'means' a relational term. In this case, *that*-clauses would require a referent. While the question which of these approaches we should endorse is important for further research, it is not a question that I will be concerned with here. It seems to me, though, that the availability of these options shows that the account could plausibly be compatible with different

approaches to the compositionality of 'means *that*' depending on the further commitments one will want to endorse regarding *that*-clauses. Note, though, that in both cases, a *deflationary* account of *that*-clauses will require to deflate further notions (e.g. 'extension' and 'reference' in the cases above). I do not take this to be a problem in the context of my investigation, though, as an expressivist who wants his account to fit with truth-conditional semantics will need those anyways. I'd like to thank an anonymous referee for drawing me out on this issue.

18. Proponents of this view are e.g. Ned Block (1986), Hartry Field (1978), and Gilbert Harman (1999). It is related to inferentialism in that both emphasize role for content, but differs from inferentialism in that it emphasizes causal-functional, rather than inferential role (Brandom [1994] is the most well-known proponent of inferentialism). Note that the label 'conceptual role *semantics*' is misleading, given that the account explains in virtue of what mental states have their contents and so takes up the space in the philosophy of mind that *meta*-semantic accounts take up in the philosophy of language.
19. What follows is, of course, only a rough sketch of the account.
20. As already remarked in fn. 12, I fill this theoretical gap in (Köhler 2017).

Acknowledgements

I owe special thanks to Matthew Chrisman, Guido Ehrhardt, and Mike Ridge for numerous conversations on the topic of this paper and for their more than generous support. For comments and discussion, I would also like to thank Vuko Andrić, Cameron Boult, Lars Dänzer, Christoph Fehige, Ben Ferguson, Simon Gaus, Susanne Mantel, Geoffrey Sayre-McCord, Robin McKenna, Stephan Padel, Joey Pollock, Huw Price, Peter Schulte, Christine Tiefensee, as well as an anonymous referee for the *Canadian Journal of Philosophy*, and audiences at work in progress events in Edinburgh and the Practical Philosophy Workshop in Saarbrücken. I owe the title of the paper to Robin McKenna.

References

Baker, Derek, and Jack Woods. 2015. "How Expressivists Can and Should Explain Inconsistency." *Ethics* 125: 391–424.
Blackburn, Simon. 1993. "Attitudes and Contents." In *Essays in Quasi-Realism*, edited by Simon Blackburn, 182–197. Oxford: Oxford University Press.
Blackburn, Simon. 1998. *Ruling Passions*. Oxford: Oxford University Press.
Block, Ned. 1986. "Advertisement for a Semantics for Psychology." *Midwest Studies in Philosophy* 10: 615–678.
Brandom, Robert. 1994. *Making It Explicit. Reasoning, Representing, and Discursive Commitment*. Cambridge, MA: Harvard University Press.
Charlow, Nate. 2014. "The Problem with the Frege–Geach Problem." *Philosophical Studies* 167 (3): 635–665. doi:10.1007/s11098-013-0119-5.

Charlow, Nate. 2015. "Prospects for an Expressivist Theory of Meaning." *Philosophers' Imprint* 15 (23): 1–43.
Chrisman, Matthew. 2016. *The Meaning of "Ought": Beyond Descriptivism and Expressivism in Metaethics*. Oxford: Oxford University Press.
Davidson, Donald. 1990. "The Structure and Content of Truth." *Journal of Philosophy* 87 (6): 279–328.
Field, Hartry. 1978. "Mental representation." *Erkenntnis* 13 (1): 9–61. doi:10.1007/BF00160888.
Field, Hartry. 1994. "Deflationist Views of Meaning and Content." *Mind* 103 (411): 249–285.
Field, Hartry. 2001. "Attributions of Meaning and Content." In *Truth and the Absence of Fact*, edited by Hartry Field, 157–174. Oxford: Oxford University Press.
Gibbard, Allan. 2003. *Thinking How to Live*. Cambridge, MA: Harvard University Press.
Grover, Dorothy L., Joseph L. Camp, and Nuel D. Belnap. 1975. "A Prosentential Theory of Truth." *Philosophical Studies* 27 (2): 73–125. doi:10.1007/BF01209340.
Harman, Gilbert. 1999. "(Nonsolipsistic) Conceptual Role Semantics." In *Reasoning, Meaning, and Mind*, edited by Gilbert Harman, 207–232. Oxford: Oxford University Press.
Horgan, Terence, and Mark Timmons. 2006. "Cognitivist Expressivism." In *Metaethics after Moore*, edited by Terry Horgan and Mark Timmons, 255–298. Oxford: Oxford University Press.
Horwich, Paul. 1998a. *Meaning*. Oxford: Oxford University Press.
Horwich, Paul. 1998b. *Truth*. Oxford: Oxford University Press.
Köhler, Sebastian. 2017. "Expressivism, Belief, And All That." *The Journal of Philosophy* 114 (4): 189–207.
Price, Huw. 1988. *Facts and the Function of Truth*. Oxford: Basil Blackwell.
Price, Huw. 2013. *Expressivism, Pragmatism and Representationalism*. Cambridge: Cambridge University Press.
Ramsey, Frank. 1927. "Facts and Propositions." *Aristotelian Society Supplementary Volume* 7 (1): 153–206.
Ridge, Michael. 2014. *Impassioned Belief*. Oxford: Oxford University Press.
Rosen, Gideon. 1998. "Blackburn's Essays in Quasi-Realism." *Noûs* 32: 386–405.
Shiffer, Stephen. 1996. "Language-Created, Language-Independent Entities." *Philosophical Topics* 24 (1): 149–167.
Schiffer, Stephen. 2003. *The Things We Mean*. Oxford: Oxford University Press.
Schroeder, Mark. 2008. *Being For: Evaluating the Semantic Program of Expressivism*. Oxford: Oxford University Press.
Schroeder, Mark. 2010. *Noncognitivism in Ethics*. New York: Rougtledge.
Schroeder, Mark. 2013. "Two Roles for Propositions: Cause for Divorce?" *Noûs* 47: 409–430. doi:10.1111/j.1468-0068.2011.00833.x.
Sellars, Wilfrid. 1954. "Some Reflections on Language Games." *Philosophy of Science* 21 (3): 204–228.
Sellars, Wilfrid. 1969. "Language as Thought and as Communication." *Philosophy and Phenomenological Research* 29: 417–437.
Sellars, Wilfrid. 1974. "Meaning as Functional Classifications." *Synthese* 27: 417–437.
Silk, Alex. 2013. "Truth Conditions and the Meanings of Ethical Terms." In *Oxford Studies in Metaethics*, edited by Russ Shafer-Landau, Vol. 8, 195–222. Oxford: Oxford University Press.
Wedgwood, Ralph. 2008. *The Nature of Normativity*. Oxford: Oxford University Press.
Williams, Michael. 1999. "Meaning and Deflationary Truth." *Journal of Philosophy* 96: 545–564.

Relativism and the expressivist bifurcation

Javier González de Prado Salas

ABSTRACT
Traditional expressivists want to preserve a contrast between the representational use of declarative sentences in descriptive domains and the non-representational use of declarative sentences in other areas of discourse (in particular, normative speech). However, expressivists have good reasons to endorse minimalism about representational notions, and minimalism seems to threaten the existence of such a bifurcation. Thus, there are pressures for expressivists to become global anti-representationalists. In this paper I discuss how to reconstruct in non-representationalist terms the sort of bifurcation traditional expressivists were after. My proposal is that the relevant bifurcation can be articulated by appeal to the contrast between relativistic and non-relativistic assertoric practices. I argue that this contrast, which can be specified without appeal to representational notions, captures the core intuitions behind the expressivist bifurcation (in particular, it captures the anti-realist intuitions motivating many expressivist proposals).

1. Introduction

Expressivists about normative vocabulary typically want to contrast descriptive declarative speech, which has a straightforwardly representational function, with normative discourse, where declarative sentences are used in other, non-representational ways. Thus, normative expressivism tends to be a local form of anti-representationalism (see Blackburn 2013). By contrast, pragmatists like Price (2011, 2015) recommend embracing anti-representationalism all across the board. Global anti-representationalism is motivated to a large extent by minimalist views about representational notions, according to which such notions cannot play a substantial role in our ultimate explanations of why sentences mean what they mean. Adopting minimalism is often taken to be a natural move for expressivists, perhaps even a compulsory one. Therefore, it seems that local expressivists find themselves in an unstable position: once one becomes a representational minimalist for some specific domain of declarative speech, it is difficult not to endorse minimalism globally (see Chrisman 2008; Dreier 2004; Price 2011).

My aim is to examine whether the sort of demarcation that local expressivists have in mind can be drawn in a way that respects the representational minimalism endorsed by pragmatists. In other words, I will try to reconstruct the expressivist contrast without appealing to representational notions, but by identifying relevant differences in the practical effects of declarative speech acts in the domains taken to be non-descriptive by expressivists. More specifically, I will propose that assertoric speech acts in those domains behave in a relativistic way. The distinction between relativistic and non-relativistic assertion, which can be specified in non-representational terms, would underlain the contrast pursued by expressivists about normative matters.

I start by introducing in Section 2 the challenge faced by local anti-representationalist views. In Section 3, I characterize in more detail global pragmatist approaches, and, in Section 4, I show how normative and evaluative speech can be integrated within a pragmatist framework. In Section 5 I discuss the limitations of trying to capture the alleged non-descriptive nature of normative speech by appeal to the involvement of higher-order modal operators. In Section 6 I turn to my positive proposal. I first sketch a model of relativistic assertion and then I explain how the contrast between descriptive and non-descriptive speech can be reformulated in terms of the distinction between relativistic and non-relativistic assertoric practices.

2. Expressivism and the bifurcation thesis

Expressivist theories, as I will understand them here, aim to explain why sentences have the meaning they have in terms of the mental states conventionally associated with their use – more broadly, in terms of the characteristic function of the speech acts conventionally performed by uttering those sentences. By contrast, representationalist theories of meaning explain what it is for a sentence to have a certain meaning by appeal to some representational relation between the sentence, or its use, and the world.

I will regard both theories as metasemantic proposals, in other words, as proposals about what it takes for some sentence to have certain semantic features (Charlow 2015; Chrisman 2015; Pérez Carballo 2014; Silk 2015). In a way, expressivist and representationalist metasemantics can be made compatible: there can be representationalist versions of expressivism. This will happen when the characteristic function of the relevant speech acts (or the mental states associated with them) is specified in representationalist terms. So, one could say that the function of assertions of p is to express the belief that p, and then add that believing that p is a matter of representing the world in a certain way (in short, the function of assertions of *p* would be to represent the world as being a *p*-world). This account of why *p* means what it means would be both expressivist and representationalist.

However, expressivist often want to claim that there are areas of discourse where this representationalist approach is inadequate, in particular normative and evaluative speech (and also epistemic modals or indicative conditionals). In such areas of discourse, the relevant speech acts would have a non-representational function – they would be associated with non-representational mental states. For example, normative statements tend to be associated with non-doxastic mental states with a motivational dimension (e.g. desires, plans, preferences or states of endorsing some norm). In this way, expressivism provides an attractive framework for those with antirealist intuitions about some domain. Expressivism allows one to grant that the vocabulary in the domain in question can be used to make meaningful assertoric speech acts, while denying that these speech acts are meaningful (and sometimes accurate) in virtue of there existing referents for that vocabulary, or there being facts that correspond to the contents asserted. Thus, expressivism makes it possible for the antirealist to account for our patterns of speech in the relevant domain without undertaking undesired metaphysical commitments.

Now, it seems that expressivism can only play this role in the antirealism debate if it is contrasted with an alternative realist characterization of the target area of speech. Such realist characterizations will typically be couched in representational terms: sentences in the target domain mean what they do because they are used to refer to certain entities in the world. Indeed, expressivists often want to argue that some target domain of discourse works differently than paradigmatically descriptive areas of speech. In contrast to such paradigmatically descriptive speech (e.g. speech about middle-sized dry goods), the characteristic functions of our discourse in the target area would be non-representational. The antirealist intuition behind many expressivist proposals is precisely that talking about chairs and tables is not the same as talking about, say, norms or values. In particular, a realist interpretation of the second, but not the first type of talk would involve problematic metaphysical commitments. So, those sharing these antirealist intuitions will be prone to reject that our speech about norms and values is descriptive in the same way that our speech about chairs and tables is. This distinction between non-descriptive and genuinely descriptive areas of declarative speech is what authors like Huw Price call the *bifurcation thesis* (Price 2011, 2015). Expressivists who embrace the bifurcation thesis are only local anti-representationalists (Blackburn 2010, 2013).

There are authors, however, that endorse a global anti-representationalist stance (Brandom 1994, 2000; Horwich 1998; Price 2011; Williams 2010, 2013). According to this approach, which I will call pragmatist, the explanation of why an expression means what it means should be made, in all areas of speech, in terms of its use, of its characteristic function. And, crucially, for these authors our ultimate account of the use of the relevant expressions cannot rely on representational notions. It would not be good enough to say that 'red' is used to describe things as being red. We would have to further explain what we do when describing something as red, the pragmatic impact or function of such a speech act (for instance, by specifying the norms governing that speech act in our practices).

This sort of pragmatist position can be motivated in several ways. On the one hand, some may be reluctant to accept the existence of word-world representational relations, perhaps on naturalistic grounds. In particular, it may be doubted that there is any specific, informative relation between our words and the world that amounts to a representational relation (beyond the stuttering relation specified by saying, for instance, that 'water' refers to water). On the other hand, one can argue that there are internal pressures for anti-representationalist to become global. This is because it seems natural for expressivists to accept minimalism about representational notions such as truth, reference, belief or description. I will understand minimalism as the view that whether the relevant notions apply to some area of discourse is merely a matter of whether expressions in that area of discourse are amenable to take part in certain patterns of use (without further requiring that such expressions engage in specific relations with the world). So, on a possible minimialist view of truth, that a sentence *p* is truth apt just means that it is assertable and it is appropriate to say things like 'It is true that *p*.' Likewise, according to a minimalist account of belief, believing that murder is wrong would just require that one's moral attitude is properly expressed by asserting 'Murder is wrong.'

Expressivists have good reasons to adopt representational minimalism: this allows them to account for the superficial similarity between the target area of discourse and paradigmatic descriptive speech (e.g. it will be possible to recognize the truth aptness of normative declarative sentences). The problem of opening the door to minimalism is that we stop having a clear contrast between descriptive and non-descriptive speech. At least, such a contrast cannot be traced in representationalist terms any more, for instance saying that in descriptive domains words have referents, sentences are truth apt and facts are stated. On a minimalist approach, these things will also happen in the domains targeted by the expressivist. After becoming a minimalist, thus, the natural step is to abandon local anti-representationalism and accept global pragmatism (or perhaps endorse some form of quietism). Dreier (2004) has called this the problem of *creeping minimalism* (for discussion, see Asay 2013; Chrisman 2008; Golub 2017).

In a way, global pragmatism can be seen to bring victory to the expressivist field. From a pragmatist perspective, all meaning is a matter of use, and the variety of functions of language is acknowledged: representation loses its central position in our explanations of what it is for an expression to have a certain meaning (see Price 2011). Nevertheless, some expressivist may want to preserve a genuine distinction between paradigmatically descriptive speech and other forms of declarative discourse, in particular normative discourse (see for instance Blackburn 2010, 2013). Can this demarcation be maintained within a global pragmatist framework? Maybe, but it will have to be reconstructed in non-representational terms. The relevant contrast will be a contrast in the characteristic uses and functions of declarative speech in different domains. In this paper, I explore how this contrast can be drawn. More specifically, I will investigate whether the broadly antirealist intuitions motivating many versions of expressivism can be captured by pointing to certain features of the use of declarative speech in the domains traditionally targeted by expressivists.

In Section 3 I outline a general pragmatist account of assertion. Then, I explore whether we can delineate the desired distinctions within this general pragmatist framework.

3. Global pragmatism

The view I am calling global pragmatism is a generalized use-based theory of meaning. According to this view, the meaning of all expressions is to be explained in terms of their use (of their pragmatic effects), ultimately characterized without appealing to representational notions (Brandom 1994; Price 2011; Williams 2010, 2013; for discussion, MacFarlane 2010). So, semantic features are attributed to expressions in order to codify their conventional use. Moreover, having certain semantic features is just a question, at bottom, of being used in certain ways and having certain characteristic functions. If the mental state involved in accepting a sentence is taken to be a feature of its use, pragmatism becomes a generalization of expressivism.

Note, however, that the connection between semantic features and use does not need to be direct. In particular, semantic values do not need to be identified with characteristic functions, mental states expressed or other features of use (see Charlow 2015). It is only necessary that the relevant features of the use of an expression can be derived, in a context, from its semantic value.[1] So, pragmatism understood in this way is a metasemantic thesis, connecting the attribution of semantic values to an expression with its use. The picture I have in mind is as follows (for proposals in a similar spirit, see Charlow 2015; Chrisman 2015; Yalcin 2011). Semantics is in the business of ascribing (compositional) semantic values to expressions (e.g. truth values at a context and index). The semantic value of a sentence determines, in a context, what can be called the informational upshot of its utterance, its contribution to the conversation – for instance, what proposition is put forward when asserting the sentence.[2] Finally, pragmatic theory studies the conversational effects of the use of a sentence, its characteristic function (e.g. the conversational effects of making an assertion with a certain content). Non-representational pragmatism requires that there is a suitable relation between the semantic value of a sentence and its characteristic use (specified in non-representational terms).

In principle, pragmatist metasemantics may be compatible with different semantic frameworks. To be sure, certain semantic theories make the connections with use more perspicuous. For instance, in dynamic semantics, the characteristic conversational effects of utterances of a sentence can be directly read off from the semantic features assigned to the sentence (see Charlow 2015; Starr 2016; Veltman 1996). However, at least in many cases, the same phenomena can be described by combining a static semantic theory with dynamics at the pragmatic level – that is by assigning static semantic values and adding bridge principles that determine the conversational effects of uttering sentences with such semantic features (Rothschild and Yalcin 2017).

For my purposes here, I do not need to choose a specific semantic theory. I will only impose the pragmatist metasemantic requirement that the attribution of semantic features is suitably connected with an explanation of the use of sentences. My focus will be on examining the characteristic conversational effects of speech acts performed by uttering the relevant sentences (more specifically, those conventional, public effects that are directly determined by the linguistic rules governing the use of words). My ultimate goal is to explore whether it is possible to specify, without appealing to representational notions, a contrast between the characteristic effects of paradigmatically descriptive speech and of evaluative discourse (and the other types of discourses targeted by expressivists).[3]

Let us begin by considering a simple, Stalnakerian model of the conversational effects of assertions (Stalnaker 2014). In this sort of model, the state of the conversation at a certain time is characterized by the common ground of the conversation at that moment, that is by the information mutually presupposed by the participants of the conversation. An assertion would be a proposal to update the common ground by adding a proposition to it. It is customary to characterize the information in the common ground in terms of the worlds compatible with such information (i.e. the possible worlds left open in the conversation). Adding propositions to the common ground would have the effect of ruling out those worlds incompatible with the proposition asserted.

Taking this general model of assertion as a starting point, one may try to develop a non-representationalist characterization of the pragmatics of assertoric discourse, for instance along the lines of Brandom's inferentialism (1994, 2000). According to Brandom, when a speaker makes an assertion, she becomes committed to the proposition asserted and to the propositions inferable from it (using as potential collateral premises the rest of the propositions she is committed to). Similarly, if the speaker is entitled to undertaking a commitment to some proposition, she also counts as entitled to a commitment to the propositions following from it. Moreover, two propositions count as incompatible when an entitled commitment to one of them automatically precludes being entitled to the other one. The state of the conversation would be specified by a conversational scoreboard that keeps track of the commitments and entitlements acquired by the speakers; the conversational score registers the propositions accepted in the context of the conversation and whether there is entitlement for such an acceptance.[4] An assertion would be a proposal to update the conversational score: by taking an assertion on board, the audience revises their commitments and entitlements.[5]

It is natural to think of assertoric updates in a Brandomian model as additive: when accepting a proposition, speakers acquire commitments (and, if entitled, also entitlements), which are added to the conversational score. Nevertheless, appealing to the notion of incompatibility, this updating process can also be interpreted in an eliminative sense. The idea would be that the acceptance of a proposition potentially reduces the set of propositions compatible with the speakers' commitments. This sort of inferentialist view can also be formulated in terms of worlds. We just have to say that a proposition p is associated with the set of p-worlds, the set of worlds compatible with p.[6] So, if q follows from p, then a commitment to taking the world to be a p-world would bring a commitment to taking it to be a q-world as well. Thus, the inferential role of the proposition p would explain what it is for a world to be a p-world.

In accordance with the pragmatist project, Brandom aims to describe the conversational impact of assertions without appealing to representational notions. In order to do so, he characterizes the dynamics of assertoric speech in terms of our normative practices of assessing each other and of attributing entitlements and commitments – what he calls scorekeeping, following Lewis (Brandom 1994, ch. 3; Lewis 1979).[7] For instance, if you assert p, and then you assert something incompatible with it, the other participants in the practice (acting as scorekeepers) are entitled to treat you as doing something inappropriate, something you had no entitlement for. In this way, the pragmatic effects of assertions are determined by the social norms governing scorekeeping, which are specified without the involvement of representational concepts.

In principle, Brandom's pragmatist characterization applies to assertoric speech in all domains, including paradigmatic descriptive areas of discourse. Brandom's proposal, thus, is an example of a non-representationalist account of the conversational effects of assertoric speech in general. It is not my purpose here to argue in favor of Brandom's theory. I will just assume for the sake of argument that such a theory, or something in a similar pragmatist spirit, can be made to work. What I want to do is to see whether it is possible to provide a pragmatist reconstruction of the distinction between descriptive and normative speech, once this sort of general non-representational account of assertoric discourse is in play. I will start by consider how normative and evaluative speech can be integrated in the model of assertion I have been sketching.

4. The pragmatics of normative discourse

Think of normative and evaluative sentences like:

(1) One ought to help one's friends
(2) Venice is a beautiful city

A pragmatist can deal with such sentences in a straightforward way. It can simply be said that, when one of these sentences is asserted, the proposition expressed is added to the common ground. In an inferentialist model, this would involve acquiring a commitment to such a proposition and to those inferable from it. For instance, if you are committed to the claim that beautiful cities should be preserved, then accepting (2) commits you to accepting that Venice should be preserved. The pragmatist could even say that, when (2) is added to the common ground, worlds in which Venice is not a beautiful city are ruled out by the presuppositions of the conversation (i.e. the possibility that Venice is not beautiful becomes incompatible with the commitments undertaken by the participants in the conversation).

It should be stressed that the pragmatist's appeals to the notions of proposition, truth or fact do not carry metaphysical weight. The idea of correspondence to the facts does not play a substantive role in the pragmatist's ultimate story about why sentences mean what they mean. Indeed, given the pragmatist's minimalist understanding of the notions of truth and fact, it is a trivial observation that assertable sentences are truth apt and are in the business of making factual claims about the world.[8] Insofar as one is prepared to assert (2) one should be prepared to assert 'It is a fact that Venice is a beautiful city' or 'It is true that Venice is beautiful.' Note, in particular, that the notion of proposition appealed to in this pragmatist account would also be thin or deflationary. Whether the utterance of a sentence expresses a proposition would just be a matter of whether the speech act has the characteristic effects of an assertion and is evaluable for truth.

It may be useful for certain purposes to refine the characterization of the conversational state, so that it does not just reflect generally the possible worlds compatible with the common ground. For instance, one can also keep track explicitly of the (moral, aesthetic, gastronomical) preferences or values of the speakers (see Silk 2015). Similarly, one can distinguish a normatively neutral specification of possibilities (i.e. a specification in which no information about values, norms or preferences is included) and a classification of such possibilities in accordance with their normative or evaluative features (e.g. whether they are permissible possibilities). Instead of just saying that there is a possible world in which Mary is wrong in not helping her friend Peter, we would first specify a possibility in which Mary does not help her friend Peter, and then we would classify such a possibility as impermissible. So, the state of the conversation would be characterized by means of two separate parameters, the first one tracking a set of open possibilities specified in a normatively neutral way (call them 'worlds') and the second one providing a classification of these open possibilities as permissible or impermissible (see Charlow 2015; Starr 2016).[9]

Once these finer distinctions are introduced, one might be tempted to think that descriptive sentences can be differentiated as those whose acceptance leads to updates that rule out worlds (specified in a normatively neutral way), but do not affect the selection function that classifies worlds according to their permissibility. Non-descriptive sentences would be associated with other types of updates, in particular updates that modify the permissibility selection function (Starr 2016, 387). Now, introducing these distinctions may be illuminating for some purposes but, by pragmatist lights, it is not enough to capture the purported difference between genuinely descriptive and non-descriptive discourse. It will not do just to label the information registered by the first parameter of the scoreboard as 'descriptive' or 'factual' and the information in the second parameter as 'non-descriptive' or 'normative'. These distinctions presuppose the relevant bifurcation between descriptive and non-descriptive information, rather than explain it. The pragmatist still needs to show that these labels are not merely arbitrary, but reflect pragmatically significant differences in the conversational effects of using each type of sentence (and, crucially, it should be possible to characterize such differences in non-representational terms, without presupposing the contrast between descriptive and non-descriptive information).

A possible way of reconstructing the bifurcation thesis within an inferentialist, pragmatist framework is by appeal to the Humean intuition that normative thought and discourse is distinctively linked with the motivation and justification of actions. In this way, Chrisman suggest drawing the relevant contrast by focusing on the role played by normative discourse (in particular, ought-claims) in practical reasoning (Chrisman 2008; for discussion, see Tiefensee 2016). The idea is that only normative claims (e.g. 'I ought to cook dinner'), and not merely descriptive ones, can directly provide entitlement to perform some action (e.g. to cook dinner). Moreover, according to Chrisman's suggested view, normative claims can only be inferred from premises including further normative or practical claims. Thus, from a set of merely descriptive premises, a normative conclusion would not be inferable. This would capture the common idea that normative attitudes are required for motivating and justifying action.

This is the sort of difference pragmatists should be after. What distinguishes normative claims, on Chrisman's (2008) view, is their connection with action (and with other normative claims). We do not need to invoke representational notions to characterize this connection. So, this is an appealing proposal for the pragmatist. However, this way of drawing the bifurcation thesis is arguably too limited (as Chrisman 2015 has come to acknowledge) and potentially problematic (see Tiefensee 2016). I think, therefore, that it is worthwhile to explore further ways of characterizing the contrast between descriptive and non-descriptive speech. One first reason for this is that it is controversial whether actions can only be motivated and justified by explicitly normative considerations. Several authors argue that standard descriptive considerations often justify, and also motivate actions (for instance, Alvarez 2010; Dancy 2000). For example, the fact that a car is approaching may justify and motivate one not to cross the road. Actually, Brandom himself (2000, 89–92) maintains that the premises of non-enthymematic pieces of practical reasoning may be entirely descriptive, and not involve explicitly normative concepts.

Certainly, many expressivists will share the Humean intuition that merely descriptive attitudes cannot do all the work in motivating and justifying actions (after all, this sort of intuition is often offered as support for expressivism about normative speech). Nevertheless, I take it to be preferable to remain as neutral as possible on this debate. Moreover, as Chrisman himself points out (2015, 179–182), it is not clear that the same direct connection with the motivation and justification of actions is observed in relation to all types of ought-claims. Consider, for instance, ought-claims about the past. Arguably, such claims do not play a direct role in motivating the agent's current actions – although they may be appealed to in order to justify past actions. It is also questionable whether a direct connection with motivation and justification of action always takes place in other forms of evaluative discourse (e.g. 'Her paintings are very elegant'). At any rate, it seems that the link with action is far less prominent in other areas of discourse that many expressivist will want to situate in the non-descriptive side of the divide, for instance, speech involving epistemic modals or indicative conditionals (Chrisman 2015, ch. 7).

In what follows I examine other ways of demarcating the division between genuinely descriptive discourse and other forms of assertoric speech. I start by discussing whether this division can be drawn by appeal to the distinctive impact of modal claims on the conversational state.

5. Test dynamics

Normative speech often involves modal operators, such as 'ought' and 'may'. Indeed, modal operators seem to play a central role in many of the areas of discourse targeted by expressivists (e.g. epistemic modals). It may be argued that modal sentences behave in a characteristic way, which distinguishes them from basic declarative sentence. Roughly, the intuition is that the correctness of modal claims does not depend (or not only) on how the actual world is, but on features of certain possible situations. So, 'You may visit the museum for free' is true if some permissible world is such that you visit the museum for free (even if in the actual world perhaps you decide to go to the cinema instead).

Is it possible to appeal to the distinctive behavior of modal operators in order to develop a pragmatist-friendly bifurcation thesis? It seems that one could try to contrast genuinely descriptive sentences with declarative modal sentences, which do not provide information about the way the actual world is, but do something else instead (see Charlow 2015, 18–19; Chrisman 2015; Veltman 1996). In this way, Chrisman (2015) argues that modal operators are associated with 'metaconceptual operations' in which more basic contents are manipulated. Following Sellars and Brandom, Chrisman fleshes out this idea from an inferentialist perspective, suggesting that sentences involving modal operators have as their characteristic function to allow us to make inferential connections explicit: on Chrisman's proposal, modal sentences get their 'content from being usable to acknowledge inferential connections between more basic items rather than to refer to things in the world' (2015, 197).

The distinctive behavior of modal sentences can be characterized in a more precise way within the sort of model of assertion sketched above. According to simple accounts of assertion, the assertion of standard declarative sentences introduces information in the conversation, by adding a proposition to the common ground (or, equivalently, by ruling out worlds). Several authors argue that modal sentences are associated with a different type of update instruction (Charlow 2015; Starr 2016; Veltman 1996). Assertions of such sentences would not introduce new information (or a least not only), but rather impose a *test* on the conversational state. Performing a test amounts to checking whether the conversational state has certain features. If the test is passed, the conversational state remains as it was (it is not updated). Otherwise, we get a defective conversational state. A defective conversational state calls for modification, if the conversation is to proceed. However, the modal sentence does not specify which particular modification has to be implemented in order to overcome the defectiveness of the conversational state.

Take as an example 'Mary ought to help Peter'. On the view under consideration, accepting this sentence involves checking whether all the open worlds that are classified as permissible in the conversational state are worlds in which Mary helps Peter. If this is the case, the test is passed. Likewise, 'The keys must be in the kitchen' tests that all open worlds in the conversational state are such that the keys are in the kitchen.

The crucial distinction here is between enforcing a property on the conversational state and testing whether the state has such a property (Charlow 2015, 36–37). For instance, when 'The keys are in the kitchen' is accepted, all worlds in which the keys are not in the kitchen are ruled out from the common ground. Thus, the property that all open worlds are such that the keys are in the kitchen is enforced on the conversational state: the conversational state is directly modified in a way that ensures that it has that property. By contrast, an assertion of 'The keys must be in the kitchen' leads to checking whether the conversational state has the relevant property (i.e. being such that in all open worlds the keys are in the kitchen). So, in tests the property in question is not directly enforced, but checked.

A natural reaction to a failed test is to accommodate, that is to modify the conversational state in a way that makes it pass the test. In the example of 'The keys must be in the kitchen', this will typically involve eliminating those open worlds in which the keys are not in the kitchen. Thus, the conversational state ultimately derived from the acceptance of the modal sentence may be the same as the state directly resulting from updating on the sentence 'The keys are in the kitchen'. It must be stressed, however, that the path to this final state is different in each case. The updating rule associated with the non-modal sentence directly instructs one to eliminate the worlds incompatible with the keys being in the kitchen. In other words, the semantic value of the sentence determines that the conversational state has to be updated in this way. By contrast, the semantic information of the modal sentence only specifies what test is to be performed, but not how the conversational state is to be modified after the failure of the test. When a test fails, the subsequent revision of the conversational state proceeds via accommodation: speakers modify the conversational state so that the sentence uttered can be accepted without rendering such conversational state defective (or else, they reject the sentence uttered). This process of accommodation is not directly guided by the semantic features of the sentence uttered, but by broader conversational rules concerning rational attitude-revision.

So, as long as there is a pragmatically significant difference between changes to the conversational state introduced via updating instructions encoded semantically and changes introduced via accommodation, the pragmatic profile of modal sentences will be clearly distinguishable from that of other declarative sentences (Charlow 2015, 36–38). It seems, therefore, that by embracing test semantics for modals the pragmatist is in a position to differentiate the characteristic uses of paradigmatically descriptive discourse and discourse involving modal operators (in particular, speech about obligations and permissions).

Can the contrast between descriptive and non-descriptive speech be recast in terms of this distinction between tests and eliminative updates? I think that there are reasons to remain cautious about the scope of this proposal. The problem is that not all instances of declarative speech typically taken to be non-descriptive involve modal operators. More specifically, normative and evaluative speech does not always include modal, intensional operators. There are many evaluative sentences in which the relevant evaluative expressions seem to constitute ordinary first-order predicates, rather than expressing higher-order operators (this is acknowledged in Chrisman 2015, ch. 7). Arguably, this is the case with 'cruel' in 'Mary is very cruel', 'tasty' in 'Artichokes are tasty', or 'beautiful' in 'Venice is a beautiful city.' Treating these sentences as involving higher-order operators seems to be unmotivated and ad hoc. Therefore, appealing to the distinctive conversational effects of modals would not allow us to differentiate these evaluative sentences from other declarative sentences involving ordinary first-order predicates. A possible option is to argue that only normative sentences that include modal operators (e.g. 'ought') should actually be seen as contrasting with paradigmatic descriptive speech. Evaluative discourse about goodness, tastiness or beauty would be, according to this view, on the descriptivist side of the divide. While this is a possibility, it seems that it will not be appealing to those with expressivist inclinations – after all, 'beauty' and 'good' are among the standard targets of expressivist proposals.

The distinction between tests and eliminative updates, therefore, is not enough to draw a general division between paradigmatic descriptive speech and other forms of assertoric discourse, including evaluative claims with no modal operators. In the next section, I explore the possibility of reconstructing the bifurcation thesis in terms of the contrast between relativistic and non-relativistic assertoric practices. This way of reformulating the bifurcation thesis allows one both to deal with first order evaluative predicates and to capture the anti-realist intuitions behind expressivism.

6. Relativism

According to the simple model of assertoric speech sketched above, assertions are proposals to add a proposition to the conversational common ground. From this point of view, we can say that two assertions are incompatible when, for any possible non-defective conversational state, the simultaneous addition to the common ground of the two propositions asserted makes the conversational state defective. In this way, when two speakers make incompatible assertions they would be proposing that the common ground is updated in incompatible ways. The two updating proposals cannot be both accepted in relation to the same common ground, on pains on getting a defective conversational state.

In standard assertoric practices, only one of two incompatible assertions can be correctly accepted in relation to a given conversational state – that is, only one of two incompatible propositions can be correctly added to the common ground. In Brandom's terminology, when two propositions are incompatible speakers cannot be actually entitled to accept both of them. This idea can be expressed in terms of a truth correctness-standard governing assertoric practices: asserting *p* is correct only if *p* is true (Kölbel 2008, 10). In general, out of two incompatible propositions only one can be true, so only one can be correctly asserted.

Let us make the plausible assumption that correctness-standards have normative force, so that an incorrect performance is impermissible or inappropriate (Whiting 2009). If this is so, then at least one of two speakers asserting incompatible things is doing something impermissible. This is why assertoric disagreement generates a normative tension (see Price 2003). When one makes an assertion that is incompatible with a previous assertion by another speaker, one is challenging that speaker's entitlement to make her assertion (Brandom 1994). So, disagreeing assertions lead to an unstable conversational state – there are normative pressures to revise such a state in order to move back to a situation of agreement.

The resulting picture is that of assertion as a practice governed by norms, in particular a norm that prohibits asserting something false. Arguably, this basic norm gives rise to the requirement to retract an assertion that is false, given that asserting falsities is impermissible (MacFarlane 2014, ch. 5; Price 2003; Whiting 2013). Furthermore, in principle it will be appropriate to challenge, criticize or reject a false assertion – more broadly, it will be appropriate to treat asserting something false as impermissible (Brandom 1994; MacFarlane 2005, 2007).[10] These sorts of normative constraints (and perhaps others) characterize the speech act of assertion.

Assuming this general framework for assertion, we can now describe specifically the properties of relativistic assertoric speech. I will follow here the main ideas of MacFarlane's account of relativism (2005, 2007, 2014).[11] In accordance with pragmatist metasemantics, MacFarlane thinks that the attribution of relativist semantic features to a sentence is only vindicated if it is suitably connected with relevant aspects of the use of that sentence (MacFarlane 2007, 2014, ch. 5; an alternative pragmatist rendering of relativism can be found in Shapiro 2014).[12] Thus, we need to specify how relativistic assertoric practices work.

The basic norm of standard assertion applies as well in relativistic discourse: it is impermissible to assert something false. The main difference in relativistic assertion is that the truth values of propositions are not perspective-independent; therefore, the correctness or permissibility of an assertion is not perspective-independent either. In non-relativistic domains, if a proposition is *actually* false as evaluated from a certain perspective, it will also be false from any other perspective or context of evaluation. So, a false assertion will be properly assessed as impermissible from any perspective in the practice. By contrast, in relativistic discourse, an assertion that is actually true as evaluated from a certain perspective can be actually false in relation to a further perspective of evaluation. As a result, there will be no perspective-independent answer to the question of whether an assertion is false, and thereby impermissible. Assume, for instance, that discourse about personal taste is relativistic. Then, the proposition 'Artichokes are tasty' can be true in relation to the perspective of evaluation of someone that likes artichokes, but false in relation to the perspective of someone who does not like them.

Appealing to the notion of truth in relation to a context of assessment, the basic norm of assertion can be reformulated as follows: asserting p is permissible, as assessed from context c', only if p is true in relation to the context of assessment c' (and the context of utterance c).[13]

In a similar way, we can formulate norms for relativistic retraction (MacFarlane 2014, ch. 5) and challenges or rejections (MacFarlane 2007). The idea is that a speaker in a context c' ought to retract an assertion that is false in relation to that context of assessment c'. Likewise, a speaker in a context c' may permissibly challenge or reject an assertion that is false as assessed from context c'. These norms are a generalization of the norms for retraction and challenges in non-relativistic domains.[14]

What we find in relativistic domains is that there does not need to be a perspective-independent way of determining which of two disagreeing agents is right. It may happen that, from the perspective of a first agent, it is actually permissible to make an assertion that, from the perspective of a second agent, is actually permissible to reject or challenge.[15] So, in relativistic domains it can be the case that, from the perspective of some agent, it is permissible to add a certain proposition to the common ground, whereas it is impermissible to do so from the perspective of other participants in the conversation. These sorts of disputes in relativistic domains can only be settled by adopting some evaluative perspective: there is no neutral way of solving relativistic disagreements.

6.1. Relativism and expressivism

My proposal is that, in general, assertions in the areas of discourse traditionally targeted by expressivists behave in a relativistic way. Thus, in the target domains agents still put forward their views in the form of assertions (and often express their beliefs in doing so), but these assertions are relativistic. This association between relativist assertion and the areas of discourse addressed by expressivists opens a clear path for a pragmatist reconstruction of the bifurcation thesis. The distinction between non-relativist (i.e. absolutist) and relativist assertoric practices allows the pragmatist to recover the contrast between declarative sentences used in a genuinely descriptive way and declarative sentences receiving non-descriptive uses (for instance, in normative discourse). This proposal has at least some initial plausibility, given that most areas of discourse targeted by expressivists have also received a relativistic treatment (see MacFarlane 2014 for a detailed review). In particular, it should be noted that modal speech – which, as discussed in Section 4, has been taken to be a source of non-descriptive assertions – lends itself naturally to a relativistic analysis (MacFarlane 2014, ch. 10–11).

Indeed, relativistic assertion captures to a large extent the anti-realist, non-descriptivist motivation behind most expressivist proposals. As we have seen above, relativistic disputes cannot be adjudicated in a neutral way, but only from inside one of the perspectives potentially engaged in the debate – there is no external viewpoint from which it can be determined what side of the dispute is right. So, if normative discourse worked relativistically, then one could only give a verdict about some first-order normative controversy from the perspective of some endorsed system of norms of values.[16] There is a sense, therefore, in which relativistic disputes are not about how the world is, but rather about what evaluative perspective to adopt (e.g. what values to endorse). It is in this sense that assertoric discourse in the domains targeted by expressivists can be said to be 'non-factual' or 'non-descriptive'. Of course, in keeping with the minimalism favored by pragmatists, we will still be in a position to talk about (monadic) truth, descriptions and facts in relation to such domains, but these will be relativistic facts: what the facts actually are will depend on the perspective of evaluation. Thus, the debate between realist and anti-realist accounts of a given domain of discourse would become a debate about whether assertions in such a domain are governed by relativistic norms (rather than about whether fact-talk is warranted in that domain).

One may wonder what is the point of relativistic speech. Why would we use assertoric speech in areas of discourse where our primary aims are not representational or descriptive? A plausible answer is that we do so in order to take advantage of the normative mechanisms afforded by assertoric practices. Assertoric challenges tend to impose normative pressures on the addressee, insofar as they express disapproval (the agent making the challenge presents herself as taking the addressee to be doing something impermissible). In this way, assertoric speech is a systematic and effective way of creating normative frictions that promote the coordination and alignment of our attitudes (see MacFarlane 2007, 2014). As Macfarlane (2007, 30) puts it: 'Perhaps, then, the point of using controversy-inducing assessment-sensitive vocabulary is to foster coordination of contexts.'

The idea, therefore, is that in domains where there is a point in attuning our attitudes, it will make sense to resort to assertoric speech. In this way, it is not so much that we can use assertions in areas of discourse that aim to describe the world, but rather that when we want to introduce the normative friction associated with assertoric disagreement, we will tend to make use of assertion (and thereby, the relevant area of discourse will automatically count as descriptive in a minimalist way). So, as Price argues, it is the application of the norms of assertoric practice 'which creates the disagreement, where initially there was mere difference' (Price 2003, 17). Of course, speakers are not always obliged to become subject to the normative pressures of assertoric speech. It is often possible to elude assertoric disagreements by retreating to reports of one's attitudes or claims that are explicitly relativized to perspectives (e.g. 'I like artichokes', 'Artichokes are tasty for me').[17]

One of the main virtues of the relativistic approach I am sketching is its theoretical parsimony: it does not require a radically different account of assertion and the semantics of declarative sentences specifically tailored for the domains of discourse targeted by expressivists. Speech in these domains would co-opt the normative mechanisms of regular assertion, so we can retain much of the standard analysis of assertoric discourse (rather than having to appeal to additional normative mechanisms, such as disagreement in non-doxastic attitudes or metalinguistic negotiation). In particular, we can keep understanding assertoric speech acts in these domains as proposals to add propositions to the common ground. For instance, by asserting 'It is wrong to steal books from the library', I propose to rule out from the common ground those worlds in which it is permissible for you to steal books from the library (or, equivalently, I propose to rule out from the permissibility set those worlds in which you steal books from the library). In this way, the attitude directly expressed in typical instances of relativistic assertions would just be a (relativistic) belief. Perhaps the ultimate goal of the speech act is to express some further attitude, such us the endorsement of some system of norms and values, but this would be done indirectly, rather than as part of the characteristic function of the speech act.

Presumably, by presenting yourself as believing that the world is such that it is impermissible for you to steal, you present yourself as endorsing a system of norms that make that action impermissible. So, relativistic assertion may be an indirect way of expressing non-doxastic attitudes, but this would be done just by resorting to the standard mechanisms of assertoric practices, without having to introduce further linguistic machinery.[18] Expressivist models, therefore, can be reformulated in a simple way within a relativistic framework. In other words, relativism can be seen as an implementation of the expressivist project without high theoretical costs.[19] By contrast, other proposals would require more radically revisionary accounts of our linguistic practices – for instance, treating sentences with first-order evaluative predicates as actually involving modal operators (as discussed in Section 5).

6.2. Identifying relativistic practices

Of course, even if relativist assertion is governed by the same types of norms as standard assertoric speech, the point I am trying to make is precisely that there is a significant practical difference between both forms of assertoric discourse, and that this difference may ground a pragmatist reconstruction of the bifurcation thesis. The relevant practical difference is that, as explained above, in relativistic assertion disputes cannot be settled in a perspective-independent way. So, an external observer studying a relativistic practice would find disagreements in which there seems to be no potential fact or piece of evidence that would adjudicate the dispute in a manner acceptable to all (rational) debaters.

To be sure, it is not clear that one can assess a relativistic dispute from a genuinely external point of view. Arguably, evaluating the merits of some position in a relativistic debate can only be done by adopting oneself a particular assessing perspective. And from the inside of a practice it is difficult to ascertain whether such a practice is relativistic or rather absolutist (Cappelen and Hawthorne 2011, 460–461; MacFarlane 2014, 199–200; Shapiro 2014, 145). After all, participants in a relativistic practice will assess some assertions as correct because, from their perspective, they actually seem to be so. This is this same that happens in a non-relativistic, absolutist practice: agents treat as correct what seems correct from their perspective. The subjective experience of agents, then, will be very similar when participating in a relativistic and a non-relativistic practice. However, this does not need to be problematic for my proposed reconstruction of the bifurcation thesis; indeed, it is as it should be, in view of the entrenched, recalcitrant metaethical debates about realism. A relativistic approach allows us to do justice both to anti-realist and absolutist intuitions – and to explain why the limits between descriptive and non-descriptive discourse are often unclear.

All this does not mean that we cannot decide, on reflection, that relativism offers the best model for characterizing an assertoric practice we are part of. This will happen, for instance, if we reach the conclusion that the sorts of debates participants in the practice engage in are unlikely to find a perspective-independent resolution, and not due to some epistemological limitation, but rather because there is no potential 'smoking gun' – that is, there is no potential decisive piece of evidence that would be recognized as such by all rational participants in the debate. In those areas of discourse less prone to a relativistic analysis, there tend to be possible tests and sources of evidence whose force and significance is acknowledged by all relevant agents. So, if we are discussing the location of your keys, all parties will presuppose that direct perception of the keys on the kitchen table would provide (at least in normal circumstances) a definitive answer to the issue discussed. In this way, in order to determine whether some assertoric practice is relativistic, we can investigate whether it is suitably related to some such baseline, agreed-upon standards of correctness. Non-relativistic assertoric speech will in general be inferentially connected with practices in which there are sources of evidence that are presupposed to provide perspective-independent verdicts, such as empirical observation (see Chrisman 2011). Depending on what types of sources of evidence we are willing to count as playing this arbitrage role, we will include more or less areas of discourse in one side or the other of the divide established by the bifurcation thesis.

7. Conclusions

Traditional expressivist projects highlight the distinction between domains of discourse where declarative sentences are used to describe the world, and domains where they are used in other ways. This distinction becomes blurred when one adopts a minimalist perspective about representational notions, according to which all instances of assertoric speech automatically count as purporting to describe how things are. My proposal has been to reconstruct the distinction between descriptive and non-descriptive assertoric speech by appeal to the contrast between relativistic and non-relativistic assertion. This contrast can be specified in non-representational terms, so it offers a way of reconstructing the expressivist distinction that is available for pragmatists embracing minimalism about representational notions. Moreover, this way of reconstructing the relevant distinction works both for sentences involving first-order evaluative predicates (such as 'good' or 'beautiful') and also for higher order operators (such as 'ought'). In general, the areas of discourse where expressivism has some initial plausibility are also amenable to a relativistic analysis.

Notes

1. Compare Charlow (2015, 34): 'to know a sentence's semantic value is to be in a position to know which state of mind is constitutively involved in the acceptance of that sentence.'
2. The distinction between semantic value and informational upshot is needed because informational upshots (e.g. propositions constructed as sets of worlds)

do not always compose, whereas semantic values are standardly expected to respect compositionality (see Lewis 1980; Rabern 2012).
3. Price (2011, 2015) proposes reconstructing the relevant bifurcation in terms of the notion of 'e-representation', which would be a non-representational relation of tracking or covariance with environmental features (e-representation would be distinctive of the types of speech that the expressivists wants to classify as descriptive). My suspicion is that this notion will either turn out to be actually representational or it will not suffice to characterize descriptive speech. Anyway, I will not pursue these worries here, but rather explore my own proposal.
4. Although Brandom tends to talk of the scoreboard of individual speakers, we can consider a common conversational scoreboard reflecting the commitments and entitlements shared by the speakers, as participants of the conversation.
5. In particular, Brandom (1994, ch. 3) argues that the audience acquires an entitlement by deferral to the proposition asserted. This means that the audience's responsibility to vindicate their entitlement to the proposition (if suitably challenged) can be delegated to the speaker who made the assertion.
6. From this point of view, worlds would be characterized by maximally specific propositions, that is propositions that answer all possible questions (or at least, all possible questions relevant for the purposes of the conversation). In this way, a proposition characterizing a world will be incompatible with either p or $-p$ for any relevant proposition p.
7. Brandom's broader story includes connections between commitments to accepting propositions and practical commitments to acting in certain ways, and also connections between occupying certain perceptual positions and being entitled to accept some proposition (see Brandom 1994, ch. 4).
8. This is compatible with the existence of a technical notion of truth at a context and index playing a role in semantic theories to which the pragmatist may resort (see MacFarlane 2014; Yalcin 2011). The pragmatist is only committed to eschewing appeals to a substantive notion of truth in her ultimate account of why expressions mean what they do, not in technical explanations at the semantic level.
9. Or a set of such classifications, if we want to make room for normative uncertainty. I will leave these complications aside.
10. MacFarlane (2014) claims that retracting an assertion is a speech act made by saying things like 'I take that back'. Likewise, rejections or challenges could be seen as explicitly expressed by saying something like 'Take that back, you are wrong!'.
11. Another influential presentation of relativism is provided by Kölbel (2008, 2015).
12. This does not mean that MacFarlane is committed to an anti-representationalist version of pragmatism. It may be that the relevant practice is to be characterized by appeal to representationalist notions (see MacFarlane 2010 for discussion of pragmatist metasemantics).
13. Following MacFarlane (2014, ch. 4), I allow for the possibility that the truth value of a proposition depends both on features of the context of assessment and the context of utterance. For my purposes here, it is enough to focus on the dependence on the context of assessment. Therefore, in what follows I drop the mention to the context of utterance.
14. Note that such generalized norms can be used to give a unified account of relativistic and non-relativistic assertion. In non-relativistic domains, such norms will reduce to the non-relativistic ones, since the truth value of propositions will be insensitive to contexts of assessment.

15. Relativistic assertion so understood must be distinguished from contextualist or indexicalist speech, in which the same sentence can be used to assert different propositions in different contexts of utterance. What Harman (1975) calls 'moral relativism' is actually a version of indexicalism.
16. It is important to note, however, that asserting something like 'Stealing is wrong' does not amount to *reporting* one's endorsement of the relevant values or norms. Rather, one would be making an assertion that is true only in relation to contexts of assessment in which certain values are endorsed.
17. It may be hypothesized that in those areas of discourse where intersubjective coordination is more valuable, we will be more inclined to make use of the normative friction introduced by assertion, and we will be more reluctant to retreat to agent-relative claims merely reporting one's attitudes.
18. Of course, we need to characterize the notion of relativistic assertion, and this is likely to involve some modifications in our semantic theory. But these modifications will be reasonably conservative, and the resulting picture will be continuous with standard theories of meaning (see MacFarlane 2014, ch. 5). Note, in particular, that although relativism introduces a technical notion of truth at a context of assessment, the monadic truth predicate used in ordinary speech will still behave in a standard way (i.e. one will take assertions of 'p is true' to be permissible whenever assertions of 'p' are).
19. For discussion of the relations between relativism and expressivism, see MacFarlane (2014), Field (2009) and Stalnaker (2014).

Acknowledgements

Thanks to an anonymous referee for this journal and audiences at the Granada Workshop on Epistemic Expressivism and the 2017 EPISOC summer school for their feedback.

Disclosure statement

No potential conflict of interest was reported by the author.

Funding

This work was supported by Ministerio de Economía y Competitividad [grant number FFI2014-57258-P].

References

Alvarez, Maria. 2010. *Kinds of Reasons*. Oxford: Oxford University Press.
Asay, Jamin. 2013. "Truthmaking, Metaethics, and Creeping Minimalism." *Philosophical Studies* 163 (1): 213–232.
Blackburn, Simon. 2010. *Practical Tortoise Raising: And Other Philosophical Essays*. Oxford: Oxford University Press.
Blackburn, Simon. 2013. "Pragmatism: All or Some?" In *Expressivism, Pragmatism and Representationalism*, edited by Huw Price, 67–84. Oxford: Oxford University Press.
Brandom, Robert. 1994. *Making It Explicit: Reasoning, Representing, and Discursive Commitment*. Cambridge, MA: Harvard University Press.
Brandom, Robert. 2000. *Articulating Reasons*. Cambridge, MA: Harvard University Press.
Cappelen, Herman, and John Hawthorne. 2011. "Reply to Lasersohn, MacFarlane, and Richard." *Philosophical Studies* 156 (3): 449–466.
Charlow, Nate. 2015. "Prospects for an Expressivist Theory of Meaning." *Philosophers' Imprint* 15 (23): 1–43.
Chrisman, Matthew. 2008. "Expressivism, Inferentialism, and Saving the Debate." *Philosophy and Phenomenological Research* 77 (2): 334–358.
Chrisman, Matthew. 2011. "Expressivism, Inferentialism and the Theory of Meaning." In *New Waves in Metaethics*, edited by Michael Brady, 103–125. London: Palgrave Macmillan.
Chrisman, Matthew. 2015. *The Meaning of 'Ought': Beyond Descriptivism and Expressivism in Metaethics*. Oxford: Oxford University Press.
Dancy, Jonathan. 2000. *Practical Reality*. Oxford: Clarendon Press.
Dreier, James. 2004. "Meta-Ethics and the Problem of Creeping Minimalism." *Philosophical Perspectives* 18 (1): 23–44.
Field, Hartry. 2009. "Epistemology without Metaphysics." *Philosophical Studies* 143 (2): 249–290.
Golub, Camil. 2017. "Expressivism and Realist Explanations." *Philosophical Studies* 174 (6): 1385–1409.
Harman, Gilbert. 1975. "Moral Relativism Defended." *The Philosophical Review* 84 (1): 3–22.
Horwich, Paul. 1998. *Meaning*. Oxford: Oxford University Press.
Kölbel, Max. 2008. "Motivations for Relativism." In *Relative Truth*, edited by Manuel Garcia-Carpintero and Max Kölbel, 1–38. Oxford: Oxford University Press.
Kölbel, Max. 2015. "Relativism 2: Semantic Content." *Philosophy Compass* 10 (1): 52–67.
Lewis, David. 1979. "Scorekeeping in a Language Game." *Journal of Philosophical Logic* 8: 339–359.
Lewis, David. 1980. "Index, Context, and Content." In *Philosophy and Grammar*, edited by Stig Kanger and Sven Öhman, 79–100. Dordrecht: Reidel.
MacFarlane, John. 2005. "Making Sense of Relative Truth." *Proceedings of the Aristotelian Society* 105: 305–323.
MacFarlane, John. 2007. "Relativism and Disagreement." *Philosophical Studies* 132 (1): 17–31.
MacFarlane, John. 2010. "Pragmatism and Inferentialism." In *Reading Brandom. On Making it Explicit*, edited by Bernhard Weiss and Jeremy Wanderer, 81–95. London: Routledge.
MacFarlane, John. 2014. *Assessment Sensitivity: Relative Truth and its Applications*. Oxford: Oxford University Press.
Pérez Carballo, Alejandro. 2014. "Semantic Hermeneutics." In *Metasemantics: New Essays on the Foundations of Meaning*, edited by Alexis Burgess and Brett Sherman, 119–146. Oxford: Oxford University Press.
Price, Huw. 2003. "Truth as Convenient Friction." *Journal of Philosophy* 100 (4): 167–190.

Price, Huw. 2011. *Naturalism without Mirrors*. Oxford: Oxford University Press.
Price, Huw. 2015. "From Quasirealism to Global Expressivism–And Back Again?" In *Passions and Projections: Themes from the Philosophy of Simon Blackburn*, edited by Robert N. Johnson and Michael Smith, 134–152. Oxford: Oxford University Press.
Rabern, Brian. 2012. "Against the Identification of Assertoric Content with Compositional Value." *Synthese* 189 (1): 75–96.
Rothschild, Daniel, and Seth Yalcin. 2017. "On the Dynamics of Conversation." *Noûs* 51 (1): 24–48.
Shapiro, Lionel. 2014. "Assertoric Force Perspectivalism: Relativism without Relative Truth." *Ergo* 1 (6): 1–30.
Silk, Alex. 2015. "How to be an Ethical Expressivist." *Philosophy and Phenomenological Research* 91 (1): 47–81.
Stalnaker, Robert. 2014. *Context*. Oxford: Oxford University Press.
Starr, William. 2016. "Dynamic Expressivism about Deontic Modality." In *Deontic Modality*, edited by Nate Charlow and Matthew Chrisman, 355–394. Oxford: Oxford University Press.
Tiefensee, Christine. 2016. "Inferentialist Metaethics, Bifurcations and Ontological Commitment." *Philosophical Studies* 173 (9): 2437–2459.
Veltman, Frank. 1996. "Defaults in Update Semantics." *Journal of Philosophical Logic* 25 (3): 221–261.
Whiting, Daniel. 2009. "Is Meaning Fraught with Ought?" *Pacific Philosophical Quarterly* 90 (4): 535–555.
Whiting, Daniel. 2013. "Stick to the Facts: On the Norms of Assertion." *Erkenntnis* 78 (4): 847–867.
Williams, Michael. 2010. "Pragmatism, Minimalism, Expressivism." *International Journal of Philosophical Studies* 18 (3): 317–330.
Williams, Michael. 2013. "How Pragmatists Can Be Local Expressivists." In *Expressivism, Pragmatism and Representationalism*, edited by Huw Price, 128–144. Cambridge: Cambridge University Press.
Yalcin, Seth. 2011. "Nonfactualism about Epistemic Modality." In *Epistemic Modality*, edited by Andy Egan and Brian Weatherson, 295–332. Oxford: Oxford University Press.

ⓐ OPEN ACCESS

Perspectival representation and fallacies in metaethics

Max Kölbel

ABSTRACT
The prevailing theoretical framework for theorising about representation construes all representation as involving objective representational contents. This classic framework has tended to drive philosophers either to claim that evaluative judgements are representations and therefore objective, or else to claim that evaluative judgements are not really representations, because they are not objective. However, a more general, already well-explored framework is available, which will allow theorists to treat evaluative judgements as full-fledged representations (thus doing justice to their representational aspects) while leaving open whether they are objective. Such a more general conception of representational content is exemplified, e.g. by Lewis's 'centred contents' and Gibbard's framework of 'contents of judgement', thus it is not new. I shall start in §1 by introducing the more general framework of perspectival contents and then illustrate in §2 how awareness of it can help expose the fallaciousness of certain widely used forms of argumentation in metaethics.

1. Perspectival representational contents

1.1. Representation

All representation minimally involves representing things as being some way. If things are as represented, the representation is accurate or correct. For example, a representation might represent things in general as being such that there are cats, or it might represent a particular cat as being large, amusing or hungry. We will here be interested in certain types of representation, namely representations that are mental states, such as beliefs, or linguistic acts, such as assertions.

Uncontroversial examples of representational mental states or linguistic acts would be, for example:

(B1) My belief that there are cats.

(B2) My belief that Apolo is a cat.

(B3) My belief that my neighbours have a cat.

(B4) My belief that Apolo is my neighbours' cat.

(U1) My utterance of the sentence 'There are cats.'

(U2) My utterance of the sentence 'Apolo is a cat.'

(U3) My utterance of the sentence 'My neighbours have a cat.'

(U4) My utterance of the sentence 'Apolo is my neighbours' cat.'

For one reason or another, the following mental states and linguistic acts are not uncontroversial examples of representations:

(B5) My judgement that Apolo is amusing.

(B6) My judgement that it is bad to leave Apolo alone in the flat.

(U5) My utterance of the sentence 'Apolo is amusing.'

(U6) My utterance of the sentence 'Leaving Apolo alone in the flat is bad.'

I think I could have equally characterized the mental states (B5) and (B6) as my *beliefs* that Apolo is amusing and that locking him in is bad respectively. I chose the term 'judgement' in order to have a term that is more neutral and is not associated with certain assumptions that are usually made about beliefs in the context of non-cognitivism, namely that beliefs are descriptive, representational, truth-apt, objective, etc.

Why should these examples be controversial? I suggested above that representations represent things as being some way, and that they are accurate or correct just if things are as represented. If that is all there is to representation, then (B5), (B6), U5) and (U6) should qualify as representations, for each of them seems to represent things in some way, and each of them will be accurate or correct if and only if things are as they have been represented.

However, the trouble starts when we specify how things are represented by a given representation (and thereby also specify what would be required for the representation to be correct). It seems that B2 represents Apolo as a cat, and that B2 will therefore be correct just if Apolo is indeed a cat. Similarly, we might say, B5 represents Apolo as amusing, and it should be regarded as correct just if Apolo is indeed amusing. However, at this point, some will say that whether B5 is correct depends not just on how things are with the object of representation,

Apolo, but also on how things are with me, the owner of B5. To see this, compare a further mental state, and corresponding utterance:

(B7) Your judgement that Apolo is amusing.

(U7) Your utterance of 'Apolo is amusing.'

Let us suppose that at the time of B5, my dispositions to be amused are such that Apolo is (at the time of B5) liable to amuse me, but that your dispositions (at the time of B7) are such that he will not amuse you. It would seem, then, that B5 is correct, while B7 is not. Nevertheless, both B5 and B7 can be described as representing the same object, Apolo, in the same way, namely as amusing. So, if we accept this description of the representational content of B5 and B7 (they both represent Apolo as amusing), then clearly the correctness of B5 and B7 does not depend only on how things are with Apolo, the object of representation. It seems to depend also on how things are with the owner of the mental state in question, for it is the difference between me and you (the respective owners of B5 and B7) that accounts for the difference in correctness.

Some philosophers think that we cannot, therefore, construe B5 and B7 as representing things in the same way, i.e. as having the same representational content.[1] On this kind of view, representational contents must be construed in such a way that if two representations (that occur in the same world) have the same content, then it cannot be that one is correct, but the other is not. Representational content, on this conception, determines correctness. Or perhaps I should precisify: given a state of the world, representational content determines representational correctness.

1.2. The classic conception

This sort of conception is in the tradition of Frege, who stipulated that *thoughts* (his analogue of contents) were to determine a truth-value, and did not allow that anything short of determining a truth-value could qualify as a thought (Frege 1918). On this conception, representational contents are by definition objective: if anyone believes such a content correctly at any time, then any belief with the same content, no matter by whom or at what time, will also be correct (assuming that truth is necessary and sufficient for correctness). Let's call this the 'classic conception', and let's call representational contents construed to meet this constraint 'classic contents'.

On the classic conception, then, if we are to say that B5 is correct while B7 is not, we *have to* construe them as having distinct representational contents, i.e. as not representing things in the same way. For example, on the classic conception, one might say that B5 and U5 represent Apolo as amusing *me*, while B7 and U7 represent Apolo as amusing *you*, thus assimilating B5 and B7 to B3 (or U3): my belief that my neighours have a cat does not have the same content as B8 (U8):

(B8) Your belief that your neighbours have a cat.

((U8) Your utterance of 'My neighbours have a cat.')

even though you would use the same words to express B8 (as in U8), or to ascribe it to yourself ('I think my neighbours have a cat.'). In the case of B3 and B8, we are less tempted to say that they share the same content, for we would not use the same words to specify how they represent things as being. This was different in the case of B5 and B7: both can be correctly described (by me, you or anyone else) as representing Apolo as amusing. On the classic conception, however, this description is not complete and masks a difference in representational content and B5 and B7 should be treated as having contents, respectively, like those of B9 and B10:

(B9) My belief that Apolo amuses me.[2]

(U9) My utterance of 'Apolo amuses me.'

(B10) Your belief that Apolo amuses you.

(U10) Your utterance of 'Apolo amuses me.'

1.3. Perspectival content

The classic conception, however, is not the only option. There is no compelling reason for stipulating that representational content must determine correctness (i.e. is objective by definition). Alternative, perspectival conceptions drop this requirement, so that we can, after all, maintain that the way B5 and B7 represent things as being is the same. Both B5 and B7 represent Apolo as amusing, but they do so, as it were, from different perspectives. On this conception, then, whether a representation with a certain representational content is correct can depend on who represents and at what time. We might say: whether it is correct to represent things a certain way, whether it is correct to believe a certain representational content, depends on the identity of the thinker and the time of thinking. In other words, this conception operates with perspectival contents, contents the correctness of believing which depends on a perspective or standpoint. For our purposes, we can think of perspectives as ordered triples of a thinker, a time and a posible world. On this conception, while a content (and the world) alone do not determine a truth-value, a content does so relative to a perspective.

I proposed initially that representation minimally involves representing things as being a certain way and that representations are correct iff things are the way they are represented as being. The classic conception adds a further objectivity requirement, namely that the ways things are represented as being can only be specified in a certain way, namely such that if two representations share the same representational content, they cannot differ with respect to correctness. Construing representational contents as perspectival involves maintaining the essential feature of representation but dropping the classic constraint on representational content. As a result, the perspectival approach will allow us to classify B5 and U5 as representations.

B6 and U6 – the judgement and claim that leaving Apolo alone in the flat is (morally) bad – are subject to similar worries as B5 and U5, in so far as there are philosophers who argue that the correctness of moral judgements may, in addition to depending on facts concerning the objects of moral evaluation, depend on features of the judge, such as her system of moral norms, or that of her community. Those who argue this will have options that are analogous to the ones just discussed for B5 and U5: adopt a classic or a perspectival conception.[3]

Besides allowing B5/U5 and B7/U7 to be uncontroversially classified as representations, *and* as representations with the same content, the perspectival approach also permits more *differentiation* in some cases of uncontroversial representations. Thus, we can distinguish between the content of B3 and the content of B11, while arguably the classic conception does not:

(B11) My belief that MK's neighbours have a cat.

It would also allow us to treat, for example, B9 and B10 as having the *same* content: they both represent the owner of the belief as being amused by Apolo. Of course this will be another case where correctness depends not only on how things are represented as being, but also on who does the representing.[4]

1.4. What is at stake?

It is not obvious what, if anything, is at stake in the choice between classic and perspectival conceptions of representational content. In my view, the situation is best described as follows.

Focus on our minimal starting point: representations represent things as being some way and they are correct iff they represent things as they are. However, there are many different respects of similarity that one could usefully focus on when thinking about how representations represent things as being and the conditions under which they would be correct. In some respects, B3 and B8 are similar: both of them represent the thinker's neighbours as having a cat. Both of them are representations that are correct just if the thinker who has the representation has neighbours who have a cat. A perspectival conception of content allows modeling this similarity as sameness of content. The proponents of the classic conception may well be interested in this kind of similarity too, they do not, however, want to capture this respect of similarity in terms of sameness of content. Instead, they try to abstract from a different respect of similarity, namely that obtaining between B3 and B11: both represent the same object (MK's neighbours) as being the same way. The respect of similarity they are interested in entails sameness of correctness status: any two representations similar in this respect are also similar in respect of correctness. This means that the classic conception needs to capture the earlier mentioned similarity between B3 and B8 in a way that does not require sameness of content.[5] As long as each conception is able to offer alternative ways of modelling similarities that are captured by the other, there seems to be nothing substantial at issue between the two approaches.

I conceded that similarities captured as sameness of content on perspectival conceptions can be described in other ways on classic conceptions. However, are perspectival conceptions conversely able to model everything classic conceptions can model? Yes, they can. Let us focus for a moment on a well-known, simple and elegant implementation of the classic conception: the conception of contents as functions from possible worlds to truth-values (or, equivalently, sets of possible worlds). Compare this classic notion of content with a corresponding perspectival notion of contents as functions from 'centred worlds' to truth-values, where centred worlds are simply ordered pairs $<w, c>$ consisting of a world w and a center c (where centres are in turn construed as ordered pairs of thinkers and times). David Lewis (1979) has shown that *this* perspectival notion is a generalization of *this* classic notion, in the following sense: Amongst all the perspectival contents some are what has been called 'boring'[6] or 'portable'[7]: the centre-component of each centred world is irrelevant for the value of the function, because if the value of the function is truth for some centred world $<w, c>$, then it is truth also for every centred world $<w, c'>$ with a different centre, but the same world. Or if we think of contents as sets: a set P of centered worlds is *portable* just if: for all centers c and worlds $w, <c, w> \in P$ only if for every center $c', <c', w> \in P$. Now, for each classic content C, there is exactly one portable perspectival counterpart P, such that $w \in C$ iff for some (or all) centres $c, <w, c> \in P$. Since there is exactly one counterpart portable centred content for each classic possible-worlds content, and counterparts share all the theoretical properties that do any work in the classic conception,[8] the framework of centred contents can do everything the classic framework can do.

Lewis's point seems to hold not only for unstructured contents, but for any conceptions of classic and perspectival structured content which are such that the only difference between them is that the classic conception imposes an extra condition of objectivity, and thereby rules out all except the portable ones amongst the perspectival contents.[9] For we will then again be able to find exactly one counterpart perspectival content for each classic content, which shares all the theoretically relevant properties. Thus, whatever else we think a content needs to do in addition to determining conditions under which it can be correctly believed: a perspectival version is just a generalization and can do everything its classic counterpart can do.

While this result is good news for the perspectival conceptions, it by no means decides which conception we should adopt. A theorist who is only interested in using her representational contents to explain phenomena that can be explained by classic contents, and who reserves other resources for other phenomena (or is not interested in them) can of course rationally stick to the classic conception.

Even if I am right, and the choice between the two frameworks is a matter of stipulation and a pragmatic choice, it will make a rhetorical and presentational difference whether we do or do not allow non-objective representations. Those convinced that evaluative thought is non-objective, in the sense that correctness depends on one's perspective, standpoint etc., may have a harder time selling their view if they are forced to say that evaluative thought does not qualify as representational (as they would be on the classic view).

The mere rhetorical or presentational significance of the choice, however, can mislead if the category of representation (as classically delimited) is erroneously imbued with further significance. For example, if it is assumed that everything that shares certain patterns of behaviour with paradigm representations should also (on pain of explanatory disunification) be a representation. This would be a fallacy, and demonstrably so, if there is an alternative notion of representation available that would restore explanatory uniformity. The second part of my paper attempts to diagnose such a fallacy.

2. Fallacies in metaethics

2.1. Introduction

I want to illustrate that our choice of notion of representational content – classic or perspectival – can mislead us into substantial philosophical mistakes. I believe that mainstream thinking in metaethics in the last half-century or so has been misguided by the narrow classic picture, because it makes certain metaethical views (non-cognitive ones) appear less unified. The basic theme is the one already mentioned: if we regard all representation as involving objective content, then our conceptual framework, our terminology, portrays anything that is otherwise a bona fide judgement, but lacks such a content, as something categorically different: as not a representation or as lacking proper representational content.

I suggested above that the matter is merely terminological: if we stipulate that representation must involve classic contents, then instead of arguing whether the contents of certain representations are objective, we'll be arguing whether certain mental states are or are not representations. That approach may be rhetorically unfair (to those who have to argue that certain bona fide judgements are not genuine representations), but as long as we do not imbue our choices of conceptual and terminological framework with substantial, perhaps metaphysical or explanatory, significance, we are completely free to choose as we wish. However, it is sometimes hard to remember later on that certain bits of framework that one has grown fond of were in fact the result of a stipulation that one could revoke at any time. The familiarity of notions employed in a theory (e.g. classic content) may also count as an explanatory advantage, but it is at most an historically contingent advantage that can vanish without residue as rival notions become more familiar.

This is all highly abstract. In order to fill this abstract possibility with concrete life, I will now show how awareness of the perspectival content framework can expose some well-known forms of reasoning in metaethics as fallacious. The fallacious reasoning I have in mind is frequently exhibited in the family of objections against metaethical non-cognitivism and expressivism that is associated with the label 'Frege-Geach point'.

I shall first outline a certain non-cognitivist/expressivist outlook with an emphasis on those aspects that are important for my point. Here I will distinguish non-cognitivism: a view about the nature of the mental states one might call 'moral judgements', from expressivism: a view specifically about moral language. Then I shall outline some conclusions drawn from the Frege-Geach point that exhibit a fallacy to which I think our stipulation of classic representational contents can lead. In order to demonstrate that I am not merely taking down a straw man, I shall then show how even the most sophisticated and sympathetic engagement with expressivism, namely Mark Schroeder's, is guilty of a version of this fallacy. Finally, I shall outline a rudimentary theory of 'judgements', understood as those representational mental states that have perspectival contents.

2.2. Non-cognitivism

Metaethical non-cognitivism is a view about the nature of moral judgements, namely the view that moral judgements are non-cognitive mental states. Paradigm examples of cognitive mental states are beliefs, while paradigm examples of non-cognitive mental states are desires or preferences. Thus non-cognitivism is a view about a certain class of mental states, namely the class of moral judgements. It is often pointed out that the term 'judgement' is ambiguous between an act-sense and a state sense. It is here used in the state-sense: it denotes a state of mind, i.e. an opinion or conviction, rather than a mental act of judging.

Expressivism, as I shall explain below, is a view about moral language which, even though usually motivated by non-cognitivism, is a clearly separable idea. Unfortunately, it is not usually clearly separated. For some reason, the canonical or textbook formula widely used to characterize non-cognitivism, emotivism and expressivism is as 'the view that moral judgements express non-cognitive attitudes'. This formula ('The Formula') does not make sense on either of the two senses of 'judgement' I just distinguished. For neither does anyone intend to characterize a view according to which one mental *state* expresses another, nor does anyone intend to characterize a view according to which one mental *act or episode* expresses another. What the many users of The Formula clearly intend is the view that some overt act or behaviour, such as that of *making a moral statement*, expresses a non-cognitive attitude. Thus, the only way to make sense of 'judgement' in The Formula is to take it in a third sense, namely as denoting an overt act of making a claim or statement. Understood in this way, The Formula does contain a decent enough characterization of what I shall call 'expressivism' below, but this third sense of 'judgement' is highly unusual and therefore potentially confusing. I shall stick to 'judgement' in the state-sense and stay away completely from The Formula. Instead, I shall do as I did above and characterize non-cognitivism as the view that moral judgements *are* non-cognitive states, while characterizing expressivism as the view that moral statements, i.e. utterances of moral sentences, *express* non-cognitive states.

A quick reminder of the typical motivations for non-cognitivism will help us get the right perspective on this family of views. Let me distinguish metaphysical, epistemological and psychological motivations. *Metaphysical*: if moral judgements were cognitive states, i.e. beliefs, then they would aim to represent how things are objectively. Accordingly, any correct moral judgements would be correct because they represents some aspect of objective reality correctly. Therefore cognitivism, if combined with the view that some moral judgements are correct, requires there to be aspects of reality that make moral judgements true: moral facts. This is regarded as problematic by philosophers with a naturalist outlook who also think that there is no naturalistic reduction of moral values.

Epistemological: relatedly, if cognitivism is true and some moral judgements do indeed represent moral facts correctly, then how do we acquire knowledge of such facts, given that there seems to be no suitable empirical or a priori form of justification available.

Psychological: if we accept a Humean picture of the mind, then beliefs or cognitive states (the outputs of a Humean faculty of reason) cannot by themselves motivate thinkers to act. Beliefs only serve to inform our desires and preferences, but without any desires or preferences they would be completely motivationally inert. Combined with motivational internalism about moral judgements, the Humean picture therefore motivates non-cognitivism: if moral judgements in conjunction with certain beliefs, do motivate us in the absence of any further motivating mental states (desires, preferences), then they must themselves be on the non-cognitive side of Hume's divide.

Based on these typical motivations, let me make some observations that will be relevant later in §2.9.[10] The non-cognitivist's claim is that moral judgements are non-cognitive mental states. Given the psychological motivation, these non-cognitive mental states must fall on the motivating side in a Humean picture of the mind. Thus, the idea is that judgements in general divide into cognitive (motivationally inert) and non-cognitive (intrinsically motivating) ones, and that moral judgements in particular (perhaps alongside other types of value-judgement) fall on the motivating side. The important point to retain here is that non-cognitivists are committed to a specific claim of discontinuity between moral judgements (and perhaps some other value judgements) and other judgements, concerning their motivational features: moral judgements fall on the motivational side of Hume's divide between reason and passion.

Similarly, the epistemological motivation commits the non-cognitivist to the view that not all judgements admit of straightforward empirical justification, and that only those that do should be regarded as cognitive. Ayer, for example, points out that moral intuition would not qualify as an appropriate source of empirical justification, because there is no way to settle the matter when two different thinkers' intuitions conflict. The metaphysical motivation also relies on the assumption that cognitive states (beliefs), when successful, correspond to objective aspects of reality, i.e. facts. Thus, the epistemological and metaphysical motivation seem to require that cognitive states correspond to, and (when true) are made true by, objective aspects of reality, for which there is an empirical method that could settle conflicts effectively.

To summarise, the non-cognitivist seems committed to three kinds of difference between moral and cognitive judgements: (a) moral judgements do not, like cognitive judgements, represent aspects of objective reality, (b) the method used to justify moral judgements cannot effectively settle inter-subjective disagreements, as empirical methods in science (supposedly) can, and (c) moral judgements are not, like beliefs, motivationally inert. As long as the non-cognitivist retains her specific claim of discontinuity between moral and other types of judgement, she is free to view the wider category of judgements as otherwise highly continuous.

2.3. Expressivism

As already mentioned briefly, expressivism is a thesis about moral language that naturally complements non-cognitivism. It seems undeniable that in some good sense declarative sentences, or their utterances, express judgements. Thus, the sentence 'Gambling is a lucrative business.' serves to express the judgement that gambling is a lucrative business, and the sentence 'Gambling is bad.' serves to express the judgement that gambling is bad. What does it mean to say that a sentence serves to express a mental state, or perhaps more accurately, that we can utter a sentence and thereby express a mental state? There are many things one could say here. Minimally, the claim that a sentence, or utterances of it, express a mental state seems to be a characterization of an aspect of the sentence's conventional meaning. We might say further, and still fairly generally, that the sentence, by virtue of its conventional meaning, is suitable for performing a certain speech-act that requires, as a condition on the speech-act's sincerity, that the sentence-user have the mental state. This much should be fairly uncontroversial.[11]

Expressivism, now, seems to be built on this fairly uncontroversial assumption that sentences are meant (in some sense) for the expression of mental states. It seems sensible to say that moral sentences like 'Gambling is bad.' serve to express moral judgements in precisely the sense just mentioned. If moral judgements are non-cognitive mental states, as the non-cognitivist claims, then moral sentences express non-cognitive mental states. This is the expressivist's thesis. It follows from non-cognitivism on the simple assumption that moral sentences serve to express moral judgements.

Looked at in the way I just did, expressivism is not a particularly exciting addition to non-cognitivism. However, it immediately looks more interesting once we place it in the context of some surrounding assumptions about language. Let us consider the following assumptions:

A1 Declarative sentences express beliefs.

A2 Declarative sentences are assertoric (i.e. they serve, in virtue of their meaning, for the performance of assertions).

A3 Assertions aim at objective truth (they have objective contents).

The expressivist has to deny A1, because expressivism is the thesis that some declarative sentences, namely moral declarative sentences, do not express beliefs, for they express non-cognitive states. A2 and A3 can be seen as background assumptions that motivate A1. If the expressivist does not deny A2, then at least she has to deny A3.[12]

Thus, the interest of expressivism lies in its denial of A1, which is the result of either denying A2 or A3. This is regarded by many as a theoretical cost, because a certain account of meaning and conversation seems at first sight to depend on these assumptions being true. The expressivist's denial of A1 and either A2 or A3 threatens to throw over board some valuable and sucessful theories of meaning and conversation. The family of objections surrounding Geach's Fregepoint and Unwin's negation problem spell out this worry in more detail, as we shall see in a moment.

But the expressivist need not give up any of the advances that may seem to be encapsulated in A1–A3. The expressivist could, for example, simply accept A1*, A2 and A3*:

A1* Declarative sentences express judgements.

A2 Declarative sentences are assertoric (i.e. they serve, in virtue of their meaning, for the performance of assertions).

A3* Assertions aim at correctness (they have perspectival contents).

These alternative assumptions about declaratives allow the preservation of everything worth preserving in established theories of meaning and conversation. To see this, let us now examine Geach's Frege point and related objections in a little more detail.

2.4. Geach's Frege point against expressivism

Geach (1960, 1965) targeted expressivist claims like the following:

(E1) The meaning of the moral predicate 'bad' consists in the fact that it can be used to condemn, or express disapproval of, something.

Thus, Geach's target is a proposal about moral *predicates* rather than the expressivist claim about the meaning of moral *sentences* that I have been discussing. However corresponding claims about moral sentences can presumably be derived from E1:

(E2) The meaning of the moral declarative sentence 'Gambling is bad.' consists in the fact that it can be used to condemn gambling or to express disapproval of gambling.

Geach objected (i) that there were many occurrences of the predicate 'bad' in which it cannot be used to condemn anything – for example when occurring embedded in the following sentences:

(G1) Gambling is not bad.

(G2) If gambling is bad, then seducing others to gamble is bad.

(G3) Is gambling bad?

On these occurrences, the expressivist's meaning analysis cannot be correct: neither of these sentences can be used to condemn gambling or express disapproval of it. Moreover, Geach pointed out (ii) that we can't say that the meaning of 'bad' changes from unembedded uses to embedded uses as in G1–3. For if we say that, then (for example) the valid argument from:

G4 Seducing others to gamble is not bad.

and G2 to G1 as conclusion comes out as *not* of valid *modus tollens* form, but rather as a mere equivocating *modus tollens* look-alike. However, the argument is clearly valid, and it seems to be a perfect instance of *modus tollens*.

Geach's diagnosis was that the expressivist's thesis E1 does not take into account the difference between mere predication and assertion. When 'bad' is predicated of gambling and the resulting content is asserted, we get a sentence that asserts badness of gambling. However, 'bad' is also predicated of gambling in G2 and G3, but without asserting the predication we do not get an assertion of badness (Geach 1960, 223; 1965, 464).

In effect, Geach's point is that, in order to challenge the established account of the function of 'bad' and 'gambling is bad', it is not sufficient for the expressivist only to offer a speech-act analysis of the predicate 'bad' in simple declarative sentences, or to say what mental state such sentences express. For the challenge to be effective, the expressivist's alternative account needs to say something about the unchanging contribution the predicate 'bad' makes on all its occurrences. For this is what the established account does: it is a systematic account that tells us how the propositional content of sentences containing 'bad' result from the meaning of 'bad' and that of other constituent expressions. The communicative function of sentences (e.g. making assertions, expressing belief) then results from the account of the propositional content together with the type of sentence it is (declarative, interrogative etc.).

To take the simplest case, the established account will say that G1 has as its content the negation of the proposition that gambling is bad, where the negation of a proposition *p* is simply the proposition that is true in all those cases in which *p* is not true. Thus, the expressivist needs to say likewise what contribution the negation is making on her account.

Geach's point is well taken and essentially correct. The fallacy I am going to diagnose occurs en route to the further conclusion, drawn by many theorists, that the expressivist cannot meet Geach's challenge.

2.5. Unwin's negation problem

Unwin's negation problem (Unwin 1999) extends Geach's challenge for expressivism to non-cognitivism. Geach is asking for an account of the meaning of moral expressions that works for all possible embeddings of these expressions. Unwin's negation problem concerns the expressivist's and non-cognitivist's account of the non-cognitive mental states expressed by complex moral sentences. Unwin focusses on negation as the simplest case of embedding, but the problem can be raised equally for other forms of embedding and the corresponding mental states expressed. The problem is this: the expressivist claims that to judge that gambling is bad is to disapprove of gambling. For someone to fail to judge that gambling is bad, correspondingly, should then be construed as failing to disapprove of gambling. However, what is it, then, to judge that gambling is not bad? It couldn't be disapproval of not gambling, because merely thinking that gambling is not bad does not commit one to thinking that not gambling is bad. So it looks like the expressivist has to introduce a further non-cognitive attitude, say *toleration*, in order to account for the judgement that gambling is not bad: it is the same as tolerating gambling:

(N1) Nick judges that gambling is bad. = Nick disapproves of gambling.

(N2) Nick does not judge that gambling is bad. = Nick does not disapprove of gambling.

(N3) Nick judges that gambling is not bad. = ? (proposal: = Nick tolerates gambling.)

(N4) Nick judges that not gambling is bad. = Nick disapproves of not gambling.

Thus, the non-cognitivist, in order to deal with all four states of mind N1–N4 needs to introduce a further non-cognitive attitude, *toleration*.

However, what should be the systematic contribution of negation in thought that allows us to predict that thinking that gambling is bad is disapproval of gambling while thinking that gambling is not bad is the attitude of tolerating gambling? Moreover, similar questions can be raised about other forms of complex thought or embedding, thereby forcing the non-cognitivist-expressivist to resort to further, unsystematic postulations of additional attitudes.[13]

2.6. Response: distinguishing force and content

How can the expressivist respond to Geach's challenge? How can the non-cognitivist respond to Unwin's negation problem? Geach's own diagnosis seems sensible. Established theories distinguish the compositional contribution a predicate makes to the content of sentences (predicating a property of something) from the ultimate, and composite, effect that the predicate has when it is used assertorically and without being embedded (attributing the property). If we claimed that 'bad', in virtue of its meaning, serves to attribute the property of badness, we would get into the same kind of trouble as the expressivist who claims that 'bad' serves to condemn, or to express disapproval. 'Bad', when simply predicated of something and then asserted, can be plausibly claimed to attribute badness. But when embedded in negation, a conditional, a disjunction, etc. it will often generate a content asserting which will clearly not amount to attributing badness (see G1, G2). And even a simple predication of 'bad' does not serve for the attribution of badness unless the result is asserted (see G3).

The problem exposed by Geach, therefore, is simply that the expressivist, who claims that 'Gambling is bad.' serves to condemn or express disapproval (E2), must separate the content-determining compositional function of 'bad', which it has in all contexts in which it is used with the same sense,[14] from the effect 'bad' has only when used unembedded and asserted. In other words, the expressivist should drop or modify E1, and treat E2 as a derivative fact that results from the compositional meanings of all the syntactic elements in 'Gambling is bad.', including its assertoric force indicator (mood, word order). The expressivist should say that on the one hand there is the general effect of the assertoric mood of the sentence, which it has wherever it occurs. On the other hand there is the content one can assert by using the sentence 'Gambling is bad.' (which is negated in G1, which occurs as the antecedent of G2 and which it shares with G3). This content is determined by the content-determining semantic features of the sentence's syntactic elements. Instead of E1, the expressivist could claim, say, that the content-determining function of 'bad' is to predicate the *feature* of badness (where 'feature' is supposed to be more general and less committal than 'property'). That would be just as (un)informative as the line according to which 'bad' predicates the property of badness. Talk of 'predicating features' would need to be further explained, just as talk of predicating properties does. This further explanation will need to underpin E2 and the expressivist's general claim that moral sentences serve to express non-cognitive attitudes (just as Geach's talk of predicating properties would ultimately underpin the general view that moral sentences serve to express beliefs).

An answer to Unwin's negation problem (and its generalization to other forms of complex moral thought) would already be contained in such an answer to Geach's challenge. For it will involve separating out in all moral judgements the content from an attitude of acceptance. For example, disapproval of gambling will be factored into a judgeable content, that gambling is bad, and an attitude of acceptance. Negated, conditional, disjunctive, etc. moral judgements will be analysed as functions of simpler judgeable contents, and even atomic judgeable contents will be constructed from simpler elements that can re-occur in other contents ('concepts').

This kind of answer to Geach and Unwin has had the benefit of being forcefully and clearly presented by Mark Schroeder in a series of papers (e.g. 2008a, 2008b) and in his book *Being For* (2008c). In Schroeder's work, the attitude of disapproval of gambling expressed by 'Gambling is bad.' is factored into a general moral attitude of acceptance or endorsement (called 'being for') and a judgeable content, explicated as 'blaming for gambling', something that one can merely consider without being for it – just as one can predicate without attributing. That the content is *blaming*, rather than, say, praising, caning, thanking or whatever is the compositional contribution made by the expression 'bad', and this is the contribution it always makes, even in the various embedded contexts (e.g. G1–3). This takes care, very nicely, of Geach's challenge and Unwin's negation problem.

Despite being clearly indicated by Geach, this sort of approach curiously has not been particularly prominent in the literature about expressivism (Gibbard 1990, 2003 are exceptions). This is probably because expressivists (and their opponents) where for a long time stuck on E1, the idea that moral predicates are force-indicators, and did not genuinely consider the possibility of factoring the contributions made by the constituents of moral sentences in the more straightforward way suggested by Geach and expounded by Schroeder.[15] Historically, this may well be due to the influence of authors like Hare (1952, 1970) and Blackburn (1984, 1988), who both started with the idea that the linguistic function of moral predicates like 'bad' was fundamentally different from that of descriptive predicates, as they found it in authors like Ogden and Richards (1946), Ayer (1936/1946) or Stevenson (1937).

2.7. Fallacies 1

I now want to point out two tempting but fallacious lines of reasoning into which the classic conception outlined in part 1 can mislead us. I leave it to the reader to determine the extent to which these fallacies have in fact occurred. It is enough for my purposes, to establish that these forms of reasoning are indeed fallacious.

Geach's challenge draws attention to the fact that when we give an account of the meaning of an expression, the account should (i) cover all possible occurrences of the expression. In other words, the account of meaning should be *compositional*: we should be able to derive the meaning of complex expressions from the meanings of their constituent parts. Moreover, this compositional account should (ii) correctly predict/explain which sequences of (utterances of) sentences constitute formally valid arguments.

Standard frameworks for modelling meaning deliver (i) and (ii) and involve a classic conception of content. The composititional meaning involves assignments of meanings to (some) simple expressions and some compositional rules that specify how the meaning of compound expressions are determined by the meanings of constituent parts. In this way, the theory assigns to each sentence (or sentence in context) a classic content. Such contents are, or at least determine, functions from the possible state of the world to truth-values.

The compositional rules and semantic assignments predict certain logical properties and relations: the contents of some sentences (in context) are true at every possible state of the world (*logical necessity*). Some sentences are such that if their contents (in a given context) are true at a certain state of the world, then the content of another sentence (at that context) must also be true at that state of the world: *logical consequence*. If a certain pattern of constructing a series of sentences <$S1, S2, ..., Sn$> always yields sequences of contents <$C1, C2, ..., Cn$> such that $C1, C2, ...$ is true at a state of the world, then Cn must also be true at that state of the world, then we say that that pattern is a *valid argument form*.

As a matter of historical fact, such compositional semantic theories have been first articulated for formal languages; and in so far as theorists have been interested in natural languages, they have been interested primarily in fact-stating discourse, especially in scientific discourse (consider, e.g. Russell's and Frege's motivations). Given this historical background, it is only natural, that the notions of content they used were classic: whether it is correct to believe such a content depends only on the state of the world (not on who believes or when). Suppose, now, that we regard these theories as successful, at least within their narrow range of application.

Now consider the following argument:

F1 The compositional and logical patterns of behaviour of paradigmatic beliefs and their linguistic expressions are correctly modelled by assigning them classic contents.

F2 Non-cognitive mental states do not have classic contents.

F3 The compositional and logical patterns of behaviour of moral judgements and their linguistic expressions are the same as those of paradigmatic beliefs and their linguistic expressions.

C1 So, moral judgements are not non-cognitive mental states.

This argument is not yet deductively valid: it ignores the possibility of a non-classic explanation for the compositional and logical patterns of behaviour of moral judgements and their expressions (despite the similarity of the explananda). Something like this gap in the argument was recognized by Susan Hurley (1984) and she articulated an additional constraint: ordinary modus ponens arguments and moral modus ponens arguments clearly have the same valid form, they are valid for the same reason. So it is upon the expressivist to ensure that her explanation preserves this uniformity of explanation. Adapting this lesson to our purposes, we might add a further premiss in Hurley's spirit:

> F4 The compositional and logical patterns of behaviour that beliefs and moral judgements and their linguistic expressions share, must receive a uniform explanation.

The argument from premises F1–F4 to conclusion C1 does look tempting: we already have a correct theory for descriptive beliefs and their expression (F1), but the shared behaviour of moral judgements and descriptive beliefs should receive a uniform explanation (F3 and F4), however, the correct theory of beliefs cannot be used for non-cognitive states (F2). So, since we already have the correct treatment for descriptive beliefs, a treatment that does not work for non-cognitive states, we can't say that moral judgements are non-cognitive states (not without violating F4).

But there is a mistake: even if the classic account mentioned in F1 is correct, it may still be a special case of a more general account, an account which could offer a uniform explanation for the shared pattern of behaviour but still be compatible with moral judgements not being cognitive.

To see this, focus on a further silent premiss, which is needed to establish C1:

> F5 There is no uniform explanation of the shared behaviour that is compatible with non-cognitivism (and with the correctness of the classic explanation).

This silent premiss is clearly unwarranted, and it can be shown to be false by looking at part 1 above. There are uniform non-classic explanations of the relevant patterns of behaviour of both cognitive and non-cognitive representations. Classic contents are special cases in the perspectival content framework, and the explanations needed for the shared patterns of behaviour do not rely on anything not true also of these special cases.

For concrete illustration, suppose the classic theory mentioned in F1 operated with classic contents that are functions from worlds to truth-values, and that the definition of logical consequence used to explain cases of valid inference was this: A content Cn is a consequence of contents $C1, C2, \ldots,$ $=_{def}$ for all worlds w: if the $C1, C2, \ldots$ all have the value true at w, then Cn also has the value true at w.

Suppose further that we now generalize to a perspectival conception on which contents are functions from centred worlds to truth-values. Then each of the earlier classic contents has a unique objective counterpart in our new framework (see §1.4 above): for each original classic content C, its perspectival counterpart C^* fulfils the following condition: for all worlds w and centres c, $C^*(<w, c>) = $ truth iff $C(w) = $ truth.

We can then adopt the following generalized definition of logical consequence: A content Cn is a consequence of contents $C1, C2, \ldots,$ $=_{def}$ for all centred worlds $<w, c>$: if the $C1, C2, \ldots$ all have the value true at $<w, c>$, then Cn also has the value true at $<w, c>$.

Clearly, any explanations of cases of logical consequence in the classic framework can be translated into equally good explanations in the extended perspectival framework. But the extended framework can accommodate beliefs and utterances with non-objective contents. The explanations offered for behaviour shared between moral judgements and descriptive beliefs will be uniform.

It is easy to overlook the silent and false assumption F5, if one forgets that nothing compels us to use a classic conception of representational content.[16]

2.8. Schroeder's fallacy

Mark Schroeder has done a lot to improve our understanding of the Frege-Geach point: as already mentioned, he has moved the focus away from the less promising (but once prominent) expressivist approaches that start from E1. Moreover, he has articulated a proposal that implements this advice by separating a general non-cognitive acceptance attitude 'being for' from the specific contribution made by 'bad' and other moral predicates to the contents that can be the objects of the general attitude of being for (see Schroeder 2008c. Compare also Silk 2014). However, Schroeder argues that his own solution to the Frege-Geach problem does not ultimately work. As we shall see, his reasoning to this conclusion also contains a fallacy that is quite tempting to those brought up on the classic view.

Schroeder argues that his own solution works only if we consider purely normative (moral) thought and language by itself. But in fact, we form complex thoughts (and sentences) involving both moral elements and descriptive ones. We can think, for example, that either Ed didn't steal the money, or he ought to be punished; or that if carbon dioxide emissions cause global warming, then emitting carbon dioxide is bad.[17] The following two sentences seem to serve for expressing such thoughts:

(M1) 'Either Ed didn't steal the money, or he ought to be punished.'

(M2) 'If CO_2 emissions cause global warming, then emitting CO_2 is bad.'

Dealing with such mixed thoughts and claims, he thinks, would require that the expressivist 'allow that all sentences express the same general kind of attitude' (2008a, 597). I concur. But Schroeder continues as follows:

> For cognitivists, this is easy to do, for the attitude is simply belief. But for expressivists, this turns out to be tricky. For descriptive sentences, according to expressivists, express beliefs. So if they are to express states of being for, then it must turn out that beliefs are really states of being for – that belief needs to be analyzed in terms of a non-cognitive attitude. (2008a, 597. See also 2008c, 91–92, for a very similar passage.)

Schroeder is arguing that the following two options are exhaustive:

I all declarative sentences express belief.

II all declarative sentences express 'being for' (Schroeder's general non-cognitive attitude).

Option I is not acceptable to the expressivist. Option II seems radical and surprising, as Schroeder himself observes. It would involve, for example, as Schroeder is proposing, that the descriptive sentence 'Grass is green.' serves to express the non-cognitive attitude of 'being for' directed at the content of 'proceeding as if grass is green'.[18] However Schroeder spends the remainder of his book exploring how the expressivist could best defend this view, i.e. that all (declarative) sentences express non-cognitive states of being for, and that analogously beliefs are also really non-cognitive states. The final verdict he reaches, after detailed discussion, is negative: ultimately expressivism fails.

If I have done my job well, readers of this paper will have easily spotted Schroeder's fallacy. Of course there is a third option that Schroeder has not considered:

> III All sentences express a general attitude of which belief and non-cognitive attitudes are species.

There is a general kind of attitude – call it 'judgement', for example – which falls into two mutually exclusive subspecies: cognitive and non-cognitive judgements. The answer is simple for those who have stepped back a little bit from the classic view, and who have present in their minds the notion of a perspectival content, which is a generalization of that of a classic content. The next and final section will flesh out this view.

I believe that this illustrates once more that the decision to adopt a classic notion of content, while not pernicious in itself, can make it hard to see the uniformity of a certain class of mental states: judgements.[19] Even though the class of judgements contains both beliefs and non-cognitive states, it is nevertheless importantly uniform in just the way needed: all judgements are states with perspectival representational contents.

2.9. The positive account: judgements as states with perspectival contents

I have claimed that non-cognitivists can perfectly coherently regard the class of judgements as uniform in all respects besides those that make up the cognitive/non-cognitive divide on which their defining thesis is based (see §2.2 above). What, then, might be those respects of uniformity amongst all judgements? Let me sketch a reasonable view (but one that does depart from some central elements of the Humean picture of Human psychology).

All judgements differ from other mental states or mental dispositions in that they involve the employment of concepts and that they are subject to rational norms. Another way of saying this, of course, is to say that they have contents, for contents serve, amongst other things, to model the conceptual and rational relations amongst different judgements (or other contentful mental states). This differentiates judgements from certain non-contentful, non-rational mental states, such as certain moods or feelings, for example the feeling of giddiness or the feeling of anger (at least on a non-cognitive contrual of those feelings).

Judgements differ from other conceptual and contentful states in the kind of rational norm that governs them. Judgements are governed by norms of correctness: their contents determine what conditions need to hold for a judgement with that content to be correct. Thus, a judgement to the effect that the water is boiling is correct iff the contextually relevant water is indeed boiling. My judgement that the taste of the coffee is pleasant will be correct iff I will normally be pleased by the contextually relevant coffee. This norm of correctness, in turn, gives rise to general norms of rationality: the requirement to avoid judgements with inconsistent contents and the requirement to avoid judgements not obtained with correctness-conducive methods.

Desires or hopes may also have content, but in so far as they are subject to norms of rationality or correctness, these norms play a different role. For example, suppose I have an instrumental desire to acquire Dr Gordon's Hair Elixir, which is based on the belief that applying Dr Gordon's Hair Elixir to one's scalp will boost hair growth and the more fundamental desire to have fuller hair. Then my instrumental desire for the elixir might be incorrect or irrational because my belief in the elixir's effectiveness, on which the desire is partly based, might be incorrect or irrational. Thus, while other contentful mental states may be subject to certain derivative constraints of correctness or rationality, only judgements are non-derivatively subject to such constraints. [20]

This story, while reasonable, diverges from Hume's at a key point: Hume thought that only beliefs, or the mental states produced by the faculty of reason, were subject to (underived) rational norms, while the passions, i.e. non-cognitive states, were not subject to underived rational constraints at all. Thus, in Hume's picture, the division between the intrinsically motivating states and motivationally inert cognitive states coincides with the division between the mental states that are subject to underived rational norms and those that are not. My 'reasonable view' thus emphatically allows for rationally constrained judgements that are nevertheless on the motivational side of Hume's divide.[21]

I believe that all these general features of judgements can be modelled perfectly within a perspectival content framework. Let us begin with the distinction between beliefs and non-cognitive attitudes, that is so dear to the non-cognitivist's heart. The most obvious proposal is to distinguish those perspectival contents that comply with the classic constraint: i.e. if accepting such a content is correct for one thinker at one time, then it is correct to accept it for any thinker at any time. Call this subclass of perspectival contents 'objective'. Then one good starting point would be to say that judgements with objective contents are beliefs, while non-cognitive judgements have non-objective contents.

Why should some of the judgements with non-objective contents be intrinsically motivating, as is required by the psychological motivation for non-cognitivism (§2.2)? This is because the correctness of accepting a non-objective content will depend not just on the aspects of reality represented, but also on features of the judge. In the case of judgements of pleasantness, this is fairly straightforward: in order for my judgement that the taste of that coffee is pleasant to be correct, the coffee needs to be such that my dispositions are such that under certain normal conditions I experience pleasure when drinking the coffee. In so far as pleasure is an end in itself, such a judgement will constitute a motive, *ceteris paribus*, to prefer the coffee in question to other options that do not produce pleasure.

Hume's thought that motivational states are rationally unconstrained can be partially preserved: those features of thinkers at times on which correctness may depend when contents are non-objective will often be features that are not subject to thinkers' rational control. In this sense, the reasonable picture can retain a non-rational aspect of intrinsically motivating judgements.

The moral case is more complicated: what are to be the requirements on the judge if she is to be correct in her judgement that gambling is bad? There are many options. Some may base moral judgements on certain general individual preferences (such as a desire to promote pleasure, happiness, justice or what have you). Others may have a more social view of moral norms and tie the individual's interests somehow to the values prevalent in that individual's society. This is not an issue to be decided here: all we need to show is that there are plausible proposals on each of the outlooks that might combine with a non-cognitivist view (like the ones just mentioned). Perhaps what is required in an individual, in order for that individual's judgement that gambling is bad to be correct, is that gambling have a tendency to prevent the realization of that person's moral goals. Then that would explain why judging gambling to be bad is *ipso facto* a reason to avoid gambling. For if the judgement is correct, then the avoidance of gambling will avoid something that prevents the realization of that judge's moral goals.

Why should beliefs, i.e. judgements with objective contents, be epistemologically less problematic than judgements with non-objective contents? The epistemological problem that Ayer saw with an empirical account of the justification for moral claims, construed as irreducible was this: if moral judgements were based on 'intellectual intuition', then we would get conflicting intuitions and have no way of settling the conflict (1946, 108–109). Any adequate method for justifying judgements with objective content will not suffer from this defect: since adequate justification tracks correctness, correctness for one is the same as correctness for anyone, anything that is an adequate method for me is also an adequate method for you – as long as the content is objective. Thus while that does not guarantee that we have an effective method for every objective question, it at least guarantees that once we have exchanged our justifications and agreed on what are adequate methods, we will share the same view. In the case of non-objective contents, this is not guaranteed. Here, what tracks correctness for you may not track it for me. Thus the reasonable view makes room for the kind of epistemological asymmetry that traditionally motivates non-cognitivism.

Finally, the metaphysical motivation for non-cognitivism (given non-reductivism): why should correct judgements with non-objective contents be less metaphysically comitting than judgements with objective contents? Assume, minimally, that reality consists in those aspects of the world that we all share and to which all our judgements are answerable. Then it seems clear that those judgements that have objective contents, if correct, represent those aspects of reality that all thinkers are answerable to, while judgements with non-objective contents, even if correct, may not describe an aspect of reality that everyone faces or is answerable to.[22]

I hope that this concluding sketch has put some flesh on the bones of the abstract idea of a mental state that is defined as a state with a perspectival content – a judgement – , and on how it can play the role needed by the non-cognitivist expressivist route I have recommended.[23]

Notes

1. For example Frege (1918), Wright (1992, 91–93, 2005, 170), and Moore (1997) imposes the same constraint on contents, but construes representation more liberally, allowing that a representation could be what he calls 'perspectival'.
2. Treating B5 and B9 as having the same representational content has its problems, of course. But I do not want to enter this discussion here. My main purpose here is to characterize the classic and the perspectival conceptions of representational content as alternatives. The second part of the paper will then identify some substantial conclusions that may be derived from the choice between the approaches. I have offered arguments in favour of the perspectival approach to content in many places, including Kölbel (2013, 2014, 2015a).
3. And arrive, respectively, either at a view similar to Harman's (1975), Dreier's (1990) or Björnsson and Finlay's (2010) indexical relativism or at one similar to the invariant moral relativism outlined in Kölbel (2015b).
4. Wanting to distinguish the contents of B3 and B11, as well as treating B9 and B10 as having the same content, correspond to the classic motivations for introducing perspectival contents (also often called 'de se contents'). Two loci classici are Perry (1979) and Lewis (1979).
5. For example: while B3 and B8 attribute possession of a cat to different people, the people in question are the believer's neighbours in each case.
6. See Egan (2007).
7. See Kölbel (2013).
8. The primary role of representational contents is that they must determine necessary and sufficient conditions for when it is correct to have a representation with a given content. Classic contents and their centred counterparts determine the same such conditions.
9. See Dreier (1999) for a nice recipe for transforming unstructured perspectival contents into structured ones.
10. I will not be assuming that every non-cognitivist must have all these motivations at once. All I am saying is that typically non-cognitivists have one of these motivations. There are also some important metaphysical motivations that I

have not mentioned, such as the argument that if there were moral facts and properties, it would be hard to explain why they should supervene on non-moral facts and properties (this argument, again, is directed against non-reductivist forms of cognitivism only).

11. In order to accept this much, one does not need, for example, to follow the programme of Green and Bar-On, who claim that linguistic meaning is in general based on such expressive properties (see, e.g. Bar-On 2013; Green 2007).

12. See Kölbel (2013) for some proposals for the dynamics of conversation when assertion is not construed as aiming at objective truth and the contents of assertion are not objective (not 'portable').

13. See Blackburn (1988); who postulates an attitude of toleration in response to Hale (1986, 1993); who objects. See also Schroeder (2008a, 2008b, 2010) for a good account of how Unwin's challenge generalizes to other forms of embedding.

14. I.e. not, e.g. when used in the slang sense, in which it predicates something like attractiveness.

15. Even though Kölbel (1997) distinguishes the 'force-indicator approach', which keeps E1, from the 'content-indicator approach', which drops E1 and pursues the solution here proposed. It emerges that the latter is more elegant and that the former, when executed viably, leads to something structurally similar to the latter. Still, the focus is on the former, thus exemplifying the prevailing tendency to regard force-indicator approaches as the more typical forms of expressivism. Similarly, Kölbel (2002), ch. 6.8, explicitly classifies Gibbard (1990) as not genuinely pursuing an expressivist agenda, precisely because of disanalogies with the E1 approach.

16. I suggested in part 1 that the choice between classic and perspectival conceptions is a pragmatic decision that can have no substantial consequences. So how would one deal with this problem on a classic conception? To start with, presumably, one would have to deny F2 and find some suitable classic contents even for non-cognitive states.

17. I am assuming that the question of whether global warming is caused by CO_2 emissions is a descriptive one. Those who accept a non-cognitivist account of causation should choose a different example.

18. I believe that Schroeder saddles the expressivist with an (additional) unnecessary problem at this point: the construction he chooses for descriptive declarative sentences F(a) as expressing being for proceeding as if F(a) is not symmetrical to the construction he chooses in cases where F is a moral predicate: here he will say that the sentence expresses being for F-ing a (where F-ing = blaming for if F = 'bad'). The asymmetry at the level of attitudes expresses is mirrored at the level of the proposed expressivist logical forms for descriptive and moral sentences. I believe that many of the problems he subsequently detects for the expressivist are the result of this unfortunate and unmotivated choice.

19. I myself have been, to some extent, a victim of this effect: In Kölbel (1997), I considered roughly the expressivist theory here proposed (under the label 'content-indicator approach'). I suggested then that expressivists pursuing this agenda would need to develop a more general novel theory of content, and that that theory would probably need to be an inferential role theory, i.e. a theory that does not rely on compositionally specified truth-conditions. I now know better: as we saw in the first part of this paper the theory of perspectival contents can perfectly well take one of the habitual truth-conditions-specifying forms: it just needs to add a further parameter of variation of truth-value, such as a location or centre.

20. Many readers will ask (and will have asked throughout) how my *correctness* is related to *truth*. I can't treat this question adequately here, so let me just gesture in the direction of a possible answer: truth is a special case of correctness, namely the correctness of a representation with an objective content. This would work well with a view of truth as objective truth, on which a non-cognitivist would then be entitled to deny that moral judgements are truth-apt. There also seems to be a (minimal) truth concept that we apply across the board to objective and non-objective contents. Moreover, there also seem to be truth-like concepts that we employ in formal semantics. These different concepts of truth need to be distinguished. For more on this, see Kölbel (2008a, 2008b).
21. I am aware that it may seem terminologically odd to call certain contentful judgements 'non-cognitive'. For often the label 'cognitive' is used precisely to mark out the features of contentfulness and being subject to rational constraints. I am nevertheless sticking to the term because the position discussed here is non-cognitivism. That is why in §2.2 above I spent some time investigating the significance of the non-cognitivist thesis by reviewing the typical motivations for non-cognitivism.
22. I believe that this 'reasonable view' is broadly in line with Gibbard's view articulated in *Wise Choices, Apt Feelings* (1990).
23. I am very grateful to the editors, Matt Bedke and Stefan Sciaraffa, of this special issue for their very useful critical feedback, which has helped improve this paper. Thanks also to a very critical audience at the 2017 *Representation & Evaluation* conference in Vancouver, including especially Matthew Chrisman, Jamie Dreier, Anandi Hattiangadi, Gurpreet Rattan, Stefan Sciaraffa, Mark Timmons. Thanks also to audiences at Barcelona and Salzburg, where versions of this paper were presented and discussed in June and November 2017.

Disclosure statement

No potential conflict of interest was reported by the author.

References

Ayer, Alfred J. 1946. *Language, Truth and Logic*. 2nd ed (1st ed 1936). London: Victor Gollancz.
Bar-On, Dorit. 2013. "Origins of Meaning: Must We Go Gricean?" *Mind & Language* 28: 342–375.
Björnsson, Gunnar, and Stephen Finlay. 2010. "Metaethical Contextualism Defended." *Ethics* 121: 7–36.
Blackburn, Simon. 1984. *Spreading the Word*. Oxford: Clarendon Press.
Blackburn, Simon. 1988. "Attitudes and Contents." *Ethics* 98: 501–517.

Dreier, Jamie. 1999. "Transforming Expressivism." *Noûs* 33: 558–572.
Dreier, James. 1990. "Internalism and Speaker Relativism." *Ethics* 101: 6–26.
Egan, Andy. 2007. "Epistemic Modals, Relativism and Assertion." *Philosophical Studies* 133: 1–22.
Frege, Gottlob. 1918. "Der Gedanke. Eine Logische Untersuchung." *Beiträge zur Philosophie des deutschen Idealismus* 1: 58–77. English translation as "The Thought: A Logical Inquiry", *Mind* 65 (1956), pp. 287–311.
Geach, Peter. 1960. "Ascriptivism." *Philosophical Review* 69: 221–225. Reprinted in his *Logic Matters* (1972), pp. 250–54, Oxford: Blackwell.
Geach, Peter. 1965. "Assertion." *Philosophical Review* 74: 449–465. Reprinted in his *Logic Matters* (1972), pp. 254–69, Oxford: Blackwell.
Gibbard, Allan. 1990. *Wise Choices, Apt Feelings*. Oxford: Oxford University Press.
Gibbard, Allan. 2003. *Thinking How to Live*. Boston: Harvard University Press.
Green, Mitchell. 2007. *Self-Expression*. Oxford: Oxford University Press.
Hale, Bob. 1986. "'The Compleat Projectivist' (Critical Study of Blackburn 1984)." *Philosophical Quarterly* 36: 65–84.
Hale, Bob. 1993. "Can There Be a Logic of Attitudes." In *Reality, Representation and Projection*, edited by Crispin Wright and John Haldane, 337–363. Oxford: Oxford University Press.
Hare, Richard M. 1952. *The Language of Morals*. Oxford: Oxford University Press.
Hare, Richard M. 1970. "Meaning and Speech Acts." *Philosophical Review* 79: 3–24.
Harman, Gilbert. 1975. "Moral Relativism Defended." *The Philosophical Review* 84: 3–22.
Hurley, Susan. 1984. "Frege, the Proliferation of Force, and Non-Cognitivism." *Mind* 93: 570–576.
Kölbel, Max. 1997. "Expressivism and the Syntactic Uniformity of Declarative Sentences." *Crítica* 29: 3–51.
Kölbel, Max. 2002. *Truth without Objectivity*. London: Routledge.
Kölbel, Max. 2008a. "'True' as Ambiguous." *Philosophy and Phenomenological Research* 77: 359–384.
Kölbel, Max. 2008b. "Truth in Semantics." *Midwest Studies in Philosophy* 32: 242–257.
Kölbel, Max. 2013. "The Conversational Role of Centered Contents." *Inquiry* 56: 97–121.
Kölbel, Max. 2014. "Agreement and Communication." *Erkenntnis* 79: 101–120.
Kölbel, Max. 2015a. "Relativism 1: Representational Content." *Philosophy Compass* 10 (1): 38–51.
Kölbel, Max. 2015b. "Moral Relativism." In *Routledge Encyclopedia of Philosophy*, Taylor and Francis. doi:10.4324/9780415249126-L099-2. Accessed 29 January 2018. https://www.rep.routledge.com/articles/thematic/moral-relativism/v-2
Lewis, David. 1979. "Attitudes *De Dicto* and *De Se*." *Philosophical Review* 88: 513–543. Reprinted in David Lewis, *Philosophical Papers* vol. 1, Oxford: Oxford University Press, pp. 133–59.
Moore, Adrian. 1997. *Points of View*. Oxford: Oxford University Press.
Ogden, C. K., and I. A. Richards. 1946. *The Meaning of Meaning*. 8th ed. (1st ed. 1923). New York, NY: Harcourt, Brace & World.
Perry, John. 1979. "The Essential Indexical." *Noûs* 13: 3–21.
Schroeder, Mark. 2008a. "How Expressivists Can and Should Solve Their Problem with Negation." *Noûs* 42: 573–599.
Schroeder, Mark. 2008b. "What is the Frege-Geach Problem." *Philosophy Compass* 3 (4): 703–720.
Schroeder, Mark. 2008c. *Being for: Evaluating the Semantic Program of Expressivism*. Oxford: Oxford University Press.
Schroeder, Mark. 2010. *Noncognitivism in Ethics*. London: Routledge.

Silk, Alex. 2014. "How to Be an Ethical Expressivist." *Philosophy and Phenomenological Research* 91: 47–81.
Stevenson, Charles L. 1937. "The Emotive Meaning of Ethical Terms." *Mind* 46: 14–31.
Unwin, Nicholas. 1999. "Quasi-Realism, Negation, and the Frege-Geach Problem." *Philosophical Quarterly* 50: 337–353.
Wright, Crispin. 1992. *Truth and Objectivity*. Cambridge, MA: Harvard University Press.
Wright, Crispin. 2005. "Relativism about Truth Itself: Haphazard Thoughts about the Very Idea." In *Relative Truth*, edited by Max Kölbel and Manuel García-Carpintero, 157–185. Oxford: Oxford University Press.

Two nondescriptivist views of normative and evaluative statements

Matthew Chrisman

ABSTRACT
The dominant route to nondescriptivist views of normative and evaluative language is through the expressivist idea that normative terms have distinctive expressive roles in conveying our attitudes. This paper explores an alternative route based on two ideas. First, a core normative term 'ought' is a modal operator; and second, modal operators play a distinctive nonrepresentational role in generating meanings for the statements in which they figure. I argue that this provides for an attractive alternative to expressivist forms of nondescriptivism about normative language. In the final section of the paper, I explore ways it might be extended to evaluative language.

1. Introduction

Some metaethicists are impressed by the idea that normative statements (e.g. saying what someone ought to do) differ fundamentally from statements describing reality. This idea has founded a fecund research program in twentieth century metaethics including the development of emotivist, prescriptivist, projectivist, and (most recently) expressivist views. The sorts of expressivism currently on the market are highly sophisticated, inspiring great ingenuity even amongst their critics in thinking about the function of normative/evaluative language and the relations between this and normative/evaluative thought.[1] In my view, however, there is a different and better way to get to the idea that normative statements do not describe reality.

This alternative is based on the dominant view in deontic logic and formal semantics that ought-statements should be treated as expressing a type of modal judgment.[2] More specifically, in this literature, ought-statements are commonly regarded as 'weak' necessity claims, where context determines the flavor (moral, prudential, teleological, epistemic) of weak necessity. A different and older tradition in the philosophy of mind and language was impressed by the idea that there is a fundamental difference between representing empirical facts and making modal judgments concerning various ways in which things might necessarily or possibly be. For example, considering the content of judgments about the world as it can be represented in our experiences, Kant wrote, 'The modality of judgments is a quite special function of them, which is distinctive in that it contributes nothing to the content of the judgment' ([1787] 1998, 209). And considering the propositional content of judgments conceived of as representations of reality, Frege wrote, 'By saying that a proposition is necessary I give a hint about the grounds for my judgment. But, since this does not affect the content of the judgment, the form of the apodictic judgment has no significance for us' ([1879] 1967, 13).

Developing this tradition's insight about modality suggests treating ought-statements as nondescriptive *because they are modal* (rather than because they are emotive, prescriptive, projective, or expressive). This is the kind of view of 'ought' I favor as a foundation for a nondescriptivist view about normative thought and discourse.[3] Because of its contrasting explanation of why normative language is nondescriptive, I have been reluctant in my own work in metaethics to adopt the label 'expressivist' despite agreeing with many expressivist arguments against descriptivist views in metaethics. Kant and Frege didn't think modal statements express anything like prescriptions, noncognitive attitudes, or planning states, but they do seem to have regarded them as nondescriptive because they performed some function in our thought and talk different from describing reality. To draw out this contrast with the expressivist tradition in more detail, there are two questions I want to explore here.

First (and mainly), even if we agree with Kant that the modality of a judgment contributes nothing to the content of that judgment, or we agree with Frege that saying a proposition is necessary does not affect the content of the judgment that it is true, it is obvious that we should not say that 'ought' contributes nothing to the *meaning* of statements in which it figures. (For what it's worth, I think it is most charitable to interpret Kant and Frege as making claims about the *descriptive* content of these judgments.) This raises the question: if 'ought' considered as a modal doesn't contribute to the descriptive content of the statements in which it figures, how does it affect their meaning? (Sections 3 and 4).

Second (and much more tentatively), the expressivist tradition offers various unified explanations of why normative *and* evaluative statements are nondescriptive, but a modal-operator account of why ought-statements are not descriptions of reality does not extend naturally to evaluative statements. Words such as 'good', 'bad', 'better', and 'worse' are not plausibly understood as modal operators in any usual sense. This puts pressure on a metaethics based on the modal-operator account of ought-statements to abandon the natural assumption that normative and evaluative statements are nondescriptive for

2. Normative and evaluative statements as nondescriptive; some historical lessons

When I say that some metaethicists, including myself, are impressed by the idea that describing reality differs from saying what anyone ought to do or evaluating things as better and worse, I think it is important to recognize that most of these metaethicists would recognize a prominent descriptive use of words such as 'ought' and 'good'. This was already hinted at by Ayer, who distinguished between the use of such words to describe the moral sense of a particular community and their use as 'normative ethical symbols'. In fact, on a careful rereading of *Language, Truth and Logic*, one can get the sense that Ayer regarded most uses of words such as 'ought' and 'good' as descriptive (1936). On his view, many uses of these words are sociological descriptions of the morals of some group of people or descriptions of the verdicts of some normative system that conversational participants are assuming for the sake of conversation. It's only when we get to the business of discussing what one *really* ought to do or what is *really* good that his verificationism about meaning led him to deny that the words carry descriptive content.

We shouldn't dwell on Ayer's verificationist reasons for making this distinction, but I do think we should recognize a use of words such as 'ought' and 'good' where one is, in effect, describing the verdicts of some set of norms or values applied to some case. We should set aside these uses of 'ought' and 'good' in attempting to explain why normative and evaluative statements differ from straightforward descriptions of reality.

With that distinction in place, Ayer famously argued that the use of 'normative ethical symbols' is purely expressive, neither adding to nor subtracting from the descriptive content of the rest of the statement in which they figure (if it already had one). This has seemed implausible to many metaethicists. How could a word be meaningful and yet have no effect on the descriptive content of statements in which it figures? But we have pretty clear examples of this in ordinary language. The word 'fucking' in 'The fucking kids trashed the park,' is plausibly viewed as a purely expressive word. It's not a qualification of 'kids', used to pick out a specific group of kids; rather it's a way for the speaker to express a negative attitude towards the kids who trashed the park. This statement still carries the descriptive content *that the kids trashed the park*, it's just made using a word that adds an extra expression of negative attitude towards the kids. On a charitable interpretation of Ayer, this is like what 'normative ethical symbols' do in most statements containing them.

Even when charitably interpreted, this idea is not credible, for many well-known reasons. The logical properties of normative and evaluative statements seem to turn on their use of 'ought' and 'better' in a way that statements involving the expressive use of 'fucking' do not.[4] Nevertheless, in moving beyond Ayer's emotivism, we shouldn't reject the idea that words can figure meaningfully in statements without contributing to the descriptive content of those statements; and a statement containing one of these words can still be descriptive, even if it also performs some other discourse role in conversational dynamics (because of the nondescriptive word in it). Ordinary uses of the sentence 'The fucking kids trashed the park' are still plausibly regarded as describing something the kids did.

Hare's (1952) prescriptivism offers a radically different model for the role of normative and evaluative words. He thought they functioned somewhat analogously to markers for imperatival mood. A common account of the meaning of imperatives treats them as containing two elements: a descriptive content and a 'make-true' operator on this content. The idea is that imperatives are linguistically suited to prescribe rather than describe because they involve a semantic operation on a piece of descriptive content turning it from something that can be put forward as true to something that can be put forward as to be made true. For example, 'Kids, clean up the park!' might be said to carry the descriptive content *that the kids clean up the park*, but the imperative is not usable to describe reality in this way; rather it is usable to prescribe to the kids a complex action which would make this descriptive content true. This is why imperatives are often said to have satisfaction conditions rather than truth conditions. The situation is a bit more complicated for normative statements, according to Hare, but his core thought seems to have been to treat 'ought' in statements such as 'The kids ought to clean up the park' as operations on embedded descriptive content that make it usable to prescribe action which would make the embedded content true.

Even when charitably interpreted, this idea is also not credible as a thesis about normative and evaluative statements. Sentences deploying 'ought' and 'good' are linguistically embeddable in propositional contexts (e.g. under 'believes' and 'might') that do not embed imperatives. However, we shouldn't reject the thought that words can have their meanings in part because of how they function as operators on descriptive content rather than contributors to descriptive content. With Hare, we might want to say that such statements 'carry' descriptive content but they do not describe reality as matching this content. I think this lesson is crucial for making sense of the idea that ought-statements are nondescriptive because they are modal.

3. 'Ought' as modal operator

Some metaethicists might think that 'ought' is a descriptive word, describing a relation between agents and actions. For example, an ordinary use of 'You ought to call your mother' might be said to describe you as being obligated to perform the action of calling your mother. But, even if that looks halfway plausible in this case, it cannot be right as a general thesis about the word 'ought'. There are many 'flavors' of 'ought', not all of which have anything to do with agents and actions; and even for a more relaxed version of the relational view to work, the ought-relation would have to be multifarious to the point of gerrymandering. No agent is plausibly related to an action in 'As they left an hour ago, they ought to be home by now.' And even if we think there are agents responsible, the relation that would be described by 'There ought to be no childhood starvation' would have to be quite different from the relation putatively described by 'You ought to call your mother.' Moreover, we make general normative evaluations about how people feel, as in e.g. 'One ought to feel sympathy for the bereaved' where it's very hard to see how this could be plausibly construed as describing a relation that is similar to any normative relation between an agent and an action.

In response to these counterexamples to the relational view, some have suggested that 'ought' is ambiguous – maybe sometimes describing a relation between agents and actions, other times describing a relation between agents and their attitudes, and still other times describing outcomes as highly likely in light of some implicit body of evidence or some state of affairs as overall best.[5] But the dominant view in semantics is that 'ought' – like other modal words – is not ambiguous but context sensitive More specifically, it is context sensitive in the way that many intensional operators are. These are usually treated as linguistic devices that shift the circumstances relative to which various pieces of embedded semantic content are to be semantically evaluated. Context provides input to the kind of shift that takes place.

This is not the place to get into the general theory of intensional operators, but it might suffice to say that allowing that some bits of language are non-extensional is crucial for making progress towards the ideal of compositionality in our theoretical models the semantics of natural languages; and the existence of operators capable of shifting the circumstances under which some embedded piece of content is to be evaluated semantically as part of compositional processing of language is at the heart of all model theoretic semantic accounts that have any hope of achieving the ideal of compositionality.[6] This is the semantic role of intensional operators, and modal words are commonly thought to be paradigm examples of intensional operators.

In philosophy, this idea is perhaps most familiar from discussion of the epistemic possibility modal 'might'. Consider a standard use of 'Sally might be at home.' Assume, vagueness aside, it is the case either that Sally is at home or that Sally is not at home. In this case, it appears misguided to say that 'might' in this statement describes a relation Sally stands in to being at home. Rather, the standard view is that this word operates on the propositional content it embeds (*that Sally is at home*), evaluating this propositional content as true in at least one set of circumstances consistent with the relevant body of evidence.

If we appeal to possible worlds to model various circumstances under which a propositional content can be evaluated, we could generate a simple

MODAL RULE FOR 'MIGHT':$[[\text{might } p]]^e$
$= T$ iff p is true at some of the e-compatible worlds

where e-compatible worlds are the worlds consistent with the relevant body of evidence. There is considerable debate about how the relevant body of evidence for might-statements is negotiated, but the more general idea is clear enough. The word 'might' functions not to represent a relation but rather to shift semantic interpretation of the proposition it embeds, in effect directing interpreters to evaluate this proposition for truth not at the actual world but at all possible worlds compatible with some body of evidence. For instance, with typical uses of 'Sally might be at home' the modal rule for 'might' suggests one evaluate whether the proposition *that Sally is at home* is true at all circumstances compatible with some body of evidence.

There are complexities in extending this intensional semantics to 'ought' that I don't want to get into here.[7] However, it's enough for my purposes below to fixate on a simplified intensional operator view about 'ought' that treats it as a necessity modal rather than a possibility modal and allows a two-factored determination of the set of worlds relevant for modeling the circumstances at which its embedded content is to be evaluated.[8] If we do so, we get something like this simple:

MODAL RULE FOR 'OUGHT':$[[\text{ought } p]]^{fg}$
$= T$ iff p is true at all of the fg-compatible worlds

where f and g are contextually negotiated parameters determining, respectively, the background conditions and an identification of top ranked worlds relative some ranking of worlds, e.g. in terms of moral ideality, prudential betterness for some agent, probabilistic likelihood given some evidence, etc.

For example, take a use of 'Peter ought to live in southern Spain' considered as a claim about achieving best quality of life. We could (as a first pass anyway) model semantic interpretation of this statement as follows:

p: Peter lives in Southern Spain

f: restrict to possible worlds where Peter lives in Europe, has a portable job, etc.

g: identify the remaining worlds that are prudentially best for Peter, where this is a resultant of lifestyle, food, opportunities for meaningful relationships, etc.

Then the ought-statement is true iff the fg-compatible worlds are ones where p is true.

The attraction of the modal rule for 'ought' is its unity, flexibility, and similarity to semantic rules proposed for other modal words. By treating 'ought' as a context sensitive weak necessity modal, we can predict fairly plausible truth conditions for all of the different flavors of ought-statements mentioned above without massive gerrymandering. The relatively simple rule doesn't restrict application to agents and actions; and it can make sense of the different ways background conditions and ways of ranking things affect the semantic processing of various ought-statements in context. Moreover, assimilating words like 'ought', 'should', and 'must' to universal quantification over possibilia and words like 'might', 'may', and 'could' to existential quantifications over possibilia allows for an attractive explanation of what these words have in common qua modal auxiliaries.

4. 'Ought' as a modal and descriptive content

Going forward, let's assume the modal rule for 'ought' is roughly correct. How does that affect the issue of whether ought-statements are descriptions of reality? Here are two apparently competing answers:

First: if the modal rule is roughly correct, ought-statements have truth conditions. So, like other statements with truth conditions, they can be believed true and they can be known. This means ought-statements describe a way reality could be. To be sure, since 'ought' is not a relational predicate, ought-statements shouldn't be treated as *ordinary* descriptions of a relation. We need an alternative account of what they describe; we should develop an account of the pieces of reality the description of which grounds 'ought's semantic contribution to the sentences in which it figures. If we are realists about possible worlds and the relations amongst them, then we can say ought-statement describes a region of modal space: what's true in all of some set of possible worlds. If we're skeptical of modal realism, we can still recognize various real relations of normative necessitation and view ought statements as describing these.

Second: if the modal rule is roughly correct, 'ought' is a modal operator. Modal operators do not function to describe things in reality. This means that 'ought' does not add descriptive content to the statements in which it figures. But surely it has meaning. Ayer's expressive and Hare's prscriptive accounts provide two early and inadequate accounts of its meaning. However, Hare was closer to right: As an intensional operator, 'ought' is more like markers for imperative mood than the expressive use of 'fucking'. It functions to shift the role of the descriptive content it embeds, meaning that ought-statements 'carry' descriptive content but do not put this forward as a description of reality. The idea that ought-statements sometimes *prescribe action rather than describe reality* seems plausible as part of the story, but this is too narrow to work as a general account. We need a more general alternative account of what ought-statements do; we should develop an account of the conceptual role of 'ought' that grounds its semantic contribution to the statements in which it figures.

Something like the first answer is fine for uses of 'ought' that Ayer would have regarded as describing the verdicts of some assumed system of norms. I think we should be skeptical of the reality of 'regions of modal space', but talk of what's true in various possible worlds can be a useful way to model the content of statements describing real relations of necessitation, and verdicts following from some assumed system of norms might be viewed as a real relation of necessitation. Perhaps many or even most uses of 'ought' are like this. Certainly, in contexts where one could preface the use of 'ought' with phrases such as, 'According to the values of capitalism ...' or 'On a Christian way of looking at this ...' In these cases, it makes sense ask: 'But what ought I really to do, think, or feel?' suggesting that there's a difference between describing the verdicts of some system of values or norms and making a genuinely normative statement. Indeed, arguably, many uses of 'ought' are pro tanto, in the sense that one makes an ought statement intending to contribute to someone's reasoning about what to do, think, or feel, but one still allows that the verdict could be undercut, overridden, or erased by other truths about what one ought to do, think, or feel. In these cases, the speaker might be viewed as describing what follows from (or is normatively necessitated) by some system of values or norms, without yet endorsing those verdicts as winning in the end.

If we accept that descriptivist view for some uses of 'ought', why not accept it for all uses of 'ought'? After all, descriptivism offers a simple account of why the modal rule for 'ought' generates the correct truth conditions (insofar as it does): those truth conditions articulate what ought-statements describe (e.g. what is necessitated and how it is necessitated). As already suggested, however, many feel an intuitive difference between describing the verdicts of some system of norms and making a genuinely normative statement. Moreover, if one is skeptical of posits of real relations of 'all things considered' or 'just plain' normative necessitation as part of the fabric of reality, we'll want some view other than descriptivism for genuinely normative statements, on pain of viewing much normative discourse as being in error.

How could we accept the modal rule for 'ought', which predicts truth conditions, and not view all ought-statements as descriptions of reality? To answer this question, it may be helpful to take a step back and consider what we're doing when we develop semantic rules such as the modal rule for 'ought'. These are meant to be parts of a semantic model capable of predicting semantic contents for whole sentences that are compositional in the sense that the content of the whole sentence is a function of the content of the parts and the way these parts are put together. This is viewed by philosophers of language and linguistic semanticists as crucial for explaining the learnability and productivity of language. However, these models don't tell us how to interpret them (e.g. they deploy terms such as 'true' and 'refers' but they don't include a theory of truth or reference). For this reason, I would say that philosophy of language includes the project of explaining what it is in virtue of which statements and their parts have the semantic contents that the best compositional semantics says they have. Because it is not part of (compositional) semantics, I classify this project as 'metasemantic'. It's part of our overall theory of meaningfulness, though it's probably going to appeal to elements of metaphysics, philosophy of mind, psycholinguistics, pragmatics, decision theory, cognitive ethology, evolutionary game theory, etc.

Sometimes I suspect that the uncommitted end up accepting a descriptivist account of all 'ought' statements for lack of an alternative to the representationalist idea that truth conditions tell us how reality has to be in order for the statement to be true. What we need to avoid this easy slide to descriptivism is an alternative metasemantic framework with the space to treat some uses of 'ought' as descriptive and others as nondescriptive.

One way to make this space is to interpret a semantic model's predictions of a statements' truth conditions as telling us *not* how reality has to be for the statement to be true *but rather* what thoughts a speaker has to have in order to be using this statement in accordance with the core communicative rules of the language. For example, if someone says 'Grass is green' most semantic models will predict that this statement is true iff grass is green – a prediction we might then interpret as an articulation of the thought one has to have in order to be using this statement in accordance with the core communicative rules of the language (e.g. sincerity rules and meaning rules).

To get a version of nondescriptivism about genuinely normative ought-statements, one needs then to add that some thoughts are not representations of reality. For, of course, most philosophers want to say that the thought that grass is green is representational of the way reality is. However, representationalism needn't be correct for all thoughts. For example, when it comes to the thought that Sally might be at home, the more natural view is that this though is not directly about reality but rather some sort of qualification of one's epistemic position with respect to Sally's location (which 'in reality' is either in the house or not).

A sophisticated expressivist way of combining these two ideas would be to argue that the thoughts a speaker has to have, in order to be using genuinely normative ought-statements in accordance with the core communicative rules of English, are nonrepresentational because these thoughts have a desire-like direction of fit, ultimately being more like conditional plans or universalized preferences than beliefs about how reality is.[9] Insofar as we are impressed by the intuition that there is an important difference between describing how the world is and saying what someone ought to do, this sophisticated expressivist metasemantics for ought-statements provides a way to endorse the modal rule's predictions about the truth conditions for ought-statements while denying that these statements are always descriptions of reality.[10]

Unlike many other metaethicists, I'm not very moved by the idea that thoughts can be divided into the belief-like and desire-like, with attendant different 'directions of fit' with reality and different roles in practical reasoning. It's not that I doubt the utility of the direction-of-fit metaphor, but I suspect many thoughts fall somewhere in between, having both or neither direction of fit, in some sense and I think the categories *belief* and *desire* are not usefully aligned to this distinction.

Consider, for example, the epistemic 'ought'. For reasons already alluded to, the usual use of 'They left an hour ago, they ought to be there by now,' seems no more descriptive than an all-in normative use of 'You ought to call your mother.' However, with epistemic modal statements, I think it is considerably strained to say that these statements don't describe reality *because they express thoughts with a desire-like direction of fit with reality*. No, the reason they don't describe reality seems to me to have much more to do with the way language can be used in conversation to position ourselves epistemically with respect to the truth of some proposition. Moreover, I suspect that many of the same reasons we might want to be nondescriptivists about ought-statements apply to other modal statements (might-statements, must-statements, etc.). So I long for some more general explanation of why the thoughts expressed by genuinely normative ought-statements (the content of which the sophisticated expressivist takes to be articulated by predictions of the modal rule for 'ought') are not representations of the way reality is; and this explanation needs to be compatible with the idea that there are uses of 'ought' that are descriptive of assumed systems of values or norms.

So that's the main reason why I'm not inclined to go the expressivist route. In seeking an alternative, it can be instructive to ask what a sophisticated form of prescriptivism about 'ought' would look like in this context? The original prescriptivist position was that normative ought-statements don't describe reality but put forward some descriptive content as to be made true (for reasons that generalize). We might bring this in line with a different metasemantic interpretation of the predictions of the modal rule for 'ought' by claiming that the predictions a semantic model makes for truth conditions tell us not (i) what speakers have to think in order to use ought-statements in accordance with the core communicative rules of the language, but rather (ii) what speakers are committed to in virtue of using ought-statements to make assertions in ordinary discursive practice. Then, we could use (iii) to turn the original prescriptivist position into a metasemantic interpretation of the modal rule for 'ought' by suggesting that, while some statements are descriptive in committing speakers ontologically to a way reality is, other statements are prescriptive in committing speakers practically to acting and reacting in accordance with particular prescriptions and whatever they entail.

On this sophisticated form of prescriptivism, the predictions of the modal rule for 'ought' would be interpreted as articulations of the practical commitments carried by ought-statements in ordinary discursive practice. For example, the modal rule for 'ought' predicts that a normative use of 'You ought to call your mother,' is true iff you call your mother in all possible worlds consistent background conditions including your practical situation which are ranked highest by moral ideals. Our sophisticated prescriptivist would not interpret the reference here to possible worlds and moral ideals representationally, rather she would interpret this prediction as telling us something like the following: someone who asserts this ought-statement in ordinary discursive practice is practically committed in a moral way to acting in accordance with the prescription *call your mother!* across some range of circumstances (whatever circumstances are consistent with the background conditions including the practical situation of the 'you' to whom he is speaking). If we want to include a reactive element to this, perhaps we could add that this includes the speaker being committed not only to calling his own mother if in relevantly similar circumstances but also to blaming his audience for not calling her mother in the circumstances in which she currently finds herself.

So far, however, this looks like it has the same problems as the sophisticated expressivist view. It doesn't work well for epistemic uses of 'ought', and it doesn't extend well to other modals such as 'might' and 'must'. Moreover, there are apparently normative uses of 'ought' that are not comfortably assimilated to the idea of prescribing action. What practical commitment is one undertaking, conceived as endorsing the legitimacy of particular prescriptions, when one says 'There ought to be less childhood death and disease'? It's not impossible to answer this question, but most answers strike me as a stretch.

I think these problems can be overcome (but I'm not sure!) by modifying the alternative metasemantic view to be one about commitments to *think and reason in particular ways* rather than commitments to act in accordance with particular prescriptions.[11] This idea generates an account of why the modal rule for 'ought' generates the correct truth conditions (insofar as it does), an account which is comparable in terms of simplicity to that provided by descriptivism: those conditions articulate what ought-statements commit a speaker to, how they have to think and reason in order to satisfy the implicit conceptual commitments affirmed by using 'ought' to make an assertion in normal discursive practice.

To develop this, consider might-statements first. When a speaker makes a might-statement, we can view her as implicitly affirming a commitment to think and reason in particular ways: roughly, to avoid thinking or reasoning in ways that would be inconsistent with the proposition embedded in the might-statement being true. Whether it is acceptable to commit in this way depends on what is ruled out by the body of evidence counting as 'relevant' on the conversational score. Whatever exactly this is, we could conceive of an articulation of the truth conditions of a might statement (i.e. a prediction made in terms of existential quantifications over possible worlds consistent with a body of evidence) as an attempt to spell out which ways of thinking and reasoning the speaker has implicitly affirmed commitment to in making the might-statement.

For example, when a speaker says 'Sally might be at home,' he is committed to not thinking that Sally is at work and to not reasoning in ways that presuppose that Sally is not at home. This commitment is of course defeasible. If he later gets really good evidence that Sally is at work, the speaker is certainly allowed to think that Sally is at work. It's just that the commitment undertaken with the previous might-statement must then be abandoned (even if only implicitly).

So, on this view, the commitment articulated by a statement of the truth conditions for a might-statement is not a practical commitment in the traditional sense of being a commitment to act (moving our bodies towards some end) in in accord with some prescription. But it is also not an ontological commitment to reality being a particular way. Rather it is a commitment to thinking and reasoning in some way.

Could a similar view about 'ought' retain the virtues of the sophisticated expressivist and prescriptivist views while avoiding their problems? To do so, because 'ought' is more flexible than 'might' in the way it can take many flavors (moral, prudential, teleological, epistemic), we'd need to enrich our conception of the ways one can commit oneself to thinking and reasoning. What were previously conceived as practical commitments to act in accordance with some prescription could now be conceived as commitments to reason practically in certain ways, e.g. taking certain considerations to be decisive reasons for acting. This could help with genuinely normative statements such as 'You ought to call your mother.' However, we could also allow for commitments to thinking and reasoning with preferences, e.g. taking certain considerations as reasons for preferring things (even if these never connect to someone's ability to act). This could account for statements such as 'There ought to be less childhood death and disease.' Similarly, we could allow for commitments to thinking and reasoning with credences, e.g. taking certain circumstances to be reasons for assigning a high credence to particular propositions. This might help with statements such as 'They left an hour ago, they ought to be there by now.'

Initially this might look like a hodgepodge, but the general idea is unified: interpret the truth conditions predicted by the modal rule for 'ought' as articulations of the commitment implicitly affirmed by one who uses the statement to make an assertion in ordinary discursive practice, where this commitment is not conceived, in the first instance, as an ontological commitment to the way reality is but rather a commitment to think and reason in some way. Importantly, however, some commitments to think and reason in some way *are* ontological. They're commitments to think and reason as if reality is some particular way. So this metasemantic view is nonrepresentationalist in the sense that *not all* statements are treated as true just in case reality is some particular way, but it still allows that some (even many) statements are true just in case reality is some particular way. So if Ayer is right that some uses of 'ought' are best conceived as descriptions of the verdicts of the moral sense of some community or some assumed system of values, then this account can make sense of these statements as descriptive. But it does so while preserving theoretical space to make sense of other ought-statements as nondescriptive. What this means is that it has promise of being the general account of that in virtue of which sentences have the meanings that our best compositional semantic account will predict them to have, while nonetheless avoiding commitment to global representationalism about truth-apt statements (something we already wanted to avoid because of might-statements).

5. 'Good' as a measurement of value

At the beginning of this paper, I advertised my view about the meaning of normative statements as more inspired by Kant and Frege on modality than emotivists, prescriptivists, and expressivists on morality. I also suggested that this alternative route – via the idea that modal concepts are nonrepresentational – to a nondescriptivist view in metaethics doesn't extend straightforwardly to evaluative statements. This is because evaluative terms are not modals, and it's not natural to treat them as intensional operators. Relatedly, evaluative terms rarely embed whole propositions, such that it might make sense to explain their conceptual role in terms of some kind of formal modification of the propositions they embed rather than in terms of ordinary contribution to the propositional content of the statements in which they figure.

Some philosophers will see this as a big lacuna in my metaethical view. If one's metaethical nondescriptivism applies to normative words such as 'ought' but not to evaluative words such as 'good', then hasn't one failed to defend a nondescriptivist view of the concepts targeted by metaethical inquiry? After all, Moore (1903, ch. 1) was originally focused on judgements about things being *good*, not about what someone *ought* to do, and this is what sparked the familiar debates between nonnaturalists, expressivists, error theorists, and naturalists. Why should we care about a nondescriptivist view about normative statements if that view cannot be extended to a similar view about evaluative statements?

I understand the worry in these questions, but I don't share it. I think it would still represent an interesting form of nondescriptivism in metaethics if normative statements were treated as nondescriptive, but evaluative statements were treated as descriptive. Such a view would respect the *is-ought gap*; it would continue to allow that ought-judgments play a distinctive role in practical deliberation; and it would arguably respect some of the intuitions behind open-question style arguments that originally moved Moore and Ayer. For these reasons, I am sometimes inclined to combine nondescriptivism about 'ought' with some sort of sophisticated relativism about 'good'. However, I also think the above discussion makes space for a weak form of nondescriptivism about 'good', which I shall explore in this section.

Semantically, statements about something's being good seem to be very similar to statements about something's being tall or cold. Words such as 'tall', 'cold', and 'good' are vague gradable adjectives with thresholds. A good start towards articulating the semantic rules governing them would include something like this:

SCALAR RULES $[[x \text{ is tall}]]^c = T$ iff $tall(x) > threshold_c(tall)$
$[[x \text{ is cold}]]^c = T$ iff $cold(x) > threshold_c(cold)$
$[[x \text{ is good}]]^c = T$ iff $good(x) > threshold_c(good)$

Where the function *tall*, *cold*, and *good* take items and returns a measurement of how tall, cold, or good they are in some scale for measuring height, temperature, or value (e.g. feet, degrees Fahrenheit, or weighted preference satisfaction) and the function $threshold_c$ takes measurement functions and returns a threshold degree on the corresponding scale (e.g. how many feet, degrees F, or weighted preferences an item can have and still not be truly said to be tall, cold, or good).[12]

As we know, scalar adjectives are generally context sensitive in the sense that how tall, cold, good, etc. something needs to be in order to be truly said to be, tall, cold, good, etc. will vary from conversational context to conversational context; and even within context vagueness can mean that there are borderline cases. Moreover, as Geach (1956) stressed, most if not all uses of these adjectives need implicit (if not explicit) determination of the category of thing being evaluated before we have any idea what is being said. So, before context can even shift the threshold, it needs to fix the category of items being evaluated as tall, cold, good, etc.[13]

So it is obviously wrong to think that saying something is tall, cold, or good is to provide a context-independent description of reality. However, once context does its work, it is very natural to see ordinary uses of at least some of these adjectives as straightforwardly descriptive. After all, saying that LeBron James is tall in a context where we're talking about all men or that Vancouver is cold in a context where we're talking about North American cities in January would normally be regarded in metaethics as paradigmatic descriptive statements. These are precisely the kinds of statements with which expressivists contrast normative and evaluative statements.

For this reason, representationalism would seem to provide the default interpretation of the scalar rules for 'tall' and 'cold'. The representationalist view, recall, is that the rules above are correct (assuming they are) because they articulate how reality must be in order for the relevant statements to be true. It's important to note, however, that the predicted truth conditions for statements about something's being tall or cold include reference to a measurement scale and threshold. This is provided by context of utterance, and so part of what these statements describe – assuming that they are descriptive – is how something relates in its degree of height or temperature to the threshold on a contextually determined scale.

Turning to the scalar rule for 'good', does the plausibility of the representationalist-cum-descriptivist view about 'tall' and 'cold' mean we should also embrace a form of metaethical descriptivism, according to which the scalar rule for 'good' is interpreted as articulating the *evaluative* way reality has to be in order for the relevant statements to be true? Maybe, but there does seem to me to be a difference between describing the verdicts of some way of measuring value and making a genuinely evaluative statement.[14] One can make the former without endorsing the verdicts, whereas the latter seems to carry some conceptual connection to what there is reason to do, think, or feel. We can all recognize that, as a murder weapon, poison is good, without being forced to accept that there is any reason to use poison to murder or to admire those who do so. And someone who really thinks that saving for their retirement is good would seem to be irrational or unreasonable or deluded if they deny any preference or inclination to save for their retirement.

Above, I argued that a broader nonrepresentationalism could make sense of descriptive *and* nondescriptive uses of 'ought'. The idea was to interpret the truth conditions predicted by standard semantic rules articulating something other than the way reality has to be in order for the relevant statements to be true but also to allow that this 'something other' could sometimes but not always carry ontological commitment. Even though I'm inclined to think that 'good' is used descriptively more than 'ought', this theoretical structure can clearly be extended to cover both descriptive and nondescriptive uses of 'good'.

One way to do this would be to use a sophisticated form of expressivism. That is, we might interpret the scalar rule for 'good' as telling us what thoughts someone has to have, in order to be using good-statements in accordance with the core communicative rules of English. But we go on to argue that, while some thoughts that something is good are thoughts about the way reality is, not all thoughts that something is good need to be like that. More precisely, for those uses of 'good' that look to be descriptions of the verdicts of a contextually supplied system of values (e.g. 'As a murder weapon poison is good'), the sophisticated expressivist says that these thoughts are representational and the statements expressing them are ontologically committing. However, that leaves room for the expressivist to argue that other uses of good (e.g. 'Saving for retirement is good') express thoughts that are not representational. What makes them nonrepresentational? Maybe the expressivist can convince us that these thoughts play a distinctive functional role in our cognitive economies more like sophisticated preferences than representations of reality.[15]

This sophisticated form of expressivism is attractive for the way it can accept the semantic similarity between 'tall', 'cold', and 'good', and for the way it can use the scalar rule for 'good' to treat some good-statements as descriptive and other as nondescriptive. However, it does commit the expressivist to developing a particular view about the nature of the thoughts expressed by genuinely evaluative statements. A nondescriptivism about 'good' more in line with the nondescriptivism about 'ought' outlined above can be less committal about the psychology of evaluative thinking (even if it has to be more commital about the normative structure of thinking and reasoning). If we think that genuinely evaluative uses of 'good' are the ones that carry some conceptual connection to what there is reason to do, think, or feel, then we could try to write that connection into the commitments we think are implicitly affirmed by someone making a good-statement.

Recall, from above, that my preferred alternative to sophisticated expressivism is a metasemantic view that interprets the truth conditions predicted by our best semantics as articulations of how someone making that statement in ordinary discursive practice is committed to thinking and reasoning. This applies to both descriptive and nondescriptive statements. For statements we think are descriptive, we add an account of how someone making the statement is committed to thinking and reasoning, where this *includes* thinking that reality is some particular way or reasoning as if there is something in reality corresponding to the statement. For statements we think are not descriptive, we add an account of how someone making the statement is committed to thinking and reasoning, where this *excludes* thinking and reasoning about the way reality is. For ought-statements, it was natural to focus on practical commitments, commitments to do certain things (though not all ought-statements are practical). For good-statements, it may be more natural to focus on attitudinal commitments, commitments to feel particular ways, in particular to prefer certain things in certain ways.

The resulting picture is one in which both evaluative and descriptive uses of 'good' are assigned the same semantic rule (where the scalar rule for 'good' above is a first approximation). But we don't interpret this rule as telling us what reality has to be like for the relevant statements to be true or what thoughts one who makes the statement has to have in order to conform to the core communicative rules of the language. Rather we interpret this rule as telling us how someone making that statement in ordinary discursive practice is committed to thinking and reasoning. When the good-statement is descriptive, they are committed to thinking and reasoning about reality in some particular way; when the good-statement is nondescriptive, they are committed to thinking and reasoning in other ways about what to do, think, and feel.

6. Conclusion

I began this paper by contrasting the route into a nondescriptivist view about 'ought' offered by Frege and Kant on modality with the more familiar route in metaethics offered by emotivists, prescriptivists, and expressivists. I suggested that the former is attractive for how it hews more closely to the standard intensional semantics for 'ought' and fits with broader metasemantic observations about the linguistic and conceptual role of other modal words such as 'might'. I suggested, however, that a sophisticated expressivist could also provide a metasemantic interpretation of the modal rule for 'ought' capable of funding a kind of nondescriptivism about genuinely normative ought-statements. Moreover, both of these views could make sense of Ayer's observation that some uses of words such as 'ought' are descriptive of the verdicts of particular systems of values that are assumed for the purposes of some conversation, even if not endorsed by the speaker.

So we might conclude that, if one wants a form of nondescriptivism about genuinely normative ought-statements, there are two available routes. The Kant-Frege route may look unattractive for how it doesn't extend straightforwardly to evaluative uses of words such as 'good'. The traditional metaethical project was to explain normative *and* evaluative thought and talk; so providing an account of one of these that doesn't extend to the other is a lacuna in one's overall metaethical view. And since the sophisticated expressivist story about normative thought and talk can be extended to evaluative thought and talk, we might think that's a reason to prefer the Ayer-Hare route to a nondescriptivist view in metaethics.

In the final section of this paper, I sought to deflect this objection. I don't have a settled view about evaluative thought and talk. But I think there are ways of developing a non-expressivist form of nondescriptivism so that it covers 'good' as much as it covers 'ought'. So, in the end of the day, the deciding factor between these two ways of developing a nondescriptivist account of normative and evaluative thought and talk will be broader considerations having to do with what one thinks is foundational to a theory of meaningfulness and concept possession/use. Since I am skeptical of attempts to divide mental states into 'belief-like' and 'desire-like,' and more generally since language is a (mostly) public and observable phenomenon whereas mind is a (mostly) private and inferred phenomenon, I tend to like the non-expressivist route to a nondescriptivist account of normative and evaluative thought and talk. It is one which moves attractively from the inferential/conceptual structure of language to the psychological structure of thought, rather than the other way around.

Notes

1. See Sinclair (2009) and Chrisman (2011) for discussion of the history and some relatively recent developments.
2. Portner (2009, chs. 2–3) contains a great introductory discussion; see also Chrisman (2015) for an introduction.
3. It is the view I defended in Chrisman (2012a) and have developed in more detail in Chrisman (2016a) and (2016b).
4. For different versions of this argument see Dreier (1996), Unwin (1999), Schroeder (2008), and Blome-Tillman (2009).
5. See Humberstone (1971) and Schroeder (2011) for a view in this vein. See Chrisman (2012b) for critical discussion.
6. See Heim and Kratzer (1998, ch. 12) and Von Fintel and Heim (2007).
7. I address some of these in more detail in ch. 5 of Chrisman (2016a), where I argue that there is an agentive use of 'ought' embedding prescriptive content which is not propositional, and I explain a way to capture the relative weakness of 'ought' compared to 'must'.

8. This two factored account is the idea pioneered by Kratzer (1981). See Portner (2009, ch. 3) for general introduction and Chrisman (2015) for introduction to the case of deontic modals.
9. Chrisman (2016a, ch. 5, 2016b). See Ridge (2014) for a sophisticated development of this approach within a 'hybrid' expressivist framework that is capable of embracing the modal rule for 'ought' and treating some ought-statements as descriptive and others as nondescriptive.
10. What about embedded uses of 'ought'? On the one hand, this might be a question about the semantic content of complex statements, such as 'If you ought to call your mother, then you ought to charge up your phone.' If so, the answer is relatively easy: the modal rule predicts truth conditions for complete ought-sentences like a general truth-conditional semantic model attempts to do for any declarative sentence. These predictions must then be integrated with the model's treatment of sentential connectives, such as 'if-then' to predict truth conditions for the whole complex sentence in which the simpler sentences figure. To be sure, it is a matter of considerable controversy in compositional semantics how 'if-then' works, but as long as it takes truth-conditional complements, the modal rule for 'ought' will be able to integrate with a rule for 'if-then' to produce truth conditions for the complex sentence. On the other hand, however, the question about embedded uses of 'ought' could be a metasemantic question about what grounds our semantic model's predictions of the truth conditions for complex 'if-then' statements. This is a very difficult question, but one that is perhaps even more difficult for representationalists than nonrepresentationalists. It is sometimes claimed in compositional semantics that ordinary language conditionals are covert modals, in which case some of the same descriptivist and nondescriptivist ideas explored here about 'ought' might be explored in developing a metasemantic interpretation of 'if-then'. But there are also other possible metasemantic accounts of 'if-then'.
11. In Chrisman (2017), I explain how this might be incorporated into a conceptual role account of meaning for the sorts of expressions of interest to metaethicists.
12. Compare Kennedy (2007).
13. See Thomson (2008) for a worked out version of this view addressing many of the shortfalls of Geach's own suggestion but continuing in a similar spirit.
14. Also 'good' unlike 'tall' and 'cold' seems to be multidimensional. I will largely ignore this here, but it provides another path to a nondescriptivim about 'good': perhaps some contexts do not determine how the various dimensions of value are to be weighed in determining whether something is good. In such cases, the function of good-statements might not be to describe something's value but to set a standard for weighing competing values. See Plunkett and Sundell (2013) for further discussion of this metalinguistic use of vague and context-sensitive adjective and some of the implications it has for metaethics.
15. Compare Silk (2015) and Köhler (forthcoming).

References

Ayer, A. J. 1936. *Language, Truth and Logic*. London: V. Gollancz.
Blome-Tillman, Michael. 2009. "Non-Cognitivism and the Grammar of Morality." *Proceedings of the Aristotelian Society* 103 (1): 279–309.
Chrisman, Matthew. 2011. "Ethical Expressivism." In *Continuum Companion to Ethics*, edited by Christian Miller, 29–54. New York: Continuum.
Chrisman, Matthew. 2012. "'Ought' and Control." *Australasian Journal of Philosophy* 90 (3): 433–451.
Chrisman, Matthew. 2012. "On the Meaning of 'Ought.'" In *Oxford Studies in Metaethics*, vol. 7, edited by Russ Shafer-Landau, 304–332. Oxford: Oxford University Press.
Chrisman, Matthew. 2015. Deontic Modals. *Routledge Encyclopedia of Philosophy*.
Chrisman, Matthew. 2016a. "Metanormative Theory and the Meaning of Deontic Modals." In *Deontic Modality*, edited by Nate Charlow and Matthew Chrisman, 395–430. New York: Oxford University Press.
Chrisman, Matthew. 2016b. *The Meaning of 'Ought': Beyond Descriptivism and Expressivism in Metaethics*. New York: Oxford University Press.
Chrisman, Matthew. 2017. "Conceptual Role Accounts of Meaning in Metaethics." In *The Routledge Handbook of Metaethics*, edited by Tristram McPherson and David Plunkett, 260–274. New York: Routledge.
Dreier, James. 1996. "Expressivist Embeddings and Minimalist Truth." *Philosophical Studies* 83 (1): 29–51.
Frege, Gottlieb. (1879) 1967. "Begriffsschrift, eine der arithmetischen nachgebildete Formelsprache des reinen Denkens (Halle a. S.: Louis Nebert)." [Concept Script, a formal language of pure thought modelled upon that of arithmetic.] In *From Frege to Gödel: A Source Book in Mathematical Logic*, translated by S. Bauer-Mengelberg, edited by J. van Heijenoort, 1879–1931. Cambridge, MA: Harvard University Press.
Geach, P. T. 1956. "Good and Evil." *Analysis* 17: 33–42.
Hare, R. M. 1952. *The Language of Morals*. Oxford: Clarendon Press.
Heim, Irene, and Angelika Kratzer. 1998. *Semantics in Generative Grammar*. Blackwell.
Humberstone, I. L. 1971. "Two Sorts of 'Ought's.'" *Analysis* 32 (1): 8–11.
Kant, Immanuel. (1787) 1998. *Critique of Pure Reason* (translated and edited by Paul Guyer & Allen W. Wood). Cambridge: Cambridge University Press.
Kennedy, Christopher. 2007. "Vagueness and Grammar: The Semantics of Relative and Absolute Gradable Adjectives." *Linguistics and Philosophy* 30: 1–45.
Köhler, Sebastian. forthcoming. Expressivism, Meaning, and All That. *Canadian Journal of Philosophy* ,
Kratzer, Angelika. 1981. "The Notional Category of Modality." In *Words, Worlds, and Contexts*, edited by Hans Eikmeyer and Hannes Reiser, 38–74. Berlin: de Gruyter.
Moore, G. E. 1903. *Principia Ethica*. Mineola, NY: Dover Publications.
Plunkett, David, and Tim Sundell. 2013. "Disagreement and the Semantics of Normative and Evaluative Terms." *Philosophers' Imprint* 13 (23): 1–37.
Portner, Paul. 2009. *Modality*. Oxford: Oxford University Press.
Ridge, Michael. 2014. *Impassioned Belief*. Oxford: Oxford University Press.
Schroeder, Mark. 2008. "How Expressivists Can and Should Solve Their Problem with Negation." *Noûs* 42 (4): 573–599.

Schroeder, M. 2011. "Ought, Agents, and Actions." *Philosophical Review* 120 (1): 1–41.
Silk, Alex. 2015. "How to Be an Ethical Expressivist." *Philosophy and Phenomenological Research* 91 (1): 47–81.
Sinclair, Neil. 2009. "Recent Work in Expressivism." *Analysis* 69 (1): 136–147.
Thomson, Judith Jarvis. 2008. *Normativity*. Chicago, IL: Open Court.
Unwin, Nicholas. 1999. "Quasi-Realism, Negation And the Frege-Geach Problem." *The Philosophical Quarterly* 49: 337–352.
Von Fintel, Kai, and Irene Heim. 2007. *Intensional Semantics*. Unpublished Lecture Notes, Cambridge, MA.

The unity of moral attitudes: recipe semantics and credal exaptation*

Derek Shiller

ABSTRACT
This paper offers a noncognitivist characterization of moral attitudes, according to which moral attitudes count as such because of their inclusion of moral concepts. Moral concepts are distinguished by their contribution to the functional roles of some of the attitudes in which they can occur. They have no particular functional role in other attitudes, and should instead be viewed as evolutionary spandrels. In order to make the counter-intuitive implications of the view more palatable, the paper ends with an account of the evolution of normative judgments as exaptations of the cognitive structures that underlie beliefs.

Normative noncognitivism is a negative theory: it holds that normative judgments lack representational contents and are therefore not beliefs. Formulating a satisfying positive theory requires saying more about what moral attitudes actually are. To that end, noncognitivists have traditionally looked to the motivational capacity of moral judgments and have focused on straightforwardly predicative forms such as *insurance fraud is wrong* and *charitable donations are morally exemplary*. Moral judgments compel us to engage or refrain from engaging in actions without help from ancillary desires.[1] Though noncognitivism can be developed in a number of ways, I will treat this motivational strain as representative.

Noncognitivists are known to face challenges in making sense of moral attitudes other than straightforwardly predicative moral judgments. The Frege-Geach problem, which addresses logically complex moral judgments, is the most well-known challenge. However, noncognitivists require characterizations of a range of other attitudes.

---

*This paper benefitted from comments by Adam Thompson, Derek Baker, David Faraci, Tristram McPherson, William Melanson, and two anonymous referees, as well as audiences at the Philosopher's Cocoon and Minds Online conferences.

In this paper, I will sketch a systematic strategy for characterizing moral attitudes. My approach differs from most extant noncognitivist views in that I don't aim to rationally vindicate the behavior of our moral attitudes or earn the right to realist practice and discourse. Instead, I aim only to provide an account of what distinguishes these attitudes. I hope that once this account is fleshed out, their behavior will be shown to be understandable.

In short, I propose that moral attitudes can be divided into primary and derivative classes. The primary moral attitudes admit of traditional noncognitivist characterizations. The derivative moral attitudes are identified by non-semantic similarities with members of the primary class. Namely, they involve the same constituent components. This dichotomy allows for a 'recipe semantics' of moral attitudes, which characterizes them by their inclusion of components that have distinctive functional roles in a restricted set of contexts.

The resulting noncognitivist view shares some of the spirit of error theory: I will suggest that the derivative moral attitudes are accidental byproducts of the cognitive structures underlying the primary moral attitudes. The parallels between moral and propositional attitudes result from their syntactic commonalities. Moral concepts enjoy the same syntactic freedoms as other concepts, even if they don't have coherent functions in all of the contexts in which they occur.

I will begin in Section 1 by cataloguing the attitudinal complexities facing noncognitivists. In the second, I will present an account of our propositional attitudes to frame my proposal about moral attitudes. In the third, I will explain how a recipe semantics could be used to characterize moral attitudes. In the fourth, I will conclude with a speculative account of the cognitive evolution of moral judgments that makes a recipe semantics plausible.

1. A menagerie of moral attitudes

Cognitivists hold that moral judgments, such as the sort expressed by (A), can be characterized as beliefs with a certain moral content.

(A) It is wrong to collect trophies of endangered species.

The judgment expressed by (A) takes a proposition about the distribution of a certain property (*wrongness*) as its object. Cognitivists disagree about the nature of this property, but they agree that the world must meet definite conditions in order for (A) to be true.

In contrast, noncognitivists hold that such judgments have no special representational contents. There is no property that we ascribe to acts in judging them wrong. Rather, in judging an act wrong, we adopt a conative attitude towards it. According to this approach, moral judgments are *moral judgments* not because of their representational content, but because of their motivational force.

An account of straightforwardly predicative forms of moral judgments won't tell us much about the nature of logically complex forms. Consider (B), which employs 'wrong' under the scope of a negation.

(B) It is not wrong to collect trophies of extinct species.

The attitude expressed by (B) is not motivational in the same way as the attitude expressed by (A), so an account of straightforwardly predicative moral judgments will not carry over to negational judgments. We are not moved to act solely because we believe that something is *not* wrong.

Negation is the only most basic form of logical complication.[2] The same problem also arises for conjunction and disjunction, as in the attitude expressed by (C), and quantification, as in the attitudes expressed by (D) and (E).

- (C) Human beings either have a special moral status or it is wrong to test cosmetics on animals.
- (D) Everything you did today was more wrong than the thing you did before it.
- (E) Most killings are deeply morally wrong.

Quantification hasn't received the same attention as conjunction, disjunction, and negation, but it is equally problematic.

In addition to ordinary quantification, moral judgments can also take plural and generic forms, such as the attitudes expressed by (F) and (G).

- (F) The wrongs that the colonists did to the natives were more varied and numerous than the wrongs that the natives did to the colonists.
- (G) Wrongs are a stain upon the moral character of decent people.

Geach was especially interested in conditionals, since they play an important role in moral arguments:

(H) If lying is wrong, then getting your little brother to lie is wrong.

Although there are truth-functional interpretations available for these conditionals, they are widely thought to be inadequate. The indicative conditionals found in moral judgments like that expressed by (H) are subject to the same considerations that motivate non-truth-conditional interpretations of indicative conditionals in other contexts. This means that the problems created by conditionals are not quite like the problems created by logical operators.

Moral judgments can take the form of subjunctive conditionals, as expressed by (I), and can involve tense, as expressed by (J).

- (I) If it had been wrong to bring children into this world, we would not have done it.
- (J) Abortion is as wrong today as it was fifty years ago.

Noncognitivists must also account for the existence of mixed normative judgments. Mixed normative judgments, such as the attitudes expressed by (K) and (L), combine different flavors of normativity within a single attitude.

(K) You ought (epistemically) to know when you did wrong.
(L) You should (rationally) keep track of what you shouldn't (morally) do.

Finally, noncognitivists owe an explanation of moral attitudes other than judgment. Not only can we judge that actions are wrong, but we can wish that they were permissible, regret that we acted immorally and hope that we chose the right thing, wonder whether utilitarianism or deontology is correct and be more confident in one than the other, find some moral principles intuitive, imagine fictional scenarios where different moral principles hold, and suppose novel moral principles for the sake of arguments.

We must make sense of these other attitudes just as we must make sense of moral judgments. An account of what it is to judge that an action is wrong will not tell us what it is to hope that we did the right thing or wonder whether what we did was obligatory. It makes no sense to suppose ordinary conative attitudes for the purposes of arguments (though we can suppose that *we have* these conative attitudes).

Although the problems involved in logical and other semantic contexts are different from the problems created by other moral attitudes, the threat they pose is the same. Noncognitivists would be best served by a general account of the nature of these attitudes.

2. Context and meaning determination

Since moral attitudes are so similar to propositional attitudes, any inquiry into the former ought to start with the latter. In this section, I will present some assumptions about the cognitive structure of ordinary propositional attitudes in preparation for the recipe semantics that I provide in the next.

On the view to be assumed, our propositional attitudes involve relations to cognitive representations whose representational contents are determined by the representational properties of their parts. Those parts can be individuated by means of non-semantic properties and can receive their representational content from their function in special contexts. I will describe each of these ideas in turn.

2.1. *The representational theory of mind*

According to the Representational Theory of Mind (RTM)[3], ordinary propositional attitudes involve relations to mental representations whose contents are propositions. The type of attitude that results from tokening a mental representation depends upon the way in which it is tokened. For instance, to believe a proposition might be to token a representation of that proposition in a certain way and to use representations tokened in that way in deciding how to act to satisfy one's goals.

Those who accept RTM need a psychosemantic account of the associations between mental structures and propositions. I will assume a teleological theory (e.g. Dretske 1995; Millikan 1984; Papineau 1984): roughly, mental representations have their representational contents by virtue of being designed to represent that content. This theory won't differ from its competitors on points relevant to my argument, and so readers may substitute their own preferred psychosemantics wherever appropriate.

2.2. Compositional representations

Representations can be either structured or unstructured. Structured representations are composed of constituents with their own representational contents. Natural language sentences are structured, since both sentences and words represent. Maps are also structured, since they have sub-regions with representational content (Blumson 2012). I will assume that mental representations are structured and I will refer to the ultimate constituents of individual mental representations as 'concept tokens'. The bare term 'concept' will be reserved for types of concept tokens.

Structured representations are typically compositional in the sense that the representational contents of the parts help to determine the representational contents of the whole. The representational contents of concept tokens do not determine how they (as neurophysiological entities) can be combined, even if their contents will have a say in whether the combinations they enter into are meaningful (Stich 1983). Semantic properties simply aren't the right sort of property to play that role, any more than the representational content of a LEGO head explains why it fits snugly onto a LEGO torso and not a LEGO horse.[4]

Non-semantic – 'syntactic' – properties enable the combination of some concepts and not others. As a result, there may be syntactically viable combinations of concept tokens that are semantically incoherent.

2.3. Orthographic identities

By supposition, concept tokens acquire meanings from their designed functions. The designed functions of concepts depend upon the their behavior in some range of contexts, and so it is necessary that concept tokens have identities that are preserved across contexts in order to ground their representational contents. Quine's (1960) radical interpreters could rely on the phonological properties of 'gavagai' to re-identify the word in different contexts. Their task would have been impossible had the sound of the word varied arbitrarily with each use. The same goes for cognitive semantics: representational contents could not be assigned to the components of an attitude if those components could not be re-identified. The difficulty is not merely epistemic; patterns of use must underlie semantic values.

Since they are used to assign representational contents, the properties that identify concept tokens from context to context must be non-representational. Given the analogy with written language, I will refer to such properties as 'orthographic'. Orthographic properties might be closely associated with syntactic properties, but they need not be the same.[5]

2.4. Spandrel contexts

Our concepts may or may not have a designed function in every context in which their syntactic properties permit them to occur. Phenotypical traits often outstrip the requirements of their designed function. Natural selection exerts imprecise forces, and adaptations that are helpful in one context may also have effects elsewhere. This means that many phenotypic traits are byproducts – 'spandrels' – of selection for other traits.

Suppose that that we identify the concept *horse* as a concept whose designed function is to track the properties of horses by figuring into representations of horses. It isn't part of the designed function of the concept *horse* to distract us when we are bored, but its tokens can be employed to this end. This use need not count against the concept's designed function, as the concept may not have been designed *not* to be used as a distraction. Instead, its function may be given by its contributions in the context of certain kinds of attitudes, such as beliefs and desires, and it may have no functions in others, such as daydreams. If this is the case, then these other contexts are spandrel contexts for the concept.

3. Recipe semantics for moral attitudes

In Section 5, I developed a view on which propositional attitudes involve mental representations. I suggested that individual mental representations can be identified across contexts by virtue of their orthographic properties. I now propose extending this idea to moral attitudes. I will start by broadening the notion of mental representation to allow for non-representational variants. Then I will provide a recipe semantics for daydreams to serve as an analogue for my view about moral attitudes. Finally, I will turn to my proposed recipe semantics of moral attitudes.

3.1. Presentations

The orthographic properties of non-mental representations can be divided into resemblance classes. Written words, for instance, are individuated by their shapes. These shapes are distinctive, but they share more in common with each other than they do with spoken words. Written English sentences also share features (across different typefaces and handwriting styles) that distinguish them from sentences in Arabic or Greek. An 'orthographic class' is a set composed of entities whose orthographic properties resemble each other and that includes a system of representations as a subclass. There are orthographic classes for English sentences, road maps, stock tables, and bar graphs.[6]

Membership in an orthographic class is determined by the orthographic properties of the potential member and the corresponding properties of other members. Representationality is not a prerequisite for membership. Many members of orthographic classes have no representational significance. Take this stanza from Lewis Carroll's Jabberwocky:

'Twas brillig, and the slithy toves

Did gyre and gimble in the wabe:

All mimsy were the borogoves,

And the mome raths outgrabe.

These sentences belong to orthographic classes that also contain English sentences, but since many of the words have no established meaning, they do not represent.

Any member of an orthographic class is a 'presentation'. Representations are often presentations, but presentations need not be representations. The sentences in Jabberwocky are non-representational presentations.

Non-representational mental presentations are conceptually coherent: they are presentations that fail to meet contingently-satisfied conditions for representing. If minds use representations in their propositional attitudes, they may also use non-representational presentations in other attitudes. Not every attitude that acts something like a belief has earned a semantic value. This opens up the possibility that moral attitudes involve non-representational presentations in just the way that propositional attitudes involve representations.

3.2. The presentational theory of mind

According to RTM, propositional attitudes are relations to mental representations. If beliefs involve relations to mental representations, moral judgments plausibly involve relations to mental presentations. Beliefs and moral judgments are quite similar (Horgan and Timmons 2006), and so it would be surprising if they were implemented in fundamentally distinct ways.

Now my proposal: *straightforwardly predicative moral judgments are attitudes that involve relations to complex structured presentations that contain non-representational concepts whose proper function is not to represent but instead to influence action (in that context)*. These concepts are moral concepts and they are syntactically compatible with representational concepts in the same way as representational concepts are with each other. Since the designed function of neither the whole presentation nor its constituent moral concepts is to represent, neither is representational. But since moral concepts convey an action-directing function in the context of straightforwardly predicative moral judgments, they are also not functionless.[7]

3.3. A recipe theory of daydreams

Philosophers of mind have traditionally focused on attitudes, such as belief and desire, that play an important role in influencing behavior. Not all of our attitudes are like this. Daydreams are not. This means that many strategies for characterizing propositional attitudes cannot be fully generalized. Contra functionalism, we cannot make sense of what it is to daydream about a particular situation in terms of what that daydream does in our mental life. In order to understand these states, we may need to approach them as byproducts of other cognitive faculties.

I propose that the representational properties of daydreams ought to be understood through their parts and how those parts are used elsewhere. We can't identify a concept token as a concept of a horse, for instance, solely by its deployment in daydreams. Instead, we must look to how the same sort of concept token is used in other cognitive contexts, such as perceiving horses, having beliefs about horses, and organizing intentions regarding behavior toward horses.

A daydream gets its content by employing concepts that play important roles in other contexts. These concepts are recognized by the orthographic properties of their tokens. A concept token of a horse in a daydream represents a horse only insofar as it was designed to have a certain representational content in other contexts. The fact that a dream is of a horse and not a teapot results from the fact that the same concept tokens employed in the dream have the function of keeping track of the properties of horses on other occasions.

3.4. A recipe semantics for moral attitudes

In Sections 1 and 2, I suggested that straightforwardly predicative moral judgments involve a special kind of mental presentation. In the present, I will explain how to extend this characterization to handle more complex moral attitudes.

Moral concepts are characterized by non-representational proper functions that operate in the context of straightforwardly predicative moral judgments. In order for a concept token to be a token of a moral concept, it must be designed for a certain use in certain contexts. Given that concept tokens can be recognized in a variety of contexts based on their orthographic properties, and given that they need not have functions in all of the contexts in which they occur, it is easy to systematically extend this account to handle other moral attitudes.

The general strategy is to characterize attitudes with recipes for constructing them – i.e. in terms of the ingredients that must be combined to produce the attitude. The ingredients may be characterized by their designed function in other contexts. There need not be anything distinctive about these attitudes beyond the parts from which they are made. They may lack a function and have no important role in cognition.

Just as with daydreams, the concepts that populate our moral attitudes may get their contents from other contexts. In particular, moral concepts may be characterized by their role in straightforwardly predicative judgments and have no particular semantic characters in general.[8]

3.5. Hope

Perhaps the most promising applications of this approach are to moral attitudes other than judgments. Noncognitivists must make sense of what it is to have moral hopes, to be uncertain about moral issues, and to make moral suppositions for the purposes of arguments. With a recipe semantics, we can easily explain what makes these attitudes moral attitudes.

According to RTM, propositional attitudes involve relations to mental representations. By assumption, differences in kinds of propositional attitudes correspond to differences in the relationships taken to mental representations. To believe something and to desire it involve taking different relations to the same content. Just as with concept tokens, these relations need an orthographic identity in order to support a complex pattern of use. Each belief involves an orthographically identifiable relation to an orthographically identifiable presentation, each desire involves a distinct orthographically identifiable relation to an orthographically identifiable presentation, and so on.

If hopes are a basic propositional attitude, then we can expect that there will be a separate orthographically distinctive property that characterizes the relations we have to the representations we hope to be true. Even if hoping is characterized by its functional role within our cognitive lives, the realizer playing that role may be distinctive in a non-semantic way.

If our minds employ moral presentations and we relate to them in the same orthographically distinctive way that we relate to the representations that we hope, then we can count as hoping them as well, even though they lack representational content and do not have quite the same functional role as ordinary hopes. A moral hope is created by combining a presentation including a moral concept with the orthographic relation special to hope. There need be no deeper essence for moral hopes.

3.6. Negation

Negational moral judgments are the sorts of judgments that we typically express with negations of moral predications. They appear to be logically inconsistent with straightforwardly predicative moral judgments. For instance, the judgment *immigration restrictions are not wrong* is a negational moral judgment that appears to be inconsistent with the judgment *immigration restrictions are wrong*. This inconsistency has been thought to create substantial problems for noncognitivists (Schroeder 2008; Unwin 1999), and has received a lot of attention in recent years (e.g. Baker and Woods 2015; Schwartz and Hom 2015; Shiller 2016; Sinclair 2011).

Noncognitivists have tried to characterize negational attitudes by their relation to their unnegated counterparts: they are states that are in some way incompatible (Blackburn 1988; Gibbard 2003; Horgan and Timmons 2009). This incompatibility might be explained by the characteristic functional role of the attitudes. For instance, the functional roles of straightforwardly predicative and negational moral judgments might be to direct us to realize mutually unsatisfiable states of affairs.

Critics have cast doubts on whether noncognitivists can locate attitudes with the relevant sort of incompatibility. The chief worry is that the incompatibility must be essential to the attitudes and must accommodate the distinction between logical and non-logical forms of inconsistency (van Roojen 1996).

Negational moral judgments are not the strongest candidates for a recipe semantics, and adopting a recipe semantics would not preclude us from characterizing straightforward predicative moral judgments and their negations in ways that account for attitudinal inconsistency. However, noncognitivists can also make use of a recipe semantics to characterize negational moral judgments and doing so helps explain the appearance of inconsistency.

On a recipe semantics, negational moral judgments might be characterized as attitudes that involve presentations with a special sort of negation concept. A negational moral judgment involves a presentation that includes a negation concept token as a constituent. Though the negation concept is designed to play a certain function in the case of representations, it need not play that specific function in other presentations and so it may have no special function or representational content whatsoever in the context of moral presentations. What identifies the moral judgment as a negational moral judgment is the presence of a constituent with a specific function in other contexts.

It is plausible that the characteristic function of negation concepts is to invert representations: a representation governed by a negation concept has the opposite satisfaction conditions as its unnegated content. This function is restricted to representations. The concept may not have this function in all of its syntactically viable contexts. In the context of moral judgments, in which there are no satisfaction conditions to invert, the negation concept may have no more function than 'not' in 'it was not brillig'. Instead, it simply feeds another component into the presentation.[9]

Characterizing an attitude is one thing. Accounting for its behavior is another. This paper is specifically focused on offering a schema for characterizing moral attitudes, but the viability of these characterizations will depend in part on how they can account for the behavior of the attitudes. When it comes to negational moral judgments, the key feature to be explained is the appearance of inconsistency.[10]

The appearance of inconsistency probably does not depend on an implicit grasp of the semantics of moral attitudes. On the contrary, the appearance may result from the presence in moral attitudes of the same non-semantic mechanisms that generate genuine inconsistency in other situations.

Even in its spandrel contexts, the presence of the negation concept may color our introspective view of the attitude. Since it generates inconsistencies in so many other contexts, the negation concept could produce the appearance of inconsistency in moral attitudes and thereby lead us to treat the attitudes in which negation concept tokens occur as spandrels in the same way we treat the attitudes in which they play their proper role. In other words, we may project the inconsistency-generative appearance of negational concepts from their primary contexts to their spandrel contexts.

We can extend this explanation to handle the logicality of attitudinal inconsistency. Noncognitivists and their critics have realized that it is helpful to attribute some structure to moral attitudes (Baker and Woods 2015; Schroeder 2008) in order to explain logical inconsistency. The recipe semantics achieves this through attributing syntactic structure and the presence of distinctive concepts in the cognitive presentation. Moral attitudes often appear inconsistent because they have the form of inconsistent attitudes, and the considerations that deprive them of representational meanings are subtle.

This structure even permits a shallow sense of logical validity. While moral claims may only be truth-evaluable in a deflationary sense themselves, any substitution of representational concepts for moral concepts in a 'valid' moral argument would produce a truth-preserving argument. Moral arguments can have a valid form, since the structure of their logical concepts can guarantee representational truth preservation. Of course, moral arguments are importantly different from their propositional analogues, but their logical form might explain why they are compelling in the same way. It is unsurprising that we should be inclined to view moral arguments as akin to non-moral arguments, especially given our tenuous introspective grasp on their semantics.[11]

3.7. Comparisons with existing views

By adopting a recipe semantics, we avoid the need to attribute representational contents or essential functional characters to attitudes other than straightforwardly predicative judgments. Straightforwardly predicative moral judgments establish the orthographic properties that other attitudes must share in order to count as moral attitudes. There is no semantic core to moral attitudes in all their guises. They are moral attitudes because a subset of the attitudes with the relevant orthographic properties (i.e. containing a orthographically identified moral concept) play the role characteristic of straightforwardly predicative moral judgments.

It is consistent with this approach that many kinds of moral attitudes have representational contents or functional characters – all that the recipe semantics requires is that these properties are not what qualifies them as moral attitudes. However, once we secure the morality of moral attitudes without recourse to a shared content or functional role, there is little reason to demand contents or functional roles for any particular attitudes. This makes my approach very different from traditional approaches to the problem, and for attitudes other than straightforwardly predicative moral judgments, it may more closely resemble error theory (Joyce 2001; Mackie 1977). The attitudes themselves are not mistaken in the way error theorists suppose, but our higher-order judgments about them are deeply mistaken.

3.7.1. Traditional expressivism

Traditional noncognitivists such as Simon Blackburn (1988) and Allan Gibbard (2003) have developed elaborate views with the aim of vindicating aspects of moral practice – of earning the right to realist forms of practice and discourse. The prominence of the Frege-Geach problem has led to a focus on moral argumentation and the logical relations between our attitudes. The standard line is to interpret apparently logically inconsistent attitudes as involving some sort of opposing and mutually unsatisfiable commitments.

The view about negational moral judgments suggested in Section 2 takes a very different tact. Instead of aiming to vindicate the relations between moral attitudes, it provides an explanation of how we might be led to treat them as we do. It is plausible, for reasons presented below, that some of our attitudes play no important roles in our psychology. If these aspects of moral psychology do not need intelligible rationales, than we should be satisfied with non-rationalizing explanations of moral practice.

The key point is that in denying moral attitudes special semantic contents, we need not surrender any of the cognitive machinery responsible for our use of (and intuitions about) propositional attitudes. Propositions are abstract objects we use to help us think about neurological processes. Strictly speaking, they do not contribute to the functioning of the underlying neural machinery. We impose propositions on top of this machinery in order to fit it within our folk psychological and normative schemes, but if our schemes break down, it is more likely because of the limitations of the abstracta than the machinery.

This view will fair poorly if our goal is to support the greatest number of pre-theoretical intuitions, for it contradicts a common perspective on morality. However, error theories play a special role in philosophical methodology: intuitions that can be effectively explained away are not intuitions whose satisfaction counts for much. If we can effectively explain our moral intuitions by means of syntactic features of moral attitudes, then we should let the semantic cards fall where they may.

3.7.2. Hybrid expressivism

Forms of hybrid expressivism (Ridge 2014; Schroeder 2013; Toppinen 2013) that marry cognitive and noncognitive states have recently become popular. On these views, moral judgments involve both beliefs and noncognitive states. Judging that an act is wrong, for instance, might be analyzed into believing that the act has a certain non-moral property and disapproving of all acts with that property. Hybrid views have the advantage of capturing the behavioral similarity of moral attitudes with both cognitive and noncognitive states within a traditional psychological framework.

Hybrid expressivism may not differ so much from the view on offer in terms of the kinds of cognitive structures that it attributes to moral judgments. Both views will allow that belief-like attitudes take part in moral judgments. They will disagree, however, primarily[12] on the meta-semantic question of whether those belief-like structures have full representational contents. The motivation for the recipe semantics is the thought that moral concept tokens lack representational contents because they fail to meet the conditions necessary to represent. Hybrid expressivists must deny this.

The primary drawback to hybrid views is that they require representational contents for our moral beliefs. In order to accommodate the diversity of moral views, the most promising versions of hybrid expressivism have been forced to adopt a kind of relativism in which the representational contents of moral judgments (the parts involved in beliefs) are relativized to the judge's particular moral standards (Ridge 2014).

In many moral judgments, it is not hard to find reasonable representational contents to assign. The problem is that the approach is committed to finding a non-normative content of this sort for every moral judgment: in order to judge an action wrong, an individual must judge it to have some particular negatively regarded property. Similarly, it must be impossible to hope that an action was right without hoping that it had some specific positively regarded property.[13]

The attribution of relativized contents is unnecessary. The primary value of assigning contents to these attitudes is that it allows them to be fit within a familiar rationalizing psychological picture. It is not worth going to great lengths to read robust representational contents into moral attitudes, given the potential of non-semantic explanations to achieve the same ends. If we don't need to attribute representational contents to understand our attitudes, we shouldn't go out of our way to do so. So, if the project of explaining the similarities between moral judgments and beliefs in terms of their syntactic properties pans out, then we don't need to assign representational contents.

4. Belief, exaptation, and moral judgments

The value of this recipe semantics depends on how plausible it is that some of our concepts appear in spandrel contexts. While it is coherent for concepts that have a function in one context to appear in spandrel contexts, it may still count against a theory to be forced to this conclusion.

We are able to combine concept tokens in the ways that we do because of their syntactic properties. The semantic properties of our concepts, which depend partly on their historical or counterfactual behavior, cannot themselves fully explain how it is that we are able to use them to produce attitudes with the characteristic behaviors of propositional attitudes.

Cognitivist and noncognitivists alike require explanations of the forms our attitudes take. Cognitivists face the challenge of explaining how we can form diverse beliefs. Jerry Fodor has argued for a solution invoking the structure rather than the content of our attitudes (Fodor 1998, 2008; Fodor and Pylyshyn 1988). Fodor explains our systematic and productive attitudinal capacities in terms of a cognitive system of recombinable units. The purported functional differences provide little reason to think that the challenge of accounting for all of our attitudes will look much different for noncognitivists. The mechanisms that determine unit combinability are orthogonal to the properties that convey these units their semantic values.

Nevertheless, it might be doubted that our moral concepts have syntactic properties that allow them to be combined into attitudes without functions. How is it that we're able to hope that we did the right thing, if the concept *right* doesn't make any specific semantic contribution to the attitude?

The evolutionary history of moral attitudes can make these syntactic properties unsurprising. What follows is one story of how this history may have gone. It isn't the only viable story, but it can still ward off serious worries about postulating spandrel moral contexts.

4.1. Coordinating social expectations

Our tendency to moral behavior is surely the product of evolutionary forces.[14] Full-fledged moral attitudes play an important role in regulating our behavior, and the behaviors they produce contribute to our fitness. It is fitter for us to reciprocate acts of kindness and cruelty and to act altruistically toward our kin.[15] However, full-fledged moral attitudes are not necessary to produce this sort of behavior. Moral sentiments suffice. We could have evolved to feel grateful, vindictive, protective, and magnanimous without having anything that looked quite like moral judgments.

Moral judgments are complex and sophisticated attitudes. On the surface, they appear to rely on the same mechanisms that underlie our capacity to formulate complex representations, even if they are not representational. If moral sentiments are capable of driving moral behavior by themselves, why do we also have the capacity to judge actions to be right or wrong?

One explanation is that moral judgments evolved to enable us to coordinate social expectations.[16] They not only play a role in guiding moral behavior, they also increase social flexibility. They give us the cognitive resources necessary to formulate, assess, and communicate norms that can regulate our sentiments. We can voice the moral rules we agree to obey, and learn the rules others favor following. Furthermore, if we are flexible and open to influence by others, we can ensure that the rules that govern our community are a compromise of the interests of its members. This makes it easier to accommodate changing social structures and power dynamics.

In the rough and rapidly changing world of the upper palaeolithic, moral flexibility would have been advantageous. Our species spread out quickly to environments as different as Ice Age Europe and Polynesia (Henn, Cavalli-Sforza, and Feldman 2012). The new ways of life required for survival in these environments created novel social dynamics in an evolutionary instant. Furthermore, the cognitive advances that allowed for this expansion also forced our ancestors to deal with new interpersonal issues relating to property, contracts, debts, and punishments, and fueled the change from small and relatively unspecialized egalitarian family communities to large hierarchical societies of highly specialized strangers (Boehm 2012). Fixed moral sentiments would have been a handicap.

4.2. Exaptation

A system of normative attitudes for coordinating attitudes would not have sprang up overnight. Chimpanzees and bonobos, our closest relatives, may have some rough analogues to moral sentiments, but they have nothing clearly recognizable as judgments about morality. They recognize some social expectations and are able communicate with each other about their observation in very basic ways. As far as we know, they are not capable of formulating, evaluating, and communicating anything as complex as social rules (von Rohr, Claudia, and van Schaik 2011). Our nearest cousins might have some sense of reciprocity, permission, and obligation, but they do not reason, discuss, or negotiate them in the way that we do.

Our ancestors almost certainly would have started making cognitively sophisticated moral judgments only after their split with our nearest cousins some six million years ago, and the greatest cognitive changes most likely came in the last fifty to two hundred thousand years. In that period of time, cultures sprang up, art and religion developed, tool use drastically advanced, long distance trade commenced, and sophisticated forms of language probably evolved.[17]

It makes sense that moral attitudes (as opposed to our moral sentiments) were largely a product of this time period, and if so, they must have evolved extremely quickly. Our pre-moral ancestors would have had much to gain by coordinating social expectations about behavior. This would have produced an evolutionary pressure to allow for such flexibility. This pressure would have set to work on a cognitive system with a stock of propositional attitudes including beliefs and desires. Moral judgments might have emerged *sui generis*, but it seems far more likely that they would have been spun off from existing attitudes. It is easier to co-opt – 'exapt'[18] – existing structures than to build them from scratch: there is evidence (Anderson 2010) that many aspects of cognition make use of the resources of older cognitive functions. Beliefs and desires seem like the two best candidates for the original source material of moral attitudes, and there are some reasons to favor the former over the latter.

Moral judgments might have arisen as exaptations of beliefs because of the advantages they afford: perhaps the structural flexibility and logical relations available to beliefs were helpful in moral reasoning and discourse. If so, then it is possible that logical connectives had an important function and that logically complex attitudes need a richer characterization than is provided by a recipe semantics.[19] However, while this might explain why it is better for us to have moral judgments that are structurally similar to beliefs, it cannot explain how a trend initiated in that direction. Why were incipient moral attitudes formed from beliefs, rather than desires?

The primary reason to favor the hypothesis that moral attitudes developed from beliefs is that beliefs about social regulations are the best candidates for precursors to moral judgments. Our ancestors were probably thinking and conversing about collective expectations for at least as long as they have been reasoning about norms. The states that play the most similar functional roles in promoting social coordination are beliefs about social roles and expectations.[20] Evolutionary forces pushing toward non-representational moral judgments would have likely moulded these states.[21]

Our pre-moral ancestors might have started with ordinary beliefs about social rules and regulations: they judged actions according to their social appropriateness within their community and expressed these judgments with simple language. Generation by generation, they became increasingly disposed to form attitudes that functioned not to simply represent social standards, but to motivate them to adopt these standards. Gradually, the set of standards they were motivated to adopt might have come to differ from those that were accepted by their society. The divergence between what was accepted by individuals and what was accepted by other members of their society could have grown to a point where the attitudes fell outside of the range of representationality, especially if they came to have a use in influencing those standards, and not just reflecting them.

Our concept tokens employed in tracking rules and social regulations combine normally with negation, conjunction, quantification, generics, conditionals, tense, and other attitudes. *If our moral concepts exapted from these representational concepts, then they could easily continue to share some of their syntactic properties.*

This is supported by the rapidity of the development of moral judgments. It is quite possible that we only started internalizing social regulations as moral judgments in the last fifty thousand years (This is especially plausible if moral attitudes are the result of cultural evolution rather than biological evolution). Retaining the capacity for superfluous attitudes does us no harm, and selection has not yet weeded these attitudes from our cognitive repertoire. Even if they have no function, they may still prove useful.

This is far from the only story to be told about the origins of our moral attitudes, and it may well be false in many of its details. However, its plausibility undermines concerns about whether syntactic properties could allow moral concepts to appear in spandrel contexts. The fact that moral judgments display the same syntactic properties as beliefs without having a clear function is not a major problem for the view.

5. Conclusion

In this paper, I have argued that noncognitivists can provide a recipe semantics for a variety of moral attitudes. Moral judgments involve moral concepts. Moral concepts are characterized by the roles they play in the context of moral judgments. Moral concepts can be identified in spandrel contexts by their orthographic properties. The other moral attitudes, including both complex moral judgments and non-judgment attitudes, can be characterized in terms of their orthographic similarities to straightforwardly predicative moral attitudes.

Many of our moral attitudes may be byproducts. The logical relations that we attribute to them need no underlying rationale, and the appearance that such attributions are deserved may instead result from the historically accidental syntactic viability of logical concepts in moral attitudes.

This thesis does not entail that our attitudes are mistaken. Nothing should hold us back from putting cognitive spandrels to good use. There is also nothing wrong with treating attitudes as if they were logically inconsistent, and so we need not change our moral practices, even if we discover that some of the relations we intuit between moral attitudes are not supported by anything essential to the attitudes themselves.

Despite not requiring any change to our moral practices, the proposal does give up something of our folk conception of moral psychology. Insofar as we seek to substantiate the folk conception of morality in our metaethics, this must be seen as a drawback. While the lack of particular explanatory meaning-determined rationales for the behaviors of moral attitudes may be disconcerting, they can be accounted for by the rapid evolutionary development of ordinary moral judgments. If we are willing to leave some parts of our folk psychology behind, the resulting picture may be the best path forward for noncognitivists to simultaneously understand the diversity and unity of moral attitudes.

Notes

1. A.J. Ayer (1936) and Simon Blackburn (1984) treated moral judgments as a special sort of approval and disapproval. Charles Stevenson (1937) described them as a species of interest or partiality. Allan Gibbard (2003) compared them to plans. Mark Timmons and Terry Horgan (2006) suggested that they are a special non-representational species of belief. Mark Schroeder (2008) proposed (without endorsing) that they are attitudes of favoring or disfavoring attributions of blame. These views all emphasize the pressures moral judgments exert on us to act in certain ways. Some of the remaining difficulties involved in providing an adequate characterization of straightforwardly moral judgments are explored in David Merli (2008).
2. The question of logical complexity, first raised in the work of Peter Geach (1965) and John Searle (1962), has taken a prominent place in discussions of noncognitivism. Though it is typically presented under the inclusive label of *The* Frege-Geach Problem, logical complexity poses a variety of different issues. One part of the problem – the part that I focus on in this paper – is to make sense of just what sort of attitudes logical complex moral judgments are. The other parts of the problem involve explaining why logically complex attitudes relate to each other in the ways that they do, how such attitudes have logical relations such as inconsistency and entailment, and how they can figure into rationally compelling arguments. The challenges involved in all of these parts of the problem are explored in depth by Mark Schroeder (2008). I have discussed them elsewhere (Shiller 2016), and the solution I present there for this second part of the Frege-Geach problem is compatible with the solution I present here for the first part of the Frege-Geach problem.
3. This term comes from Jerry Fodor, who uses it to describe a constellation of theories (1998). I will restrict its usage to the view defined above (a view that is found, for instance, in Field [1978]): a theory that is distinct from the Language of Thought Hypothesis, which makes additional assumptions about the structure of mental representations, and the Computational Theory of Mind, which makes additional assumptions about the way that representations are handled in deliberation and reasoning.
4. Of course, representational properties are correlated with viable combinations of both concepts and LEGOs, but these properties are not explanatory except in a unificationist sense. If anything, representational contents are determined in part by what combinations are possible, rather than the other way around.
5. Friedemann Pulvermüller (2002) presents a theory that illustrates the intended difference between orthographic and syntactic properties. On his proposal, individual concepts are implemented in the brain by networks of functionally entwined neurons that selectively respond to relevant stimuli. These functional webs are themselves connected to collections of sequence detectors that act as

grammatical categories. The fact that a given web is connected to a collection of detectors typical of nouns explains why it can be put into subject position in thoughts. In this theory, concepts are distinguished by orthographic properties (dispositional firing patterns of a functional web), and how they associate with each other depends upon their distinct syntactic properties (connection strengths of the web with specific sequence detectors).
6. Orthographic classes are plentiful and many will be vague. There need not be a clear cut answer as to whether or not sentences in English and Chinese fall into the same orthographic class. They fall into some of the same orthographic classes and not others.
7. We can characterize the function of moral concepts in a variety of different ways, so this proposal is consistent with many analyses of straightforwardly predicative moral attitudes.

    It might be objected that my proposal will restrict moral judgments only to those creatures who employ presentations. I am sympathetic to this worry, and I will allow that having moral judgments may not require having presentations. Nevertheless, it is not misguided to limit our focus to creatures like us. Our way of having moral attitudes involves taking attitudes toward presentations with moral concepts.
8. Are concepts meaningless in their spandrel contexts? I want to resist the urge to say that moral concepts mean anything different in spandrel contexts than in the contexts in which they have a function. Representational concepts are not meaningless in their spandrel contexts precisely because they borrow their meaning from their functional contexts. For both moral and representational concepts, there is only one fundamental bearer of semantic values between the two kinds of contexts, and whatever semantic values those concepts have, they have because of their behavior in the functional contexts.

    That said, I doubt that it is possible to assign an object to count as a moral concept's meaning in both spandrel and functional contexts in the way that is possible for representational concepts. If it takes a meaning object to be meaningful, then moral concepts are not meaningful in any of the contexts in which they occur.
9. The fact that an attitude lacks a function or a meaning does not entail that it is useless. The attitude may have begun its life as a spandrel and subsequently come to be put to good use. The present value of a concept may be tangential to the properties that provide it with a coherent meaning.
10. Negated moral judgments and their unnegated counterparts may genuinely be inconsistent in the shallow sense in which two attitudes are inconsistent when we are inclined to treat them as disagreeing and perceive them as incompatible social commitments. We try not to adopt such 'inconsistent' attitudes, and expect others to expect this of us. This shallow sense of inconsistency often arises from, and cannot explain, the appearance of something deeper. Nevertheless, recognizing that such shallow forms of inconsistency may persist mitigates the unintuitiveness of denying authenticity to deeper senses. Noncognitivists have been happy to embrace minimalist interpretations of truth and content, I see little further cost to also adopting shallow interpretations of inconsistency.
11. If the contents of our moral concepts are determined by population-level regularities of concept use (Schroeter 2014), then we can have no special introspective insight into their meanings, and it is highly plausible that we might be misled by the forms of our attitudes.

12. They may also disagree about whether the motivational force of the moral attitude is provided by the belief-like structure or by a separate structure. The most straightforward way of interpreting hybrid expressivism within RTM analyzes moral judgments into two structures, but it is also possible to treat them as one structure implementing two attitudes.
13. I expand on this line of criticism in (Shiller 2017).
14. I do not mean to imply that most aspects of morality are genetic. In fact, the proposal developed here is quite a natural fit for a cultural revolution approach (Powell, Shennan, and Thomas 2009; Sterelny 2011) to explaining human behavioral changes of the last hundred thousand years.
15. Joyce (2007) provides an in depth overview of the ways that stereotypically moral behavior is fitness enhancing.
16. Gibbard (1990), Sinclair (2012), and Björnsson and McPherson (2014) advocate for a similar perspective on the role of morality. Michael Tomasello (Tomasello 2016; Tomasello et al. 2012) has also developed a two-step process in the evolution of morality in which cultural aspects of moral psychology arose with the dawn of culture, long after the appearance of cooperation-inducing components of moral psychology.
17. The possible range of dates for the evolution of cognitively modern humans spans the emergence of anatomically modern humans ~160 ka (d'Errico and Stringer 2011) and the great dispersal out of Africa ~50 ka (Klein 2008).
18. Gould and Vrba (1982) present the concept and argue that it plays an important role in evolution, including in cognition.
19. Thanks to an anonymous reviewer for raising this idea.
20. Tomasello (2016) hypothesizes that early normative judgments focused on proper role-playing in complex cooperative activities. If so, they surely trailed beliefs about what roles individuals could productively play.
21. Furthermore, is unlikely that young children are able to discern representational from noncognitive concepts. They must form attitudes in response to moral instruction very early in life, and their mature attitudes grow out of these early ones. Whatever attitudes they ultimately come to have, children probably begin classifying actions under moral categories in much the same way that they classify actions under other categories, and this probably involves the structures of belief. Later on, they adopt the subtleties of moral concepts that rob them of their representational contents, but they don't need to fundamentally refigure their existing attitudes. In this case, perhaps, ontology recapitulates phylogeny: states that start out primarily as representations of social categorizations become something more closely tied to motivation.

References

Anderson, Michael. 2010. "Neural Reuse: A Fundamental Organizational Principle of the Brain." *Behavioral and Brain Sciences* 33 (4): 245–266.

Ayer, Alfred J. 1936. *Language, Truth and Logic*. London: Victor Gollancz.

Baker, Derek, and Jack Woods. 2015. "How Expressivists Can and Should Explain Inconsistency." *Ethics* 125 (2): 391–424.
Björnsson, Gunnar, and Tristram McPherson. 2014. "Moral Attitudes for Non-Cognitivists: Solving the Specification Problem." *Mind* 123 (489): 1–38.
Blackburn, Simon. 1984. *Spreading the Word*. Oxford: Oxford University Press.
Blackburn, Simon. 1988. "Attitudes and Contents." *Ethics* 98 (3): 501–517.
Blumson, Ben. 2012. "Mental Maps." *Philosophy and Phenomenological Research* 85 (2): 413–434.
Boehm, Christopher. 2012. *Moral Origins: The Evolution of Virtue, Altruism, and Shame*. New York: Basic Books.
Dretske, Fred. 1995. *Naturalizing the Mind*. Cambridge, MA: MIT Press.
d'Errico, Francesco, and Chris Stringer. 2011. "Evolution, Revolution or Saltation Scenario for the Emergence of Modern Cultures?" *Philosophical Transactions of the Royal Society B: Biological Sciences* 366 (1567): 1060–1069.
Field, Hartry. 1978. "Mental Representation." *Erkenntnis* 13 (1): 9–61.
Fodor, Jerry. 1998. *Concepts: Where Cognitive Science Went Wrong*. Oxford: Oxford University Press.
Fodor, Jerry. 2008. *Lot 2: The Language of Thought Revisited*. Oxford: Oxford University Press.
Fodor, Jerry, and Zenon Pylyshyn. 1988. "Connectionism and Cognitive Architecture." *Cognition* 28 (1–2): 3–71.
Geach, Peter. 1965. "Assertion." *The Philosophical Review* 74 (4): 449–465.
Gibbard, Allan. 1990. *Wise Choices, Apt Feelings: A Theory of Normative Judgment*. Cambridge, MA: Harvard University Press.
Gibbard, Allan. 2003. *Thinking How to Live*. Cambridge, MA: Harvard University Press.
Gould, Stephen J., and Elisabeth Vrba. 1982. "Exaptation – A Missing Term in the Science of Form." *Paleobiology* 8 (1): 4–15.
Henn, Brenna, Luigi Cavalli-Sforza, and Marcus Feldman. 2012. "The Great Human Expansion." *Proceedings of the National Academy of Sciences* 109 (44): 17758–17764.
Horgan, Terry, and Mark Timmons. 2006. "Cognitivist Expressivism." In *Metaethics after Moore*, edited by Terry Horgan and Mark Timmons, 255–298. Oxford: Oxford University Press.
Horgan, Terry, and Mark Timmons. 2009. "Expressivism and Contrary-Forming Negation." *Philosophical Issues* 19 (1): 92–112.
Joyce, Richard. 2001. *The Myth of Morality*. Cambridge: Cambridge University Press.
Joyce, Richard. 2007. *The Evolution of Morality*. Cambridge, MA: MIT Press.
Klein, Richard. 2008. "Out of Africa and the Evolution of Human Behavior." *Evolutionary Anthropology: Issues, News, and Reviews* 17 (6): 267–281.
Mackie, John L. 1977. *Ethics: Inventing Right and Wrong*. New York: Penguin Books.
Merli, David. 2008. "Expressivism and the Limits of Moral Disagreement." *Journal of Ethics* 12 (1): 25–55.
Millikan, Ruth. 1984. *Language, Thought and Other Biological Categories*. Cambridge, MA: MIT Press.
Papineau, David. 1984. "Representation and Explanation." *Philosophy of Science* 51 (4): 550–572.
Powell, Adam, Stephan Shennan, and Mark Thomas. 2009. "Late Pleistocene Demography and the Appearance of Modern Human Behavior." *Science* 324 (5932): 1298–1301.
Pulvermüller, Friedemann. 2002. *The Neuroscience of Language: On Brain Circuits of Words and Serial Order*. Cambridge: Cambridge University Press.
Quine, Willard V. O. 1960. *Word and Object*. Cambridge, MA: MIT Press.
Ridge, Michael. 2014. *Impassioned Belief*. Oxford: Oxford University Press.

von Rohr, Rudolf, Judith Burkart Claudia, and Carel van Schaik. 2011. "Evolutionary Precursors of Social Norms in Chimpanzees: A New Approach." *Biology and Philosophy* 26 (1): 1–30.

van Roojen, Mark. 1996. "Expressivism and Irrationality." *The Philosophical Review* 105 (3): 311–335.

Schroeder, Mark. 2008. *Being For: Evaluating the Semantic Program of Expressivism*. Oxford: Oxford University Press.

Schroeder, Mark. 2013. "Tempered Expressivism." In *Oxford Studies in Metaethics 8*, edited by Russ Shafer-Landau, 283–314. Oxford: Oxford University Press.

Schroeter, Laura. 2014. "Normative Concepts: A Connectedness Model." *Philosophers' Imprint* 14 (25), 1–26.

Schwartz, Jeremy, and Christopher Hom. 2015. "Why the Negation Problem Is Not a Problem for Expressivism." *Noûs* 49 (4): 824–845.

Searle, John. 1962. "Meaning and Speech Acts." *The Philosophical Review* 71 (4): 423–432.

Shiller, Derek. 2016. "A Primitive Solution to the Negation Problem." *Ethical Theory and Moral Practice* 19 (3): 725–740.

Shiller, Derek. 2017. "The Problem of Other Attitudes." *American Philosophical Quarterly* 54 (2): 141–152.

Sinclair, Neil. 2011. "Moral Expressivism and Sentential Negation." *Philosophical Studies* 152 (3): 385–411.

Sinclair, Neil. 2012. "Metaethics, Teleosemantics and the Function of Moral Judgements." *Biology and Philosophy* 27 (5): 639–662.

Sterelny, Kim. 2011. "From Hominins to Humans: How Sapiens Became Behaviourally Modern." *Philosophical Transactions of the Royal Society B: Biological Sciences* 366 (1566): 809–822.

Stevenson, Charles L. 1937. "The Emotive Meaning of Ethical Terms." *Mind* 46 (181): 14–31.

Stich, Stephen P. 1983. *From Folk Psychology to Cognitive Science: The Case Against Belief*. Cambridge, MA: MIT Press.

Tomasello, Michael, Alicia Melis, Claudio Tennie, Emily Wyman, and Esther Herrmann. 2012. "Two Key Steps in the Evolution of Human Cooperation: The Interdependence Hypothesis." *Current Anthropology* 53 (6): 673–692.

Tomasello, Michael. 2016. *A Natural History of Human Morality*. Cambridge, MA: Harvard University Press.

Toppinen, Teemu. 2013. "Believing in Expressivism." In *Oxford Studies in Metaethics 8*, edited by Russ Shafer-Landau, 252–282. Oxford: Oxford University Press.

Unwin, Nicholas. 1999. "Quasi-Realism, Negation and the Frege-Geach Problem." *The Philosophical Quarterly* 49 (196): 337–352.

Neo-pragmatism, morality, and the specification problem

Joshua Gert

ABSTRACT
A defender of any view of moral language must explain how people with different moral views can be be talking to each other, rather than past each other. For expressivists this problem drastically constrains the search for the specific attitude expressed by, say, 'immoral'. But cognitivists face a similar difficulty; they need to find a specific meaning for 'immoral' that underwrites genuine disagreement while accommodating the fact that different speakers have very different criteria for the use of that term. This paper explains how neo-pragmatism deals with this issue while avoiding problems that arise with existing expressivist and cognitivist solutions.

1. Introduction

The point of this paper is to draw attention to an important feature of neo-pragmatism as a general philosophical method, and to appeal to this feature in solving a problem that challenges both expressivist and cognitivist accounts of moral thought and talk. The important feature of neo-pragmatism is its focus on language as a social practice, in contrast to the derivative issue of what a given individual can manage to do with a token assertion. The problem is explaining how people with different moral views can be understood to be talking *to* each other, rather than *past* each other. In the context of expressivism, this is what Tristram McPherson and Gunnar Björnsson call 'The Specification Problem': the problem of isolating a specific attitude that is expressed by the use of a given normative term (Björnsson and McPherson 2014). In the context of cognitivism, it is the problem of isolating a specific meaning that underwrites genuine disagreement while at the same time meeting what Laura Schroeter calls 'The

Flexibility Constraint': the need to accommodate the fact that different speakers will have very different criteria for the use of the relevant normative term (Schroeter 2012; See also Schroeter and Schroeter (2014, 19)).

Björnsson and McPherson offer an expressivist-friendly solution to the problem, while Laura and François Schroeter offer a more representationalist-friendly solution. I will agree with many elements of both solutions: for example, the increased emphasis on the role of the social. Moreover, I will agree with Björnsson and McPherson (as against the Schroeters) that no substantial notion of reference is required in order to make sense of moral discourse. And I will agree with the Schroeters (as against Björnsson and McPherson) that we do not have to know virtually anything about the attitudes of two speakers in order to be justified in taking them to be involved in a genuine moral dispute. The resulting neo-pragmatist co-option of what is correct in both Björnsson and McPherson's view and in the view defended by the Schroeters yields something both more general and more attractive. But before getting to that, let me explain what I take neo-pragmatism to be.

2. Neo-pragmatism

Neo-pragmatism is an approach to philosophical questions that have traditionally seemed to require us to do some metaphysics. We start out wondering what, for example, numbers or values might be, and the metaphysician calls out to us with various proposals. Really good metaphysicians manage to come up with proposals that save most of the first-order phenomena. And a subset of those metaphysicians offer proposals that identify the target of our worries with something that we are not similarly worried about. Worried about numbers? They're just sets, no different really than sets of chairs or spoons. Worried about normative reasons? They're just our desires. Worried about possibilities? They're just stories. What all these proposals share is a presupposition about what the best strategy for addressing our worries should look like. It should look like an identification of some entity or property that lies at the non-linguistic end of a reference relation. This is a very significant presupposition, and one of the neo-pragmatist's defining features is the acceptance of a picture that denies it.

What is the neo-pragmatist's contrasting picture? It is one that highlights the overt, observable aspects of our practices with sounds, marks, and signs, analogizing them with games that make use of physical pieces. One useful aspect of this analogy is that there is little temptation to think of pieces in games in terms of reference relations to anything. The neo-pragmatist picture also highlights the ways in which our linguistic practices are continuous with similar practices that other animals engage in. For example, consider the dances of bees. It is not hard to imagine a story that explains how this sort of complex information-transmitting behavior evolved, without having to appeal, at any level, to reference relations or to any other semantic notions, or even to the idea that the dances express a certain mental state. Of course, analogies with bees are unlikely even to seem relevant to someone with antecedent representationalist views about how human language works. So let me now develop an example that involves animals more closely related to human beings: non-linguistic primates.

Consider the transmission of disgust reactions in groups of non-linguistic primates.[1] Disgust is a contagious response. If one animal exhibits disgust at a certain substance for what we might call 'primary reasons' – reasons that have to do with actual physical contact with a toxic or infectious substance – a second animal who witness this reaction will acquire a disposition to be disgusted by that same kind of thing, even without the same sort of physical contact. And later on, when that second animal manifests disgust at that same kind of item, a third animal will acquire a similar disposition. Nothing in this explanation requires appeal to semantic notions, or even an appeal to the notion of belief. Moreover, it is easy to see the usefulness of the mechanism here, since it allows groups of primates to acquire the disposition to avoid certain dangerous substances, without each of them having to have a dangerous form of contact with it.

As it happens, disgust is hard to unlearn. But it would in some cases be useful for a community to unlearn it. Suppose, for example, that the initial expression of disgust at a certain item had nothing to do with the properties of that item; rather, suppose that a causally independent illness just happened to reach its nauseating peak soon after the animal put a bit of genuinely healthy fruit in its mouth. If the resulting disgust propagates through the community with nothing to check it, then this sort of food will be needlessly avoided. So let me now indulge in some primatological fiction. Suppose that there is a distinct response to expressions of disgust – distinct, that is, from the response of acquiring a disposition to be disgusted by the same sorts of items. This distinct response is manifested at expressions of disgust when they are directed at items with which the witnessing animal has had direct contact, and which have proved to be tasty and energy-providing. Call this second-order emotion 'progust'. According to my fictional account, an animal whose disgust mechanism has been calibrated to be triggered by a certain substance can have it reset by exposure to an animal that exhibits progust in response to observed disgust. The paired disgust and progust reactions together serve to get a community of primates to converge on a more useful uniformity of response-dispositions. As will emerge later, the usefulness of this sort of uniformity plays a crucial role, for the neo-pragmatist, in explaining the emergence of semantic terms such as 'true' and 'false'. Indeed, it may be useful to think of expressions of disgust as corresponding to a claim – 'That's not to be eaten' – and to think of expressions of progust as corresponding to an assessment of that first claim as false.

According to the neo-pragmatist, we should think of human linguistic practices on analogy with the dances of bees and expressions of disgust and progust. Of course human language is much richer than either of these examples. But we humans are nevertheless animals; our behavioral dispositions, including our linguistic capacities, are amenable to biological-evolutionary and cultural-evolutionary explanations. If we can sketch such explanations of the linguistic practices in which we make the assertions that raised the mystifying questions about the nature of numbers, possibilities, and values, then we should cease to be mystified about the *objects* of these sorts of assertions. That is, we should abandon the metaphysics of mathematics, possibility, and value, replacing them with explanations of the ways in which we use number language, modal language, and evaluative language.[2]

Against the neo-pragmatist program I've just described, those who are partial to more traditional metaphysical methods might initially make the following protest: 'It's all well and good to explain how we came to say such things as "There are three positive even numbers less than six", or "It is simply not possible that I could have been born as a pine tree". But, however it happens that we utter these sentences, some turn out to be *true*, and others to be *false*, and we need to do some metaphysics in order to understand what the difference is.' But this protest simply assumes what the neo-pragmatist denies: that truth and falsity are robust properties, and that they to be explained in terms of relations – including reference relations – between assertions and the entities and properties that those assertions are about. If this sort of account of truth and falsity were correct, then metaphysics might well be required to explain difference between true and false propositions. But the neo-pragmatist will favor deflationary accounts of truth and falsity.[3] That is, the neo-pragmatist will explain our use of the words 'true' and 'false' in a way that does not depend on appeal to a property of truth or falsity.

The account of truth-talk that I favor is one that has been developed and defended by Huw Price (1988, 2003). His idea is that for some behavioral dispositional states it is useful if a community converges in certain ways. For example, it is useful if everyone is disposed to count in the same way, since then the words used in counting can serve all sorts of useful functions. As a result, it is also useful to have terms such as 'false' or 'wrong' that function to correct people when their verbal behavior deviates from the useful counting pattern. And those same words – 'false', 'wrong', and so on – can be used in response to an open-ended class of other linguistic performances: ones we might call 'assertions about possibility', 'assertions about the moral status of an act', and 'assertions about the locations of objects the physical environment'. But according to neo-pragmatism, the common assertoric form – shared whether one is talking about numbers, values, possibilities, or moral status – does not owe its existence to the fact that it allows for a truth-constituting correspondence between parts of sentences – or the propositions they express – and parts of reality. Rather, the explanation of the shared assertoric form is that (a) it invites the use of words like 'true' and 'false', and that (b) one common feature of number-talk, possibility-talk, and moral-talk is that it is useful if a community of speakers converge in certain ways with respect to the assertions its members are prepared to make in those arenas. Of course, as these examples makes clear, *mere* convergence is not typically the useful thing: rather, certain foci of convergence will be especially useful.

One important kind of assertion is a description of the physical environment. Truth-assessments of these assertions can, it is true, be seen as responsive to a kind of correspondence between, on the one hand, words for things and properties and, on the other hand, those very things and properties. But it would be a mistake to take this one case – one in which a kind of causal/historical account of reference is plausibly extensionally adequate – as a model for all reference or representation. Rather, the neo-pragmatist offers a completely general explanation of our use of 'true' and 'false' (and other semantic terms) that focuses on establishing certain sorts of harmony in the states that underlie our counting things, our assessing possibilities, our evaluations of things, *and our descriptions of the physical environment*. In the latter case it turns out that the useful harmony is one in which the psychological state involves some causally mediated relations to the physical world. But even in that case the causal relations do not *constitute* the relation of reference or representation, since there is no such relation. One way of putting this point is that the causal/historical theory provides a good account of *the reference* of certain *sorts* of terms (names for physical objects and properties), but not of the concept of reference in general. By way of analogy, 'ants and grubs' is a good description of *the diet* of certain *sorts* of animals, but does nothing to clarify the concept 'diet.'

Against the view just described, a common idea among representationalists is that we should take truth-assessments of descriptions of the physical world to be making use of a notion of *genuine* truth, and that while truth-talk has a home in domains such as the normative or the modal, its function there is a *derivative* one. On this view, there is a radical difference between genuine truth-assessments and what we might call assessments of quasi-truth. The former paradigmatically apply to descriptions of the physical environment, while the latter apply to linguistic performances that have the outward form of assertion, but that actually serve to express some kind of non-cognitive attitude. But that is not the right way to think of truth-assessments, according to neo-pragmatism. Rather, according to neo-pragmatism, *all* truth-assessments are in a very important sense in the same business: helping to push a community of speakers into a useful harmony.

Given the above explanation of truth-talk, the similarity between assertions in virtue of which they all count as assertions is a very superficial one, and tells us nothing about their function. Following Wittgenstein, Price likens the similarity in the superficial grammatical form shared by all assertions to the similarity in the form of the various different handles one might find in the control room of a train.[4] What makes the handles look so similar is that they are designed to be grasped by a human hand. But what that hand does with them – pumping, putting pressure, switching from an on to an off position, rotating – can vary, as of course can the whole mechanism to which the handle is connected, and (therefore) the function of the handle in the overall operation of the train. The fact that a given handle is hand-sized and conveniently shaped tells us absolutely nothing about what the handle does or how to operate it. Similarly, Price argues that the assertoric form in human languages allows for the kind of pressures that truth-assessments provide: to put it in terms of the analogy with handles, the assertoric form allows assessments of truth and falsity to 'get a grip' on the attitudes of speakers. Because of this grip, they help push a community of speakers into a useful uniformity of attitude. But those attitudes are as various as the mechanisms to which the handles in a control room might be connected.

In explaining the relevant sense of harmony we should think of it as related to success in social action. If we all count in the same way, for example, this allows number words to function in their characteristic ways in requests, orders, descriptions, and so on. And if we are in overwhelming agreement in terms of what sorts of behavior lay one open to various sort of sanction, this allows us to go about our daily lives without having to take so many costly precautions to protect us from harm at the hands of other people. Also, of course, agreement in the states that find expression in verbal descriptions of the locations of things in physical space is hugely helpful. But the notions of truth and falsity that apply to assertions in all three domains – the arithmetical, the moral, and the physical – are the same. Roughly put, calling an assertion that p 'true' only when one could also sincerely assert that p, and calling it 'false' only when one could also sincerely assert that not p helps bring about the relevant harmony in the behaviors connected with number-talk, moral-talk, physical object-talk, and so on.

According to the neo-pragmatism I am defending, beliefs are functional states in a vast psychological architecture that includes all sorts of sensory input, and that has behavior – including verbal behavior – as output. But that characterization doesn't differentiate beliefs from sensations, desires, and so on. What beliefs share is the following: they are states that have 'characteristic assertions' that are subject to our practice of truth-assessment because of the usefulness of those practices in the domains of discourse to which the characteristic assertions belong. Moreover, the usefulness of truth-assessments depends on the usefulness of there being a convergence on beliefs within a linguistic community, which means that a given assertion cannot be both true and false. This characterization helps explain why belief is what Mark Schroeder calls an 'inconsistency-transmitting' attitude (Schroeder 2008). That is, it explains why it is problematic to hold beliefs that have inconsistent contents, in contrast to the perfectly reasonable case of wondering whether p while also wondering whether not-p. And the neo-pragmatist account of belief does this despite the fact that belief is not, in an important sense, a homogeneous category. Rather, an attitude counts as a belief if it can find expression in assertion. And what marks off assertions from questions, commands, greetings, and so on, is that they are offered up in a form that invites truth-assessments. So the neo-pragmatist does not explain why belief is inconsistency-transmitting by reference to a supposedly unified metaphysical nature of belief. Rather, what does the work is the practical usefulness of truth-assessments: assessments that presupposes that – of a pair of conflicting assertions – only one can be called 'true'.

It should be stressed that the usefulness of our practice of assertion and truth-assessment is not to be found in token cases. Making a correct assertion might well do nothing but harm; so too might informing someone else that he has spoken falsely. Rather, the benefits of having the assertions and truth-assessments can be seen when we consider whole domains of discourse, and when our view is long-term and social.

3. The specification problem

Let me now explain how the sort of neo-pragmatism I've just presented sidesteps a problem that arises both for expressivists and for more traditional normative realists. Expressivists take normative claims to express non-cognitive attitudes, rather than beliefs. Moreover, for each normative predicate, expressivists have tended to assume that there is some specific non-cognitive attitude it expresses, distinct from the attitude expressed by other normative predicates. Gunnar Björnsson and Tristram McPherson note this tendency and a certain pressure towards it (Björnsson and McPherson, 2014). The pressure stems from the need to explain what a specifically *moral* disagreement is, and why there need not be a similar disagreement between someone who thinks a certain policy *is not* morally wrong and someone who thinks it *is* stupid. This assumption of univocality in expressed attitude gives rise to a significant problem for expressivists, which takes the form of a dilemma. To the degree that the attitude we propose as moral disapproval is specific – for example, a certain type of anger based in specific aspects of its target, combined with a distinct form of approval for punishment – it looks like it will not be held by some people who make sincere and competent moral claims that a certain action is immoral. But to the degree that we make it more general – making it more like plain old disapproval – we lose the capacity to distinguish claims about moral wrongness from claims about stupidity or bad taste.[5]

The dilemma I've just described for expressivists might seem to press for a cognitivist account of moral judgment. But, as Björnsson and McPherson stress, it turns out that cognitivist accounts face quite a similar dilemma, at least if they rely on a substantial notion of reference. This dilemma is central to the well-known Moral Twin Earth arguments developed by Terry Horgan and Mark Timmons (1991). Such arguments ask the cognitivist for her theory of reference and then cook up a version of Moral Twin Earth according to which the seemingly moral language of the Twin Earthlings ends up referring to a property distinct from the property of moral wrongness to which we refer here on Actual Earth. As a result, Earthlings and Twin Earthlings will – according to the cognitivist – be talking past each other when they get into what looks like a moral dispute. But many theorists have the strong sense that this is not right: that Earthlings and Twin Earthlings are capable of having genuine moral disagreements. So it looks like cognitivists and expressivists alike will have difficulties specifying exactly what it is in the semantics of moral vocabulary that explains when we have a genuine moral disagreement, and when we don't.

If the specification problem afflicts both cognitivists and expressivists, what are we to do? In this section I will examine two attempts to deal with the issue. The first is developed by Björnsson and McPherson themselves, and is a version of non-cognitivism. The second is developed by Laura and François Schroeter, and is a version of cognitivism. Both solutions shift the focus of theorizing from individuals to communities. From the neo-pragmatist perspective this is, of course, a promising move. But I will argue that both Björnsson and McPherson on the one hand, and the Schroeters on the other, do not distance themselves sufficiently from the initial commitments of the more individualistic versions of their views. In particular, Björnsson and McPherson give a central role to a very specific attitude: paradigmatic moral judgment. And the Schroeters continue to rely on a substantive notion of reference. As I will argue, these commitments are unnecessary and constraining. When they are jettisoned, the result is a neo-pragmatic solution to the specification problem that has all the virtues of their solutions, without their liabilities.

3.1. Björnsson and McPherson's non-cognitivism

Although Björnsson and McPherson offer a solution to the specification problem on behalf of the non-cognitivist, they are certainly not traditional non-cognitivists. One of their central departures from traditional views comes in the form of a denial 'that every party to a genuine moral disagreement must share the same type of noncognitive attitude' (Björnsson and McPherson, 2014, 3). What makes them count as non-cognitivists, despite this disavowal, is that a certain kind of noncognitive attitude nevertheless plays a central role in their account. They call this attitude a '*paradigmatic* wrongness judgment,' and they think that 'nearly all of our experience with what we think of as wrongness-judgements' are constituted by encounters with this specific attitude (Björnsson and McPherson, 2014, 13). Paradigmatic wrongness judgments are characterized by five features. The first three are shared by other sorts of negative normative judgments, such as aesthetic ones, or judgments of irrationality. These include (1) aversion to the objects of the judgments, (2) person-level acceptance (this sort of acceptance distinguishes them from mere appearances, which one might regard as false or misleading), and (3) a disposition to engage with others when there are conflicts in such attitudes. There are, however, two distinctive features of paradigmatic moral judgments. First, they are grounded in a perception or belief that the target has intentionally harmed someone or violated some boundaries crucial to social cooperation. Second, they include a syndrome called 'social hostility'. This includes hostility not only towards those whom we judge to have acted wrongly, but also towards those who give expression to moral judgments that conflict with our own. Björnsson and McPherson argue that the five features of paradigmatic wrongness judgments explain why those who make such judgments will be quite accommodating in interpreting other speakers as appropriate targets for engagement in moral discussion. This allows their account of moral disagreement to accommodate quite a divergence in the attitudes expressed by two disputants (Björnsson and McPherson, 2014, 17).

What I want to argue in this section is that Björnsson and McPherson make an assumption that they need not make. And when we reject that assumption, what we get is not best viewed as a 'non-cognitivist solution to the specification problem', as they describe their own proposal (Björnsson and McPherson, 2014, 21). Rather, we get a neo-pragmatist solution. The assumption with which I am concerned is contained in the very name of the problem: the specification problem. This label suggests that what we need to look for is some specific thing – either an attitude or a property – that both (a) plays a special role in explain the meaning of a moral term and (b) at least commonly plays that role in individual uses of that term. This way of viewing the difficulty shares too much with approaches to specification problem that view it as a challenge to find the right semantic values for moral terms.

Admittedly, one might try to solve the specification problem by reference to a specific attitude without taking that attitude to play the role of a semantic value. Björnsson and McPherson might well describe their own project in this way. Nevertheless, their focus on a specific attitude that can form part of the psychology of a single person does not give sufficient weight to the fact that language – including, of course, moral language – is a social practice. As such a practice, it can serve its purpose even if most of the individuals who take part in it do not manifest the same attitude by uttering – sincerely and competently – the same sentence. Of course, in a trivial sense, they do express the same attitude: belief in the proposition expressed by the sentence. But for the neo-pragmatist, the notions of belief and proposition are to be understood in a deflationary way, and cannot be deployed in explanations of the meanings of utterances.

How will the neo-pragmatist think of moral talk, in order to avoid Björnsson and McPherson's idea that there is a specific non-cognitive attitude that is the psychological state expressed by paradigmatic moral judgment? One way is to think of moral discourse on analogy with a multi-player game. Typically the point of making a move in a game is not to express a mental state. Similarly, on the neo-pragmatist view, the point of uttering a sentence is not to express a mental state; it is to make an overt move in a social practice.

What, then, is the neo-pragmatist's solution to the specification problem? It is that we should count two people as having conflicting moral beliefs if they are in a position to make (roughly: if they are disposed to make) conflicting sincere moral assertions. If they actually address such assertions to each other then they not only have conflicting views, but are having a moral disagreement. By 'conflicting moral assertions' here is meant something quite superficial; not precisely grammatical, but almost.[6] I say 'almost', because seeing that a pair of assertions conflict sometimes requires one to employ the linguistic skills involved in following anaphoric chains, in disambiguating homophonic lexical items, in using context to fill in ellipses, and so on. Still, if the relevant claims are made by people speaking the same language, we can typically see that claims conflict just in virtue of their form.

Of course, two people need not speak the same language in order to have conflicting moral beliefs, and one might worry that the specification problem re-emerges for the neo-pragmatist at the level of linguistic practices taken as wholes. How, that is, do we know that two distinct linguistic communities have the same practice – for example, one that we might call, in our own case, 'moral discourse' – so that when they meet their members can be said to disagree (or agree) about a common subject matter? Indeed, once this inter-community question is raised, even the intra-community issue might seem problematic. How do we know that two speakers are making assertions that are both part of the same linguistic practice, and not simply using homonyms? There are a number of answers to these questions.

The first answer begins by noting that the things the neo-pragmatist is comparing – linguistic practices – are quite different from what expressivists and robust-referential-realists are comparing. The standard expressivist (not Björnsson and McPherson) needs to assure herself that two disputants, in a given token discussion, are using the moral term at the center of the dispute to express the very same non-cognitive attitude. How on Earth – or Twin Earth, for that matter – can one have any reason to believe this? Attitudes of the complex sort that expressivists typically assign to moral assertions are not visible.[7] Similarly, the robust-referential-realist needs to assure herself that somehow or other the moral term, as it emerges from the mouth of each of the disputants, is linked by the reference relation to the very same property. This is even trickier than the problem faced by the expressivist, since the reference relation is not only invisible, but mysterious and complicated as well.[8] Indeed, its very existence is a matter of dispute.

The neo-pragmatist, in contrast with the standard expressivist and realist, is comparing easily observable public practices. The question as to whether two people, raised in the same linguistic community, are engaged in the same linguistic practice when they are arguing over the moral status of some kind of act is not typically more difficult to answer than the question of whether each of the twenty-two players currently running around on the soccer field is playing the same game. It is not relevant here to protest that the only reason we find this latter question so easy is that we are familiar with soccer and similar games, and that an alien 'plunked down' into the soccer stadium would perhaps think that each player was simply doing her own thing. That is correct, but irrelevant; the neo-pragmatist is allowed to appeal to our having been inducted into various practices – both recreational and linguistic – since all he is attempting to explain is why *we* treat certain assertions as conflicting with others.

Even when we consider two completely isolated linguistic communities – as in Moral Twin Earth thought experiments – it is not hard to see how we might come to the justified conclusion that they each have their own version of what is basically the same linguistic practice. Indeed, the possibility of identifying a linguistic practice as one that concerns morality in particular is presupposed by the thought experiments that are used in order to get the specification problem going for both expressivists and realists in the first place. This is true even of Björnsson and McPherson. The recipe they use in order to generate counterexamples to the standard versions of expressivism and realism ask us to imagine communities in which the

> word 'wrong' functions much as our word 'wrong' does: as a term of criticism that plays a distinctive role in deliberation and social coordination. The term is used to characterize a very similar range of actions, and there are very similar controversies about its proper extension. (Björnsson and McPherson, 2014, 8)

Their appeal to 'a distinctive role' here reveals that Björnsson and McPherson are not worried about identifying the role that moral vocabulary plays in our social practices. They would not, after all, have been happy talking about 'a distinctive attitude' expressed by our moral judgments, or 'a distinctive property of actions' referred to by our moral terms.

Björnsson and McPherson's use of the phrase 'a distinctive role' suggests that they are assuming that we know that role when we see it. And I think this assumption is not particularly problematic, since we *can* see it, unlike invisible attitudes, reference relations, or abstract referents. This capacity to note the role a term plays need not be deployed to recognize genuine disputes *within* a linguistic community. The reason for this is that the default assumption – the default way of playing the game – is that two speakers who make superficially contradictory moral claims in the same language are disagreeing; that they are using a term that has a shared role and a univocal meaning in the language.[9] The capacity to note the role of a term in a language comes into play primarily when we consider translation, or thought experiments involving distinct linguistic communities: whether English speakers and Spanish speakers, or English speakers and twin-English speakers.

The neo-pragmatist focus on linguistic practices as social phenomena explains the truth of Björnsson and McPherson's claim that

> intuitions about agreement and disagreement in wrongness-judgements seemingly require neither specific substantive assumptions about cognitive content, nor specific substantive assumptions about non-cognitive attitudes. (Björnsson and McPherson, 2014, 12)

But in an important contrast with Björnsson and McPherson, the neo-pragmatist emphasizes the role of language. Björnsson and McPherson often write as if the important things, in explaining particular cases of agreement and disagreement, are the psychological states of a pair of judgers, rather than the claims they do or would make. Consider their suggestion that we should think of moral judgments as functional kinds, on the model of hearts or automobiles. On this view moral judgments will include, in the first instance, paradigmatic moral judgments and, also, various sorts of deviations from that paradigmatic case. In offering this suggestion they claim to be explaining our 'rough tendencies to treat various attitudes as wrongness-judgements' even when they lack certain paradigmatic features – just as we classify dead hearts as hearts and wheel-free cars as cars (Björnsson and McPherson, 2014, 28). There is no mention of language here, and one gets the very strong impression that Björnsson and McPherson understand moral assertions derivatively, as expressions of moral judgments, which are doing the real explanatory work.

One way of seeing the plausibility of the neo-pragmatist's linguistic re-casting and co-option of Björnsson and McPherson's account is to note certain suspicious elements in their own explanation of the nature of paradigmatic moral judgments. Is it really true that someone who makes a moral judgment is even *typically* disposed to engage with the moral judgments of others, as they claim? Moreover, the distinctive grounds of paradigmatic wrongness judgments simply don't seem essential to a judgment being a moral one – though many of us think they are essential to their being *true*. Recall, the distinctive grounds are, according to Björnsson and McPherson,

> intentionally harming or risking harm to others or things that they care about, and failing to respect certain boundaries that play a central role in sustaining social cooperation. (Björnsson and McPherson, 2014, 15)

But there are loads of moral judgments about sexual matters that do not fit this pattern, and they need not be regarded as inviting divine smiting either, which might – depending on the form that smiting took – put an end to social cooperation. Some people seem simply to think that masturbation, pre-marital sex, and homosexuality are wrong. What explains Björnsson and McPherson's controversial claims about the nature of paradigmatic moral judgment? It is that when one looks for the shared features of even paradigmatic moral judgments understood as *attitudes*, one is bound to distort the phenomena. What really does the unifying is to be found at the level of linguistic practice.

One response to worries about the specificity of the attitude Björnsson and McPherson describe might be a reminder that what they are concerned with is not what is typical, but what is paradigmatic. That is, they could claim that moral judgments based in purely sexual matters are non-paradigmatic. But this is to ignore their claim that paradigmatic moral judgments constitute 'nearly all of our experience with what we think of as wrongness-judgements'? (Björnsson and McPherson, 2014, 13). Moreover, even overlooking this fact, the worry would then be that they are using 'paradigmatic' in a technical way that robs it of explanatory power. Of course *some* people make judgments with the five features they list. But why is that meant to be important for understanding what moral judgment is supposed actually to *be*, if loads of people make non-paradigmatic ones? This will be especially pressing if we want to hold that two people, each of whom makes quite differently-constituted *non*-paradigmatic moral judgments, can nevertheless be rightly regarded as having a genuine dispute.

What Björnsson and McPherson do seem to me to show is that it is no surprise that many people who make moral judgments will be quite liberal in interpreting other people as making conflicting judgments. I agree that morality is 'a practice with a purpose,' and that the purpose is to sustain certain patterns of social interaction that minimize harm (or something like that). As a result, it's no surprise that when someone who makes paradigmatic moral judgments encounters someone who makes judgments that resemble paradigmatic ones sufficiently closely, the paradigmatic judger will be willing to engage in moral discussion. Such willingness plausibly serves the *purpose* of the *practice*.

Where Björnsson and McPherson seem to me to go wrong is in eliding the purpose of the practice as a whole with the purpose of each token moral judgment or assertion. This elision emerges in their appeal to the analogy with functional kinds such as hearts and cars. They analogize these functional kinds with moral judgments, and not with the *practice* of moral judgment. That is how they explain why a non-motivating moral judgment nevertheless counts as a moral judgment. But the function of moral discourse is best viewed at the level of the whole practice. Indeed, it simply cannot be achieved in any other way.

Because the purpose of the practice of moral discourse is served by the whole practice, and not by individual utterances, there is no call to identify necessary and sufficient conditions for paradigmatic individual moral judgments, as there is a need to explain what a paradigmatic heart or car is. What we can say instead is that there are moral assertions because, given what human beings are like, the language of morality – thought of as a social practice – serves a purpose, and can be taught from one generation to the next. The neo-pragmatist easily sidesteps the specification problem because the focus of attention is not on the semantics of particular moral assertions. Rather, it is on the language game of morality as a whole. And one can make a move in that practice for a host of quite distinct reasons, and with a host of quite distinct attitudes.

Before moving on, let me mention an interpretation of Björnsson and McPherson's paper that I have not discussed. I have been writing as if their goal was the relatively ambitious one of providing a non-cognitive account moral judgment that solves the specification problem. In contrast to this reading, one might take their paper as intended only to explain why it is no surprise that those who make *paradigmatic moral judgments* often engage in moral discussion with those who make other sorts of judgments – judgments that might *or might not* be moral judgments. The functional account they offer might be taken not as an account of moral judgments in general, but only of *paradigmatic* moral judgments. And Björnsson and McPherson might simply be taken as silent as to what counts as a moral judgment that is not paradigmatic. Call this the 'modest reading' of their paper.

Against the modest reading, of course, is Björnsson and McPherson's explicit definition of paradigmatic moral judgments as possessing the five features described above, and their claim that moral judgments form a functional kind (Björnsson and McPherson, 2014, 13–14). Moreover, there is admittedly something odd about taking deviant cases – like the moral judgments of young children, depressed people, and psychopaths – as *paradigmatic*, which we would have to do if the functional account they offer is interpreted as an account of only paradigmatic moral judgments. On the other hand, there are places in which Björnsson and McPherson do describe *paradigmatic moral judgments* as constituting a functional kind – including in the abstract of their paper (Björnsson and McPherson, 2014, 1, 26). But regardless of whether one takes the modest reading to reflect their intentions or not, it remains a view that one might defend. The question is: how does it fare in comparison with the neo-pragmatist view?

The modest reading can fit, virtually unmodified, within a more general neo-pragmatist view. Moreover, it would benefit from being so located. Keep in mind that Björnsson and McPherson are not offering an account of moral *discourse* at all. Rather, they are offering an account of a certain functionally-defined attitude-type, and of the interactions between those who hold such an attitude and those who evince attitudes that are sufficiently similar. These interactions can be characterized as efforts to produce a greater uniformity in attitude. The neo-pragmatist can supply Björnsson and McPherson with a ready-made account of the two primary mechanisms used in such efforts: (1) assertions and (2) assessments of truth and falsity.

Neo-pragmatism can also soothe some of the dissatisfaction one might feel at the modest reading's explicit silence as to the nature of moral judgments. Partly this is because the neo-pragmatist explicitly rejects two impulses that generate the dissatisfaction. The first is the impulse to want metaphysical answers to questions such as 'What is the nature of a moral judgment'. And the second is the impulse to take language as merely the *clothing* of thought, rather than as the primary phenomenon. Moreover, the neo-pragmatist actually has something like an answer to the question of when it is someone is making a moral judgment. According to the neo-pragmatist, if a person makes a sincere and competent moral assertion, that person has expressed a moral judgment. What Björnsson and McPherson contribute to this answer is partial explanation of existence of moral discourse in the first place, as well as an explanation of the tolerance that certain participants in that discourse will exhibit in interpreting others as worth engaging with in moral discussion.

NORMATIVITY AND THE PROBLEM OF REPRESENTATION 149

3.2. Laura and François Schroeter's community-referential account

Laura and François Schroeter solve the specification problem for cognitivists by solving a more general problem: explaining how people with very different criteria for the use of a referring term can nevertheless be taken to be talking about the same thing. In offering their explanation, the Schroeters explicitly reject the central assumption of what they call 'the template model' of concept identity (Schroeter and Schroeter (2014, 4–5); See also Schroeter (2012, 186–187)). The template model holds that concept identity, and therefore the possibility of genuine agreement and disagreement, is type-identity of something internal to a pair of speakers: for example, it might be identity of reference-fixing criteria, or of the non-cognitive attitude expressed by the relevant term, or of the pattern of inferences accepted as conceptually justified. Against this, the Schroeters hold that the basic unit to which we ought to be assigning a semantic value is a socially and temporally distributed linguistic tradition.

The basic conceptual tool the Schroeters employ in constructing linguistic traditions is what they call 'the appearance of *de jure* sameness': the subjective appearance of obvious, incontrovertible and epistemically basic sameness of subject matter (Schroeter 2012, 181). Appearances of this sort characterize what is going on in a case in which you and I are talking with each other about the Provost by using her given name. They also characterize what is going on in such a conversation when I use the word 'she' in such a way that the anaphoric link is to the Provost's name. They do *not* characterize what is going on when I use the phrase 'the positive square root of sixteen' and you say 'that is, four'. So an appearance of *de jure* sameness is something that represents the referents of two phrases more closely even than an assertion of necessary identity. It involves, as the Schroeters put it, something more like the total absence of what Frege would call 'a cognitive difference'.

In our conversations with each other – and in reading books, watching television, and otherwise producing and consuming language – appearances of *de jure* sameness of topic link together a vast multitude of token uses of terms into what the Schroeters call a 'representational tradition' that extends, often, far into the past.[10] Representational traditions are messy things, since the token uses of the relevant terms are produced by people with quite widely divergent criteria for the use of the term, and some of the utterances may well be assertions that are blankly false and wildly confused. Still, representational traditions, taken as wholes, allow for charitable interpretations: interpretations that seek to identify 'the most important practical and theoretical interests that have been subserved by the categorizing practices', and that yield, in favorable cases, univocal referents (Schroeter and Schroeter 2014, 14 n. 22). These interpretations also end up classifying some appearances of *de jure* sameness of topic as *mere* appearances: as when I misinterpret your claim about your cat, Genghis Khan, as a claim about the leader of the Mongol empire. When we exclude these *mere* appearances, what remains are *genuine* relations of *de jure* sameness of topic. The equivalence classes of token uses linked by this 'cleaned up' relation all express the same concept, allowing for agreement and disagreement about a common topic.

On reflection a number of important points of similarity between the neo-pragmatist and the Schroeters should be apparent. The neo-pragmatist, like the Schroeters, questions the usefulness of an individualistic metasemantics, and focuses instead on linguistic practices and their purposes. Moreover, the Schroeters' use of the notion of apparent *de jure* sameness in order to explain when two people are talking about the same thing results in a view that is extremely neo-pragmatist friendly. That is because appearances of *de jure* sameness of topic depend essentially on the sort of overt features of language on which a neo-pragmatist will also focus when explaining language as a social practice. Here, for example, are two of the ways the Schroeters describe such appearances:

> [T]he psychological mechanisms that generate the initial appearance of *de jure* sameness in conversation are not directly sensitive to sameness of core topic-fixing criteria – they're sensitive to the syntactic and pragmatic features that allow us to parse sentences.
>
> [I]n parsing another person's speech, you automatically hear their use of a familiar English expression as pertaining *de jure* to the very same topic you yourself associate with that expression.[11]

The Schroeters' strategy for solving the specification problem depends crucially on the two theoretical commitments they share with the neo-pragmatist: a focus on the linguistic community as a whole, and a focus on its overt, public aspects. It is by focusing on overt linguistic phenomena – the 'public practice' of language – that they avoid thinking of appearances of *de jure* sameness as resulting from some sort of comparison of the subject-specific topic-fixing criteria two different people are using. In this way these sameness-appearances are very different from, say, appearances of sameness of shape. Things appear the same in shape because we compare the two shapes. In contrast, the Schroeters think we regard ourselves as talking about the same topic as someone else because of much more superficial – largely syntactic – features of that person's speech. And the essential appeal to the community as a whole comes when the Schroeters select, as the unit of semantic interpretation, the whole body of token uses of particular phrases that are linked together across time and people by the appearance of *de jure* sameness.

The point of contention between the Schroeters and the neo-pragmatist has to do with the notion of reference. The neo-pragmatist understands reference-talk in a deflationary way, and denies that the reference relation – if we want to call it a relation at all – can bear any theoretical weight. The Schroeters, on the other hand, seem to rely on it. True, they allow the formal possibility that the best interpretation of moral discourse might not involve reference. But they think this possibility is unlikely to be realized, for the following reason:

> rationalizing interpretation [of a linguistic tradition] is biased in favor of a traditional, context-invariant realist interpretation of normative concepts because [certain] realist assumptions are central to our normative thought and talk. (Schroeter and Schroeter 2014, 22)

This is a crucial claim, since these realist assumptions include 'that a single property is picked out by all competent subjects independently of their idiosyncratic interests or circumstances'. The Schroeters take this univocal 'picking out' (i.e. reference) to explain how it is possible that 'we correct, refine, and precisify prior categorizations in light of this reflective theorizing'. This goes against standard versions of expressivism and speaker-relativism. And I think that the Schroeters think that it also goes against neo-pragmatism. But if neo-pragmatism is on the table, no appeal to these sorts of 'realist assumptions' can push it off, even if they make use of the notion of 'picking out'. The neo-pragmatist can endorse any realist presuppositions the Schroeters offer, given her endorsement of deflationary accounts of truth, reference, belief, and related notions. Indeed, it is notoriously difficult to find a criterion of realism that the neo-pragmatist cannot accept. In any case, the Schroeters have certainly not provided one.

Why do the Schroeters take moral talk to be representational? They seem to think it is part of the best explanation of the fact that normative discourse looks like it does – involving genuine disagreement, argument, and so on:

> if you assume that we are all co-referring on normative questions, there will be direct epistemic pressure to take others' testimony at face value, to give credence to their normative reasoning, and to work toward resolving interpersonal disagreements through distinctions, justifications, and rationales that are intersubjectively acceptable. Without such a presumption of stable co-reference, it's not obvious that these virtuous epistemic practices would be warranted. (Schroeter and Schroeter 2014, 22–23)

It is clear here that the Schroeters are placing genuine explanatory weight on the notion of reference. But the neo-pragmatist can explain the warrant for our epistemic practices without such an appeal. According to the neo-pragmatist assertoric discourses exist precisely because by opening us up to correction by others they serve to get a community into a useful uniformity of psychological states. That is, we have such things as assertions precisely because of the utility of those practices in which we exercise the dispositions the Schroeters identify as the epistemic virtues. Referential talk is the *result* of these virtues being virtues in the domains of arithmetic, probability, descriptions of the environment, morality, and so on.

If the Schroeters gave up the idea that truth-aptitude and objectivity require finding a reference, their view would be both more general and more powerful. Vindicating truth-aptitude and objectivity would be a matter of showing that the epistemic practices we employ as a community in resolving disputes about a topic can be expected to yield convergence in all but borderline cases, at least under favorable circumstances. This would allow empirical argument to be *one* of those epistemic practices in *some* cases – for example, when we are talking about natural kinds, or about the location of a certain restaurant – but it would also allow mathematical proof to count as such a practice, as well as the distinctive sorts of arguments we use in normative disputes.

Here is one final reason for the Schroeters to abandon their reliance on reference and endorse neo-pragmatism. As they themselves admit, their view makes it impossible for causally isolated linguistic communities to share any concepts. The reason for this is that their model 'makes real causal-historical connections a necessary condition for concept identity' (Schroeter and Schroeter 2014, 18 n. 28). As a result, no alien race could even possibly have the concept of the integers, or of space, or of time, let alone the concept of moral wrongness. And this would be true even if they had concepts that functioned *exactly like* ours, with the *same referents*. So the Schroeters reject the presupposition of moral Twin Earth thought experiments. Earthlings and Twin Earthlings are, on their view, incapable of having genuine moral disagreements, at least until their concepts change.

The Schroeters have some responses to the above worry that may serve to blunt its force, but it would be better not to have to face it at all. And the neo-pragmatist does not face it. For the neo-pragmatist, as for the Schroeters, the question of concept identity has to do with how we use the word 'concept'. But because the Schroeters take the concept of 'concept' to be referential, they are compelled to find a referent to validate it. But the neo-pragmatist is not so compelled. As a result, it is possible for the neo-pragmatist to avoid the present worry while agreeing with the virtually all of what Schroeters say in explaining our judgments of sameness of topic within a linguistic community – including the way in which appearances of *de jure* sameness of topic fit into the picture. Indeed, their view supplements Price's own story about the ways in which truth-assessments produce useful convergence in attitudes within a linguistic community. But the neo-pragmatist can also point to the characteristic usefulness – and therefore the aptness – of truth-assessments of the accuracy of translations. Thus they can say that the English word 'wrong' perfectly translates the Twin English word 'wrong', so that they mean the same thing and are associated with the same concept. True, such assessments require us to make judgments of identity at the level of linguistic practices taken as wholes – such as the practice of counting, or of assessing probability, or of making moral judgments. But as I have already argued, in section 3.1, this is not especially problematic.

4. Conclusion

Neo-pragmatism avoids the worries that each of the two views I've discussed in this paper might raise about the other. Björnsson and McPherson might worry that in relying on primarily syntactic features of sentences to generate the appearance of *de jure* sameness of topic, the Schroeters fail to do enough to indicate how we should go about the rationalizing interpretation that will exclude some of these appearances as *mere* appearances. And the Schroeters might worry that in giving paradigmatic moral judgments such a central role in their account, Björnsson and McPherson fail to give competent speakers the kind of latitude they really have with respect to the content and affect those speakers associate with moral terms. Neo-pragmatism avoids both of these problems by shedding the unnecessary commitments that lead to them. It avoids relying on a substantive notion of reference that threatens to limit the sorts of explanations the Schroeters can give of the purposes of moral discourse. And it avoids relying on the idea that there is some special attitude to which we need to appeal in explaining what counts as a genuine moral judgment.

The criticisms the neo-pragmatist levels at both the non-cognitivism of Björnsson and McPherson and the cognitivism of the Schroeters are by no means devastating. Quite to the contrary, I think that it should not be too difficult for them to abandon the assumptions I have been criticizing: (1) the idea that there is a privileged non-cognitive attitude to which we should appeal in explaining moral judgment, and (2) the idea that we need to appeal to a substantive notion of reference to explain the efficacy of the epistemic virtues in the moral domain. What remains, in the case of Björnsson and McPherson, is an explanation for the extent of our willingness to engage with others on moral matters, even when it is clear to us that their moral classifications are quite different from our own. And what remains, in the case of the Schroeters, is an explanation of the cognitive architecture that underwrites our assertoric practices. The neo-pragmatist can embrace both of these explanations. And the hope is, as with other embraces, that it will be returned.

Notes

1. For a philosophically useful presentation of the origin of actual human disgust, see Kelly (2011). I am simplifying and therefore distorting the facts somewhat, but not in ways that have any dialectical importance.
2. See Sepielli (2016, 286) for a nice implicit argument that this is going to be the least controversial strategy.
3. This is not an a priori constraint. Rather, it is the result of the application of neo-pragmatist techniques to these notions.
4. Wittgenstein (1953, §12), quoted in Price (2008, 132).
5. This issue is the focus of an exchange between Blackburn (1991a, 1991b) and Sturgeon (1991).
6. Compare the discussion of Laura and François Schroeter below, and see Schroeter and Schroeter (2014, 7, 11).
7. See Gert (2002) for more discussion of this fact as part of an argument against moral expressivism.
8. Compare Schroeter (2012, 189) and Schroeter and Schroeter (2014, 7–8). I'll consider the Schroeters' own cognitive-realist-friendly solution to this difficulty in the next section.

9. This point has some similarity to Laura Schroeter's (2012) claims about the appearance of de jure sameness of topic, though, as I discuss below, the neo-pragmatist will re-cast talk of such appearances into talk of competence with a linguistic item.
10. For obvious reasons, the neo-pragmatist is likely to prefer the phrase 'assertoric tradition'. I suspect the Schroeters also ought to use this phrase, given that they explicitly hold that the correct interpretation of a representational tradition might in some cases not involve representation.
11. Schroeter and Schroeter (2014, 7, 11). It is true that the Schroeters claim that their view privileges the level of thought rather than linguistic communication (2014, 8). But I think that careful attention to their solution to the specification problem falsifies this claim.

Acknowledgement

For helpful discussion and written comments on earlier versions of this paper, many thanks to Matt Bedke, Jamie Dreier, Diana Heney, Tristram McPherson, François Schroeter, Laura Schroeter, and Stefan Sciaraffa.

Disclosure statement

No potential conflict of interest was reported by the author.

References

Björnsson, Gunnar, and Tristram McPherson. 2014. "Moral Attitudes for Non-Cognitivists: Solving the Specification Problem." *Mind* 123: 1–39.
Blackburn, Simon. 1991a. "Just Causes." *Philosophical Studies* 61: 3–42.
Blackburn, Simon. 1991b. "Reply to Sturgeon." *Philosophical Studies* 61: 39–42.
Gert, Joshua. 2002. "Expressivism and Language Learning." *Ethics* 112: 292–314.
Horgan, Terence, and Mark Timmons. 1991. "New-Wave Moral Realism Meets Moral Twin Earth." In *Rationality, Morality, and Self-Interest*, edited by J. Heil, 115–133. Lanman, MD: Rowman and Littlefield.
Kelly, Daniel. 2011. *Yuck!: The Nature and Moral Significance of Disgust*. Cambridge, MA: MIT Press.
Price, Huw. 1988. *Facts and the Function of Truth*. New York: Blackwell.
Price, Huw. 2003. "Truth as Convenient Friction." *Journal of Philosophy* 100: 167–190.
Price, Huw. 2008. "The Semantic Foundations of Metaphysics." In *Minds, Ethics, and Conditionals: Essays in Honour of Frank Jackson*, edited by I. Ravenscroft, 111–140. Oxford: Oxford University Press.

Schroeder, Mark. 2008. *Being For: Evaluating the Semantic Program of Expressivism*. New York: Oxford University Press.

Schroeter, Laura. 2012. "Bootstrapping Our Way to Samesaying." *Synthese* 189: 177–197.

Schroeter, Laura, and François Schroeter. 2014. "Normative Concepts: A Connectedness Model." *Philosopher's Imprint* 14: 1–26.

Sepielli, Andrew, 2016, "Moral Realism Without Moral Metaphysics," *Oxford Studies in Metaethics* 11: 265–292.

Sturgeon, Nicholas. 1991. "Contents and Causes." *Philosophical Studies* 61: 19–37.

Wittgenstein, Ludwig. 1953. *Philosophical Investigations*. New York: Macmillan.

Building bridges with words: an inferential account of ethical univocity

Mark Douglas Warren

ABSTRACT
Explaining genuine moral disagreement is a challenge for metaethical theories. For expressivists, this challenge comes from the plausibility of agents making seemingly univocal claims while expressing incongruent conative attitudes. I argue that metaethical inferentialism – a deflationary cousin to expressivism, which locates meaning in the inferential import of our moral assertions rather than the attitudes they express – offers a unique solution to this problem. Because inferentialism doesn't locate the source of moral disagreements in a clash between attitudes, but instead in conflicts between the inferential import of ethical assertions, the traditional problem for expressivism can be avoided. After considering two forms of inferentialism that lead to revenge versions of the problem, I conclude by recommending that we understand the semantics of moral disagreements pragmatically: the source of univocity does not come from moral or semantic facts waiting to be described, but instead from the needs that ethical and semantic discourses answer – a solution to the problems of what we are to do and how we are to talk about it.

1. Introduction

Moral disagreement is, we think, ubiquitous. We find it in the seminar room, at the dinner table, and pretty much everywhere on our social media feeds. But metaethicists have trouble explaining these disagreements. When fundamentally disparate sorts of considerations drive our moral judgments, how is it that we are to understand moral disagreements *as* moral disagreements, instead of just instances of people talking past one another? How can we account for the sense that such disagreements are genuine? What's needed is an account of the meaning of our moral language that establishes a 'semantic common ground'

(Merli 2007b, 26) for interlocutors – if we don't mean the same thing with the words we're using, we can't have a genuine disagreement. Metaethicists need an account of the *univocity* of moral language.[1]

Consider the problem as it appears for moral expressivism. Expressivists maintain that moral utterances express non-cognitive states. Our moral judgments are more like desires than beliefs, they argue, so expressivists can understand univocity in terms of the potential harmony or disharmony between the attitudes being expressed by disputants. But because they model disagreement in terms of a kind of conative clash, the viability of their account of univocity hinges on the identification of the particular kind of conative attitudes all moral claims function to express. This is problematic; we can imagine having genuine disagreements with 'atypical' agents who make moral claims without being in the appropriate mental state.

In this paper, I set out to argue for a metaethical position that maintains the principal appeal of expressivism – what I will call its deflationary advantages – but does so without running into this problem. What's needed is a deflationary approach that does not account for the meaning of ethical claims as a function of the attitudes they express. Such an approach is available: metaethical inferentialism.

I proceed as follows: In Section 2, I explain the appeal of deflationary approaches, both in metaethics and elsewhere. In Section 3, I explain how the possibility of conative variation makes univocity problematic for expressivists. In Section 4, I offer inferentialism as a deflationary alternative to expressivism, and argue that because this position doesn't explain the meaning of moral claims in terms of the mental states they express, it offers us a tempting way to avoid problems associated with expressive accounts of univocity. In Section 5, I consider two ways of explicating the link between use and meaning: *dispositional* and *regulatory*. I argue that both face a problem of inferential variation that echoes the expressivists' difficulty with conative variation. In Section 6, I argue that these problems stem from an inflationary assumption about meaning talk itself. I suggest a deflationary alternative: *normativism* about meaning. This approach is uniquely well equipped to deal with the dangers that variation poses for giving a univocal treatment of moral communication.

2. Background: the appeal of deflationism

A traditional realist approach to metaethics has a seemingly straightforward account of genuine disagreement: when interlocutors have a moral disagreement, that's because there's some moral property that they're both referring to.

Adam: Eating meat is wrong.

Amy: No, it's not wrong at all.

Adam thinks the property of wrongness attaches to the act of eating meat; Amy doesn't. So long as we can give an account of how our moral predicates 'lock on' to the same properties, we can explain why this is a genuine disagreement. Now, it turns out that it's actually a bit tricky to account for this mutual locking on – explaining how diverse speakers are connected to the same moral properties even when they have fundamental disagreements about their extensions.[2] I'll ignore these issues here; for my purposes, it will suffice to note that traditional moral realism faces a more basic problem, one that stems from its essentially *inflationary* approach.

An inflationary metaethics is any one in which moral properties or facts play an ineliminable role in the explanation of moral discourse. The idea is that our moral expressions aim to represent moral facts, and that these facts act as *truthmakers* for our moral claims or judgments. Accordingly, this truthmaker would play a crucial role in the inflationist's account of Adam and Amy's disagreement – each of them is making a claim which will turn out to be true only if it accurately represents the moral nature of eating meat. But positing moral facts in this way brings with it a host of well-known metaphysical and epistemic worries. The challenge for the inflationist lies in figuring out just what sort of things moral facts are supposed to be, and placing them within a scientifically respectable worldview.[3] Whether she can fulfill this metaphysical desideratum or not, the inflationist also has to contend with epistemic and practical questions: How is it that we hairless, language-using apes come to learn about these moral truthmakers, and how do these moral facts come to influence how we decide to behave?

A tempting response to these worries is to go deflationary. Instead of asking, 'What is the nature of moral properties?', the deflationist asks, 'What are we *doing* when we make moral claims like this?' If we can answer the latter question, we might find that a satisfying explanation of moral thought and practice that doesn't hinge on the answer to the former question. In contemporary metaethics, the dominant answer to this question comes from expressivists, who hold that what we're doing, fundamentally, is expressing conative attitudes – roughly speaking, we are booing or hooraying the eating of meat. The expressivist foregoes an explanation of the nature of moral properties or facts, and instead gives an account of the practical significance of moral assertions.

I call expressivism 'deflationary' to highlight its connection to deflationism in other domains. There are many of these – in ethics, but also in epistemology, modality, and theories of truth. The hallmark of such approaches is the turn away from inflationary questions about *truthmakers* – about the facts or properties that are ontologically required for an assertion or thought to be true. Deflationists instead step back to ask the *pragmatic* question: What purpose is served by thinking and talking about these things – about morality, knowledge, necessity, truth? So, a deflationary approach to epistemology might look past questions about the necessary and sufficient conditions for knowledge itself, and instead focus on how knowledge claims help us keep track of who is reliable and why.[4] Modal deflationists don't attempt to understand modal claims in terms of truthmakers like possible worlds, but instead favor explanations of how our talk about necessity and possibility helps to make explicit the conditions under which particular concepts can be applied.[5] Deflationists about truth deny that there is some interesting property that all true statements must share; they instead explain our use of the truth predicate as a 'disquotational device', one that frictionlessly moves us from the assertion *p* to the assertion '*p* is true'.[6] In each of these deflationary accounts, the basic approach is to prefer a *functional* account of how we use certain types of expressions over a *representational* account that demands an investigation into the truthmakers for those expressions. The hope is that a proper understanding of this function will give a satisfyingly natural account of the discourse in question and the part it plays in our lives, but will also deflate the epistemic and metaphysical worries that bedevil inflationary approaches.

On an expressive account, moral claims get their meaning by expressing evaluative attitudes, and these attitudes are more akin to desires than beliefs. Expressivists argue that because moral language functions primarily to express mental states – and not to report on a domain of moral facts – we can give a naturalistically respectable explanation of moral discourse that doesn't appeal to any problematic moral truthmakers. This is the appeal of deflationism, in metaethics and elsewhere: by focusing on the practical matters that drive a discourse, we won't get mired in questions about what sorts of properties or facts the claims in such a discourse are supposed to reference.

3. Genuine disagreement for expressivists

The expressive account of moral disagreement can be read off of two central theses:

(*Mentalism*): the meaning of moral claims comes from the mental states that these claims express

(*Non-cognitivism*): unlike beliefs, these states do not primarily function to describe some moral aspect of the world, but instead, like desires, they play some sort of non-cognitive or conative role.

To keep its deflationary credentials, an expressivist account of disagreement cannot start from the truth-making assumption that there is some property an act has (or lacks) that disputants disagree about. Instead, an expressivist explanation of disagreement must work through an account of the attitudes moral claims function to express. Expressivists understand disagreement in terms of the expression of non-cognitive mental states that have a kind of incompatible practical significance. Interlocutors disagree when they are expressing conative states that systematically lead to behavior that puts them at odds with one another.

We might, for example, follow Stevenson (1937) in modeling ethical disagreements on clashes between our interests, instead of our beliefs:

> Disagreement in interest occurs when A has a favorable interest in X, when B has an unfavorable one in it, and when neither is content to let the other's interest remain unchanged ... A. "Let's go to a cinema to-night." B. "I don't want to do that. Let's go to the symphony." A continues to insist on the cinema, B on the symphony. This is disagreement in a perfectly conventional sense. They can't agree on where they want to go, and each is trying to redirect the other's interest. (Stevenson 1937, 27)

Moral claims conflict in the same way – because they express attitudes that clash in their practical implications for our behavior. We read their content as contradictory as a result of this clash. We might think of these mental states as if they were jigsaw puzzle pieces from the same box; they 'fit' with one another because they systematically share practical implications for how we behave.

Given that the notion of mental states being expressed does so much work for expressivists, we must ask: Exactly what sort of conative state are we supposed to be expressing when we make moral claims? It won't do to simply assert that moral claims express interests, as Stevenson seems to suggest; when I say, 'The Star Wars prequels were awful', I'm expressing a kind of interest (in never watching them again, say), but for all that I'm not making a moral claim. It also won't do to just contend that moral assertions express *moral* interests. This may be true, but it illuminates nothing about what sets moral interests apart from other kinds of interest, like prudential or aesthetic interests.

It turns out that this challenge – the Moral Attitude Problem, or MAP (Miller 2003, 43–51) – is a major obstacle for expressive accounts of morality. David Merli (2007b) points out that the expressivist response must meet two criteria: it must give an account of the attitude in question that is specific enough to differentiate it from other kinds of normative claims (aesthetic or prudential, say), but also be general enough that it doesn't render moral disagreements that we intuitively take to be genuine as instances of equivocation. We see that Stevenson's suggestion fails the former criterion; expressivists have to be sure that the account they give is specific enough that it differentiates moral attitudes from non-moral ones. But they must also meet the latter criterion; their account of the moral attitude must be general enough to make sense of the robust diversity of participants in genuine moral disagreements – we don't want an account of mental states that rule out disputants that our commonsense intuitions would rule in as participants to a real disagreement.

The danger here is that the more exact the expressivist's specification is, the more open she becomes to counterexamples. For example, Allan Gibbard analyzes moral attitudes as endorsements or rejections of the rationality of feeling guilt or resentment towards an act (1990, 42). So, in our example above, Adam endorses the rationality of feeling this way towards eating meat, and Amy rejects it. Plausibly, if he's in favor of that emotional reaction and she's against it, they're expressing mental states that could lead to incompatible behavior in a way that's in line with the general expressive account of genuine disagreement. But what if guilt isn't at the heart of Amy's judgment? What if what she's really expressing with her claim is a rejection of the rationality of feeling disgust at those who eat meat? What if she's from a culture where judgments about the appropriateness of shame are fundamental to morality? Or maybe she's one of those dreaded amoralists – someone whose moral judgments are motivationally inert because they don't express any particular conative attitude.

The worry generalizes. For *any* proposed attitude, it seems we can imagine engaging in what appears to be a genuine ethical dispute with someone who doesn't in fact have that attitude. This may be because our interlocutor is an amoralist, or because she is an iconoclast whose moral claims don't reflect common sensibilities, or because she is suffering from *akrasia* or cynicism and so doesn't have access to the relevant dispositions, or it can be because she comes from a culture whose members characteristically express significantly different attitudes with their moral assertions. This is the problem of 'conative variation' for expressivists. Above, I suggested that expressivists can think of disagreement in terms of the mental states being expressed by interlocutors having the appropriate practical 'fit', like puzzle pieces from the same box. The problem of conative variation forces us to consider situations in which interlocutors are drawing their tiles from different boxes, and so lay down pieces that don't have the right kind of fit. The implication is that such engagements are equivocal: because our interlocutor is expressing a different sort of mental state than we are, he is – according to (*Mentalism*) – making claims with different meanings than ours, and 'in order to engage in real agreement or disagreement, we must mean the same thing by our terms; otherwise we are simply talking past one another' (Merli 2007b, 26). If the meaning of moral claims comes from the attitude they express, the question of whether or not interlocutors engaged in an apparently genuine disagreement are in fact talking past one another is entirely hostage to *both of them having the right kinds of attitudes*. This suggests there is a tension between our common-sense intuitions about moral univocity and whatever theoretical commitments an expressivist might make in specifying the attitude moral claims function to express.

The MAP generalizes, too. Metaethicists of any stripe must deal with the potential conflicts between (1) their theoretical commitments, whatever they may be, regarding the foundation of meaning for moral claims, and (2) our common-sense judgments about ethical univocity, which seem to systematically outstrip these commitments. David Merli (2007a, 2007b, 2009) points out that this gives us a way to undermine accounts of genuine disagreement across the metaethical spectrum; let us call it *Merli's Strategy*:

> Once a theory puts its chips on one particular aspect [essential to all] moral judgment, it must struggle to account for cases of what appear to be moral judgments without that favored characteristic. Our views about what counts as a real moral claim and what does not, and about what counts as genuine moral dispute, seem

> to be sensitive to a cluster of features, any one of which can be removed without destroying the crucial intuitions. This leaves us with a sort of counterexample-generating algorithm: once a theory provides a delineation of what is really central to moral judgment, we can go to work constructing problematic cases. (Merli 2007b, 28)

The danger that the MAP presents for the expressivist is clear and compelling. In order to give a plausible, informative account of moral language, expressivists need to specify the mental states that moral judgments express. This has to be detailed enough to show why these judgments are unique, but the more specific the account is, the more exposed it is to problems of conative variation. The takeaway is that this leaves the expressivist vulnerable to Merli's Strategy: our intuitions about whether or not someone should be counted as making moral assertions are orthogonal to our theoretical considerations about what attitudes they may be expressing.

4. An inferential approach

In this paper, I want to explore a different deflationary approach, one that promises to short circuit the problem by abandoning the expressivist's theoretical commitment to conative attitudes. If we deny that the meaning of a moral claim comes from the mental state it expresses, it looks like the problem won't get any traction. We won't have any obligation to specify a particular attitude that undergirds all moral discourse, because univocity won't depend on universal expression of such an attitude.

We can do this by applying Robert Brandom's general inferential account of meaning to moral claims. The inferentialist shares with the expressivist her deflationary commitments, but instead of adopting an expressivist account of the meaning of moral claims, she explains the meaning of such expressions in terms of their location within a network of inferential relations.[7] Roughly speaking, the meaning of a claim is a function of what inferences would justify its assertion, and also of what further claims we should assent to if we accept it.

We can use a well-worn metaphor here, and compare the inferential norms that are meaning-constitutive for moral claims to the general norms governing the play of a game like chess. Chess pieces and chess moves only count as such against the background of general rules for the game. What transforms a piece of wood into a knight, say, are the moves it can make, and also its part within a game that is defined by certain norms. We define the game in terms of these norms, and identify pieces by the moves that are permitted within the context of these norms. If you want to know what a knight is, you have to understand the rules of chess.

With this metaphor in hand, we can think of the meanings of moral assertions in terms of the rules governing moves in a game. The meaning of moral claims will be identified by the import these 'moves' have in conversation, against a background understanding of the broader norms for moral discourse itself. So, to understand what a moral assertion means, we need to think about the network of inferences it's caught up in – the implications and entailments, consistencies and inconsistencies that it's connected to. Think again of the claim that eating meat is wrong. We identify the meaning of these words by looking at the rules that govern their use – just the same way we identify the chess pieces.

Adam's assertion: 'Eating meat is wrong.'	
Rules	Sample inferences
A person's moral assertions reveal commitments, sometimes about general moral principles we hold …	We should avoid harming sentient creatures
… and sometimes about the ways that those principles intersect with conclusions we've reached about matters of fact	Animals are sentient creatures
These commitments may be prompted by multiple lines of evidence …	Anyway, eating meat is bad for the environment
… and, when expressed, can themselves prompt us to worry about hitherto unconsidered moral possibilities	Maybe I should become a vegan
Finally, and essentially, our moral convictions aren't just beliefs we form about the way the world is – they lead us to form resolutions to act in a different way, to be a different sort of person, and to form new reactions (such as resentment, punishment, or praise) to others' behavior. Adam's assertion has implications for what he's going to do next	I'm going to start making my friends feel really guilty during meals!

You can see that these inferences neatly divide into two categories: What justifies Adam's assertion, and what sort of other beliefs and commitments it justifies (indicated above in the dark background). Following Brandom (1994), we can understand these relations as the 'upstream' inputs that entitle us to make a claim, and the 'downstream' outputs that such a claim licenses, respectively. Again, one of the essential rules of playing this language game is that moral assertions have direct implications for what we decide to do. Upstream, we make inferences from our principles and beliefs; downstream, moral assertions can lead to new types of behavior.

Our ability to keep track of the inferential import of one another's claims only makes sense, Brandom argues, within the socially-embedded practice of asking for and giving reasons for our assertions. This is the language game we play together that enables meaningful discourse:

> In asserting a claim one not only authorizes further assertions, but commits oneself to vindicate the original claim, showing that one is entitled to make it. Failure to defend one's entitlement to an assertion voids its social significance as inferential warrant for further assertions. It is only assertions one is entitled to make that can serve to entitle others to its inferential consequences. (Brandom 1983, 641)

Taken as a metaethical proposal, inferentialism urges us to understand the meaning of our moral claims by locating their role within an interlocking structure of linguistic responsibility and license. We undertake a commitment to answer challenges to our assertions, to give reasons that justify them, and if these challenges are met (or are never issued), we enjoy entitlement to make further inferences from these assertions, and to share license for these further inferences with others. The meaning of a moral expression falls out of its place within such a practice.

As a deflationary approach, inferentialism denies that we need to cite moral properties or relations in order to explain the meaning of moral assertions. Michael Williams' (2010) meta-theoretical explanation of meaning in deflationary theories gives us a framework to explain the meaning of expressions without adverting to their truthmakers. To give such an account, he argues, we must first look to the functional roles characteristically played by the terms of a discourse – for moral discourse, we consider terms such as 'ought', 'wrong', 'good', 'bad', and so on. The inferential norms that govern our use of such terms will be those that enable the terms to fulfill these functional roles. And these roles in turn are best understood in terms of the overall pragmatic aim that moral discourse serves in our lives. This gives us an order of explanation for the meaning of moral terms that eschews both the notion of correspondence to truthmakers and the expressivist emphasis on mental states: The meaning of a moral term like 'bad' is given by the inferential norms that govern it; these norms make sense in light of the broader pragmatic roles that are particular to our moral thought and discourse.

A thorough exploration of the function that moral discourse has in human life lies outside of the scope of this paper, but the most likely explanation of the usefulness of moral language will tie it to the role it plays in facilitating cooperative social behavior. For a highly social, language-using species there is an obvious advantage to a discourse that regulates uncooperative behavior: it promotes our collective chances for evolutionary success.

> By providing a framework within which both one's own actions and others' actions may be evaluated, moral judgments can act as a kind of "common currency" for collective negotiation and decision-making. Moral judgment thus can function as a kind of social glue, bonding individuals together in a shared justificatory structure and providing a tool for solving many group coordination problems. (Joyce 2006, 117)

Moral discourse offers us a potential counterpoint to the selfish impulses that would drive individuals to uncooperative behavior in situations when cooperation would be mutually beneficial. It also gives us a platform for negotiating social behavior by appealing to agreed-upon principles.

Once we've shown that the inferential roles associated with moral expressions arise from the pragmatic role they play (rather than the truthmakers they represent) no metaphysical or epistemic accounting is necessary. This means that a deflationary inferentialism shares the same advantages expressivism enjoys over inflationary metaethics. There is a *prima facie* case for favoring this inferential conception of meaning over the expressivist's, though, owing to its relative simplicity. As we saw above, to give an adequate account of why some moral assertions express incompatible content, an expressivist must first explain what sorts of mental states these assertions express, and then go on to explain how it is that such attitudes ground a kind of pragmatic clash that gives rise to incompatibility. The inferentialist loses the attitude, and so can take a more direct route, simply accounting for the inferences that moral assertions license without taking an explanatory detour through the mental states being expressed. Indeed, much of the recent literature criticizing expressivism has focused on the tangled knot of suppositions and commitments regarding the nature of moral attitudes that the expressivist must untie in order to account for various semantic relationships between moral claims.[8] By taking an inferential approach, we can cut cleanly through this knot, because inferentialists don't need to show anything about attitudes being expressed or their relationship to meaning and inferential import.

Inferentialism doesn't locate the source of moral disagreements in a clash between attitudes, but instead in conflicts between the inferential import of the moral claims in question. Inferentialists can explain the same kind of disagreement-grounding pragmatic clash that expressivists locate in the conflict between non-cognitive attitudes, by noting the behavior-guiding aspects of moral inferences themselves. Amy thinks eating meat is permissible; Adam argues it's wrong. They have a genuine disagreement because the inferences they're committed to endorse types of behavior that are incompatible.[9] Adam is against eating meat; Amy is okay with it.[10] This is the source of their disagreement.

Because inferentialists can account for univocity without referring to particular attitudes, the MAP doesn't get traction. If we can gesture convincingly at the sorts of inferential norms that serve the function of moral discourse, we can then go on to explain univocity in terms of sharing these norms: interlocutors are engaged in genuine disputes just when the moral assertions they make share the appropriate inferential properties; their terms share meanings just when they're bound by the same inferential rules.

5. The problem for inferential accounts

At first glance, then, we might think that the inferentialist's stance towards the MAP should be a lot like the atheist's stance towards the Problem of Evil: in both cases, the problem dissolves because neither the atheist nor the inferentialist posits the entities that raised the issue in the first place. But we're not out of the woods yet. Inferentialists argue that the meaning of moral expressions is ultimately explained by our rules of use for them, so just as the expressivist owes an account of the mental states expressed by moral assertions, the inferentialist has to give an account of the inferential rules that govern these assertions. In the following sections, I'll consider three different conceptions of these rules: *dispositional*, *regulatory*,[11] and *normative*. The dispositional conception of inferential rules, we'll see, leads to an inferential version of the MAP. The regulatory conception faces a dilemma: it either has the same problem as dispositionalism or it relies on a naturalistically suspect notion of the norms governing use. In the penultimate section of this paper I will argue that the final approach, normativism, gives a uniquely satisfying response to worries about inferential variation.

5.1. Dispositional

Dispositional forms of inferentialism hold that it is either speakers' actual use of terms or their dispositions to employ terms in certain ways that establish the meaning-constitutive rules that govern our use of these concepts. Ned Block, for example, understands the inferential role of an expression as its causal role

> in reasoning and deliberation and, in general, in the way the expression combines and interacts with other expressions so as to mediate between sensory inputs and behavioral outputs. (Block 1986, 93)

An explanation of the meaning of an assertion is therefore reducible here to natural facts about an agent's psychology – her disposition to make certain inferences. The rules that govern inferences are rules of thought in an individual's head.

The problem with this is that our judgments of what qualifies as a moral claim are not exhausted by the circumstances and consequences a speaker might endorse for her assertion.[12] Something can qualify as a moral claim even if it doesn't comport with a particular kind of dispositional pattern. Take for example the case of Thrasymachus,[13] who in his dialogue with Socrates argues that justice is no great moral good – that indeed the unjust are to be admired. Thrasymachus defines justice as the advantage of the stronger. If Socrates and Thrasymachus are evoking fundamentally different inferential dispositions when they use the term 'justice', and the meaning of the term comes from the inferences it is connected to, this seems to entail that Socrates and Thrasymachus are not in fact having a dispute, since they're using (the Greek word for) 'justice' to mean different things.

This is a variation on Merli's Strategy, at the level of inferential rule instead of attitude. The MAP for expressivists works because we recognize the plausibility of genuine disagreements between interlocutors who express different sorts of attitudes. If we read the rules of inference off of the behavioral significance individuals attach to moral expressions, and if it is these rules that fix the meanings of our moral assertions, then inasmuch as different speakers use their terms with different inferential commitments, they mean different things with their words. Our judgments of what qualifies as a moral claim are not exhausted by our considerations of the sorts of upstream and downstream inferential implications we considered in Section 4. Something can qualify as a moral claim even if it doesn't comport with a particular kind of inferential pattern. The MAP has returned in a new guise, this time as a worry about variance not in conative attitude but in inferential significance.

5.2. Regulatory

On a regulatory account, the meaning of our expressions is given not by the inferences we are disposed to make, but by the inferential rules which govern our claims. Assertions mean the same thing because they are regulated by the same set of rules. Adopting this account of inferential meaning would undermine worries about eccentric speakers like Thrasymachus – or the amoralist – who deploy moral language without the disposition to make the normal sorts of inferences. What qualifies their use of moral expressions as univocal with our own is a mutual liability: even if we do not make the same inferences from our claims, we *should*.

A regulatory conception hold that claims of meaning are justified by appeal to the meaning-constitutive norms that regulate our use of moral expressions, instead of extant use-regularities or dispositions. Consider again the metaphor from chess: engaging in a norm-governed practice like chess is a matter of being answerable to these rules. Someone can count as playing chess even if she isn't disposed to follow all of its rules – it's enough that she's held liable to the norms of a public rule-governed practice. A player who does not know how to capture *en passant* plays badly, but plays nonetheless. Likewise, someone can count as using moral language even if he doesn't have all of the appropriate inferential dispositions. So, when the amoralist says something like, 'Murder is wrong', we take his assertion to mean the same thing as it would coming from our own mouths, even though he says it without the right kind of attendant behavioral dispositions. This is because the publically held standards of correct use for that assertion include (among many other things) a defeasible motivation to avoid murder.[14]

But this approach to meaning is also problematic. On this account, our assertions mean the same thing because they are governed by the same rules. But how are we to conceive of these rules? Where do they come from? The regulist faces a dilemma: these norms are either constituted in some way by a community's inferential patterns, or they aren't. The latter option resurrects the problem of variation; the former undermines the inferentialist's deflationary advantages.

We can highlight the problems with these options if we consider the possibility of intercultural or diachronic disagreements. Consider for example the following regrettable passage:

> If a man has sexual relations with a man as one does with a woman, both of them have done what is detestable. They are to be put to death; their blood will be on their own heads. (Leviticus 20:13, New International Version)

We take ourselves to be in disagreement with this verdict. But how does the regulatory view account for the shared meaning that is a precondition for genuine disagreement? When faced with eccentric individuals like Thrasymachus or the amoralist, the regulist can defer to community-wide inferential norms that such individuals are violating. But it's quite plausible in this case that the Levitical author is not using idiosyncratic inferential patterns; his moral judgments are a reflection of the inferential standards of his community.

Here is the first horn of the dilemma, then. The moral expressions of the Levitical community answer inferential patterns that are different from our own. (For example, these patterns include justifications for the claim that we would not accept, e.g. that a vengeful God abhors homosexuality.) This is the same problem Thrasymachus presented, but pitched now at the communal instead of the individual level. Worryingly, it looks like the regulatory view would undermine our conviction that we actually disagree with this passage: after all, both we and the Levitical author are using moral expressions that are governed by different inferential rules, and in contrast to the case of the merely eccentric speaker, we can't easily explain this difference in terms of some common set of publically held norms to which we're all obviously liable. Merli's Strategy once again rears its ugly head.

On the other horn of the dilemma, we might conceive of these rules *transcendentally*, in such a way that the inferential rules come apart entirely from how people actually use (or used) language.[15] The regulatory view works by connecting meaning to the inferential rules to which we are liable. So, for it to render disputes like this one univocal, it needs to be the case that even though our own actual inferential patterns do not match up with those of the Levitical community, it's still the case that (somehow) they are both governed by the same set of inferential rules. But in appealing to rules that transcend linguistic dispositions, we're in danger of violating the naturalism that motivated our deflationary metaethics in the first place. The problems that arise with this conception of meaning echo the issues that plague realist accounts of moral truths: how are we to understand the truthmakers for these rules? Are they Platonic or natural? If the latter, what kinds of natural facts (if not use-regularities) constitute these normative facts? If the former, how is it that we language users come to enjoy the access to these rules that are necessary for meaningful communication? And how would we know that the same rules apply to the Levitical community that apply to our own?

6. Normativism: a deflationary account of meaning

Up to this point, we've been considering accounts of meaning that share an inflationary assumption: that there are some features of linguistic reality that, whatever they are, our meaning claims aim to represent. The idea is that if '*X* means the same as *Y*' is true, there's some fact about the world, some truthmaker in virtue of which the claim comes out true – whether these are facts about mental states, about the dispositions of individuals or communities, or facts about norms that somehow exist separately from those dispositions.

As we've seen with expressivism and the varieties of inferentialism proposed so far, theoretical considerations about the nature of these semantic truthmakers puts us in a position of tension with our common-sense intuitions about what qualifies as a genuine moral disagreement. If we want to account for meaning in a way that grants an immunity to Merli's Strategy, we should change our tactics. Instead of first committing ourselves to a theoretical meaning-giving feature of moral discourse, and then checking for counterexamples that would defeat this conception, we should instead ask ourselves what is happening when we make judgements of univocity in the first place.

To proceed in this way is to make the same deflationary turn toward meaning that the expressivist took towards morality, and that we saw in Section 2 has also been pursued by deflationist approaches to epistemology, modality, and theories of truth.

> Just as a deflationary theory of truth denies that there is any deep and substantive answer to the question of what the property of truth consists in ... deflationism about meaning denies that there is any special (non-semantic) property of *meaning F* to uncover the nature of, enabling us to say in general what meaning F consists in. (Thomasson 2015b, 189)

This shouldn't be taken as denial that there are facts about meaning, though. A deflationary approach to meaning does not entail that there are no facts of the matter about whether or not a given disagreement is univocal. Here again, the normativist can take inspiration from the expressivist, and marry her account to deflationary conceptions of truths and facts. The idea is that, on a deflationary reading, one can move from the sentence, 'X means Y', to the sentence, 'It is true that X means Y', or 'It is a fact that X means Y', without adding any real content to the original claim. If we can make sense of the first of these claims, we can make sense of the last two also. The normativist (like the expressivist) can thereby make claims to semantic (or moral) truths without relying on semantic (or moral) truthmakers. Again, the basic deflationary approach is to prefer a *functional* account over a *representational* one. Instead of asking about the nature of these truthmakers, we should ask what we're doing when we make these sorts of assertions.

This is what the inferential normativist does for questions of meaning. According to normativism, 'semantic claims do not talk about 'normative entities' attached to expressions, they *prescribe* how to handle the expression in the proper way' (Peregrin 2012, 97). So, if we judge that some distant community uses a term with the same meaning as one of our own, we're not thereby describing some regularity or disposition or set of transcendent rules for that community. What we're doing fundamentally is not making a *description*, but instead a *prescription* – when we say two expressions, X and Y, mean the same thing, we are licensing the inferences attendant upon X to Y (and vice versa). This is because 'meaning talk is primarily used to provide normative guidance for inferential behavior' (Lance and Hawthorne 2008, 138).

> In translating, we are not ... trying to describe a foreign community as it is in itself. Rather, we are trying to form one large community where previously there

were two. We are trying to make communication, discussion, and argumentation possible; ... we are trying to make possible the sort of cognitive openness that is largely taken for granted in any unified speech community. (Lance and Hawthorne 2008, 63–64)

Perhaps chess gives us a misleading metaphor for how rules of use relate to meaning. After all, the norms governing chess aren't metaphysically mysterious. They are written in rulebooks. There's no difficulty explain how these norms inform actual play, either; it is simply a matter of understanding the kinds of sociological facts revealed in games of chess. But there is no rulebook for a language. Unlike chess play, our judgments of synonymy are sensitive to practical considerations, the sometimes-dynamic ways that our use of words connects to our ways of living.

If we need a game metaphor, we should think instead of a pickup game of beach soccer.[16] There is no rulebook for such a game. Our play itself informs the rules to which we hold ourselves and other players liable. If the beach players endeavor to state these rules, they will be attempting to precisify, adjudicate, or just make explicit what is already implicit in their practice. We count as players in virtue of being sensitive to the rules, but these rules evolve dynamically, and are apt to assimilate particular features of that day's game: have we been worried about offsides so far? Should we count that rock as out-of-bounds, or is it too close to the shoreline? This is a better metaphor for the relationship between meaning and rules of use; the meanings of expressions sometimes assimilate certain aspects of the evolution of the discourse in which the expressions appear.

The normativist and the regulist agree that our meanings are answerable to norms, but because normativism takes a deflationary approach to meaning itself, we needn't hold out for an account of the metaphysical grounds of these norms. Instead of asking what the norms are, we ask how we use them. So, for example, our understanding of how to appropriately use morally loaded terms like 'person' and 'fairness' is answerable to the conclusions that have come from an evolving moral discourse, e.g. about who should be counted as a person and why. We need an account of meaning that does justice to the way in which norms are liable to particular features of use. Such an account doesn't cash out in terms of truthmakers for meaning claims, but instead in terms of a sensitivity to the shifting pragmatic implications of our judgments of synonymy. 'A meaning-claim gains its normative authority ... from the difference it would make to subsequent practice to respect and enforce the norms it expresses' (Rouse 2014, 35).

So, let's think again about the implications of a univocal treatment in moral discourse.

Adam: Eating meat is wrong.

Amy: <No, it's not wrong at all.>

Adam makes a moral assertion, with its attendant upstream and downstream implication, some of which I explicated above. Amy makes her own claim, and this claim carries its own network of implications. Now let the angle brackets indicate that she speaks a foreign language. Adam must consider whether to treat theirs as a genuine disagreement. If he does so, he is bringing those inferential networks into contact with one another, by endorsing a uniform treatment of the entitlements and commitments that come with their assertions. He is in effect inviting Amy into the language game he is playing. This then is an opportunity for both of them to demonstrate that their commitments to the respective claims were justified. In moral discourse, challenges like this can often be valuable platforms for the exchange of information and reasoning – and maybe for a cooperative exploration of the principles and beliefs that brought them to disagree in the first place.

Such a translation isn't just the identification of identical patterns of use; *it is the building of a communicative bridge*. It is a way to invite interlocutors into a mutual realm of persuasion, argumentation, and cooperation. This also shows what we do when we judge that our moral expressions are *not* univocal. We deny ourselves a platform for communication. We cut ourselves off from negotiating with one another and restrict the tools we can use to influence behavior – without moral discourse, we must resort to bribes, trickery, threats, or the outright use of force.

If Adam and Amy keep this bridge open, though, they maintain the possibility of persuasion. Perhaps he convinces her that his original assertion was justified, and so as a result, Amy takes on a belief that has a similar inferential profile to Adam's. This will have implications not just for what she comes to believe, but also on what she decides to do next. As we've seen, this is one of the special hallmarks of moral language. One of the things she might decide to do is spread the word to other parties, because moral discourse is a game we all play together: offering our thoughts on what's right and wrong, justifying, challenging, questioning, and adjusting these thoughts – building and partaking in the discourse that comes out of this practice. Again, all of this ethical discussion and thinking isn't just about changing and reaffirming our beliefs, but also essentially in deciding about how we're going to behave. In the moral language game, ideas and arguments can propagate into the zeitgeist and provoke important social movements. Moral discourse is a coordination device for social creatures, for whom cooperative behavior is crucial for survival. For Adam and Amy, as with all of us, the payoff of treating their disagreement as genuine is potentially huge. Recall Williams' suggestion that the norms governing a discourse are responsive to the function that discourse plays in our lives. If moral discourse functions to facilitate the negotiation of our behavior, as I've suggested, we can now see why it makes sense that our judgements of ethical univocity are so robust.[17]

None of this entails that the view I'm advocating will always recommend judgments of univocity, though. Perhaps we can take a cue from Merli, and try to imagine situations that *wouldn't* recommend a univocal treatment. If we imagine a moral-ish discourse stripped of one or some of the rules I associated with our moral assertions in Section 4, we might find our intuitions pulled in different directions.[18] So, for example, we could learn of some community that regularly engages in a type of discourse that like our moral discourse, informs practical decision-making and prompts critical reflection, but unlike our discourse, does so a way that never (tacitly or otherwise) involved any appeal to overarching principles. We might wonder whether or not the thought and practice that has grown out of their discourse should be counted as moral thought and practice. This would amount to wondering whether or not we should be reading some of the assertions within that alien discourse as having the same inferential import as some of our moral assertions – to wondering if treating our assertions as inferentially uniform is worth the effort. But the takeaway from normativism about meaning is that there is no Archimedean point outside of these sorts of considerations to look for universal principles for synonymy.

At this point, the reader may worry that I've conflated two questions: 'Under what conditions are disagreements actually univocal?' and 'Under what conditions does it make sense for us to treat disagreements as univocal?'[19] I begin this paper by promising a response to the former question, the complaint goes, but instead only deliver a response to the latter. It's important to note the sense in which this worry is question-begging. It assumes that the only adequate explanation of sameness of meaning is inflationary – that we should only be satisfied when we've been given a general account of what makes it the case that two claims to mean the same thing. But this is just the assumption being challenged by a normativist approach, which argues that once we've given an account of when it makes sense to treat an argument as a genuine disagreement, there's nothing left to explain.

The payoff of this approach is that it gives us a response to the challenge posed by Merli's Strategy. This is because the challenge began by taking a given specification of the attitudes or rules that ground moral meaning, and then searches for counterexamples wherein the given specification cannot account for our intuitions of univocity. Taking a deflationary approach to meaning itself shields the normativist from this worry. Any time the normativist is asked 'Do *X* and *Y* mean the same thing, for these people, in this context?' she will not need to read the answer off from her theoretical commitments regarding truthmakers for meaning claims – since she doesn't have any. She instead attends to whatever might be pragmatically salient to the question. When we judge that a moral interlocutor means the same thing we do with his words, this is not because we've discovered that he's answering the same inferential norms that we are, but because we've identified his discursive practice in terms of its success or failure as an alternative approach towards the same goal our moral language has: the management of coordinated group behavior for social and selfish creatures. Because we see our expressions as aiming at the same discursive goal, we see a reason to build a bridge between the inferences to which we are both liable. This reverses the inflationary order of explanation: Instead of positing inferential rules as theoretical meaning-giving entities to which our meaning claims aim to correspond – and then testing them against our intuitions about univocity – we recognize that our meaning claims and the inferential rules they reveal are a way of *making explicit* the practical judgements that inform these intuitions.[20] Merli's Strategy threatens other theories of meaning with potential counterexamples; this strategy is defanged by a normative approach, which transforms the threat into an invitation to imaginatively explore what matters to us.

Metaethical inferentialism shares the basic deflationary advantages of expressivism. We needn't posit the kind of relationship between representation and truthmaker that inflationary approaches do. For the metaethicist, that means we don't have to explain how our moral assertions lock on to some aspect of the world, and we don't have to give any account of moral properties. With the deflationary approaches, all of that goes away. If you want to understand how moral thought and discourse functions, the interesting work isn't to investigate moral truthmakers and how they fit in with all the other natural properties that science posits. The important thing is to investigate us, we hairless apes, and how we use language to figure out how to live together.

Normativist inferentialism in metaethics has the same kind of deflationary payoff for questions of meaning and genuine disagreement. This approach to meaning has the added advantage of undermining Merli's Strategy. The very intuitions that drive judgments of sameness of meaning (i.e. intuitions about whether or not a disagreement is a potentially fruitful opportunity for working out issues of how to live together) are the ones that make sense of moral discourse's functional role in our lives. Claims of synonymy endorse decisions to tie ourselves to common inferential rules for terms. These endorsements are normatively governed – not, as the regulist would have it, by reference to existent communal norms, or to norms that float free of patterns of use – but by the same pragmatic considerations that inform our intuitions about moral univocity. *We take disputants to be using the same terms when we see the negotiated assimilation of inferential commitment as one that is conducive to decisions about how to live together.*

7. Conclusion

My aim in this paper was to offer a solution to the problem of univocity for metaethical deflationists. This problem arose for expressivists once we recognized that their theoretical commitments regarding ethical meaning-makers cut orthogonally to our intuitions about genuine moral disagreements. I've pointed a way out of this problem: first, we recognize that an expressive account of meaning isn't our only option as deflationists. Instead of identifying meaning with the expression of a distinct moral attitude, an inferential approach sees the meaning of an expression in terms of its place within a network of inferential patterns. Metaethical inferentialism sidesteps the MAP because the semantic account it offers doesn't depend on a specification of which attitudes are singularly moral.

I then considered the possibility of a revenge version of the problem for inferentialists. At its strongest, the question is: how are we to account for our intuitions of univocity between denizens of cultures where the use of moral terms seems to be governed by substantially different inferential rules? We can avoid this problem too, by taking a deflationary approach to meaning claims themselves. Normative inferentialists understand questions of synonymy as questions about whether or not the same inferential norms should govern a linguistic form, where this normative question can only be answered by reflecting on the pragmatic needs that would be served by an affirmative answer.

This approach gives us a new way to think about moral univocity. It accounts for the felt intuitions we have about genuine moral disagreements, and does so without positing any inflationary moral or semantic facts that our different discourses are somehow tracking or failing to track. We count disputes as genuine, not because there is some (moral or semantic) truthmaker to which the disputants' assertions are answerable, but because doing so licenses us to hold them liable to inferences that are conducive to moral decision-making. This perspective urges us to understand the semantics of moral disagreements pragmatically: the source of univocity does not come from moral facts waiting to be described (or, as the expressivist would have it, moral attitudes being expressed), but instead from the needs that ethical and semantic discourses answer – solutions to the problems of what we are to do and how we are to talk about it.

Notes

1. I will treat these two problems – explaining sameness of meaning and explaining genuine disagreement – interchangeably. For an alternate approach, see Plunkett and Sundell (2013).
2. See Merli (2007a).
3. Cf. Price (2011).
4. See Chrisman (2011) and Field (2009).
5. See Thomasson (2007).
6. See Horwich (1999).
7. See Bar-Bar-On and Chrisman (2009), Chrisman (2010).
8. See for example Schroeder (2008), Dreier (2009).
9. Of course, not all moral disagreements directly settle questions about what to do. Disagreements in such cases may not be about what we should do immediately, but might instead be about the principles that inform what we would do. See Warren (2013, ch. 5) for an inferential account of disagreement in such situations.
10. Accounting for the incompatibility between Adam's judgement that eating meat is forbidden and Amy's judgement that it is permissible is a noted difficulty for expressivists. See Warren (2015, especially pp. 2877–2879) for an argument that inferentialism is well-situated to solve this problem.

11. Brandom (1994) uses the terms 'regularist' and 'regulist' for these conceptions, respectively.
12. Here I repurpose David Merli's (2009, 540–545) arguments against Ralph Wedgwood's Conceptual Role Semantics. Though Wedgwood's metaethics is explicitly inflationary, Merli's arguments have equal force for a deflationary, dispositional version of metaethical inferentialism.
13. See Sturgeon (1986, 115–142).
14. This is a nice potential upshot of the inferential approach: a rather tidy resolution of the internalism/externalism debate about moral motivation. See Chrisman (2010, esp. 118–119).
15. See Lance and Hawthorne (2008, 186–187).
16. See Lance and Hawthorne (2008, 218), Thomasson (2015a, 250–251).
17. Similar points are made by Tersman (2006, Ch. 6) and Bjornsson and McPherson (2014), who argue that it makes good evolutionary sense that we allow for a lot of latitude between divergent interlocutors in our judgments of moral univocity.
18. Cf. Bjornsson and McPherson (2014, 9–10).
19. Thanks to an anonymous reviewer for pressing this point.
20. In the conclusion of his (2007b), Merli gestures at a possible avenue to solve the MAP:

    > We might try to preserve our intuitive ascriptions [of moral univocity] by rejecting views that make participation in moral discourse hinge on any one member of the cluster of features that affect the attribution of moral concepts … According to one way of developing a view of this sort, facts about whether speakers share meanings are constituted, not tracked, by our best interpretations. In other words, our interpretive norms are fundamental. Hence there is no possibility of a gap between facts about what speakers mean and how they are best interpreted. (Merli 2007b, 54)

    Setting aside the worry that Merli is calling for our best interpretations to be taken as truthmakers for moral claims, I believe much of what I argue for here is consistent with this approach.

Acknowledgments

The author would like to thank Ryan Lake, Ben Yelle, Nick Wiltsher, Thomas Brouwer, Lionel Shapiro, Joseph Rouse and Amie Thomasson for a number of helpful discussions of the issues covered in this paper.

References

Bar-Bar-On, D., and M. Chrisman. 2009. "Ethical Neo-Expressivism." In Vol. 4 of *Oxford Studies in Metaethics*, edited by Russ Shafer-Landau, 133–165. Oxford: Oxford University Press.

Bjornsson, G., and T. McPherson. 2014. "Moral Attitudes for Non-Cognitivists: Solving the Specification Problem." *Mind* 123: 1–38.
Block, N. 1986. "Advertisement for a Semantics for Psychology." *Midwest Studies in Philosophy* 10: 615–678. Reprinted in Stephen P. Stich and Ted A. Warfield, eds., *Mental Representation: A Reader*, Oxford: Blackwell, 1994.
Brandom, R. 1983, November. "Asserting." *Noûs* 17 (4): 637–650.
Brandom, R. 1994. *Making It Explicit: Reasoning, Representing, and Discursive Commitment*. Cambridge, MA: Harvard University Press.
Chrisman, M. 2010. "Expressivism, Inferentialism, and the Theory of Meaning." In *New Waves in Metaethics*, edited by Michael Brady, 103–125. Palgrave-Macmillan.
Chrisman, M. 2011. "Is Epistemic Expressivism Incompatible with Inquiry?" *Philosophical Studies* 159 (3): 323–339.
Dreier, J. 2009. "Relativism (and Expressivism) and the Problem of Disagreement." *Philosophical Perspectives* 23 (1): 79–110.
Field, H. 2009. "Epistemology Without Metaphysics." *Philosophical Studies* 143 (2): 249–290.
Gibbard, A. 1990. *Wise Choices, Apt Feelings: A Theory of Normative Judgment*. Cambridge, MA: Harvard University Press.
Horwich, P. 1999. *Truth*. 2nd ed. New York: Oxford University Press.
Joyce, R. 2006. *The Evolution of Morality*. Cambridge, MA: MIT Press.
Lance, M. N., and J. Hawthorne. 2008. *The Grammar of Meaning: Normativity and Semantic Discourse*. Cambridge: Cambridge University Press.
Merli, D. 2007a. "Moral Convergence and the Univocity Problem." *American Philosophical Quarterly* 44 (4): 287–313.
Merli, D. 2007b. "Expressivism and the Limits of Moral Disagreement." *The Journal of Ethics* 12 (1): 25–55.
Merli, D. 2009. "Possessing Moral Concepts." *Philosophia* 37 (3): 535–556.
Miller, A. 2003. *Introduction to Contemporary Metaethics*. Cambridge: Polity.
Peregrin, J. 2012. "Inferentialism and the Normativity of Meaning." *Philosophia* 40: 75–97.
Plunkett, D., and T. Sundell. 2013. "Disagreement and the Semantics of Normative and Evaluative Terms." *Philosopher's Imprint* 13 (23): 1–37.
Price, H. 2011. *Naturalism Without Mirrors*. New York: Oxford University Press.
Rouse, J. 2014. "Temporal Externalism and the Normativity of Linguistic Practice." *Journal of the Philosophy of History* 8: 20–38.
Schroeder, M. 2008. *Being For*. Oxford; New York: Oxford University Press.
Stevenson, C. L. 1937. "The Emotive Meaning of Ethical Terms." *Mind* XLVI (181): 14–31.
Sturgeon, N. 1986. "What Difference does it Make if Moral Realism is True?" *The Southern Journal of Philosophy* 24 (Supplemental Issue): 115–141, cited in Merli (2007): 32–33.
Tersman, F. 2006. *Moral Disagreement*. Cambridge: Cambridge University Press.
Thomasson, A. L. 2007. *Ordinary Objects*. New York: Oxford University Press.
Thomasson, A. L. 2015a. *Ontology Made Easy*. New York: Oxford University Press.
Thomasson, A. L. 2015b. "Deflationism in Semantics and Metaphysics." In *Metasemantics*, edited by Alexis Burgess and Brett Sherman, 185–213. Oxford: Oxford University Press.
Warren, M. D. 2013. *Lightweight Moral Realism: Objectivity and Reasoning without Heavyweight Facts*. Open Access Dissertations. Paper 1138. http://scholarlyrepository.miami.edu/oa_dissertations/1138.
Warren, M. D. 2015. "Moral inferentialism and the Frege–Geach Problem." *Philosophical Studies* 172 (11): 2859–2885.
Williams, M. 2010. "Pragmatism, Minimalism, Expressivism." *International Journal of Philosophical Studies* 18: 317–330.

Keeping track of what's right

Laura Schroeter and François Schroeter

ABSTRACT
In this paper, we argue that ordinary judgments about core normative topics purport to attribute stable, objective properties and relations. Our strategy is first to analyze the structures and practices characteristic of paradigmatically representational concepts such as concepts of objects and natural kinds. We identify three broad features that ground the representational purport of these concepts. We then argue that core normative concepts exhibit these same features.

1. Introdution

In this paper, we argue that ordinary judgments about core normative topics purport to attribute stable, objective properties and relations. Normative concepts such as the concept of being morally right resemble paradigmatically representational concepts of ordinary objects, artifacts, or natural kinds in purporting to pick out stable features of the world. Of course, the presumption of successfully picking something out in thought may be mistaken: it may turn out that there is no phlogiston or moral rightness. Our point is that such discoveries overturn our initial implicit understanding of the relevant concepts.

Our strategy is to first identify which aspects of conceptual competence ground representational purport and then show that these features are shared by normative concepts. In Sections 2 and 3, we offer a general characterization of concepts as cognitively basic ways of keeping track of a topic in thought and talk. We explain how this distinctive cognitive role is tied to both cognitive significance phenomena and to subpersonal cognitive mechanisms for managing information. In Section 4, we focus on paradigmatically representational concepts such as concepts of objects and natural kinds. We identify three broad features of our conceptual practices that ground the representational purport of these concepts. In Section 5, we argue that normative concepts exhibit these same features.

2. Keeping track of a topic

There's an important distinction in the philosophy of mind between thinking about the same topic and thinking about that topic *as* the same. To get a feel for the distinction, consider two cases. Suppose you've encountered Bernard J. Ortcutt on separate occasions and formed thoughts about that very individual – that he's a spy and that he's a pillar of the community – without being in a position to recognize that it's the same person. You might decide to report Ortcutt's suspicious activity to a responsible person like Ortcutt. In this case, you're thinking about the same man but your thoughts don't represent him *as* the same. In contrast, consider the expanding body of beliefs you've accumulated about Donald J. Trump. In this case, you have no difficulty recognizing sameness of topic among your thoughts. Reading news about Trump's latest tweet, for instance, might prompt you to remember how Trump behaved as a candidate and to conclude that Trump is living up to your fears. In this train of reasoning, you're thinking of the same man *as* the same. This intuitive contrast between thinking of the same topic again and thinking of the same topic *as* the same is marked in commonsense psychology with talk of concepts: you have two different concepts of Ortcutt, but just one concept of Trump.

Given its role in grounding our intuitions about concepts, it's important to be clear about the epistemic distinction between the two cases. We'd like to highlight four epistemic signatures of thinking of a topic *as* the same (Schroeter 2012). First, it seems *obvious* that the topic of your thoughts all concern the same person: there's no need for reflection or reasoning before you engage in inferences that trade on the presumption that there's just one topic in question. Indeed, the question of sameness simply doesn't arise as long as you're engaged in ordinary object-level ruminations on the topic: your focus throughout is simply on Trump himself. Second, sameness of topic seems *rationally indubitable*: it would be crazy to doubt whether Trump is Trump. As long as your attention remains focused outwards on the world rather than on your own representational states, the question of sameness seems closed. Third, the sameness of topic seems *epistemically basic*: no object-level evidence about Trump could help justify your assumption that Trump is Trump. Fourth, the appearance of obvious and indubitable sameness disappears when you engage in *meta-level reflection* about your thoughts. To formulate an open identity question about the Trump case, you just need to step back from your object-level perspective and ask a meta-cognitive question: e.g. whether this thought represents the same individual as those other thoughts do, or whether this man (the man represented by this occurrent belief) is the same person as that man (the one represented by those beliefs).

Notice that this distinctive epistemic signature also occurs in communication. If a friend asks you whether you think Trump will be impeached, you'll understand her question *as* pertaining to Trump – the man who is the topic of many of your own attitudes. As long as you retain your ordinary object-level perspective focusing on the world, it will seem obvious and rationally indubitable that Trump (the man she asked about) is Trump (the man who tweeted, seemed unelectable, etc.).

Similar observations hold for your thinking about kinds, properties, relations, normative statuses, etc. Consider a children's game of tag, where the status of being 'it' (i.e. being the person whom all the other players try to avoid) is passed from one player to another via being caught and tagged by whoever is currently 'it'. When you succeed in tagging someone new as 'it' in your game, you see that person as acquiring the very same 'it' status that you previously had. And when she complains that she wasn't really tagged so that you're still 'it', you immediately understand her complaint as pertaining to the very same status that you associate with that term. Indeed, it seems obvious and rationally incontrovertible that the same topic is in question. This is why the belief she's expressing – that you're 'it' – seems to directly logically contradict your own belief that you're *not* 'it'.

We've argued elsewhere that thinking about a topic *as* the same is explained by subpersonal cognitive mechanisms (Schroeter 2012; Schroeter and Schroeter 2014). We must have some cognitive mechanisms for bundling together information-carrying states that allow us to consciously focus on features of our environment as topics of thought, to recognize these features again, to amass new information about them and weed out mistaken information, to keep different information bundles segregated from each other, and to retrieve information from the same bundle when engaged in reasoning about a topic. These various cognitive abilities amount to an information-management system that binds and segregates information-bearing states about features of our environment. The person-level epistemic signature of thinking of a topic *as* the same is best seen as a manifestation of the underlying dispositions that structure our perspective as thinkers.

The metaphor of a mental filing system is useful in clarifying the basic structure of the subpersonal mechanisms that ground these dispositions.[1] In your office filing cabinet, particular manila file folders serve to bind together a changing bundle of documents and keep it separate from other similar bundles in the other files. Whenever you reach for a particular file (say, your [John Perry] file) your default assumption is that all the documents in it will pertain to the same topic (e.g. they're all papers written by Perry). You may, of course, discover that this default assumption is incorrect: there could be a paper by Kaplan that has slipped into your [Perry] file. So to find out whether your default assumption is mistaken, you'll need to step back and actually examine the different document in the file to see if they match the rest of the documents in the file. But it would defeat the whole purpose of a filing system if you *always* had to compare the content of individual documents before you took them to pertain to the same topic. The key advantage of a well-maintained filing system over a giant disorganized pile of documents is that you can, in general, know that co-filed documents pertain to the same topic *before* actually reading them. So long as you've been a reasonably careful filer who only puts new stuff into existing files when it's appropriately similar to the stuff already in the file, your disposition to treat everything in the same file as pertaining to the same topic will be warranted and the exercise of that disposition will normally suffice for knowledge of sameness of subject matter. Moreover, organizing your information in files allows you to accumulate and store a whole lot of interesting new information, to access it efficiently, and monitor it for mistakes. And the stability of the files, together with your conscientious updating practices, helps explain the sense in which your filing system involves stable topics despite the constant changes in the actual contents of your files.

Mental files are structurally analogous. The central idea behind the file metaphor is that many of our consciously accessible thoughts are organized in a similar way: they are bound together (or co-indexed) by topic. For any topic you're capable of focusing on in thought, you have an evolving bundle of information-carrying states – attitudes and cognitive dispositions – that you're automatically disposed to treat as pertaining to the same topic. The mental file metaphor suggests that you have a system of subpersonal mechanisms that serve to bind a body of informational states together and keeps that body separate from other bodies stored in the system. So a particular mental file is just *a binding mechanism*, like a manila file folder, that bundles together different information-carrying states in such a way that those states are automatically treated as pertaining to the same topic by your cognitive system.

This file metaphor nicely captures the structure of thinking about a topic *as* the same. By placing the explanation at the subpersonal level, mental file accounts explain why the appearance of sameness is obvious, indubitable and epistemically basic when we use a single file to think about the world. The model also helps explain why this epistemic signature disappears when we formulate explicitly meta-level questions about whether particular thoughts pick out the same semantic contents. In effect, mental files prejudge the question of sameness of content among mental states, so you need to step back from using the same file if you want to formulate a coherent question of sameness of topic.

Because the mental filing structure captures the epistemic signature of concepts, one might be tempted to simply identify mental files with concepts. But this would be a mistake. There are several problems with this simple proposal. To begin with, we haven't specified how mental files are individuated diachronically or counterfactually. Since concepts can be shared over time and across counterfactual circumstances, the mental file proposal is at best incomplete. A natural way to develop the file model of concepts would appeal to causal-historical relations linking files over time and between individuals. Tracing the links established by the appearance of obvious and indubitable sameness of topic linking individuals' mental files at a time with their past files and with those of others would allow us to demarcate diachronic and interpersonal *filing traditions*. Such traditions reflect the participants' own implicit epistemic perspective on guaranteed sameness of topic (see Schroeter and Schroeter 2014).

But there are still structural mismatches between continuous mental filing traditions and concepts. For instance, concepts have their semantic contents essentially, but mental files do not. Mental files are subpersonal cognitive mechanisms, which can acquire different semantic interpretations due to changes in the external circumstances or to changes in the body of attitudes bound together. A single continuous filing tradition with 'Madagascar' or 'water' could shift its semantic content over time, but such a shift would constitute a shift in the concept (Burge 1988; Evans 1973; Schroeter and Schroeter 2014). The relational nature of these filing traditions also raises problems. Sameness of concept seems to be an equivalence relation (reflexive, symmetric and transitive), but the fact that filing traditions can merge or split will generate failures of transitivity (Fine 2007; Pinillos 2011).

Nevertheless, we've argued that there is an internal connection between mental files and concepts. Concepts, we suggest, are individuated by the semantic disambiguation of our mental filing traditions. In effect, concepts are representational state types demarcated by semantically fine-tuning our filing traditions. The basic unit for semantic interpretation is the filing tradition as a whole, not token elements of thought considered independently. When an entire tradition has two (or more) equally justified interpretations, ideal semantic interpretation will seek to partition that tradition in such a way that each cell in the partition can be assigned a univocal interpretation. Disambiguated filing traditions capture the direct epistemic relations forged among token elements of thought by a mental filing system while at the same time assigning a univocal semantic content to all tokens within the same partition.[2]

For present purposes, the distinction between mental filing traditions and concepts won't matter. Our question is how our basic ways of keeping track of a topic can generate representational purport. The possibility of shifts in representational content and worries about defining equivalence relations are orthogonal to this central concern.

3. Concepts vs Fregean senses

Our model of keeping track of a topic in thought turns on subpersonal cognitive mechanisms that bind informational states at a time, over time and between individuals. The resulting binding relations explain both our cognitive ability to keep track of information *as* about the same topic and the resulting person-level epistemic signature of thinking of a topic *as* the same. This relational approach to concepts is very different from the more familiar Fregean sense model, which appeals to matching patterns of substantive understanding.

Two token words express the same Fregean sense just in case each token is governed by the same pattern of understanding, which suffices to fix the same semantic content for each token (relative to specified facts about the empirical context of use). So if two token uses of 'water' are each governed by precisely the same implicit reference-fixing criterion, the thoughts expressed by those tokens are guaranteed to co-refer (assuming that they occur in the same historical environment). A precise match in criteria, moreover, is supposed to explain Fregean cognitive significance phenomena: why it sometimes seems obvious, indubitable, and epistemically basic from the thinker's point of view that there is just one topic in question.

Critics have raised numerous worries about the adequacy of this Fregean model. Do we really have indubitable commitments that are rich enough to uniquely determine the semantic content? Could such criteria really be shared over time and between individuals? Would a perfect match in implicit criteria really be obvious? In short, it's far from clear that the Fregean model can fully explain the epistemic signature of keeping track of a topic *as* the same (see e.g. Byrne and Pryor 2006; Fine 2007; Kripke 1980; Putnam 1970, 1973; Schroeter 2017; Stalnaker 1990).

For the purposes of this paper, we'd like to highlight the core structural difference between the relational model of concepts and the Fregean model of sense. As we've seen, Fregean senses are individuated by matching criteria for using an expression (perhaps together with contextual factors). In contrast, a relational model of concepts has no structural commitment to a precise match in topic-fixing criteria. What explains the direct epistemic appearance of sameness is being linked to the same tradition, which is consistent with open-ended variation in substantive understanding over time and between individuals (Schroeter 2012; Schroeter and Schroeter 2014). And even when there is a precise match in individuals' topic-fixing criteria, that match does not suffice for competence with the same concept on the relational model: there must still be a relevant causal-historical link between individuals' mental files for those individuals to share a concept.

It's also worth stressing a difference in scope between Fregean sense and concepts. The Fregean's focus on linguistic meaning encourages one to think of concepts as rules governing the correct use of particular expressions. But our understanding of concepts as *ways of keeping track of a topic in thought* is much more restrictive. You may not be thinking about any topic at all when you respect conventional criteria for using expressions. Consider the case of indexicals. Linguistic conventions governing 'here' do not correspond to a *concept* in the sense of keeping track of the same topic *as* the same. The ability to use 'here' is not an ability to focus our attention on the topic of *hereness* as such and to treat all 'here' thoughts *as* pertaining to that same topic. Hereness is not a topic of ordinary thought. Instead, 'here' is used to pick out different topics on different occasions: particular uses direct our attention to the location of the utterance. What we keep track of in thought and talk are the locations themselves – Melbourne, or Vancouver, or Angell Hall – not the relational property of being the location of an arbitrary speaker. But mastering semantic rules governing 'here' does not entail a conceptual capacity to keep track of Melbourne or Angell Hall as such. So linguistic competence with the meaning of 'here' doesn't require *conceptual* competence in the sense we've been articulating: the ability to keep track of a particular topic in thought.

4. Mental files and representational purport

In this section, we take a closer look at the distinctive cognitive and epistemic practices associated with concepts of paradigm representational topics like (i) ordinary physical objects and (ii) natural and artifact kinds. Our aim is to isolate the aspects of our conceptual practices that ground their representational purport. This will put us in a position to ask whether our ways of keeping track of core normative topics like being morally right and being all told right exhibit the same representational purport.

Our conceptual capacity to represent *ordinary physical objects* entails a rich set of abilities that single out persisting physical individuals *as such* and allows us to think of them *as* the same across different episodes of thought. We want to bring out three key features of the mental filing system, which we take to ground the representational purport of our concepts of ordinary objects.

Long-term binding and storage: A central function of concepts of individual objects is to allow for learning about a particular individual over time. To fulfill this role, a mental filing system requires mechanisms for stably binding persisting attitudes and cognitive dispositions together over time. A mental filing system allows for the accumulation of a body of information about an object's nature and history that can be stored and later redeployed in perceptual recognition or offline reasoning about the object.

Unlike perceptual tracking of objects, concepts bind information derived from different sensory modalities, testimony, and inference, which may be formatted in different ways. Your mental file for that particular ambulance, for instance, may bind visual indices tracking that object in your visual field, auditory perceptions of the noise of the siren, an awareness of your own emotional response to the object, a rich bundle of beliefs and inferential dispositions that constitute your implicit conception of what kind of thing an ambulance is (e.g. it's a spatio-temporally continuous physical object, it has the characteristic physical and social functions of ambulances), and standing object-specific attitudes about this particular ambulance (e.g. its being from your local hospital, it's the one driven by your friend Al). All of this information can be thought of as propositional attitudes (e.g. imaginings, beliefs, questions, intentions, even perceptions that the object is instantiated) or cognitive dispositions (e.g. recognitional, inferential, or motivational dispositions) bound to the very same mental file. Mental files integrate these different states and make them available to conscious reasoning *as* pertaining to the same topic. This integration of persisting attitudes and dispositions allows you to recognize the incoming information *as* pertaining to the same objects – an ability that underwrites both induction and learning about particular individuals as such.

Epistemic oversight: Our conceptual thinking is subject to reflective epistemic oversight to ensure coherence and stability of topic. As we learn more about an object, we acquire more ways of reidentifying it. The more you learn about Donald J. Trump (his changing appearance over time, his business and political associations, his family history, etc.) the more new ways you have of deciding when that individual has been involved in some event you learn about. A growing bundle of attitudes and dispositions means that you'll be disposed to add new information on the basis of many different kinds of evidence. With each new addition to the bundle, however, there is greater potential for both internal inconsistencies and variation in the external sources of information. Managing such a flexible information-bundling system thus requires epistemic vigilance.

In non-reflective creatures, incompatibilities among beliefs might be resolved through a simple battle among dispositions, with stronger credences within the creature's overall understanding winning out over weaker ones. As reflective thinkers, however, we seek to integrate different elements in our conception of a topic and are actively on the lookout for internal inconsistencies. Along the way, we reflectively refine our understanding in ways that allow us to home in on the features we judge most relevant to our background interest in the topic. For instance, we might discover that the cause of our 'Trump' beliefs for the past forty years is not an individual human being but a robot controlled from Moscow. Or we might discover that the whole 'Trump' story was a giant media hoax. In that case, what is Trump? The young tycoon? a robot? a fictional character? nothing? When we try to answer these questions, we are implicitly revising our earlier conception of the topic. The correct verdict is not determined by simply letting our strongest prior credences win out: instead we justify one verdict over others by reflecting on our own interests and priorities to determine which feature of the world has been most relevant to our practice in trying to keep track of something as Trump (see Schroeter and Schroeter 2015).

Reinterpretation: A mental filing system generates the appearance of a stable topic over time despite revisions in one's bound attitudes and dispositions. Consider an occurrent memory of Trump descending his golden escalator to announce his candidacy. The memory presents itself as a direct window on your past judgment from which it derives: it seems obvious and indubitable that there's just a single topic over time. At the same time, your [Trump] file binds this memory to a bundle of contemporary attitudes and dispositions, many of which you did not have back then. Even if you've changed your conception of

Trump, you 'read back' your current conception as the correct way of identifying the topic of your earlier thoughts. In effect, revisions in your understanding of the topic are treated as a reinterpretation of the content of your past thoughts. If you now think that Trump is a robot, then you'll take your memory to be about that robot, and you'll take your prior beliefs that Trump was a human being to be false beliefs about that robot. Thus, your mental filing system can generate the appearance of stability of topic even through radical changes in substantive understanding of the topic.

It's important to see that 'reading back' your current conception of a topic as giving the content of your past thoughts isn't an arbitrary imposition of your current perspective onto your past self. On the contrary, it reflects core epistemic commitments of your past self. After all, you never took your conception of the topic to be infallible. If you had, you would not have been disposed to refine your conception of the topic in the light of empirical inquiry and reflection. In revising your conception of Trump, you saw yourself as correcting your prior conception. And reading this correction back into your understanding of your past thoughts vindicates your general epistemic ambition to keep track of a genuinely interesting and important feature of your environment. Far from changing the topic, then, reinterpretation seeks to identify the topic you were aiming at all along. If your reflective epistemic oversight has been successful – if it has identified criteria that you would have continued to endorse after ideal, empirically informed reflection – 'reading back' your reinterpretation is actually the most charitable interpretation of the semantic content of your past thoughts (Schroeter 2008; Schroeter and Schroeter 2014).

The three key features of our internal mental filing system can be extended to the interpersonal level via stable lexical meanings. Names in a public language can trigger the immediate appearance of sameness of topic that's structurally analogous to stability of topic over time. When you hear someone else use a name in a sentence like, 'Trump is a moron', you automatically hear their claim *as* pertaining to the same topic as the one you associate with that name. This epistemic signature of obvious and indubitable sameness is grounded by stable subpersonal mechanisms for linguistic interpretation that recruit the mental file you associate with 'Trump' to interpret the content of others' claims. The result is an interpersonal mental filing system, in which appropriately linked individuals have a coordinated mental filing tradition with the three key features we highlighted above:

Long-term binding and storage: Coordinating their internal mental filing systems allows members of a community to vastly expand the body of bound information available to each individual. Others' beliefs are taken *as* pertaining to the same topic, allowing for direct logical agreement or disagreement and direct acceptance of testimony. Given a baseline of epistemic trust and cooperation within the community, this direct semantic coordination affords a vast improvement over isolated individuals' abilities to learn about particular topics as such.[3]

Epistemic oversight: Although we have a prima facie disposition to trust others' testimony, we need epistemic vigilance to deal with conflicts among individuals' commitments. Just as we take our own pool of standing attitudes into account in this process, we need to take the communal pool of attitudes into account in refining our understanding of the content of our own mental files. Given the greater variability among bound attitudes within a linguistic community, the need for oversight is particularly pressing for shared filing traditions.

Reinterpretation: Any revisions in one's own understanding of the topic are presumed to apply to all bound states. In effect, you 'read back' your own current understanding of the topic as providing the correct interpretation of what all of us have been thinking about all along. In the intra-personal case, the correct interpretation should be justifiable from your past perspective. Similarly, in the interpersonal case, the correct interpretation should be mutually justifiable from the perspective of all those to whom it is applied (Schroeter and Schroeter 2014, 2015).

These three features – long-term binding, epistemic oversight, and reinterpretation – capture our ways, as reflective thinkers, of managing our subpersonal system for accumulating empirical information *as* pertaining to particular objects. Let's now focus on the question of representational purport. How exactly do these three features ground the representational purport of a mental file?

Let's start with long-term binding. It's not obvious that mental files – whose function is to present thoughts *as* pertaining to the same topic – must always involve long-term accumulation of information about the nature of that topic. Recall our earlier example of 'being it': in this case, one might argue that there is an internal binding device, like a mental file, that simply serves to coordinate action schemas across individuals at a time, so that we're disposed to do and expect certain things depending on who is 'it'. Such a coordinating practice doesn't require any ability to accumulate a stable body of information about the topic – i.e. assumptions about the nature of itness itself or a body of contingent facts about that status. In that case, there is little pressure to interpret mastery of 'being it' as an ability to represent the abstract status *as such*, as opposed to interpreting it as a mere expressive device for practical interpersonal coordination.

Another contrast case would be perceptual tracking of objects. Zenon Pylyshyn has argued that we have 'visual indices' that bind incoming streams of visual information into discrete units, which we track across the visual field (Pylyshyn 1989, 2007). It would, of course, be appropriate for an external interpreter to describe these visual indices as 'tracking', 'locking onto', or 'representing' the objects which cause the incoming stream of information they bind together. But ascribing representational purport to visual indices seems unwarranted. We take representational purport to be a person-level phenomenon that must be grounded in the internal structure of the thinker's conscious perspective. Visual indices are merely subpersonal mechanisms automatically triggered by fleeting proximal stimuli: they do not persist beyond a single episode of perceptual tracking, and so do not afford long-term storage for bound information. From the thinker's conscious perspective, they are merely attention-grabbing aspects of their visual experience.[4]

In contrast, a mental file associated with a name like 'Trump' serves to accumulate and store a rich and stable body of empirical information *as* pertaining to a single topic. In effect, the thinker is mining the world for more information about a putatively stable topic. The growing body of information is used in outward-directed engagement with features of the environment: re-identifying the feature *as* the same on different occasions, redeploying accumulated information to that case, and storing information derived from these new cases. Thus, long-term information storage via a mental filing system can set up an informational feed-back loop for accumulating new information about specific features of the environment. From the thinker's conscious perspective, this accumulation of information from the world is *presented as* all pertaining to a stable topic. This combination of stable topic and outward directed epistemic activity in gleaning new information provides rich internal grounds for attributing representational purport. From your internal perspective, you are actively using your [Trump] file to isolate and learn about a stable feature of the world.

This representational purport is strengthened by epistemic oversight of one's mental filing system. Two aspects of oversight are crucial here: (i) coherence and (ii) epistemic ambition.

Maintaining coherence within a file is consistent with the lack of representational purport. In a mental filing practice with 'being it', for instance, we have a coherence requirement that only one person can be judged 'it' at a time. So if two players claim that different individuals are 'it', they will feel pressure to resolve the dispute by relying on the implicitly grasped rules of the game. For instance, a conflict over who's 'it' might generate an argument over who was really tagged. But it doesn't follow their thoughts purport to represent the status of itness itself. As we noted, competent users of the term need not have any ability to focus on the status as such in thought or accumulate information about it. Seeking to resolve contradictions does not alter this lack of representational purport.

But when we have a mental file with long term information storage, like that associated with 'Trump', epistemic oversight aims for a much richer type of coherence in substantive understanding. Given that your 'Trump' thoughts purport to represent a single topic, there is rational pressure to ensure that you have a coherent overall understanding of that topic: e.g. what kind of thing Trump is, his history, habits, and other characteristics. You'll typically have some implicit 'guiding conception' of what kind of thing Trump is, which constrains your understanding of coherent possibilities. If you take Trump to be a physical object, for instance, you assume that he's located in space and time, causally unified at a time and over time, that he traces out a continuous spatiotemporal path, that the relations between his parts are stable, etc. (Dickie 2010, 227). Given this guiding conception, it is incoherent to suppose that Trump was in two places at one time. A guiding conception structures your overall understanding of a topic. As a consequence, it helps focus the general outward-directed representational purport of your mental file on a particular aspect of external reality: a persisting physical object. From your own perspective, your 'Trump' thoughts purport to represent an object, a particular human being, rather than a human kind in general or Trumpish behaviour.

The second aspect of reflective oversight is epistemic ambition. What we mean by this is that you don't take your current guiding conception to be a fail-safe guide to the nature of the topic you're thinking about. As a rational epistemic agent, you have an interest in keeping track of genuinely interesting and relevant features of the world, as opposed to mere ontological shadows of your current guiding conception. For instance, you could discover that Trump is not in fact an ordinary empirical object – perhaps Trump is just a fictional character played by multiple actors. Although this type of radical revision in guiding conceptions is rare, it is in principle justifiable on the basis of your prior epistemic ambition and the actual empirical history of your filing tradition. This radical corrigibility of your guiding conception reflects your implicit commitment to representing objective features of the world rather than projections of your current categorizing criteria.[5]

This commitment to objective representation is also manifest in the third feature we highlighted, Reinterpretation. When you 'read back' your revised understanding of Trump as giving the content of your past thoughts (and those of others), you're implicitly treating earlier divergent conceptions as *mistaken*. That is, you take your current understanding to be a correct characterization of the very same topic you and others were thinking about all along.

By itself, a disposition to treat your past self (and others in your filing tradition) as mistaken about a topic does not entail a commitment to stable representational purport. It could just be a manifestation of 'bad manners' – foisting your current standards onto others without regard for what's relevant from their point of view. In fact, some theorists suggest our linguistic practice with 'tasty' is governed by a convention mandating this type of bad manners: individuals rely on their own current standards of taste to claim that anyone with different standards have false beliefs about what's tasty (Kölbel 2002; MacFarlane 2014). The proposed 'bad manners' convention for 'tasty' would coordinate expectations about how to express gustatory preferences, without committing participants to a property with stable instantiation conditions picked out by all uses of the expression. The practice is thus like the one we imagined for 'being it': there's interpersonal coordination without representational purport.

The hallmark of objective representational purport here is not reinterpretation per se, but the epistemic norms that govern reinterpretation. The substantive understanding that you 'read back' must be justifiable to other perspectives within your tradition. Holding your reinterpretations to mutually justifiable epistemic standards indicates that you're treating your filing tradition as representing stable, intersubjectively relevant features of the world. This standard of mutual justifiability is met in our practice with proper names. To be warranted, a conclusion that Trump is in fact a fictional character played by multiple actors can't simply rest on an idiosyncractic taste for conspiracy theories rejected by others. Both the empirical facts and shared background interests that have sustained your filing tradition are relevant to determining whether such conclusions are warranted. In general, our judgments about the falsity of our prior conception are backed by a commitment to finding a mutually justifiable interpretation of the semantic content of 'Trump' judgments.

In sum, we have suggested that the representational purport of our mental filing system for ordinary objects is *richly grounded in the thinker's own perspective*. Together, the three key features of this system – (1) long-term binding, (2) epistemic oversight, and (3) reinterpretation – allow the thinker to gather information about individual objects, whose essential nature she may not fully understand, and to correct mistakes about their nature and history. Long-term binding allows for outward-directed accumulation of information about a stable topic over time. Epistemic oversight and reinterpretation seek to refine our current understanding of the topic while holding ourselves and others to mutually justifiable standards of correctness. This process of self-regulation is organized around an implicit 'guiding conception', which places substantive coherence requirements on the subject's understanding of the topic. Epistemic ambition and mutual justifiability aim to refine the thinker's current understanding to arrive at a coherent understanding of objective features that are relevant to shared background interests. These more holistic epistemic standards can justify revisions to one's current guiding conception. Overall, the core features (1) – (3) ground the *objective representational purport* of our mental filing system for ordinary objects: they manifest our internal efforts to keep track of objective features of the environment that are relevant to our projects and purposes.

Singular thought is the parade case for motivating and explaining how our practices in managing a mental filing system can ground objective representational purport. But we find similar practices with other topics that we keep track of and learn about. Natural kinds like being a horse and artifact kinds like being a moped are clear cases in point. The way we think about these kinds requires a filing system that respects the same three key features we identified as grounding representational purport in the case of our conceptual representation of objects – long-term binding, epistemic oversight, and reinterpretation of a shared mental filing tradition.

We have stable bodies of standing attitudes and cognitive dispositions about topics like horses or mopeds, which we use to identify new instances of the kind and to learn more about that kind. So we must have mental files that bind and store these persisting informational states *as* pertaining to the same topic. Moreover, this mental filing system must afford long-term binding and storage if it's to underwrite learning about the kind.

As a consequence of this open-ended learning, we need to exercise epistemic oversight to ensure the coherence and relevance of the substantive understanding in the mental file. A crucial distinction between our ways of keeping track of objects and our ways of keeping track of kinds lies in our guiding conception of the topic. Unlike our conception of individual objects, our guiding conception of kinds does not require spatiotemporal continuity among instantiations of the kind. Files that purport to keep track of kinds are governed by the presumption of *coherent instantiation conditions*. One important aspect of coherence is formal consistency: we take kinds to capture a dimension of empirical similarity shared by all instances that ensures that our file does not cross-classify cases as both in and out of the kind.

A more substantive type of coherence, however, involves a guiding conception of the specific kind in question. For instance, there's an important distinction between our guiding conception of natural as opposed to artifact kinds. Consider your [horse] file: the bundle of attitudes and dispositions grouped together involves a presumption that horses form something like a *biological species*: e.g. you implicitly assume that horses don't just share similar surface appearances but share similar biological characteristics such as characteristic modes of nutrition and reproduction, that there is some 'hidden essence' that explains these similarities and is passed on through reproduction, that kind membership supports induction to unobserved horses, that being a horse excludes being a member of other biological species (e.g. no horse is a donkey), and that being a horse figures in a hierarchical taxonomy of biological kinds (e.g. horses are grouped together with donkeys and zebras as all belonging to a higher-order biological kind (*equus*), there are distinct subspecies or breeds of horse) (cf. Bird and Tobin 2017).[6] In contrast, your mental file for mopeds is governed by a presumption that they are created by humans to function in a certain way in order to serve certain human purposes. You implicitly assume that mopeds are small two-wheeled vehicles designed for short city transport, that they have a characteristic profile that distinguishes them from related vehicles (such as cars, motorcycles and bicycles), that kinds of vehicle aren't exhaustive or mutually exclusive (there can be an intermediate case between mopeds and motorcycle, or hybrid moped/jetskis), that there's no intrinsic 'hidden essence' to mopeds – their classification depends on what they can do and what they were intended to do. These initial guiding conceptions of natural and artifacts kinds, however, can be rationally refined or rejected in the light of empirical discoveries. We could discover that the things we've been classifying as horses are really artifacts controlled by Martians, and the things we've been classifying as mopeds are really the Martians themselves. In that case, we would have good reason to revise our guiding conceptions of our two filing practices.

When we do revise our initial conceptions in the light of further reflection or empirical discoveries, we 'read back' our revised conception as giving the real content of the thoughts in our mental filing tradition. As in the case of our thoughts about ordinary objects, this sort of reinterpretation is epistemically warranted insofar as it vindicates our prior epistemic ambition: all along, we took ourselves to be keeping track of features that are genuinely important and relevant to justifying our shared filing tradition – not just projections of our current conceptions.

Together, these core features ground the objective representational purport of our mental filing system for natural and artifact kinds: our filing practices of accumulating and managing information reflect an implicit effort to keep track of stable features of the world that are relevant to our shared background interests.

5. Representational purport in the normative case

We keep track of normative properties like being morally right in thought in much the same ways that we keep track of paradigm representational topics like objects, natural kinds and artifact kinds. Over time we acquire and store a wide variety of attitudes and dispositions *as* pertaining to the topic of moral rightness: commitments about particular empirical cases, rules of thumb about what sort of features make an action morally right, procedures for adjudicating hard cases, assumptions about when one's own moral judgments may be unreliable, criteria for deciding which moral testimony is most trustworthy, theoretical assumptions about the metaphysical character of moral rightness, and so on. The public language term 'morally right' helps to bind this evolving bundle of attitudes and dispositions with those of others in our community, presenting them *as* pertaining to the same topic. Thus our shared mental filing tradition grounds long-term accumulation, storage and binding of information *as* about the property of morally rightness. As in the case of paradigm representational concepts, moreover, we exercise reflective epistemic oversight to maintain the coherence and relevance of the bound information, and we rely on our revised understanding to reinterpret the semantic content of all attitudes in our filing tradition. So the concept expressed by 'morally right' seems to fit the pattern we've identified as grounding representational purport in uncontroversial cases.

We take it to be uncontroversial that our concept of moral rightness conforms to this general pattern. And the fact that we accumulate information *as* about this topic over time provides support for the objective representational purport of our filing practice. But there may be room to worry about the reflective standards of coherence governing normative concepts. As we saw in the case of 'being it' and 'tasty', purely formal coherence and reinterpretation norms don't suffice to ground representational purport. The keys to objective representational purport at the reflective level, we suggested, are: (i) the substantive guiding conception of the topic and (ii) the epistemic ambition to track important and relevant features of the world. These two features shape our practices of reflective epistemic oversight and reinterpretation of other attitudes in our filing tradition. Without the right kind of representational discipline at the level of reflective epistemic practices, your filing practices may fall short of objective representational purport. For instance, your concept of moral rightness might just a case of 'bad manners' – using your current evolving moral standards to evaluate others irrespective of their epistemic perspectives.

However, our reflective epistemic practices do not support this interpretation of normative topics like moral rightness. Our guiding conception of moral rightness is representational in much the same ways as our guiding conceptions of objects, natural kinds or artifact kinds. A guiding conception functions as a mental model of the topic that (i) guides one's inductive practices of learning and generalizing from one case to the next and (ii) determines one's substantive standards for coherence and incoherence for the topic. It's clear that we have a rough implicit guiding conception of moral rightness. We take moral rightness to be a property of actions, agents and circumstances that supervenes on non-normative descriptive properties. Roughly, morally rightness is supposed to distinguish actions that respect the practical interests and concerns of affected parties, while weighing everyone's interests equally. Like our guiding conceptions of natural or artifact kinds, our guiding conception of normative properties seeks to identify a *stable* principle of categorization, which determines a coherent intension across all possible worlds. The intension should not cross-classify cases and *it should not vary from one episode of thought to another*. Moreover, moral rightness demarcates a genuine pattern of empirical similarity: we are able to recognize the instantiation of moral rightness on the basis of ordinary empirical facts, and this empirical recognition capacity can be projected to new cases.[7]

In addition, our reflective moral epistemology evinces the epistemic ambition to identify a genuinely important and relevant property – rather than a mere projection of our current patterns of moral understanding. We take our current conception of moral rightness to be corrigible in the light of further inquiry and reflection – not just with respect to particular cases but also with respect to general principles and even aspects of our initial guiding conception. One important impetus for such corrections is an effort to reconcile different aspects of our moral understanding through narrow reflective equilibrium: for instance, we may realize that we have been classifying similar cases differently or that our moral rules of thumb conflict. Another impetus can come from new empirical information about our psychology or our circumstances: for instance, we may come to appreciate the harms others experience from our 'jokes' or we might become convinced of the existence of a moral law-giving deity. A third impetus for correcting our guiding conception comes from reflecting on facts about our shared filing tradition. For instance, learning that others in our filing tradition assume moral rightness takes into account the interests of animals as well as humans may lead us to adjust our own conception accordingly. Or more radically, learning of the role judgments of moral rightness have played in reinforcing social hierarchies over time might justify the conclusion that moral rightness marks conventional social norms for reinforcing elite social status. These examples are intended to illustrate the ways that we take our guiding conception of moral rightness to be corrigible via holistic reflection on our filing tradition and the empirical circumstances in which it developed. This openness to correction is an indication that we take moral rightness, like paradigm representational topics, to be an objectively relevant feature of the world, and not merely a projection of our current criteria.

We'd like to emphasize that the notion of *representational purport* at stake here is a robust one. We're not simply claiming that it's appropriate for participants in the filing tradition to *speak as if* there were a stable property picked out by that tradition. We're claiming that participants are committed to there *actually being* a single stable property picked out. In thinking about moral rightness, our reflective epistemic oversight seeks a single intension that can be justified from all different perspectives within one's filing tradition and determines the intension of the tradition as a whole. In short, we are actively looking for a single, univocal intension in refining our understanding of moral rightness through wide reflective equilibrium. This stable representational purport clashes with contextualist, truth-relativist, inferentialist, and pragmatist interpretations of our concept of moral rightness. Perhaps these non-representational semantic interpretations can be supported on other grounds – but they fail to capture the internal epistemic perspective of conceptually competent thinkers.

A second clarification concerns the properties normative concepts purport to represent. The mere fact that a concept has representational purport does not entail that the feature represented enjoys a privileged metaphysical status. Consider your concept of being a moped: the represented kind doesn't play any deep role in scientific explanation and it is not metaphysically fundamental. Nonetheless, being a moped is an objective feature of the world: it's not a mere projection of your current criterion for recognizing mopeds. Instead, your conception is corrigible in the light of further information about what's important and relevant to your shared filing tradition. *Mutatis mutandis* for your concept of morally right.

We'd like to end this section with a *caveat*. Although we think that many normative concepts have objective representational purport (e.g. our concepts of morally right, all-told right and practical reason), we do not claim this is true of all normative concepts. In particular, many of the concepts expressed by 'ought' seem to lack such representational purport. Epistemic modals are a case in point: as many theorists have pointed out, there is no pressure to find a single context-invariant intension for claims about what one ought to believe.

The representational purport of normative concepts must be established on a case-by-case basis.[8]

6. Conclusion

Our claim is that from the subjective perspective of thinkers themselves, core normative concepts have objective representational purport. Like our concepts for objects and kinds, our normative concepts purport to stably represent features of the world whose instantiation conditions do not depend on idiosyncratic psychological facts about the individual thinkers deploying the concept. We have sought to show how this sort of representational purport is grounded in our practices for keeping track of a topic *as the same* over time and between individuals. More specifically, we argued that three epistemic practices are distinctive of objective representational purport in reflective creatures like ourselves. First, we have long-term binding mechanisms, which accumulate and store new information *as* pertaining to the same topic. Second, we exercise reflective epistemic oversight over these evolving bodies of information, which involves both a guiding conception that determines a stable intension and epistemic ambition to home in on a relevant feature of the world. Third, we reinterpret the content of appropriately linked thoughts via this revised substantive conception of the topic. These conceptual practices are best interpreted as an effort to keep track of objective features of the world, such as objects, kinds or properties.

Our argumentative strategy contrasts with other types of argument in favor of the representational purport of normative concepts. First, our argument does not rest on an appeal to purely linguistic data about our use of certain terms. Our primary focus is at the level of thought and we seek to analyze the cognitive structures and practices that shape our ways of thinking about particular topics as such. Second, our argument is not based purely on causal-explanatory considerations. There is a rationalizing element in our account: the best rationalizing interpretation of these conceptual practices attributes representational purport to them, even if one could provide a causal explanation of the regularities involved without mentioning representation. Third, our argument does not rest on a simple appeal to the cognitive phenomenology associated with representation or rational intuitions about direct cognitive access to objective facts. We seek to articulate the cognitive structures and epistemic practices that rationally explain these subjective appearances.

In closing, we'd like to emphasize the limitations of our thesis. Our aim has been to establish that from the thinker's perspective, many normative concepts purport to stably represent objective features of the world. But this representational purport is not guaranteed to succeed. It could still turn out that, as a matter of empirical fact, our representational ambitions for normative topics cannot be fulfilled – just as they could not be fulfilled for topics like witches or phlogiston or Zeus. So we don't take ourselves to have settled the semantic question of the content of normative concepts. However, if we are right about the representational purport of core normative concepts, rationalizing interpretation will seek to vindicate traditional context-invariant normative realism in the first instance. Anything less will fall short of thinkers' epistemic ambitions.[9]

Notes

1. For an overview of the literature on mental files see (Murez and Recanati 2016).
2. Schroeter (2007, 2008). Semantic interpretation seeks to partition an ambiguous tradition into two or more equivalence classes, each of which can be assigned a univocal interpretation.
3. Of course the attitudes and cognitive dispositions of others are not immediately available to govern your actions and reasoning. But just as standing attitudes are stored in the cognitive system in a way that codes for sameness of topic, the attitudes and dispositions of others in your linguistic community are stored in your epistemic community in a way that codes for sameness of topic. And their attitudes can be accessed via testimony and other forms of linguistic communication.
4. One might argue that visual indices have a representational function at a subpersonal level: perhaps they were *naturally selected* for providing information about particular objects or perhaps an analysis of their rational function in a cognitive system construes them as representing objects (cf. Burge 2010; Millikan 1984). Our point is simply that scientific stories of the proper function of subpersonal mechanisms do not justify attributing representational purport at the person level.
5. How can such revisions be justified by our past filing practices, if they are not grounded in a prior guiding conception? In a nutshell, our answer is that revisions are justified by rationalizing interpretation of the filing tradition as a whole. You step back from your current conception and ask which interests have been most important to justifying your filing practice with 'Trump' relative to your actual empirical circumstances. Have you succeeded in latching onto a communal tradition with that name? What interests are most central in justifying our shared interest in that tradition: that we keep track of an individual human being or that we keep track of a continuous character in a social drama? It's possible to imagine empirical circumstances where the latter answer would be more plausible. In that case, we would have empirical interpretive grounds for taking our initial guiding conception of Trump as an individual human being to be false (see Schroeter and Schroeter 2015 for more details).
6. Here again, this initial conception is defeasible: you may, for instance, discover that horses do not form a biological kind after all. It could turn out that horses are like wallabies or trees – superficial kinds demarcated by more parochial human interests that do not correspond to any deeper joints of nature.
7. The claim that normative rightness captures a dimension of empirical similarity does not establish classic naturalistic reductionism. First, empirical dimensions of similarity need not be finitely definable in the language of science. Just as there is little reason to suppose that the artifact kind chair can be finitely defined in terms of the causal-explanatory properties invoked in the natural sciences, there is little reason to suppose normative properties like moral rightness can be finitely defined in this way. Second, the idea that moral rightness demarcates a genuine empirical dimension of similarity is consistent with the core non-naturalist claim

that a further metaphysically non-natural property is constitutive of being morally right. Just as a psychological dualist claims that consciousness is not identical to the neurological property with which it is correlated (even necessarily correlated), a normative non-naturalist could claim that moral rightness is not identical to the empirical dimension of similarity which it picks out.
8. Of course, moral rightness claims can be expressed by 'ought' as well, and our understanding of moral rightness seems to mirror some modal commitments embodied in linguistic conventions governing 'ought'. But this does nothing to undermine the preceding argument for the objective representational purport of our concept of morally right, which is based on the conceptual practices that are specific to this topic. Rather, it shows that it's dangerous to theorize about the concepts expressed by 'ought' judgments purely on the basis of the linguistic conventions governing that term.
9. We'd like to thank audiences at the Vancouver conference on Representation and Evaluation and at a metaethics workshop at the Australian Catholic University for helpful feedback on earlier drafts. Special thanks to Matt Bedke, Matthew Chrisman, Garrett Cullity, Matthew Fulkerson, Josh Gert, Stefan Sciaraffa, and Nic Southwood.

Disclosure statement

No potential conflict of interest was reported by the authors.

References

Bird, Alexander, and Emma Tobin. 2017. "Natural Kinds." In *Stanford Encyclopedia of Philosophy*, edited by E. N. Zalta. https://plato.stanford.edu/archives/spr2017/entries/natural-kinds/.
Burge, Tyler. 1988. "Individualism and Self-Knowledge." *Journal of Philosophy* 85: 649–663.
Burge, Tyler. 2010. *Origins of Objectivity*. Oxford: Oxford University Press.
Byrne, Alex, and James Pryor. 2006. "Bad Intensions." In *Two-Dimensional Semantics: Foundations and Applications*, edited by M. Garcia-Carprintero and J. Macia, 38–54. Oxford: Oxford University Press.
Dickie, Imogen. 2010. "We Are Acquainted with Ordinary Things." In *New Essays on Singular Thought*, edited by Robin Jeshion, 213–245. Oxford: Oxford University Press.
Evans, Gareth. 1973. "The Causal Theory of Names." *Aristotelian Society Supplementary Volume* 47: 187–225.
Fine, Kit. 2007. *Semantic Relationism*. Oxford: Blackwell.
Kölbel, Max. 2002. *Truth without Objectivity*. London: Routledge.
Kripke, Saul. 1980. *Naming and Necessity*. Cambridge, MA: Harvard University Press.

MacFarlane, John. 2014. *Assessment Sensitivity*. Oxford: Oxford University Press.
Millikan, Ruth Garrett. 1984. *Language, Thought, and Other Biological Categories*. Cambridge, MA: MIT Press.
Murez, Michael, and François Recanati. 2016. "Mental Files: An Introduction." *Review of Philosophy and Psychology* 7: 265–281.
Pinillos, N. Ángel. 2011. "Coreference and Meaning." *Philosophical Studies* 154: 301–324.
Putnam, Hilary. 1970. "Is Semantics Possible?" In *Language, Belief and Metaphysics*, edited by H.E. Kiefer and M.K. Munitz, 50–63. New York: SUNY Press.
Putnam, Hilary. 1973. "Meaning and Reference." *The Journal of Philosophy* 70: 699–711.
Pylyshyn, Zenon. 1989. "The Role of Location Indexes in Spatial Perception: A Sketch of the FINST Spatial-Index Model." *Cognition* 32: 65–97.
Pylyshyn, Zenon. 2007. *Things and Places: How the Mind Connects with the World*. Cambridge, MA: MIT Press.
Schroeter, Laura. 2007. "Illusion of Transparency." *Australasian Journal of Philosophy* 85: 597–618.
Schroeter, Laura. 2008. "Why Be an Anti-Individualist?" *Philosophy and Phenomenological Research* 77: 105–141.
Schroeter, Laura. 2012. "Bootstrapping Our Way to Samesaying." *Synthese* 189: 177–197.
Schroeter, Laura 2017. "Two Dimensional Semantics." In *Stanford Encyclopedia of Philosophy*, edited by E. N. Zalta. https://plato.stanford.edu/archives/sum2017/entries/two-dimensional-semantics/.
Schroeter, Laura, and François Schroeter. 2014. "Normative Concepts: A Connectedness Model." *Philosophers' Imprint* 14 (25): 1–26.
Schroeter, Laura, and François Schroeter. 2015. "Rationalizing Self-Interpretation." In *Palgrave Handbook of Philosophical Methods*, edited by Chris Daly, 419–447. Basingstoke: Palgrave Macmillan.
Stalnaker, Robert. 1990. "Narrow Content." In *Context and Content*. Oxford: Oxford University Press. Original edition, (C.A. Anderson and J. Owens, eds.) Propositional Attitudes. Stanford: CSLI.

OPEN ACCESS

Solving the problem of creeping minimalism

Matthew Simpson

ABSTRACT
In this paper I discuss the so-called problem of creeping minimalism, the problem of distinguishing metaethical expressivism from its rivals once expressivists start accepting minimalist theories about truth, representation, belief, and similar concepts. I argue that Dreier's 'explanation' explanation is almost correct, but by critically examining it we not only get a better solution, but also draw out some interesting results about expressivism and non-representationalist theories of meaning more generally.

1. Introduction

Since James Dreier (2004) introduced it, the so-called *problem of creeping minimalism* has threatened metaethical expressivism. The problem is that expressivism becomes indistinguishable from realism, its arch rival, once expressivists start accepting minimalist views of various concepts like truth, reference, representation, and belief. In this paper I argue that Dreier's own solution to the problem is nearly correct, but that by critically examining it several interesting points emerge. These concern not only metaethical expressivism, but some ideas which are common in the wider debate about theories which fall under labels like expressivism, but also pragmatism and non-representationalism, and have received increasing philosophical interest in recent years.[1]

After stating the problem, I explain Dreier's solution, according to which expressivists exclude ethical facts and properties from explaining ethical meaning, while realists do not. I use an objection from Chrisman (2008) to develop three important points:

This is an Open Access article distributed under the terms of the Creative Commons Attribution License (http://creativecommons.org/licenses/by/4.0/), which permits unrestricted use, distribution, and reproduction in any medium, provided the original work is properly cited.

(1) The problem should be recast: we should distinguish expressivism from *representationalism* not realism.
(2) We should not assume too much about the ontology involved in representation.
(3) We should focus on explanation in order to solve the problem.

I then offer an alternative solution. While Dreier rightly focuses on explanation, instead of focusing on ethical facts and properties we need merely say that expressivists are distinctive in excluding representation from their explanation of ethical language and thought, as well as things that could plausibly reduce representation. Doing so is enough to protect expressivism from the problem of creeping minimalism.

I then use this solution to illuminate other solutions to the problem, and further questions about expressivism and non-representational theories of meaning more generally. I argue that given my three key points, we can answer Christine Tiefensee's (2016) worrying argument that even the most central philosophical resources of three prominent writers – Chrisman, Michael Williams, and Huw Price – cannot solve the problem. I show that these views survive Tiefensee's objections; they also give us an especially interesting insight into Price's notion of e-*representation*. These conclusions are valuable not only for understanding metaethical expressivism, but for understanding concepts from the debate about non-representationalist theories of meaning in general, a debate in which Chrisman, Williams, and Price are all engaged. Finally I answer some lurking objections to the solution, concerning the impact of minimalism.

2. The problem

The problem of creeping minimalism is that once expressivists accept minimalism about various notions including truth, reference, belief, and representation, it's hard to distinguish their view from their supposed rival, realism. The problem develops like this. The most distinctive expressivist view is that ethical language and thought differs from other kinds in an interesting way: it is in some way a different *kind* of thing to other kinds of thought and language. Expressivists have characterised this difference in various ways. They have said that ethical language is not truth-apt or descriptive; it does not express propositions, state facts, or refer to properties; ethical thoughts are not beliefs, or else they are not *representational* beliefs. This contrasts both with realism, which denies all of these claims, and with what expressivists might think about other kinds of language, such as the language we use to describe ordinary objects in our surroundings.

The problem of creeping minimalism arises because expressivists now accept so-called *minimalist* views which collapse any distinctions drawn in these terms.[2] Briefly, such views entail that even by expressivists' own standards, ethical language and thought does have the features listed in the previous paragraph. Roughly, minimalism about truth, representation, and other similar features entails that if a given sentence or thought has content that can be stated using a 'that'-clause, then it has the full range of those features. So since expressivists accept that a sentence like 'stealing is bad' means that stealing is bad, and that the corresponding thought is the thought that stealing is bad, if they also accept minimalism they will accept that 'stealing is bad' has the relevant range of features. The sentence expresses a proposition, namely the proposition *that stealing is bad*; it describes or represents stealing as bad; it is true iff stealing is bad and is therefore truth-apt; it expresses the belief that stealing is bad; it ascribes the property *badness* to stealing; if stealing is bad it expresses or states a truth or fact, namely the truth or fact that stealing is bad, and if this is so then we can say the property *badness* exists.

As Dreier notes (2004, 25), minimalism is attractive to expressivists because it allows expressivists to accommodate ordinary ethical practice, which involves talk about truth, knowledge, description and representation.[3] Expressivists think that minimalism lets them straightforwardly explain these practices, once we've explained what it is to make an ethical assertion.

The problem of creeping minimalism is that expressivists seem committed to minimalism about *all* the features which they may previously have denied apply to ethical language and thought. It is therefore difficult to distinguish between expressivism-plus-minimalism and realism. We can see this in action in particular in recent work by Simon Blackburn. On minimalist grounds, Blackburn accepts that there are ethical truths and propositions, that such things represent ethical facts (Blackburn 1998, 79), that such truths and facts can be mind-independent (Blackburn 1998, 311–312), and that ethical thoughts are beliefs (Blackburn 2010, 4). To see how far Blackburn takes this idea, note how in a recent paper, he explicitly accepts the three defining theses of Richard Boyd's moral realism (Boyd 1988), exactly as Boyd states them, saying: 'I agree to all these claims' (Blackburn 2015, 843). So, the problem of creeping minimalism goes, what is the difference between Blackburn and Boyd, between expressivism and realism, once expressivism goes minimalist? Not everybody agrees on who is affected by this problem – which philosophical view suffers if the problem remains unsolved. Some think it is a problem for expressivism; others, including Dreier (2004, 31), think it is a problem for metaethicists, of making sense of the different views on offer. Some think that it is a problem for realism; for instance Blackburn sometimes claims that given minimalism, realism loses its content (1998, 294–298). I will remain neutral on this. It's also important to note that there are two distinct aspects to the problem of creeping minimalism. One is distinguishing expressivism from its rivals. The other is making sure we do so in a way that lets expressivism keep its purported epistemological and metaphysical advantages over its rivals (see Chrisman 2008, 347). In this paper I am concerned only with the first element; the other is much more difficult.

3. The 'explanation' explanation

In his (2004), Dreier suggests a solution, which he calls the 'explanation' explanation (2004, 39). This solution distinguishes expressivism and realism by their stance not on what features ethical language and thought has, but what features *explain its content*. The 'explanation' explanation says that the difference between expressivism and realism concerns what those views say about the proper *explanation* of certain target statements, which Dreier calls 'protected normative statements' (2004, 34), like:

(E) Edith said that abortion is wrong

(J) Judith believes that knowledge is intrinsically good

He argues that expressivism and realism disagree about what constitutes the truth of statements like these – what it is in virtue of which they are true. Realists and expressivists will therefore differ over how to fill in the blank in statements like:

(E*) Its being the case that (E) consists in nothing more than _____

(J*) Its being the case that (J) consists in nothing more than _____

This is the first stage of the 'explanation' explanation: expressivists and realists differ over what will (constitutively) explain protected normative statements. Since protected normative statements are just those ascribing normative content to utterances or thought, Dreier's view is that expressivists and realists differ over what constitutively explains the meaning of ethical words – what constitutively explains the fact that words like 'good' and 'wrong' mean what they do.

Dreier then says how expressivists and realists differ over explanations of ethical meaning. On his view, realists think that what fills in the blank in claims like (*E**) and (*J**) must involve ethical facts or properties, and expressivists will disagree:

> In particular, [says the expressivist,] to explain what it is to make a moral judgment, we need not mention any normative properties. (Dreier 2004, 39)

On the other hand, a realist thinks that to explain what it is to make a moral judgement, we need to cite ethical facts or properties to which the believer is related in some way. This is the second stage of the 'explanation' explanation: expressivists and realists disagree about whether normative facts and properties are needed to explain the fact that terms like 'good' and 'wrong' have normative content.

In sum: for expressivists, an ethical sentence like 'abortion is wrong' describes abortion as wrong, expresses a belief, states a truth, and so on, but it is not *because* it does any of this that it means what it does. Similarly, a belief that abortion is wrong represents abortion as wrong, and is true iff abortion is wrong, but it is not *because* of this that it has the content *that abortion is wrong*. All those features for which expressivists accept minimalism still apply to ethical language and thought, but they play no role in explaining why it means what it does. Realists, on the other hand, will disagree with this: the fact that ethical language and thought means what it does *is* to be constitutively explained in terms of such things.[4]

This looks promising. Expressivists clearly aim to explain ethical language by saying that it expresses distinctive mental states which can be characterised entirely in terms of the effect they have on their possessor's behavioural and emotional profile, and which can be characterised without appealing to a moral reality to which these states are reactions. Expressivists often claim this as a distinctive advantage, with Blackburn arguing that his view needs 'no truck with the idea that we somehow respond to an autonomous realm of values: a metaphysical extra that we inexplicably care about on top of voicing and discussing our more humdrum concerns' (Blackburn 2010, 5). So initially it seems that the lack of appeal to ethical facts and properties is distinctive of expressivism.

Dreier's account is also supported by the literature. To support his specific focus on facts and properties, Dreier draws on Fine (2001), Gibbard (2003), and Price and O'Leary-Hawthorne (1996), but there are others in the debate who support it too. Blackburn argues that it is definitional of what he calls 'pragmatism' (which includes expressivism) that its explanation of the relevant language does not cite the ontology associated with it – the 'referents [of] its terms, or truth-makers [of] its sentences' (2013, 75). Michael Williams concurs, arguing that an expressivist explanation of ethical language will be 'ontologically conservative' (2013, 143), which just means that the explanation will not appeal to ethical facts and properties.[5] We will hear more from Price and Williams later.

The most important feature of Dreier's solution is that it neatly avoids the threat from minimalism. Expressivists can accept that there are ethical facts and properties on minimalist grounds while denying that such things are part of what explains ethical content. Believing in some facts or properties doesn't require accepting that they do any particular constitutive explanatory work. This shift to explanatory questions is what stops minimalism undermining Dreier's solution.

However, Chrisman (2008, 347–348) argues that when a belief is false, realists cannot say that what constitutes that belief is a relation between the believer and a fact. If the belief is false, there is no fact for the believer to be related to. Suppose Suzy believes that some given instance of torture *T* is permissible. Suppose *T* is in fact not permissible. No one will say that her belief consists in a relation with the fact that *T* is permissible, since no such fact exists. So realism cannot be identified as Dreier suggests, or else we could only be realists about true beliefs. This would be unacceptable, since a realist will think that the same story should be told for what explains the content of all ethical beliefs.

Chrisman then argues that Dreier can only avoid the false belief issue by appealing to representation: the realist will say that what constitutes Suzy's false belief is that she *represents T* as permissible. This is possible even though her belief is false, since thinkers can represent the world falsely. Expressivists can then deny that representation is part of what constitutes Suzy's belief, and we get our distinction.

However, Chrisman argues that this relies on a 'distinction between representational and nonrepresentational mental states' (2008, 348) which collapses given minimalism. The idea is that minimalism, in the same way as I described in Section 2, simply entails that ethical beliefs are representational, even by expressivists' own standards. It therefore collapses the distinction as drawn above.

4. Learning from the 'explanation' explanation

I think that Chrisman's objections both fail. Dreier's account does not collapse for the reason Chrisman offers, and a representation-based alternative does not collapse under minimalism. However, I think Chrisman's discussion raises some important and interesting issues concerning the problem of creeping minimalism.

I'm going to use my discussion of the above debate to argue for three claims. First, we have been conceiving of the problem of creeping minimalism in the wrong way. We should recast it, and then examine Dreier's view in light of this. Second, Dreier's solution focuses too much on the ontology of representation, and the best solution to the problem of creeping minimalism should not do so. Third, Dreier is right to focus on explanation, and doing so lets us refute Chrisman's second objection. After establishing these three points, I will argue for a solution which improves on Dreier's.

4.1. Three lessons

The first point is that we should recast the problem of creeping minimalism. We should aim to distinguish expressivism not from *realism*, but from *representationalism*. Representationalism says that ethical thought and language is best *explained* in terms of representation, that ethical thoughts are best explained as beliefs, and so on. Representationalism is not sufficient for realism. While realists typically accept representationalism, so do many non-realists. For example, error theorists are not realists, in the sense that they think there are no ethical truths or facts.[6] But they typically are representationalists: they think ethical thoughts are best explained as representational beliefs. Therefore, distinguishing expressivism from realism is not the right route: error theory differs from expressivism in exactly the same relevant respect as realism does, over whether ethical thought is belief-like and representational.[7]

This leads neatly on to the second point. We should not focus too much on the ontology invoked by representational accounts. Error theory gives us a nice route in to this point. Consider again Chrisman's first objection to Dreier: the belief that p cannot be constituted by a relation to the fact that p where it's false that *p*. A very natural reply to this is to point out that the realist will of course not think it is so constituted, but will instead say that Suzy's belief that *T* is permissible is composed of concepts, including the concept of permissibility. This concept represents things as permissible, and does so in virtue of a relation to the *property* of permissibility. This route saves Dreier from Chrisman's objection: it retains the explanatory role of ethical properties rather than ethical facts.

However, it is at the very least controversial whether all accounts of representation will take this form, of appealing to a relation with properties. Start with error theory. The property view I just outlined would commit error theorists to relations between thinkers and uninstantiated properties, perhaps necessarily uninstantiated properties. If representation means a relation with a property, since error theorists think such properties are not instantiated, they can at best say we bear relations to properties which exist but are uninstantiated. Not all error theorists would want to accept this.[8] So this is a drawback for Dreier's view, though it is not necessarily decisive.

However, error theory is just one tricky case: there is a much more general point here, namely that not all accounts of representation take the property or fact view Dreier discusses. There are plenty of representationalist views that do not. Consider a propositionalist view, which takes a belief that p to be explained in terms of the believer bearing the belief relation to the proposition ⟨*p*⟩. Some take propositions to be composed of senses or concepts, which don't require corresponding properties or entities. Such a view could treat my belief that something is F as explained by my bearing the belief relation to a particular proposition, yet it would not require my representing something as F to involve a relation between me and F-ness. Contrast this view with the expressivist, who doesn't think we have to appeal to a belief relation between me and the proposition ⟨stealing is bad⟩ in order to explain my belief.

Consider also views which say that we can believe things about non-existent objects. Le Verrier's beliefs about Vulcan are still representational in a way which expressivists think his beliefs about right and wrong are not. But it would be a stretch to think that we should account for his beliefs in terms of a relation with an existing object, since Vulcan doesn't exist. The same idea goes for uninstantiated properties. We all want to account for systematically false beliefs, for instance about magic or witches. Not everyone will want to accept uninstantiated properties *being magical* and *being a witch* to help us explain such beliefs. Finally, consider adverbialism about perception (Ducasse 1942; Chisholm 1957). Such a view says that to see something red is to see red-ly, not to bear a relation with redness. Yet this view is still clearly representationalist: this view will accept that seeing red is best explained as representing something as red.

So this is our second point: we should not commit the representationalist to a specific ontological view in order to account for representation. For any proposed ontology, there are plenty of representationalists that will reject it. And we should not rule out any particular representationalist views just to solve the problem of creeping minimalism, a problem, as Dreier says, in 'metametaethics' (Dreier 2004, 31)! This point has been obscured because of the focus on distinguishing expressivism from realism specifically, rather than from representationalism.

As such, it might seem that the best route is to say this: expressivists deny that ethical language is best explained in terms of its being representational, while representationalists affirm that it is. We then decline to say anything more specific about what representation is. Before exploring this idea and suggesting an even better alternative, recall Chrisman's second objection: isn't this proposal hopeless, since expressivists won't deny that ethical language is representational, and indeed *can't* deny it if minimalism is true?

No. The whole point of Dreier's account is that what matters is not what features expressivists think ethical language and thought *has*, but which of those features *explain* the fact that ethical language mean what it does.[9] It is not what features words like 'good' and 'permissible' have, but which of their features explain the fact that they mean *good* and *permissible*. Minimalism does not imply that the content of ethical language and thought is to be constitutively explained in terms of representation. It only implies that it is representational, in the sense that ethical language and thought can be said to represent the world. Though minimalism implies that ethical thought and language is representational, it does not imply that this fact helps to explain the protected statements Dreier identifies. Its being representational does not help to explain its meaning. So Chrisman's objection completely misses Dreier's crucial manoeuvre: the shift to explanation.

4.2. A better account

So, we should be distinguishing expressivism from representationalism rather than realism, and we should remember that the key way to do so is to read the two views in explanatory terms. Representationalists think that ethical language and thought needs to be treated as representational to be properly explained; expressivists do not. However, we should also not assume too much about the ontological commitments of a representationalist view. What, then, should we say about creeping minimalism?

The first thing to do is to make a defensive point. By adopting Dreier's explanatory focus, expressivists can defend themselves from the threat of minimalism. Minimalism was a threat because it seemed to undermine the expressivist's negative view: she can no longer say that ethical language is not representational. This threat has disappeared now: even if she has to say ethical language is representational in that it represents the world, she can deny that we should *explain* it in terms of representation. This shift to explanation neatly resolves the problem of creeping minimalism: minimalism no longer collapses the expressivist's view into representationalism.

However, at this point we might ask more about what representationalism comes to. So far I've characterised it as the view that representation is required to properly explain ethical language and thought. But this is only a first step. For starters, how do we classify accounts which don't use words like 'representation' (or 'belief' and 'description') in their theory? For instance, a reductionist view, perhaps one which reduces an ethical belief to a causal tracking state, would not mention representation in its explanation of ethical thought, yet would still clearly count as representational. More generally, on the above view, expressivism only seems to oppose those accounts which use representation as a primitive – as an unexplained explainer.[10]

The best response to this objection is that we need simply understand the expressivist's ban on explanatory roles for representation and belief as including anything which might plausibly serve as a reduction base for those things.[11] So the reductionist view above rests on the idea that causal tracking *is* representation; her explanatory chain goes:

w means *good* ← *w* represents things as good ← *w* tracks goodness

(where *w* is just a word.) The expressivist will not accept this. Representation is itself trivially entailed by *w*'s meaning *good*, which is directly explained in terms of attitudes:

w represents things as good ← *w* means *good* ← basic sentences involving *w* express intentions, plans, attitudes ...

This captures the idea that representationalists are reducing representation, while expressivists are not putting it in any explanatory capacity at all.

So, to conclude: Dreier's account is right in its basic approach, but it faces two issues. It wrongly tries to distinguish expressivism from realism rather than from representationalism, and it attributes too much of an ontological commitment to representationalist views, perhaps because its focus is more on realism.[12]

Instead we should step back, and argue that while expressivists must accept that ethical thoughts are beliefs and that they represent the world, as do ethical assertions, they need not say this in their explanation of what gives ethical thought and language its content. Expressivists say that the content of ethical thoughts and beliefs is not to be explained in terms of representation or any plausible reduction base for it. This is completely compatible with minimalism.

5. Other accounts

In my view, this alteration of Dreier's original solution distinguishes expressivism not merely from realists but representationalists in general, and does not collapse given minimalism. However, before we look at some potential issues with the new solution, it is worth applying some points from Section 4 to other work on the problem of creeping minimalism. I will examine Christine Tiefensee's arguments against three solutions to the problem. One of these solutions is

Chrisman's. The other two use two concepts recently developed by two prominent non-representationalists: Michael Williams's notion of an 'EMU' (an explanation of meaning in terms of use) and Huw Price's notion of 'e-representation'. Tiefensee argues that none of these solutions works.

Tiefensee's arguments are worth discussing for two reasons. First, her pessimistic conclusion is cause for concern: if even the sophisticated non-representationalist machinery recently set out by Chrisman, Williams and Price cannot solve the problem of creeping minimalism, we might well worry that no solution is likely to emerge soon. Second, it turns out that every key point in Tiefensee's critique can be answered by using two of the ideas I defended above: (1) by not focusing on the ontology of representation and belief, and (2) by recognising the importance of *explanation*.

5.1. Chrisman's inferentialism

With this in mind let's look at Chrisman's idea. On the basis of his criticism of Dreier, Chrisman rejects representation-based approaches to the problem of creeping minimalism. Instead he thinks we should replace representation with *inference* as the central tool for understanding expressivism (Chrisman 2008, 335). On an inferentialist view, the meaning of a sentence is constituted by its inferential role, which Chrisman takes to consist in two things: (1) what circumstances license asserting the sentence and (2) what further assertions and actions are licensed by asserting the sentence (2008, 350).

Chrisman argues that realists think ethical terms play a role in *theoretical* reasoning, whose premises give 'evidential support' to the conclusion which if true 'will usually constitute theoretical knowledge about the world' (2008, 350). Expressivists, on the other hand, will play a role in *practical* reasoning, whose premises 'provide *practical* support for the conclusion' which if true 'can constitute practical knowledge about how to interact with the world as we know it to be' (2008, 349–350, original emphasis). As such, realists and expressivists differ in that the former take ethical commitments to be theoretical, while the latter take them to be practical.[13]

However, Christine Tiefensee (2016) forcefully criticises Chrisman's account, arguing that it is just as vulnerable to creeping minimalism as other approaches. She focuses her initial objection on the distinction between practical and theoretical commitments. Consider the claim that ethical statements express theoretical commitments. According to Chrisman, this means that they express commitments which if true will constitute theoretical knowledge about the world. But Tiefensee argues that given the right minimalist theories, the expressivist will accept that ethical commitments are theoretical: given minimalism about 'true', and 'world', she says, there's no reason for expressivism to reject that true ethical commitments can constitute ethical knowledge about the world (Tiefensee 2016, 2443).

I think Tiefensee is absolutely right that expressivists can accept a minimalist version of the claim that ethical commitments are theoretical commitments. However, as with Dreier, Chrisman can reply by turning to explanation. He shouldn't say that for expressivists, ethical commitments are not theoretical. He should say that for expressivists, the fact that they are theoretical has no role in explaining them. A sentence like 'torture is wrong' has its meaning *because* it is practical, not because it is theoretical. It means what it does *because* it gives practical support for conclusions based on it as a premise. But it is still theoretical: it still gives evidential support to the conclusion, and when true it constitutes knowledge about the world. It's just that this fact plays no explanatory role whatsoever. As with Chrisman's objection to Dreier, Tiefensee's objection can be avoided with more of a focus on explanation. This isn't to say his solution is correct, just that it can avoid Tiefensee's objection.

5.2. The EMU

Michael Williams (2013) claims that the notion of an EMU – an Explanation of Meaning in terms of Use – is a good way of understanding expressivism about ethical language as well as distinguishing between non-representationalism and representationalism more generally. According to him, an EMU has three components, which I will characterise exactly as Tiefensee does (Tiefensee 2016, 2448)

(I–T) A material-inferential (intra-linguistic) component, comprising the inferential patterns in which a concept stands, thus determining its conceptual meaning.

(E–T) An epistemological component, specifying the epistemological circumstances of competent language use.

(F–T) A functional component, detailing what the concept is used for.

(I–T) is meant to specify the inferential role of a term. For instance, part of the (I–T) clause for a colour-word like 'red' will specify inferential connections between that word and other colour terms: from 'x is red' you can infer 'x is coloured', from 'x is scarlet' you can infer 'x is red', and so on. (E–T) is meant to specify the circumstances under which a speaker is licensed to make assertions using the term; for instance part of (E–T) for 'red' will specify that a speaker can use 'red' only to apply to objects which are clearly red. (F–T) is meant to tell us why we have a term of which (I–T) and (E–T) are true (Williams 2013, 135). Williams says: 'The F-clause appeals to use as expressive function: what a word is used to do, what it is useful for' (Williams 2013, 135).

Tiefensee then suggests that we could try to distinguish realism and expressivism by saying that a realist EMU will differ from an expressivist one. She sets out two EMUs which follow the above pattern, and points out where they match and where they differ. For our purposes, the crucial point is that Tiefensee thinks the difference between expressivism and realism will come down to what these views say about *tracking*. Tiefensee considers the following claim: (Tiefensee 2016, 2449, my emphasis):

(1) In a reporting use, tokens of 'x is good' express *reliable discriminative reactions* to an environmental circumstance. Their role is to keep track of goodness, in this way functioning as language entry transitions.

What this roughly means is that ethical statements express beliefs which *track* ethical properties, perhaps in the same way that we think our language about our environment tracks the objects in it.

Tiefensee argues that expressivists can accept a suitably minimalist reading of (1). On this reading the idea that ethical statements 'track the moral truth' is just the idea that some ethical statements are true, and some people are good enough that they assert more or less *only* the moral truths, and that their moral statements are counterfactually responsive to the moral truth so that, for example, *if* x had been good, they would have said that x was good, and if it had not been, they would not have said so. On this minimalist reading of tracking, an ethical truth-tracker is the person who gets the ethical truths right, and who wouldn't easily have got them wrong. Since we're assuming that expressivists can make sense of 'getting the ethical truths right', and can evaluate counterfactuals involving ethical statements, they will not deny that ethical statements track the truth in this sense.

So, Tiefensee concludes, focusing on the notion of tracking as Williams does will not distinguish expressivism and realism, because expressivists will end up asserting the same things as the realist. And though Tiefensee does not explicitly say so in this passage, this is because of a minimalist reading of 'truth-tracking', which Tiefensee calls 'i-tracking' due to its link with Price's 'i-representation', a concept we'll discuss shortly.

5.3. E-representation

Tiefensee argues that as a result of this, the only way to get a distinction between expressivism and realism is to understand the notion of tracking in (1) as 'e-tracking', which we can make sense of in terms of Huw Price's distinction between what he calls 'e-representation' and 'i-representation'. Roughly, e-representation is a causal relation between terms and their environment, while i-representation is a feature emerging from relations between terms, including inferential and causal relations (see Price 2013, 36 for a fuller explanation). As such, a term e-represents if it tracks things in world. A term i-represents if it has the inferential role required to give it assertoric content. We can then read the notion of 'e-tracking' in terms of e-representation, taking the two to be more or less the same idea.

Crucially, a term can i-represent without e-representing: a term can be used in assertions, without having the job of tracking the world. Expressivists think that ethical terms are i-representational but not e-representational. We might distinguish them on this basis from realists, who think that ethical terms are both i- and e-representational. This is just the same as saying that expressivists deny, but realists accept, that ethical terms e-track the world

Tiefensee argues that we need to explain e-representation in more detail, but that the only substantial way of doing so faces a dilemma: it yields either a characterisation of realism which expressivists can accept (thus failing to yield a distinction) or else one which realists won't themselves accept.[14] Tiefensee argues that on the best way of cashing out the notion of e-representation (and thereby, e-tracking) ethical language is e-representational just in case it has two features: (i) 'reports of the presence of goodness must be caused by goodness' and (ii) such reports 'must be default justified', i.e. 'do not require inferential support from other premises' (Tiefensee 2016, 2454). However, many realists will wish to deny (ii). Moreover, there are two readings of (i), one of which realists will reject, the other of which expressivists will accept. Either way, we don't get a distinction between expressivism and realism.

Nothing in my argument will depend on whether ethical sentences are 'default justified' so instead I shall focus on claim (i), that reports of the presence of goodness must be caused by goodness. Tiefensee begins by pointing out that non-naturalist realists, who believe in the causal inefficacy of ethical facts and properties, will reject (i). I think this is sufficient reason to reject this reading, since it fails to account for one of the two major forms of realism. However she goes on to make a further point. She argues that there are two readings of (i), the strong reading and the weak reading. On the strong reading, (i) says that 'moral properties are themselves causally efficacious and that we perceive them through a special, sensory moral faculty' (Tiefensee 2016, 2454). While expressivists will indeed deny that moral properties are like this, and therefore will deny (i) on its strong reading, Tiefensee points out that many realists will also reject (i) due to scepticism about the notion of a special sensory moral faculty. The strong reading, then, fails to be acceptable to realists, and so cannot be a necessary component of realism.

On the other hand, when read weakly, (i) seems more moderate: it says that goodness can cause reports about goodness by being identical to a natural property or properties which do all the causal work. So 'whenever we detect a causally efficacious natural property that constitutes a moral property ... we also perceive the corresponding moral property' (Tiefensee 2016, 2455). This seems more acceptable to realists. However, Tiefensee argues, it will also be acceptable to expressivists, for the following reason.

The weak reading of (i), says Tiefensee, depends on the idea that moral properties are, 'in some sense or other, nothing over and above natural properties such as causing pain' (Tiefensee 2016, 2455). Expressivists, she says, can make that claim too, though for them it will be understood as the expression of an ethical claim, about what wrongness consists in (e.g. causing pain). But if this is so, she argues, then since wrongness just is some natural property, then if those natural properties cause our ethical utterances, then it follows that ethical properties cause our ethical utterances. And so expressivists will be happy to accept (i) on the weak reading.

Tiefensee concludes that e-representation, as cashed out via (i) and (ii), cannot give us a reasonable distinction between realism and expressivism: either it will not be a distinction at all or else will yield a characterisation of realism which realists themselves will reject. It's worth noting at this point that Tiefensee also thinks of e-representation as being a mark of *ontological commitment*: those bits of language which are e-representational are the ones which carry some genuine ontological commitment, and as such are the ones for which realism is appropriate. She therefore adopts a pessimistic stance about the notion of ontological commitment here: no such notion has been cashed out which distinguishes expressivism from realism *and* which realists will accept.

To sum up, Tiefensee argues that neither Williams's EMUs nor Price's distinction between i-representation and e-representation can solve the problem of creeping minimalism. EMUs cannot help by themselves because the best EMU-based strategy uses a notion of tracking that is acceptable to expressivists when understood minimalistically. When cashed out in terms of e-representation, either expressivists will *still* accept that ethical language is e-representational, or else realists will *deny* that it is.

5.4. Replying to Tiefensee

As I mentioned earlier, Tiefensee's arguments are important because they target resources – EMUs and e-representation – given a central role in recent work by prominent non-representationalists. These arguments should worry us quite independently of the problem of creeping minimalism for *ethics*: they threaten some of the core components of contemporary non-representationalism. While I think Tiefensee's argument fails as a whole, discussing it does reveal some important lessons.

First, we must recognise that it's because Williams's EMUs are taken to be *explanations*, that Tiefensee's criticism of EMU-based strategies fails. Tiefensee claims that expressivists might be able to accept the realist's claim about tracking (1), which is part of the realist's EMU for 'good'. But if Williams's EMUs really are *explanations*, then the fact that expressivists can accept that 'good' can express reliable discriminative reactions is not enough to undermine this particular EMU strategy. More is required: expressivists need to think that (1) is part of what explains the fact that 'good' means *good*. They might accept (1) as true, but say that it doesn't belong in the EMU for 'good', because it doesn't have any explanatory role. In other words, even if you are good at tracking the ethical truth, you don't have the concept good in virtue of this fact.

Tiefensee approaches this point herself in the final footnote in her paper, claiming that 'a stronger focus on function might do the trick', though she is sceptical of this (Tiefensee 2016, n. 26, 2458). However, if we read 'function' just in the same explanatory terms as Dreier introduces and I have endorsed, then the 'stronger focus on function' Tiefensee mentions can be understood as putting more emphasis on what explains ethical meaning. And this is precisely the route I want to follow. On this view, the idea Tiefensee discusses becomes the claim that expressivists say that ethical terms 'establish language entry transitions' (roughly that they track ethical facts), but that this fact does not explain their meaning. So the EMU-based solution doesn't collapse given minimalism after all.

While Tiefensee's argument against EMUs fails, I think Tiefensee is more or less right about e-representation. Price's notion of e-representation can be used as a mark of neither realism nor representationalism. There are two reasons for this. First, whether or not a given kind of language is e-representational depends on whether it has an appropriate causal connection with the kinds of objects, properties and facts that it is meant to represent. But this cannot be a mark of realism or representationalism *in general* because there will be views which accept representationalism (and perhaps realism too) yet deny that the relevant facts and properties are causally active, as Tiefensee rightly points out. For instance an ethical non-naturalist might think that ethical language can only be explained in terms of representing the world, but that the properties and facts it represents are not causally linked to it.[15]

This is one reason we can't rest the general distinction between expressivism (or nonrepresentational pragmatism more generally) and representationalism on e-representation. The second reason is that e-representation does not have explanation built in. In other words, a piece of language may well be e-representational, but this does not entail that its meaning or use is *explained* by its being e-representational. (This is why expressivists could accept that ethical language was e-representational in Tiefensee's weaker sense.) Since I have pinned the distinction between representationalism and expressivism on the issue of what explains the content of ethical language, e-representation is not by itself going to play a crucial role – we need to include explanatory considerations too.[16] So we shouldn't think that e-representation is a mark of the difference between representationalism and expressivism in ethics. More generally, therefore, we shouldn't think that it's a mark of representationalism versus non-representationalism either.

So while Tiefensee's pessimistic argument fails as a whole, it reveals some important general points about the debate about expressivism and representationalism. Moreover, we've seen that the main moves in this debate can all be better understood and answered when we appreciate that explanation is the key to distinguishing expressivism. Dreier and Chrisman's points are best understood in these terms, and understanding Williams's EMUs in this way helps us see how we might use them to answer Tiefensee's objections.

6. Minimalism's revenge

To finish I want to discuss two spanners minimalism may yet throw in the works. First, the solution I've defended seems to make minimalism incompatible with representationalism, a consequence we should avoid if possible. Second, minimalism seems to prevent expressivists from distinguishing their opponents' views from their own. I will answer these in turn.[17]

6.1. Incompatibility?

The first worry is that minimalism about representation is incompatible with representationalism. This is because minimalism rules out explanations in terms of representation – and such explanations are definitive of representationalism. This is a common point in the literature. In a recent paper Camil Golub rejects some proposed solutions to the problem of creeping minimalism for this reason (Golub 2017, 1392f; 1406). Many writers think this point is important for the wider debate about non-representational theories of meaning.[18] While a full answer requires more space than I have, I will sketch out what I take to be the best response.

It's not clear why we should care about this supposed incompatibility. We might think that expressivists can live with it: if rival views are incompatible with minimalism, so much the worse for them. However this would make expressivists, who accept minimalism, unable to be representationalists about areas of language outside ethics, for instance about the language of middle-sized dry goods. At least some expressivists want to be representationalists in these cases, so they should try to answer this problem.[19]

The short answer is this: minimalism about representation rules out some *but not all* of the kinds of explanation which count as representationalist. Recall that in Section 4 I pointed out that representationalism includes at least two kinds of explanation: (i) those using representation as a primitive, and (ii) those using a plausible reduction base for representation. Minimalism only rules out the first of these, not the second.

While there is not enough space to fully explain why, minimalism about representation blocks the use of representation as an explanatory primitive. In particular minimalism entails that any claim of the form

> x means y because x represents the world in a certain way

is false. This is because representation is a trivial unexplanatory consequence of meaning, not the other way round. So minimalism rules out explanations of kind (i). Similarly, minimalism about *belief* rules out explanations using belief as a primitive.[20]

Minimalism also entails that representation is not reducible. Horwich takes minimalism to involve the view that the property in question is not constituted by any other property. For him this means that there is no property F such that (a) all and only representational terms have F and (b) (a) explains the facts about representation (Horwich 1998b, 104–107). Since reductionism would give us such a property, it is false if minimalism is true. As such, any reductionist view of representation is incompatible with minimalism: minimalism rules out explanations of kind (ii) above.[21]

However, this is no threat to the solution I'm defending. Expressivists aren't primitivists or reductionists about representation. They do not think that we can explain any kinds of term using representation as a primitive – they usually opt for a causal relation like causal tracking to explain middle-sized dry good terms (see Blackburn 2013; Gibbard 2015). Nor do they want to reduce representation: they don't think representation can be reduced to any one property, partly because they think that ethical terms and middle-sized dry goods terms *both* represent the world but don't do so for the same reasons. So they will not care about this incompatibility. Primitivists and reductionists won't care either: so much the worse for minimalism, they will say.

Moreover, minimalism about representation is compatible with some kinds of representationalist explanations. While minimalists cannot think that representation itself can do explanatory work, they can say that a plausible reduction base for representation can do such work, so long as they do not say that representation reduces to that base. For example, an explanation in terms of a causal tracking relation C which *denies* that representation reduces to C would be representationalist, since C is a plausible reduction base for representation. Yet since this view does not actually say that representation reduces to C, it is compatible with minimalism.[22]

More generally, explanations appealing to things which are plausible reduction bases for representation will be unaffected by minimalism about representation so long as they don't take representation as reducible to such things. So expressivists can accept minimalism about representation, yet argue that some terms, for instance, bear causal relations with the world in virtue of which they mean what they do, so long as they don't think that representation *is* or is *reducible* to those relations. Minimalism rules out some representationalist explanations, but not all of them.

What if minimalism creeps all the way to these reduction bases, for instance causal tracking? I see no reason to think it will. Consider C, the tracking relation. This doesn't bear the close conceptual relations to truth and meaning that belief, representation, and description do, in virtue of which minimalism crept to them. Nor is it part of ordinary practice to say that ethical terms causally track the world. So there's no pressure on expressivists to accept minimalism here. And so the threat of incompatibility is answered.

6.2. Unintelligibility?

The second point is that if expressivists only have a minimal notion of representation to hand, they will not be able to distinguish their own view from representationalism. This is because they will not be able to characterise representationalism, which requires a non-minimal notion. This concern rests on the idea that minimalism yields a *minimal notion* of representation; this idea is common in the literature (see e.g. Williams 2013, 131; Macarthur and Price 2007, 140; Dreier 2004).

We can understand minimalists as defining a *minimal notion* of representation, by offering definitions like

'F' represents$_M$ x iff x is F.

or perhaps, if we're willing to quantify over properties

'F' represents$_M$ things as having the property X iff X is F-ness.

Minimalists think that representation, in its ordinary sense, *just is* representation$_M$: ordinary usage of 'represents' is best explained in terms of these schemas.

However this doesn't mean that minimalists cannot *understand* non-minimal notions of representation which are defined differently, for instance a causal tracking notion defined like so:

'F' represents$_c$ things as having the property X iff uses of 'F' are caused by property X

Minimalists can understand representation$_c$. They can understand what causal tracking is. They may even think it's *sufficient* for representation in general: all terms which represent c do represent. They just think representationc isn't representation in its ordinary sense, and that it doesn't explain our ordinary use of words like 'represents'.

Nor do minimalists need to hear their rivals' theories as using a minimal notion. A minimalist can *understand* a causal tracking theorist when she says: 'ethical terms representc the world'. She's saying that ethical terms causally track the world. The minimalist doesn't need to interpret this claim by replacing 'represent$_c$' with 'represent$_M$'.[23] The minimalist just thinks the tracking claim is false. So there is no threat of unintelligibility, so long as we properly understand what it means for minimalists to 'only have' a minimal notion of representation.

So neither incompatibility nor unintelligibility threatens the solution I'm defending. Minimalism about representation neither blocks representationalism *tout court*, nor makes it unintelligible from the expressivists' point of view.

7. Conclusion

To conclude: Dreier's 'explanation' explanation distinguishes expressivism and realism by their *explanations* of the meaning of ethical language and thought. Prompted by Chrisman's ultimately unsuccessful criticism of this account, I argued for key three points. First, we should distinguish expressivism not from realism, but from representationalism. Second, we should not assume too much about the ontology involved in accounts which explain in terms of representation; Dreier's account made such assumptions because of his focus on realism not representationalism. Third, we should focus on *explanation*, as Dreier does – Chrisman's second criticism of Dreier missed this fact.

As such, I argued that expressivism is distinct from representationalism because it does not use representation, or something that plausibly could reduce representation, in its explanation of ethical thought and language. This protects the expressivist from minimalism, since she can happily accept minimalism without saying that ethical language has to be explained in terms of representation. This gives us a solution to the problem of creeping minimalism.

After doing this I showed how the key points I defended help us resolve several issues raised in the recent literature: Chrisman's criticism of Dreier, and Tiefensee's criticisms of Chrisman's inferentialism, as well as Williams's 'EMUs' and Price's 'e-representation'. I argued that Chrisman himself should simply focus more on explanation, that we should recognise that Williams's EMUs are *explanations*, and that Price's e-representation cannot be a mark of either realism or representationalism. Finally, I pointed out how on this solution, minimalism remains compatible with representationalism, and representationalism can still be intelligible to expressivists, despite worries to the contrary.

As such, a critical examination of Dreier's solution to the problem of creeping minimalism gives us not only a better solution to the problem, but some interesting results concerning philosophical concepts from the wider debate surrounding non-representationalist theories of meaning.

Notes

1. See e.g. the essays in Price (2013); Gross, Tebben, and Williams (2015); Misak and Price (Forthcoming).
2. Minimalism is sometimes called deflationism, but since not all authors identify the two, I will stick to 'minimalism' here. Thanks to an anonymous reviewer for this point.
3. See also Harcourt (2005).
4. While Dreier focuses on constitutive explanation, in principle this account could be modified to use a different notion of explanation, for instance the causal-historical notion favoured by Huw Price (2013, 20). I will disregard other senses of explanation in this paper.
5. The idea that explanation is important is increasingly common. See e.g. Gross, Tebben, and Williams (2015, 6), Price (2004, 209), Blackburn (2010, 128), Williams (2013, 128), Chrisman (2011), Ridge (2014, 103ff), Zalabardo (Forthcoming) and Toppinen (2015).
6. Here I follow David Lewis (1986, viii) and take realism to be the view that there are things, truths, properties, and so on in the relevant domain, not the view that truth in the domain is objective or mind-independent. On my view, error theorists are not realists, whatever they might think about the objectivity of ethics.
7. Why call the expressivist's opponent representationalist rather than, say, descriptivist or cognitivist? Because the recent literature has settled on representationalism as the name of the expressivist opponent. None of the many different names for expressivists, their allies, and their opponents, has ever been wholeheartedly accepted in the literature. However, representationalism seems

to be the current favourite, with several recent and influential works using it, including many of the most recent works cited in this paper.
8. While the error theorist Jonas Olson has happily accepted the property view, Bart Streumer rejects it (both in private correspondence).
9. This is perhaps what lies behind Blackburn's famous claim: '... it is not what you end up saying, but how you get to say it, that defines your "ism"' (Blackburn 1993, 7).
10. Thanks to Jamie Dreier for this objection.
11. Thanks to an anonymous reviewer for this suggestion.
12. Perhaps we could treat 'mention' as ontologically non-committing, which would allow Dreier's characterisation to include as representationalists those who say that ethical terms get their meaning by, for instance, representing-things-as-wrong. While this manoeuvre may well let Dreier's original account meet the objections made above, since Dreier's focus is on realism not representationalism, this is not the best reading of his original account. Indeed, in private correspondence, Dreier himself has maintained his focus on realism. Thanks to an anonymous reviewer for this point.
13. Note that Chrisman focuses on realism rather than representationalism, though he does make room for non-realist representationalism. He defines realism as the view which says that ethical commitments are theoretical and some of them are true (2008, 353), which leaves representationalism as the view that ethical commitments are theoretical.
14. A similar argument appears in a recent paper by Camil Golub (2017, 1400ff).
15. Perhaps we should rethink the notion of e-representation, reading it as pertaining to the 'external' world but not limiting that world to the causally active. Thanks to Huw Price for this point.
16. This is not to say that the i-/e-representation distinction is no good, nor that it cannot plays a useful role in discussions of pragmatism and representationalism, just that it can't do the work it needs to do in the solutions Tiefensee criticised.
17. Thanks to Christine Tiefensee and an anonymous reviewer for pressing these problems.
18. See Price (2015); Brandom (2013); Williams (2013); Blackburn (2013); Price (2013); Gibbard (2015); Gross, Tebben, and Williams (2015).
19. See Blackburn (2013) and Gibbard (2015), though Price (2011, 2013) has argued that they should reject representationalism completely.
20. See Horwich (1998a, 1998b); Williams (2013); Price (2011) for claims like this.
21. See Horwich (1998a, 1998b); Price (2015) for claims like this.
22. As Adams and Aizawa (2010, §4.1) point out, many of those who accept a causal theory of content think that causal relations are only *sufficient* and not necessary for meaning, and hence do not accept reductionism.
23. Compare: a behaviourist does not impose his behaviourism when interpreting a dualist's claims about the mind. When the dualist says 'mental states are not merely behavioural states', the behaviourist does not hear the absurd 'behavioural states are not merely behavioural states'. He does not reinterpret the dualist: he merely disagrees with her.

Acknowledgements

For extremely helpful discussion and comments, thanks to: Simon Blackburn, Tim Crane, Jamie Dreier, Richard Holton, Huw Price and the `lab group' in Cambridge 2013–2016,

Christine Tiefensee, Michael Williams, several anonymous reviewers, and the editor of this special issue.

Funding

This work was supported by a PhD studentship from the Arts and Humanities Research Council.

ORCID

Matthew Simpson http://orcid.org/0000-0002-4743-969X

References

Adams, Fred, and Ken Aizawa. 2010. "Causal Theories of Mental Content." *The Stanford Encylopedia of Philosophy*, edited by Edward N. Zalta (Spring 2010 edition). http://plato.stanford.edu/archives/spr2010/entries/content-causal.
Blackburn, Simon. 1993. *Essays in Quasi-Realism*. Oxford: Oxford University Press.
Blackburn, Simon. 1998. *Ruling Passions*. Oxford: Oxford University Press.
Blackburn, Simon. 2010. "The Steps from Doing to Saying." *Proceedings of the Aristotelian Society* 110: 1–13. Reprinted in his *Practical Tortoise Raising: And Other Philosophical Essays* (Oxford University Press, 2010), pp. 169–180.
Blackburn, Simon. 2013. "Pragmatism: All or Some?" In *Expressivism, Pragmatism and Representationalism*, edited by Huw Price, 59–73. Cambridge: Cambridge University Press.
Blackburn, Simon. 2015. "Blessed are the Peacemakers." *Philosophical Studies* 172 (4): 843–853.
Boyd, Richard. 1988. "How to Be a Moral Realist." In *Essays on Moral Realism*, edited by Geoffrey Sayre-McCord, 181–228. Ithaca, NY: Cornell University Press.
Brandom, Robert. 2013. "Global anti-Representationalism?" In *Expressivism, Pragmatism and Representationalism*, edited by Huw Price, 75–98. Cambridge: Cambridge University Press.
Chisholm, R. 1957. *Perceiving: A Philosophical Study*. Ithaca: Cornell University Press.
Chrisman, Matthew. 2008. "Expressivism, Inferentialism, and Saving the Debate." *Philosophy and Phenomenological Research* 77 (2): 334–358.
Chrisman, Matthew. 2011. "Expressivism, Inferentialism, and the Theory of Meaning." In *New Waves in Metaethics*, edited by Michael Brady, 103–125. Basingstoke: Palgrave-Macmillan.
Dreier, James. 2004. "Meta-Ethics and The Problem of Creeping Minimalism." *Philosophical Perspectives* 18 (1): 23–44.
Ducasse, C.J. 1942. "Moore's Refutation of Idealism." In *The Philosophy of G.E. Moore*, edited by P. Schilpp, 223–252. Chicago, IL: Northwestern University Press.
Fine, Kit. 2001. "The Question of Realism." *Philosophers' Imprint* 1 (2): 1–30.

Gibbard, Allan. 2003. *Thinking How to Live*. London: Harvard University Press.
Gibbard, Allan. 2015. "Global Expressivism and the Truth in Representation." In *Meaning Without Representation*, edited by Steven Gross, Nicholas Tebben and Michael Williams, 210–223. Oxford: Oxford University Press.
Golub, Camil. 2017. "Expressivism and Realist Explanations." *Philosophical Studies* 174 (6): 1385–1409.
Gross, Steven, Nicholas Tebben, and Michael Williams, eds. 2015. *Meaning Without Representation: Essays on Truth, Expression, Normativity, and Naturalism*. Oxford: Oxford University Press.
Harcourt, Edward. 2005. "Quasi-Realism and Ethical Appearances." *Mind* 114 (454): 249–275.
Horwich, Paul. 1998a. *Meaning*. Oxford: Oxford University Press.
Horwich, Paul. 1998b. *Truth*. 2nd ed. Oxford: Oxford University Press.
Lewis, David. 1986. *On the Plurality of Worlds*. Oxford: Blackwell.
Macarthur, David, and Huw Price. 2007. "Pragmatism, Quasi-realism, and the Global Challenge." In *The New Pragmatists*, edited by Cheryl Misak, 91–121. Oxford: Oxford University Press. Reprinted in Price's *Naturalism Without Mirrors* (Oxford University Press, 2011), pp. 228–252.
Misak, Cheryl, and Huw Price, eds. Forthcoming. *Pragmatism in Britain in the Long Twentieth Century: Proccedings of the 2014 Dawes Hicks Symposium*. London: British Academy.
Price, Huw. 2011. *Naturalism Without Mirrors*. Oxford: Oxford University Press.
Price, Huw. 2004. "Immodesty Without Mirrors: Making Sense of Wittgenstein's Linguistic Pluralism." In *Wittgenstein's Lasting Significance*, edited by Max Kölbel and Bernhard Weiss, 179–205. London: Routledge & Kegan Paul. Reprinted in his *Naturalism Without Mirrors* (Oxford University Press, 2011), pp. 200–227.
Price, Huw, ed. 2013. *Expressivism, Pragmatism and Representationalism*. Cambridge: Cambridge University Press.
Price, Huw. 2015. "From Quasi-Realism to Global Expressivism – And Back Again?" In *Passions and Projections*, edited by Robert N. Johnson and Michael Smith, 134–152. Oxford: Oxford University Press.
Price, Huw, and J. O'Leary-Hawthorne. 1996. "How to Stand Up for Non-Cognitivists." *Australasian Journal of Philosophy* 74 (2): 275–292. Reprinted in H. Price *Naturalism Without Mirrors* (Oxford University Press, 2011), pp. 112–131.
Ridge, Michael. 2014. *Impassioned Belief*. Oxford: Oxford University Press.
Tiefensee, Christine. 2016. "Inferentialist Metaethics, Bifurcations and Ontological Commitment." *Philosophical Studies* 173 (9): 2437–2459. doi:10.1007/s11098-015-0622-y.
Toppinen, Teemu. 2015. "Expressivism and the Normativity of Attitudes." *Pacific Philosophical Quarterly* 96 (2): 233–255.
Williams, Michael. 2013. "How Pragmatists can be Local Expressivists." In *Expressivism, Pragmatism and Representationalism*, edited by Huw Price, 113–128. Cambridge: Cambridge University Press.
Zalabardo, José L. Forthcoming. "Inferentialism and Knowledge: Brandom's Arguments Against Reliabilism." *Synthese*. doi:10.1007/s11229-017-1506-9.

The real and the quasi-real: problems of distinction

Jamie Dreier

ABSTRACT
This paper surveys some ways of distinguishing Quasi-Realism in metaethics (and I hope also in other areas) from Non-naturalist Realism, including 'Explanationist' methods of distinguishing, which characterize the Real by its explanatory role, and Inferentialist methods. Rather than seeking the One True Distinction, the paper adopts an irenic and pragmatist perspective, allowing that different ways of drawing the line are best for different purposes.

Introduction: the problem of distinguishing

A question that has bugged me for a while is: what is the difference between Realism, in metaethics but also elsewhere in similar areas of philosophy, and Quasi-Realism? In a moment I'll say a little about how I understand Quasi-Realism, but for now I can just gesture at Simon Blackburn's view, and I think (though this is not as clear) Allan Gibbard's, views that attempt to vindicate realist-sounding talk in ethics but rest their explanations on an expressivist groundwork. I have a view about how to answer this question, though it is not at all a confident view. I am going to articulate the view and defend it against some recent objections. However, I am not deeply committed to it, and if it turns out some other view is right and mine is wrong, my attitude will be Socratic: grateful to be corrected. I am very interested in what some self-described Pragmatists think about this issue. Some of them think the question is wrong-headed, that it is exactly the sort of metaphysical question that we ought to be moving beyond. Some of them think it is a real question but requires a Pragmatist, rather than a metaphysical answer. And some of them have settled on views quite similar to mine but with important differences. In this paper I am going to sort through these broadly Pragmatist approaches; I will not be much concerned with critique and dissent from the other side of the spectrum.

In the present context the background of the problem will be familiar, so let me summarize it. The old criteria for distinguishing metaethical expressivism (emotivism, non-cognitivism, non-descriptivism ...) from realism, particularly from non-naturalist realism, dissolve in the presence of a *deflationary* conception of some semantic and metaphysical concepts. Quasi-realists embrace this deflationary conception, partly for the same reasons that they like expressivism in the first place (namely, that the robust metaphysics of realism seems misguided with the real issues better seen 'side on', in terms of what we are doing when we say and think various thoughts rather than what those various thoughts are *about*), and partly because it is very handy for working out the Quasi-realist project, since it promises a relatively easy vindication of ordinary talk of moral facts and properties and truth and belief. So, it no longer makes sense to say that Quasi-realists don't believe there are moral facts, or that they take moral judgment to be affective and conative rather than doxastic. So what is it that they don't believe, that really real realists do? Distinguishing some inflated conception of truth or property would help: we could then mark the distinction by noting that realists think there are moral PROPERTIES, while Quasi-realists believe only in moral properties. But then the problem is how to say what the inflated things are, so no real progress is made by this move.

My favorite suggestion, following in the footsteps of Fine and Price and Hawthorne (O'Leary-Hawthorne and Price 1996; Fine 2001), among others, is to distinguish the robust version of facts and properties from the deflated one according to their explanatory role in philosophical projects.[1] In a realist story about some domain of properties, the properties in the domain figure in the explanation of a certain kind of fact. The explananda are facts in which the target properties figure 'protected', in an intensional context, and in particular they are facts about people's moral *beliefs* and about what moral sentences *say*. In a realist story, the properties figure in the explanation of these facts. What it is to believe that abortion is permissible is to stand in a certain relation to abortion and permissibility, according to realism. But Quasi-realists have a different story, one that does not involve the property of permissibility. They think we are *prescribing* when we make normative claims, and thinking about *what to do* when we have normative thoughts.[2] There is no explanatory weight borne by these normative properties in the account of what we are doing when we use normative concepts.

So that is how I try to draw the distinction. I am an *Explanationist* about the divide between the real and the Quasi-real. The bulk of the paper will be about worries and objections to Explanationism. About most of the worries and objections my attitude is irenic and accommodating; at the end I address an objection that I think is mistaken, and raise one that worries me.

Part I: many lines

In this part of the paper, I enumerate three problems posed for my version of Explanationism, each of which leads to an alternative way of drawing the border between Quasi-realism and realism. In each case I say a little about why the alternative method does not capture the distinction that most interests me, but the main point is just to see how different tests may capture different distinctions. As Camil Golub (2017) sensibly says, 'I want to avoid the trap of treating realism as something the sharp contours of which we should all be able to recognize upon reflection' (1392).

The problem of things that don't exist

Matthew Chrisman raises an obvious worry, one that I am a bit ashamed of having failed to notice (Chrisman 2008). Chrisman points out that when somebody asserts that the moon is made of cheese, we can be confident that their words and belief are not made what they are by the fact that the moon is made of cheese, since there is no such fact. But we are not thereby anti-realists, or expressivists, or anything but realists about the moon and cheese. To address this rather glaring counterexample, though, an Explanationist need only adjust the theory a bit. The explanation of the naif's belief is a matter of standing in certain relations to the moon, and to cheese; there need be no fact that verifies the belief, of course. But, as Chrisman notes, a second problem is standing in the wings. Suppose, having been disabused of the mistake about the moon, our dupe offers the opinion that Superman was born on Krypton. Now our trick doesn't help. Krypton plays no role in our explanation of the dupe's belief, for it is handicapped by non-existence. Chrisman takes it to be obvious that we should not conclude that realism about the domain of Superman talk is hopeless.

Well, in fact, I would have said that it is an open question which side of the divide is home to Superman talk. We are error theorists about such talk. And typically philosophers have placed error theory on the *anti*-realist side of the divide. I am personally ambivalent (Dreier 2010). Let me table this question for a moment to discuss why.

In unpublished work, Matthew Simpson argues that the right way to think of the distinction that we seem to have lost to deflationary forces is not the distinction between realism and anti-realism, but the distinction between Representationalism and Non-Representationalism. His case in point is the error theory, which he takes to be paradigmatically anti-realist and Representationalist. For the same reason, we might say that an atheist is an anti-realist about the domain of the divine but also a Representationalist, since she thinks of the language of divinity to be an attempt to represent real properties, only a failed attempt since she thinks there is nothing divine. John Mackie insisted that on matters of conceptual analysis his view matched Moore's or Plato's, that in saying that there are no objective values he was denying exactly what Moore and Plato were asserting, that his error theory was a theory of ontology and not meaning. If we agree with Simpson that the lost distinction is the boundary between the Representational and the Non-Representational, then it is easy to see Chrisman's point. Even if we are happy to let the Explanation criterion classify Mackie as an anti-realist, we should want him to count as a Representationalist. But then, what is *that* supposed to amount to? It's no good saying Representationalism understands normative talk as representing the world. 'Representing' is too easily deflated!

The point is not that Explanationism has failed to map the *true* distinction it was after. The real point is that there was more than one distinction, and Explanationism has (so far) articulated only one. So *one* theoretically important distinction between non-naturalist realism and Quasi-realism is, indeed, the one Kit Fine explicated in 'The Question of Realism'; but there is another we haven't yet managed to analyze. I now turn to Chrisman's own solution to the problem. While it has a philosophically satisfying feel to it, Chrisman's view faces a problem, spelled out by (Tiefensee 2016). Addressing that problem is complicated, and it will take us through waters mapped out by Huw Price and Michael Williams, and again some obstacles discovered by Tiefensee.

Chrisman's inferentialism

Chrisman suggests an *Inferentialist* approach to understanding how language works, in the tradition of Brandom and Sellars, and recently of Horwich, Price and Michael Williams. As Chrisman puts it, Inferentialism 'seeks to explain meaning (even of uncontroversially descriptive statements) in terms of inference rather than representation' ['Saving the Debate', 349]. Here an inference is a transition from sentence to sentence in a public language, rather than a bit of reasoning that takes place in someone's head. While Chrisman stresses this difference by way of contrasting Inferentialism with, e.g. Allan Gibbard's way of understanding the meaning of normative language, I suspect it turns out not to be a very important contrast for current purposes. In any case, the main point is that an Inferentialist has, according to Chrisman, a particularly nice way of characterizing the difference between the way a Quasi-realist expressivist thinks language works and the way a realist thinks it works. For the two will have quite different stories about the position that a normative sentence typically occupies within the web of inference.

Chrisman suggests that a Quasi-realist expressivist should be contrasted with realists by their insistence that normative language has a special role in inference. 'Ought' sentences, a Quasi-realist will say, and other pieces of normative language, are inferred from others with the support of *practical* reasons, and they license inferences to *actions*.[3] By contrast, theoretical sentences in descriptive language are inferred with the support of *theoretical* reasons, of *evidence*, and they license inferences to *beliefs* and *theoretical knowledge about the world*. Whereas, one must suppose, a realist will draw no such contrast. According to realism, normative language seeks to describe a special section of reality, apart from the natural world,[4] and so it must be characterized by the same patterns of inference as other descriptive language.

Chrisman, then, offers a method of distinguishing the Representationalism of realist theories from the Non-Representationalism of Quasi-realist expressivist theories from within the theoretic framework of Inferentialism. Instead of Explanationalism he rests his taxonomy on the distinction between practical and theoretical inference.

Now, there are some technical issues that will have to be dealt with rigorously before this distinction can bear weight. One of these issues is the sorting of sentences into the kind that occupy the practical inference position and those that fit into the theoretical inference slots. To illustrate the complication I have in mind, consider an example of Arthur Prior's 1960: 'Whatever all church officers ought to do, undertakers ought to do.' This statement appears to be fraught with *ought*, it is paradigmatically normative language, and thus might be expected to occupy one of the practical reasoning slots in our inferential web if Chrisman's expressivist is to prevail. But it follows deductively, as Prior notes, from 'Undertakers are church officers'. Perhaps it can be marked off by its downstream inferential consequences as practical? But any such logical consequences it has must *a fortiori* be shared by everything to the left of its turnstile, including, of course, 'Undertakers are church officers', which is not supposed to have 'immediate' practical consequences. Is expressivism thus refuted? Surely it can't be so easy!

When I call these technical problems I mean that they call for technical fixes, and I will assume some such fix is available. A promising strategy, to my mind, would be to start with (Gibbard 2003)'s fact-plan world sets, which are designed to capture the mix of descriptive and (as Gibbard puts it) plan-laden content that is ubiquitous in real life normative talk, with apparatus for extracting the distinctively practical inferential capacity of sentences from the mixture when the theory calls for it. Although Chrisman sees the semantic formalities in Gibbard's work as straying too close to a truth-conditional semantics and too far from the Inferentialist program, in fact I think the fact-plan world sets can be thought of as serving precisely the function of coding inference information, so that the semantic values of sentences turn out to be, seen from the right perspective, nothing more than inferential roles. They are like Library of Congress numbers, but more systematic, indexing positions in an algebra, with the individual fact-plan worlds as atoms. In any case, I will assume, without undue optimism I think, that the technicalities can be worked out.

There is, though, a deeper problem, one explicated by (Tiefensee 2016). The problem is that upon closer examination, it looks like Chrisman has articulated the wrong divide. It's a perfectly good divide, and of certain theoretical interest, but it is not the one that separates Quasi-realism from non-naturalist realism. For take a typical explication of the practical role of an *ought* judgment. We can use Chrisman's own example: 'We ought to put the quiche in the oven now'. In his story, a couple is reasoning about their dinner party. From facts about when the guests will arrive, they reach the conclusion about the quiche, employing obviously practical reasons, and then having reached the conclusion they go ahead and put it in the oven, a step that is on its face licensed by their acceptance of the normative sentence. But that's just the problem: it is just *obvious* that ordinary normative judgments come with practical licenses and are licensed by practical reasons. It is not a distinctive component of expressivism, but a commitment common to all sorts of metaethical views.[5] For example, there is no doubt that Scanlon accepts this practical role for judgments about what reasons people have.[6] Indeed, it would be a grievous weakness in a metaethical theory if it could not make out a distinctive practical role for normative judgment, in both thought and language. It's true that the tradition of expressivism has taken this role to be utterly central, and built its theory of meaning around it, while realists merely attempt to accommodate; but many agree that accommodation is necessary. Again, if Chrisman's point is that the expressivist approach is very much more promising than any realist theory (especially non-naturalist realism), I couldn't agree more. But that is to point to an attractive feature of expressivism rather than to define it.

Eleatic explanationism

The Eleatic view of ontology (dubbed by Price 2013) says that our official ontology admits only those objects (including properties, facts, 'objects' broadly speaking) that pull their weight in causal explanations. It is a version of Explanationism, since causal explanation is a kind of explanation. In the present context it is particularly relevant whether our explanation of how words come to denote their contents is causal explanation: when it is, we'll have a tidy test for whether the vocabulary deserves a realist construal. And if we wed Inferentialism to Eleaticism, we have another scheme of classification.

To fix ideas, let's take Michael Williams's clear explication (Williams 2013). In Williams's Inferentialist account of meaning, the meaning of an expression is given by what he calls 'Explanations of Meaning in terms of Use', or EMUs. Each EMU has three components: a summary of the inferential connections exhibited by sentences in which the expression occurs; a specification of the epistemic conditions in which the expression may be competently applied; and a story about the function of the expression, what it is used to do. When Williams outlines an expressivist EMU for the term 'good' and a realist EMU for the same term, he marks out the difference in two ways. First, perhaps most obviously, he builds into the expressivist EMU an action-guiding function; in the realist one he puts a 'tracking' function:

In a reporting use, tokens of 'x is good' express reliable discriminative reactions to an environmental circumstance. Their role is to keep track of goodness, in this way functioning as language entry transitions.

Similarly, in the realist EMU's epistemic component Williams includes this:

To master 'good' in its reporting use, the speaker must have a reliable discriminative reporting disposition (RDRD), a disposition, given appropriate motivation and conditions, to report 'x is good' when confronted with something good.

These EMU elements give 'good' a role structurally similar (though of course with entirely different inferential connections) to that of 'platinum' or 'crimson'. The point of the expression is to reliably indicate the presence of a certain property, and competence with the expression requires reliability in the user in registering the presence of the property. Here *registration, keeping track, indicating* are all naturalistic, causal relations: they are like the relations of a thermometer to the temperature. But the expressivist EMUs for 'good' include no such causal elements. So, in Williams's story, according to the Eleatic Explanationist, the expressivist doesn't get goodness in his official ontology, while the realist does.

This is a nice distinction. It captures a theoretically important difference between the way expressivists understand the meaning of normative expressions and the way most of us think of naturalistic vocabulary as getting its content. But (as Tiefensee explains), it cannot capture the distinction between realism and Quasi-realism. For many normative realists, and indeed the ones we've been most concerned to distinguish from Quasi-realists, are *nonnaturalists*, and thus do not take our normative thought to be *caused* by normative properties; they may not think of normative properties as having any causal powers whatsoever.[7] It is unsurprising that a distinction drawn by Williams to capture the difference between what normative expressions do and what natural kind terms and naturalistic property-denoting predicates do should leave a *non*naturalist realist view of normative expressions on the wrong side of the divide. Useful as this Eleatic Explanationism is, it won't play the role we are looking to fill.

Simpson's explanationism

Matthew Simpson (2017) offers a version of Explanationism designed to shore up the problems in the kind I have defended. Simpson's innovation is to focus on the explanatory weight borne in a theory of meaning by what he calls *representational* properties and relations. In this category he includes the usual deflationary suspects: representation, reference, truth, expressing belief, being about the world ... Simpson knows well that these properties and relations are ripe for deflation, and that in their deflationary guises they are perfectly acceptable to Quasi-realists: nobody will deny that 'Slavery is unjust' is *true*, or that it represents slavery as unjust, and so on. The point is that these relations will not show up in a Quasi-realist theory in any explanatory role. Quasi-realists do not explain meanings of predicates by trying to say which properties they represent, or in a Gricean mode by saying (merely) which beliefs they express. Their explanations are in quite other terms, as we know. Whereas a realist account will, Simpson argues, inevitably rest its explanation of meanings on these representational features. So, Simpson's idea is thoroughly Explanationist, in that it finds a distinction by the mark of what bears explanatory weight; but instead of the target properties and facts as *explanans*, Simpson's version looks to the very representational properties that deflationists are fondest of deflating to classify theories.

This is a lovely move. On the old view, what it is to be an 'inflated' or 'robust' property or fact is to be load-bearing in a certain kind of explanation, an explanation of representation. Deflated properties can't carry this weight. Simpson's insight is to distinguish *representation itself* into inflated and deflated versions according to the load they bear or shirk in a theory. I have two worries about this strategy.

The first is that in abstract terms it looks to be a way of distinguishing deflationist and inflationist conceptions of the semantic notions in question, and not robust vs. quasi-version conceptions of, say, moral facts. Why shouldn't we be able to combine deflationism about representation with an inflated theory of wrongness itself? Can't deflationists about truth and representation have robust theories of *anything*? Of mass, for example? But then in their theories, they will not be able to make their representational relations and properties carry explanatory weight, since the mark of deflated properties is their explanatory inefficacy. And then Simpson's criterion will count these theories as non-representational. So that seems wrong.

The second problem is that it might be quite difficult to tell whether a given theory satisfies Simpson's test for being Representational. For a theory may appeal to certain relations between words and the world, say causal relations (as in Richard Boyd's theory of natural kind terms), and state its account of meanings in those terms. The use of the word 'platinum' in our linguistic community is causally regulated by the metal with atomic number 78, and in virtue of that causal relation, a naturalistic scientific realist might say, the word has the meaning it does. Now, has our theorist relied on a Representational relation? He hasn't named his relation in Representational language, but surely the idea is that the causal regulation in question is what constitutes reference (for natural kind terms). This case is a relatively easy one: the spirit of Simpson's classification scheme calls for sorting a Boydian view into the Representationalist bin, and we can just say, 'Well, Boyd is talking about *reference*, only without using the vocabulary'. But there are sure to be trickier cases.[8]

I have now reached the end of my supply of positive suggestions for dividing Quasi-realism from non-naturalist realism. Let me pause to take stock before moving on to some Big Picture issues. My Explanationist way of distinguishing realism from Quasi-realism was by asking whether the properties and facts in the target domain explain what it is to talk and think about them. But Chrisman points out that this distinction has the error theory on the Quasi-realist side, so it does not manage to say what is distinctive about Representationalist theories.

Matthew Simpson's alternative Explanationism asks whether the representational properties and relations explain our talk and thought about the domain. Both of these versions have some fuzzy regions in their boundaries, especially in the neighborhood of error theories, rather than drawing bright lines everywhere. And Chrisman's own distinction, drawn from the perspective of Inferentialism, classifies many self-styled realists with expressivists on the grounds that they recognize the intrinsically practical role of normative concepts. Finally, Eleatic Explanationism seems to pick out something important about what we might call *naturalistic* realist vocabulary, but like Chrisman's distinction it leaves *non*-naturalist realism in the camp with expressivism.

The failure to find any single boundary criterion that classifies all the theories we know into the intuitively right categories should not, I think, worry us too much. Let us embrace the pragmatic spirit: there are many lines to draw, and each of the ones we've looked at does appear to capture a theoretically important distinction. And if I'm drawing my bullseyes around the holes my bullets pierced in the side of the barn, like the farmer in the joke, that's not cheating: articulating some theoretical distinctions can help us see *post hoc* what was important about the groupings we were taking for granted.

Part II: problems not explained away by many lines

I now turn to two final problems. I am treating them separately, because I do not see how they can be finessed in the pragmatist spirit I've just appealed to. One of them, though, I will argue is based on a confusion. The other I find more deeply worrisome.

The problem of the accommodating expressivist

Camil Golub (2017) thinks the effort of redrawing the old distinction has amounted to wasted ink. The paper takes apart a number of attempts to partition the realist from the Quasi-realist accounts, using different useful tools to do the dismantling. Golub particularly wants us to remember that certain features of theories like Gibbard's and Blackburn's are hallmarks not of expressivism but of deflationism itself (which Golub calls 'minimalism'); he is clearly quite right about this and it bears remembering. We can't distinguish Quasi-realism from realism by noting that the former and not the latter take the list of instances of schema T to be trivial tautologies; even if that is an accurate description of all expressivist theories and some realist ones, it only shows that expressivists have tended to embrace deflationism about truth more than realists have. And like me, he declines to assume that there is a single watershed awaiting our discovery. On both these issues, Golub's reminders are salutary.

When he discusses the Explanationist criterion for drawing a line, though, Golub argues that no Quasi-realist will want to deny what according to Explanationism is the defining claim of realist Representationalism. I will call this, the Problem of the Accommodating Expressivist. I want to move slowly and carefully through this part of his argument, since I am not sure I am understanding it correctly. To start with, here is what Golub thinks an Explanationist will take to be the defining claim of Representationalism:

> REALISM-CON Normative facts and properties play a substantive explanatory role in the best account of the semantic content of normative discourse.

Whether Realism-Con accurately captures Explanationism's criterion depends on what's meant by an 'account of the semantic content'. For example, in recent years there has been an explosion of interesting work in the formal semantics of deontic modals, written both by semanticists in linguistics departments as by philosophers of language. As far as I know, not a single theory in this recent corpus mentions wrongness, a primitive *ought* relation, or a property of permissibility (They tend to be about ordering sources, accessibility relations, restrictors of modal quantification, and functions from contexts to sets of possible worlds). I assume Golub does not think of this work in formal semantics as giving any 'account of the semantic content of normative discourse'; a set of possible worlds would not count as 'semantic content' in the relevant sense. So what does Golub mean?

The Explanationists Golub cites are Fine, Hawthorne, Price, me, and more tentatively Gibbard and Blackburn. So, an account of the semantic content of normative discourse ought to mean: a story about which facts are the ones in virtue of which a sentence counts as meaning what 'Abortion is morally permissible' or 'We ought to put the quiche in the oven' in fact mean in our language. Quasi-realists say that these sentences express certain attitudes (or, to bring Chrisman aboard, they are attached in certain ways to other sentences and to actions and evidence in a network of inference). But Golub seems to disagree:

> It is possible to accept EXPRESSIVISM and acknowledge at the same time the importance of representationalist talk when it comes to capturing the successes and failures of our normative commitments. It is not a tenet of EXPRESSIVISM as such that EXPRESSIVISM is more philosophically illuminating than normative discourse. Therefore, there need be no explanatory tension between EXPRESSIVISM and REALISM-CON if representationalist talk is treated as internal to normative theorizing. [1405]

It is not easy to understand what Golub is getting at. Representationalist talk is internal to normative theorizing in this way: that when someone asks how Shakespeare represents Iago in *Othello*, we may say straightforwardly that Iago is represented as thoroughly evil. In so doing we are, as Simon Blackburn says, moralizing, since we are committing to a moral view according to which the deception and conniving of the character is bad; a Machiavellian moralist might say instead that Iago is represented as powerful and realistic. And there are all the familiar points to make about the *truth* of Julia Child's instructions about how long we ought to keep the quiche in the oven, and so on. But none of this seems to be on point. How can it follow, from these familiar thoughts about the deflated conception of truth and representation in ethics, that there is no tension between expressivism and Realism-Con? For expressivists say that normative facts and properties play *no* substantive role in explaining what it is to mean that abortion is permissible.

I think Golub wants to say that there is a tautological conception of meaning, according to minimalism, the kind given maybe by the list of schema T instances, which can be used by expressivists and realists alike to explain the semantic content of normative sentences. And he thinks this is a substantive explanation. So, he concludes, expressivists can agree with realists that normative properties play a substantive role. There they are, on the right-hand side of the bi conditionals, and the left side is about the truth of the sentences, so the normative properties are entering into the truth-conditions. Golub thinks that no expressivist need deny this, so long as she is a deflationist.

I think this is badly wrong. So although it will be a detour from the main track of this paper, I will explain why it is wrong.[9] The explanation may help some understand what is going on in some contemporary debate over how to give the meanings of sentences.

In his landmark of deflationism, *Truth*, (Horwich 1998), Paul Horwich offers a theory of truth in the form of the instances, restricted somehow to avoid the contradictions generated by self-reference, of the schema: The proposition that *p* is true iff *p*. A variant of Horwich's theory could be given for a truth predicate whose primary bearers are sentences rather than propositions: 'S' is true iff S (This is again a *schema*, generating instances by replacing 'S' with a sentence). From this collection, Horwich claims, everything one needs to know about the meaning of the truth predicate, everything there is to know about how to use it, can be deduced. Someone who understood our language except for the word 'true' and its cognates (and synonyms) could become fully competent with the predicate by attending to these axioms, taking them to be 'free', meaning-giving postulates. Now, there is also a tradition, exemplified by Davidson, of understanding what it is to know a language as knowing all of the truth conditions of the sentences of that language; more realistically, knowing how, by means of one's knowledge of words and syntax, to calculate truth conditions for any given sentence. So if one knew, for each sentence, what the world had to be like in order for that sentence to be true, one would know what all the sentences mean. And we can typically (after accounting for indexicals and other expressions whose content varies with context) write out the truth conditions for a sentence just by writing the sentence: the truth conditions for 'Everest is the tallest mountain' are that Everest is the tallest mountain. So it is perhaps tempting to think that the same list that the variant of Horwich's theory uses to define truth (of sentences) can be used also to give the meaning of the sentences of the language in which the theory is written down.

But even if the collection of bi conditionals can be used in *either* way, it definitely cannot be used for both purposes together. Merging the two theories is absurd. For in Horwich's theory, each bi conditional is a *tautology*, serving to specify a bit of the meaning of 'true'. And on the other hand, in the Davidsonian theory the bi conditionals together capture what the sentences of the language mean, *which is an empirical fact*. You cannot learn German by writing down each sentence of German in quotation marks, followed by 'ist wahr', followed by '↔', followed by the sentence again, and then studying that list every night. You would have a list of sentences of German, but you would not know what any of the sentences means. And if you could learn what each of those sentences means, then of course you would not need the list![10]

No doubt all of this is obvious, but I wanted to show as pedantically as necessary that the way in which truth conditions give semantic content of a sentence is not at home in the deflationary conception of truth (for sentences). Maybe an easier way of clarifying is to suppose that all parties agree that truth is explained in a satisfactory deflationary way by the schema for propositions, and then to ask what makes a given sentence express a given proposition. What has to be true of a linguistic community, we may wonder, in order for a string of words in their language to mean that abortion is permissible? We know what sort of answer expressivists give: the community has to use the string of words to express a certain type of attitude toward abortion. Realists, on the other hand, even if they agree that communities that use 'permissible' in a way that does in fact express some attitude, will answer differently the question of what *makes* the string of words mean that abortion is permissible. They (I hypothesize) will mention a non-natural property in giving their answer.

As I understand him, Golub thinks this part of the theory is not semantics, but *meta-semantics*.[11] Against Explanationism applied to metasemantics, though, he complains that the version of deflationism we are taking for granted in this discussion 'entails that many semantic facts need no deeper explanation: for example, the fact that "Genocide is wrong" is true just in case genocide is wrong. On their view, such tautologies simply follow from the grammar of the word "true". But that is just the mistake I warned against. The semantic fact that 'Abortion is permissible' means what it does needs some explanation, indeed, one which expressivists give in a distinctive way. Think of all the trained EMUs Michael Williams needs to explain what it is for a sentence to mean *that* (even just for the simplified, toy version of the language!).

As I said, I am not sure I have understood Golub's point, but as things stand I believe the Problem of the Accommodating Expressivist is not a real problem. Serious expressivists should indeed deny that the normative subject matter itself bears any weight in semantic or metasemantic explanation.

The problem of conceptual role semantics

I now turn to the final problem. And it is to my mind the most worrisome; I honestly don't know what to think about it. The problem shows up when we think about a way of specifying meanings that is sometimes called 'Conceptual Role Semantics' (Harman 1987). It is similar in most ways to Chrisman's Inferentialism, but is more naturalistic and psychologistic. Meanings are assigned first to speakers' assertions by way of the meanings of their psychological states, and only then to sentences in a language, and the 'roles' in question are causal, psychological roles rather than normative inferential ones. Suppose we wondered whether someone in an alien linguistic community meant 'platinum' by a certain word. We would want to see how the sentences in which the word occurred were linked to other words and sentences, a word, perhaps, for 'shiny', or 'metal', or 'electricity'. Probably we would try to identify a network of inferences the speaker was inclined to follow, and then assign a bunch of meanings all at once, by Ramsification (Lewis 1970) or the like (Jackson 1998). We would also have to check to see whether the speaker or her community were acquainted with platinum, whether they had any causal contact with it, whether they could collectively recognize it. We might construct an EMU for our word 'platinum' and see whether any word in the speaker's language followed its pattern of use. Now at some point we would decide that yes, indeed, the speaker had a word we could translate as 'platinum', and then we would count her as talking about platinum. The pattern of use, the conceptual role, we would think, qualified the word as being *about* some stuff in the world around us. There would be no further question of whether, having filled the conceptual role, the word *really is* about that stuff: reference happens, as it were, automatically.

Now imagine two philosophers who start off with a straightforward inferentialist story about normative expressions. One approaches metaethics in the manner of (Gibbard 2003), the other along the lines of (Wedgwood 2007), but their starting strategy is the same. They work out the same pattern of inference, including what inferentialists call 'output-transitions' to action or intention or motivation. When an expression fits one of the patterns, one of the EMUs maybe, it will count as meaning what 'ought' means, they agree.

But when they're done with that part, the Gibbard-like theorist says, 'That's the whole story, except we can add some deflationary talk about properties and truth and the like.' Whereas the Wedgwoodish theorist says, 'So, when people speak in this way, they manage to latch on to the real, non-natural normative properties and they will count as thinking and talking about those properties.'[12] It's not that my Wedgwoodish character takes the pattern of use to be excellent evidence of some other connection people must be making to the non-natural properties. The extra bit of the theory, he thinks, comes for free, emergent. We achieve reference to the non-natural properties precisely by having expressions in our language that fit the patterns. It works analogously to the way we manage to refer to things by descriptions: we just have the description in our minds, and then it refers to whatever it is in the world that satisfies the description, automatically.

These two philosophers certainly seem to have different ontologies and different accounts of normative language, the one anti-realist and the other realist, but their explanations of what it is in virtue of which our language and thought counts as normative language and thought are the same. The extra bit the Wedgwood character tacks on is not explaining, at least not explaining the things that are supposed to matter in my taxonomy. So I am worried that I classify them together when they should be separated.

I find this rather mysterious. Maybe it's just an illusion, and there really isn't any difference – the bit that gets added on by the 'realist' story is just a kind of flourish. But it doesn't feel that way to me, so I still want to figure out what to say about the difference.

Recap

In recent literature on the problem of drawing the boundary between realism and Quasi-realism, between Representationalism and Non-representationalism, some philosophers raise objections to the criteria deployed by others. But we should be accommodating: there are many lines to draw, and many distinctions of theoretical interest, so the criteria do not conflict with one another.

Some philosophers have raised doubts about the possibility of distinguishing realist domains from Quasi-realist ones, at least under broadly deflationist presuppositions; but so far no good reason has been offered for why Explanationist criteria couldn't draw useful distinctions. One problem still worries me: whether having offered a pragmatist or expressivist style account of how, for example, the normative expressions in a language come to have the meanings they have, we could still wonder whether expressions that have those meanings *also* denote properties; that is, whether the account might still be thought incomplete by those with more realistic bent. The problem, as I see it, is not so much *how we would tell*, but rather whether there is anything at all to wonder about.

Notes

1. I now think this is ambiguous between (i) the explanatory role sorts properties into two kinds, and (ii) the explanatory role is our best evidence for which properties *really exist*, as opposed to the 'mere shadows of predicates' that are in fact no property at all. My philosophical predilection is to regard the criterion in the second way, but I have no confidence that it will even make sense in the end.
2. There is a small (I think!) problem with this formulation, which Matthew Kramer has recently pounced on; I believe I can straighten this out but it would take us too far afield (Kramer 2017).

3. Or, as I would prefer, to *intentions*; see Jonathan Dancy's ['From Thought to Action' *Oxford Studies in Metaethics* volume 9, 2014] and John Broome's (*Rationality and Reasoning*, 2013).
4. See my 'Another World' (Jamie Dreier 2015) for an attempt to understand what Thomas Scanlon means when he tells us that talk of reasons is talk of a separate realm. The puzzle is that Scanlon also takes reason talk to forge precisely the kind of inferential connection with action that Chrisman associates with expressivism, leaving it particularly mysterious what the difference is supposed to be between Scanlon's realism and, e.g. Blackburn's Quasi-realism.
5. Though not all; G. E. Moore seems not to have accepted it, and by my best reading neither does (Parfit 2011).
6. Lecture 3 of (Scanlon 2014).
7. For example (Zangwill 2006).
8. In correspondence, Simpson suggested that any relation to the extension of an expression would count as Representational, so at least the paradigmatic realist exemplified by Boyd would be sorted correctly. This does seem to help, but now there will be loose ends sticking out elsewhere. What of failed expressions, like 'phlogiston' or according to Richard Joyce, 'wrong'? They will not be characterized by relations to their extensions, since they have none. As I noted above, it's fine to say that these theories are not realist, but they are supposed to be indisputably Representationalist.
9. For more along these lines, see my 'Expressivist Embeddings and Minimalist Truth' (James Dreier 1996).
10. If you do it Horwich's way, you will have a bunch of propositions instead of sentences, but that's different: Horwich's actual theory is not supposed to be a theory of truth for sentences, in the first instance, so it does not even suggest itself as a theory of meaning. Cf. Horwich's later book, *Meaning*, which is not at all deflationary, although its theory of meaning is designed to complement deflationary conceptions of truth and reference.
11. There has recently been a flurry of interest in the idea that expressivism is a meta-semantic theory rather than a semantic theory; I cannot address that issue here, but I suspect the matter is more complicated. See Alwood (2016), Perez Carballo (2014), Ridge (2014), Ridge (2015), for some examples.
12. This is not exactly Wedgwood's view in *The Nature of Normativity*; I am oversimplifying for purposes of an easier presentation.

Disclosure statement

No potential conflict of interest was reported by the author.

References

Alwood, Andrew. 2016. "Should Expressivism be a Theory at the Level of Metasemantics?" *Thought: A Journal of Philosophy* 5 (1): 13–22.

Chrisman, Matthew. 2008. "Expressivism, Inferentialism, and Saving the Debate." *Philosophy and Phenomenological Research* 77 (2): 334–358.

Dreier, J. 2010. "Mackie's Realism: Queer Pigs and the Web of Belief", In *A World without Values*, edited by Richard Joyce, Simon Kirchin, and Stephen Hetherington, 71–86. Philosophical Studies Series. Springer Netherlands.

Dreier, James. 1996. "Expressivist Embeddings and Minimalist Truth." *Philosophical Studies* 83 (1): 29–51.

Dreier, Jamie. 2015. "Another World." In *Passions and Projections: Themes from the Philosophy of Simon Blackburn*, edited by Robert Johnson and Michael Smith, 155–171. Oxford: Oxford University Press.

Fine, Kit. 2001, June 1. "The Question of Realism." *Philosopher's Imprint* 1 (2). http://quod.lib.umich.edu/p/phimp/3521354.0001.002/1.

Gibbard, Allan. 2003. *Thinking How to Live*. Cambridge, MA: Harvard University Press.

Golub, Camil. 2017. "Expressivism and Realist Explanations." *Philosophical Studies* 174 (6): 1385–1409.

Harman, Gilbert. 1987. "(Nonsolipsistic) Conceptual Role Semantics." In *Notre Dame Journal of Formal Logic*, edited by Ernest Harman, 242–256. London: Academic Press.

Horwich, Paul. 1998. *Truth*. New York: Oxford University Press.

Jackson, Frank. 1998. *From Metaphysics to Ethics: A Defence of Conceptual Analysis*. Oxford: Oxford University Press.

Kramer, Matthew H. 2017. "There's Nothing Quasi about Quasi-Realism: Moral Realism as a Moral Doctrine." *The Journal of Ethics* 21 (2): 185–212.

Lewis, David. 1970. "How to Define Theoretical Terms." *The Journal of Philosophy* 67 (13): 427–446.

O'Leary-Hawthorne, John, and Huw Price. 1996, June 1. "How to Stand up for Non-Cognitivists." *Australasian Journal of Philosophy* 74 (2): 275–292.

Perez Carballo, Alejandro. 2014. "Semantic Hermeneutics." In *Metasemantics: New Essays on the Foundations of Meaning*, edited by Alexis Burgess and Brett Sherman, 119–146. Oxford: Oxford University Press.

Price, Huw, Simon Blackburn, and Robert Brandom. 2013. *Expressivism, Pragmatism and Representationalism*. 1st ed. Cambridge: Cambridge University Press.

Prior, A. N. 1960. "The Autonomy of Ethics." *Australasian Journal of Philosophy* 38 (3): 199–206.

Ridge, Michael. 2014. *Impassioned Belief*. Oxford: Oxford University Press.

Ridge, Michael. 2015. "Summary." *Analysis* 75 (3): 433–442.

Scanlon, Thomas. 2014. *Being Realistic About Reasons*. Oxford: Oxford University Press.

Simpson, Matthew. 2017. "Solving the Problem of Creeping Minimalism." *Canadian Journal of Philosophy* 2017: 1–22.

Tiefensee, Christine. 2016. "Inferentialist Metaethics, Bifurcations and Ontological Commitment." *Philosophical Studies* 173 (9): 2437–2459.

Wedgwood, Ralph. 2007. *The Nature of Normativity*. Oxford: Oxford University Press.

Williams, M. 2013. "How Pragmatists Can Be Local Expressivists." *In Price* 2013: 128–144.

Zangwill, Nick. 2006. "Moral Epistemology and the 'Because' Constraint." In *Contemporary Debates in Moral Theory*, edited by J. Dreier. Cambridge, MA: Blackwell.

Representing ethical reality: a guide for worldly non-naturalists

William J. FitzPatrick

ABSTRACT
Ethical realists hold (i) that our ethical concepts, thoughts, and claims are in the business of representing ethical reality, by representing evaluative or normative properties and facts as aspects of reality, and (ii) that such representations are at least sometimes accurate. Non-naturalist realists add the further claim that ethical properties and facts are ultimately non-natural, though they are nonetheless worldly. My aim is threefold: to elucidate the sort of representation involved in ethical evaluation on realist views; to clarify what exactly is represented and how non-naturalism comes into the picture for non-naturalists; and to defend worldly non-naturalism against some objections. The first question addressed is how we should model evaluation on any realist view, which should in turn guide the identification of which properties and facts are credibly regarded as 'evaluative' ones. Then the question is: what role might non-natural properties and facts play, and how are they related to what is represented in ethical evaluation? Once that is clear, we will be in a position to answer certain objections to non-naturalist realism from Jackson, Gibbard, Bedke, and Dreier. I argue that the objections all mischaracterize the role played by non-natural properties and facts on plausible versions of non-naturalist realism.

1. Introduction

Ethical realists hold that our ethical concepts, thoughts and claims are in the business of *representing ethical reality*, by representing evaluative or normative properties and facts as aspects of reality; and they hold that such representations are at least sometimes accurate. To judge, for example, that intense suffering is bad, in a way that provides impartial reasons to mitigate it, is to represent the evaluative and normative status of such suffering as part of how the world is. Or again, in correctly judging that it is morally wrong to undermine health care access for the poor and sick in order to provide tax cuts for the wealthy, we are representing the evaluative fact that such behavior possesses the evaluative property of wrongness. Some ethical realists add the further claim that ethical properties and facts are ultimately *non-natural*. As I am understanding ethical realism, such non-naturalist realists maintain that these non-natural properties and facts are nonetheless *worldly*, i.e. they are as much features of the world or aspects of reality as natural properties and facts.[1]

My aim here is threefold: to elucidate the sort of representation that is involved in ethical evaluation on plausible realist views, to clarify what exactly is represented and how non-naturalism might come into the picture, and to defend worldly non-naturalism against some objections. The first main question, taken up in Section 2, is how we should model *evaluation* on any realist view, which in turn should guide the identification of which properties and facts are credibly regarded as 'evaluative' ones – as opposed to others that are merely related in some way to them but are not themselves the evaluative properties and facts whose representation constitutes evaluation. Then the question is how the non-naturalist element enters the picture for those of us who make this move in the case of ethical evaluation. What role do non-natural properties and facts play, and how do they figure into what is represented in ethical evaluation? This issue is taken up in Section 3.

Finally, once that is clear, we will be in a position to answer certain well-known objections to non-naturalist realism from Frank Jackson (1998) and Allan Gibbard (2003, 2006), as well as more recent objections from Matt Bedke (2014) and Dreier (2015). I will argue in Section 4 that the objections all mischaracterize the role played by non-natural properties and facts.

In particular, non-naturalism does not claim that the natural properties we cite in support of evaluations 'don't really matter' and that some mysterious, unrelated non-natural properties have to be introduced to do the real justifying work (Gibbard 2003, 2006; Jackson 1998). Nor does non-naturalism construe evaluative judgment as belief about non-natural properties in any sense that would imply that we should be expected to change or abandon our first-order moral beliefs if we were to lose our metaphysical belief in non-natural properties. Neither is there any implication that it should be possible to settle first-order moral questions – perhaps in surprising ways – through some sort of direct metaphysical discovery (independent of ethical methodologies) of certain non-natural properties in the world (Bedke 2014). Finally, non-naturalist realism needn't create any special mystery about why rationality requires us to be motivated by our normative judgments (Dreier 2015).

2. Evaluation, representation, and evaluative properties and facts

We may begin with a simple axiom, which I'll call the *Evaluation-Based Condition* on identifying evaluative properties:

Evaluation-Based Condition: if there is anything truly worth calling an 'evaluative property' then this must be nothing more or less than the very property we are attributing to something in *evaluating* it (e.g. in judging that it is good or right), where the attribution of this property is what *constitutes* evaluating the thing in question.

So in seeking to identify evaluative properties in the world, we need to start by thinking about what we are doing in *evaluating* things. There are various properties relevant to evaluation, such as good-making properties, but if our concern is with the evaluative property of goodness itself, for example, then what we are after is the property whose representation constitutes evaluation, such that by attributing it to something we are thereby evaluating the thing.

Consider a simple, non-ethical example. Sharpness may be a good-making feature of a knife, but simply attributing sharpness to a knife is not by itself evaluating it. Someone could attribute sharpness to a knife while not evaluating it if she doesn't regard sharpness as good-making here, perhaps because she mistakes the knife for a bookmark, say, or because she is ignorant of a knife's function, or because she fails to understand that sharpness makes things well-disposed toward cutting. We evaluate something when we judge that it is good, which is clearly something more than judging that it is sharp (or attributing any other such property to it). Of course, in the case of a knife we will cite its sharpness as a good-making feature in support of our evaluation of it as a good knife – just as we'll cite a bookmark's sharpness as a bad-making feature in support of a negative evaluation of it as a bad bookmark. But the evaluation is more than just saying that something is sharp or not, and the property whose attribution constitutes evaluation will therefore be something more than sharpness. Similar points can be made about evaluative *facts*: anything worth calling an 'evaluative fact' must be nothing more or less than the very fact we aim to state in evaluating something, the stating of which constitutes evaluating it. So we need to understand evaluation.

Moving now to ethics, suppose we evaluate a certain activity or experience as being good. Again, we are not here simply judging that it is pleasant, for example, even if that is part of what we're doing, and even if we think (though I don't) that all and only pleasant things are good, taking pleasantness to be the sole good-making feature of activities or experiences. To judge that something is pleasant is no more to evaluate it than judging that something is sharp is to evaluate it. Someone could agree that an experience would be pleasant and yet still sensibly wonder whether it would be good to pursue, so that she clearly hasn't yet settled on an evaluation of the experience. Indeed, she might even deny outright that it would be good, explicitly rejecting the positive evaluation despite judging the experience to be pleasant.

Now this is so far just a point about evaluation and the *concept* of goodness employed in it. We cannot, with Moore (1903), move directly from this sort of 'open-question' point to claims about the nature of the *property* of goodness.

Moore famously relied on faulty assumptions about semantics and metaphysics to draw quick conclusions about the impossibility of goodness being identical to pleasantness, or more generally about the falsity of ethical naturalism.[2] We know now that despite the distinctness of the concepts of goodness and pleasantness, and of judgments about goodness and judgments about pleasantness, it is still possible, as far as *that* goes, for goodness just to be pleasantness – just as water can be H2O despite the distinctness of the concepts and thoughts about them. Moorean 'open questions' don't lead straightaway to metaphysical conclusions: the fact that we can grant pleasantness but still wonder about goodness doesn't show that the properties are in fact distinct.

While that is true, however, none of this lends any plausibility to the thought that we can actually understand evaluation and therefore evaluative properties on the model of reductive definitions in the sciences. Consider, for example, the simplistic proposal that when we evaluate activities or experiences as good we are just attributing pleasantness to them using a different concept, *goodness*, much as we have all along just been talking about H2O using the concept *water*, and have now discovered the actual nature of the referent. This has no plausibility because while it is true that one possible outcome of our evaluative activity might be the hedonistic conclusion that all and only pleasant experiences are good and worth pursuing, the evaluative activity itself is plainly not one in which we were *just talking about pleasantness* all along, attributing it to things using a different concept. That is something people could do, of course, but it has nothing to do with the evaluative concerns we have as agents, where the point is not to talk about which things have or lack a property like pleasantness while using a different concept, but is instead to inquire into what kinds of things – including but not limited to pleasantness – *have an evaluative status such that they should weigh positively in our deliberations*, having normative significance for us (Darwall 2003).

This is why we can raise evaluative questions about all kinds of things in ethical reflection, including experiences already acknowledged to be pleasant, and it is why our deliberative questions could never be settled for us by some revelation that 'goodness' happens just to refer to something like pleasantness (on the water/H2O model). Our evaluative practices reveal that our evaluative words and concepts don't work that way. If they did, they would be useless to us as rational agents occupying the deliberative perspective and trying to determine whether various pleasant things, for example, are truly worthy of pursuit. As Moore would point out, for example, we are not concerned in that capacity with asking, obtusely, whether this pleasant experience is pleasant, for example, whatever concepts we are using. Our concerns are different.[3]

This brings out a basic condition of adequacy for any account of evaluative properties:

Condition of Adequacy: Any account of evaluative properties must make adequate sense of how attributions of evaluative properties like goodness *amount to evaluation*, understood in a way that properly captures the *role* evaluation plays in the practical lives of rational agents.

And this is a rich matter when it comes to ethical evaluation. We face the world from a practical, deliberative standpoint as creatures who must reflectively decide what to do. From this standpoint, we ask questions and seek to arrive at informed judgments about what is worthy of pursuit, promotion, and respect as we make choices and act. These are questions broadly about value or goodness: goods to be sought, good ends to be pursued, and values to be respected in our interactions with the world, whether by promoting certain things or by constraining our actions in appropriate ways. The most important sorts of evaluation we engage in take place in this context, from the perspective of *deliberating agents seeking to act well, all things considered*.

My claim so far, then, is this: any account of the ethical properties and facts represented in ethical evaluation must make sense of how the representation of those properties and facts constitutes this rich form of evaluative activity, playing this role in practical life. This clearly rules out the simplistic suggestion from before. A property like pleasantness may be a good-making property, but it is not *goodness* and attributing it to something is not in itself to evaluate the thing. I have argued elsewhere that the same point holds even for more sophisticated views that might seek to identify goodness with pleasantness via functional role accounts, for example, even though their accounts of evaluation are more plausible than that of the simplistic naturalistic view above: they still involve a similar misidentification of evaluative or normative properties (FitzPatrick 2011, 2014). I will not further pursue that point here, however, but will focus instead on the positive implications of the claims made so far, if they are correct.

What sort of property, then, *are* we representing in genuine evaluation, as by attributing goodness to something, which is distinct from merely attributing features to it that happen to be good-making? In particular, what is goodness as represented in *ethical* evaluation, keeping in mind the above reflections on the nature and role of ethical evaluation in the practical deliberations of rational agents? My answer is that goodness (in the ethical sphere) is a property that amounts to an *evaluative status with normative implications, which is of concern to rational agents engaging in ethical evaluation*. I will focus here on the goodness involved in common *non-basic* claims of goodness, where goodness is attributed to something by virtue of certain good-making properties (e.g. a policy is good by virtue of enhancing fair equality of opportunity, or an experience is good by virtue of being pleasant), as opposed to the *basic* goodness of good-makers themselves (such as the goodness of pleasure, which is not itself attributed on the basis of further good-making features). The claim, then, with respect to such non-basic goodness, which is our concern in ordinary forms of ethical judgment, is this:

G: Goodness is an evaluative status things can have, by virtue of possessing certain good-making features (i.e. features that make the things that have them count as satisfying relevant evaluative standards), where things that have this evaluative status are worthy of pursuit, promotion, or respect, such that there are genuine reasons for such pursuit, promotion, or respect.[4]

It is this sort of status that is the property whose attribution (or representation as being instantiated) constitutes evaluating something in the ethical domain, which is what makes this property warrant being called an 'evaluative property'. It is not pleasantness, even if hedonism turns out to be true, but an evaluative status things have *by virtue of* being pleasant, such that they merit certain responses on our part, for which there are genuine reasons. Even a hedonist, then, should not claim that goodness just is pleasantness.[5] The claim should be just that pleasure is good and is the only thing that is (intrinsically) good, so that an activity's or experience's pleasantness is what makes it have the normatively significant evaluative status of being good and worthy of pursuit. The hedonist will then still owe an account of this alleged fact about the unconditional and exclusive good-makingness of pleasantness, or equivalently, a defense of the claim that the relevant standards of goodness – the ones of proper concern to us as deliberative beings – are such as to have that implication. And if she is a naturalist, she will have to provide an account of all this while operating entirely within a naturalistic metaphysics, not smuggling in any irreducibly evaluative or normative assumptions or claims.

Similar points apply to evaluations of actions as right or wrong, and parallel temptations toward overly simplistic identifications of properties. Evaluating an act as right is not just a matter of attributing to it a property like being happiness maximizing. That may well be relevant to rightness as a right-making property, and some may even hold that it is the only one. But saying that an act is happiness maximizing is not in itself to evaluate it as right, any more than attributing pleasantness to an experience is to evaluate it as good. To evaluate an act as right is to attribute to it the normatively significant evaluative status an act has when it has sufficient right-making properties. Rightness is then precisely that normatively significant evaluative status, the representation of which (as instantiated by the act) constitutes evaluating the act as being right, where, as before, the evaluation in question is the sort of ethical evaluation we engage in as rational agents occupying the deliberative perspective. That is,

R: Rightness is an evaluative status acts can have, by virtue of possessing certain right-making features, where acts that have this evaluative status are worthy of choice by a rational agent occupying the deliberative standpoint, and worthy of moral approval or admiration by others, such that there are genuine reasons for these things.

Even, then, if consequentialism turns out to be correct, the claim should not be that rightness *just is* being happiness maximizing, say, but rather just that all and only happiness maximizing acts are right, and that an act's being happiness maximizing is what makes it have the normatively significant evaluative status of being right and worthy of pursuit and admiration. The consequentialist will still then owe an account of this alleged fact about the right-makingness of happiness maximization, or equivalently, a defense of the claim that the relevant standards of rightness of action – the ones of proper concern to us as rational deliberators – are such as to have that implication. And if she is a naturalist, she will have to provide an account of all this while operating entirely within a naturalistic metaphysics. That is the task she faces.

3. Enter non-naturalism

Nothing so far poses any explicit threat to ethical naturalism: the point has been simply to flag certain temptations we should avoid, to indicate the more complex sorts of properties represented in evaluation as such, and to highlight the rather demanding task naturalists therefore face in accounting for those properties naturalistically. This is, however, where non-naturalism comes in, because the reason why some of us are non-naturalists is precisely that we are skeptical that the task faced by the naturalist can be satisfactorily accomplished.

The worry is that the naturalistic constraint will force undesirable compromises in our understanding of the objectivity and normative force of ethical facts and properties. I have argued elsewhere that it is hard to see how we can capture everything we might want in these respects without positing some irreducibly evaluative or normative properties and facts – where these are things that can be captured (even in principle) only through evaluative or normative concepts, due to the evaluative or normative nature of the property or fact itself (FitzPatrick 2008, 2011, 2014, forthcoming).[6] It is not hard, for example, to come up with a naturalistic account of rightness as an evaluative status related to an act's satisfying certain stipulated standards cashed out in a purely naturalistic way. But if this is to capture a notion of rightness that is genuinely objective and has categorical normative force for us as rational agents, then we also need to posit such facts as that the set of standards in question is in fact the *appropriate* one for rational human beings to build our practical lives around, having genuine *authority* for us and appropriately settling the normative questions we face from the deliberative perspective. Yet it is hard to see how any such facts, if they exist, could themselves be understood as just more natural ones.[7]

It is not my purpose here to rehearse or defend those arguments. The point is just that if we do have doubts about cashing out these background evaluative or normative claims about standards or good- or right-makingness in a purely naturalistic way, then we have two choices if we wish to maintain a realist approach: either (1) we stick with naturalism and drop the ambition of capturing such facts, giving up on robust objectivity or categoricity and settling for less, or (2) we continue to posit such facts and maintain that they are *irreducibly evaluative or normative*: they're grounded ultimately in basic *values* or *reasons* (such as human dignity, or the badness of suffering) that cannot be cashed out fully by any appeal solely to non-evaluative or non-normative properties and facts. It is this second move that brings us to non-naturalism, since it is typically thought that the natural world doesn't contain any (in principle) irreducibly evaluative or normative properties and facts, at least of the robust sort relevant to ethics.[8] So for those of us who are led to ethical non-naturalism in this way, this is how the non-naturalism comes in: we are skeptical about capturing everything we want without relying on some irreducibly evaluative or normative facts about standards or good- or right-makingness; so we posit such apparently 'non-natural' facts and properties at the bottom of all this.

4. Responses to objections

With these clarifications in place, we are now in a position to provide responses to a number of objections.

4.1. Jackson and Gibbard on the superfluousness of non-natural properties and facts

Frank Jackson suggests that non-naturalists have (for some inexplicable reason) decided that the natural features of actions we ordinarily cite as wrong-making features don't really matter after all and cannot on their own justify avoiding actions that have those features, but need to be supplemented with an additional feature that has the honor of being non-natural: that's what *really* matters and does the justifying work. He imagines the non-naturalist's thinking going like this:

> I see that this action will kill many and save no one, but that's not enough to justify my not doing it. What really matters is that the action has an extra [non-natural] property such that only ethical terms are suited to pick out. (Jackson 1998, 127)

That is, however, not at all what we think. Non-naturalists don't claim that natural properties like causing suffering and death don't 'really matter' because they're merely natural, or that they're 'not enough to justify' avoiding such actions, requiring supplementation with additional wrong-making features that are non-natural. Obviously the natural features matter, and of course it would be obtuse to suppose that ethical justification would require adding mysterious non-natural wrong-making features to the list of justifiers – as if the fact that the action gratuitously kills is not enough to make it wrong or to be avoided, and we have to suppose that it also has some obscure non-natural feature (Gibbard calls it 'exnat') in order to show that it is to be avoided.[9]

The non-naturalist's claim is instead just that we cannot fully account for the fact that the natural wrong-making features *do* obviously matter and *do* justify certain choices without appealing at some point to irreducibly evaluative or normative properties and facts. For example, we might think that we cannot fully account for the *wrong-makingness* of these natural features, as specified by a certain set of ethical standards S, without appealing to the claim that S is the correct and normatively authoritative set of standards for us to be guided by as rational human beings; and defending *that* claim may require positing basic facts about the objective dignity of persons or the badness of suffering as grounds for the correctness and authority of S. If those facts in turn seem to be irreducibly evaluative and so seem to resist accommodation within a purely naturalistic metaphysics, then we have thereby been led to non-naturalism. What is non-natural are not extraneous and obscure additional features (like 'exnat') added to the list of wrong-makers, but just irreducibly evaluative or normative properties and facts to which we appeal in accounting for the evaluative or normative significance *of* the familiar natural facts we cite in ordinary ethical justifications. All we deny is that such *metafacts* about the normative significance of such natural facts (such as their wrong-makingness) are themselves *just more natural facts* (Dancy 2006; FitzPatrick 2008, 2011, 2014); Parfit 2011; Scanlon 2014, 21, 33).[10]

We are not, then, claiming that some sort of special ethical work is done by trotting out some obscure property and announcing that it is non-natural – as if non-naturalness in itself were some kind of ethical magic that allows some random property to accomplish something that natural properties cannot. The only properties and facts we are talking about in connection with non-naturalness are plainly relevant ethical properties and facts – not some 'exnat', but just *rightness* or *goodness*, or the *badness* of suffering or the *dignity* of persons, or the fact that these things objectively ground certain ethical standards we have *reason* to live by. And there is no mystery why we should be concerned with these things in our ethical thinking, if they exist. The claim that they are non-natural is not meant to *explain why* we should be concerned with them, but is instead just a theoretical claim about the metaethical status that these already plainly relevant facts and properties have to possess if our theories are to capture a robust sort of ethical objectivity and normativity: they will have to be non-natural facts and properties because they are irreducibly evaluative or normative.

4.2. Bedke's argument from responses to loss of belief in non-natural properties

If non-naturalist ethical realism is correct then our ethical judgments represent a part of reality, specifically an ethical reality with irreducibly evaluative or normative elements, thus resisting full naturalization. There is a sense, then, in which according to the non-naturalist our ethical judgments are beliefs about non-natural properties: (1) they are beliefs about evaluative or normative properties, such as goodness, and (2) these properties are irreducibly evaluative or normative and therefore non-natural. But Matt Bedke (2014) has recently argued that ethical beliefs have the wrong sort of 'epistemic profile' to be *about* non-natural properties. He offers two related arguments to this effect, which I will consider in this sub-section and the next. The first has to do with expected reactions to the loss of belief in non-natural properties, and goes as follows.

If ethical judgments are beliefs, as the cognitive non-naturalist holds, then they should have a mind-to-world direction of fit, as with other beliefs. This means that ethical judgments should tend to drop away if one were to come to think that there is conclusive evidence that their contents are false, as with other beliefs. Suppose, then, that Amy happens upon some teenagers tormenting a cat and judges it to be wrong, but then she also comes to accept evidence against the existence of non-natural properties. In doing so, she would be accepting evidence against the existence of non-natural wrongness in particular, and so against the boys' action's having that property. So if ethical judgments were really beliefs about things like non-natural wrongness, as the cognitive non-naturalist holds, then we should expect Amy at this point to drop her ethical judgment that the action was wrong. Yet she wouldn't, and shouldn't. So, the objection goes, cognitive non-naturalism is false: ethical judgments are not beliefs about non-natural properties.

In response, however, note first that the non-naturalist does not claim that ordinary ethical judgments are *de dicto* beliefs concerning non-natural properties – as if in believing that the boys' behavior is wrong Amy is believing that some non-natural property is instantiated. Unless Amy is a philosopher, she won't even have considered such matters. The claim is only that ethical beliefs, such as the belief that an act was wrong, are beliefs about properties, such as wrongness, *of which* it is true (*de re*) that they are non-natural. Amy believes that the boys' behavior was wrong, but she needn't have any *de dicto* belief at all about non-natural properties, even if it is in fact true of wrongness (which she does have beliefs about) that it is a non-natural property. Nor need Amy have any *metaethical* belief to the effect that ethical judgments are beliefs about non-natural properties. So there is no reason why we should expect Amy to drop her moral belief about the tormenting just because she now reads a book on metaphysics and concludes that there are no non-natural properties: she needn't so far think that has any bearing at all on wrongness. So cognitive non-naturalism is not saddled with any implausible implications about how ordinary people like Amy should be expected to respond morally to accepting that there is evidence against non-natural properties: it makes exactly the right predictions.

In order to raise the sort of worry Bedke has in mind we need to imagine a different sort of case where, for example, Ben is a moral philosopher who subscribes to cognitive non-naturalist realism. Unlike Amy, Ben takes his ethical judgment to be about a non-natural property, since he takes wrongness to be a non-natural property. So now suppose that Ben subsequently has a crisis of 'metaethical faith': after reading the same metaphysics book he too concludes that there are after all no non-natural properties. Here, Bedke argues, there would seem to be an expectation that Ben's ethical judgment should drop away.

After all, if his ethical belief was explicitly a belief that a non-natural property, wrongness, was instantiated by the boys' behavior, then in now coming to accept that there is conclusive evidence that there are no non-natural properties, he has likewise come to accept that there is conclusive evidence that the content of his ethical judgment is false. Just as a belief in angels (where this is understood to be a belief about supernatural entities) should drop away once one accepts that there is conclusive evidence that there are no supernatural entities, so too Ben's ethical belief about the wrongness of tormenting the cat should drop away – even while holding fixed all his beliefs about the natural features of the case he had cited as his reasons for making that judgment (Bedke 2014, 190–191). Yet, Bedke argues, this is not what would or should actually happen. The 'metaphysical discovery' that there are no non-natural properties would and should make no difference to first-order ethical judgments, even in cases like Ben's.

Now this last claim is of course correct, but the problem is that nothing forces the non-naturalist realist to endorse such abandonment of first-order ethical judgments if one should come to think that there are no non-natural properties after all. There are in fact two ways of going forward from such a 'metaethical crisis'. One would indeed be to retain the metaethical belief that ethical judgments are about non-natural properties (cognitive non-naturalism), in which case the loss of belief in non-natural properties would indeed lead one to drop the ethical judgment as well. This is precisely what we would expect for belief in angels, for example. It is a given that angels, if they exist at all, are supernatural beings (otherwise we're not really talking literally about angels), so beliefs about angels are beliefs about supernatural beings in a sense that involves believing *that* supernatural beings exist; and if someone who once believed in angels comes to think that there are no supernatural beings, then she will (typically) abandon her belief in angels. Similarly, then, the non-naturalist *could* take that path with regard to ethical beliefs after ceasing to believe in non-natural properties. But there is no reason to think that he should, and there is in fact a far more plausible alternative available.

This second, better alternative upon losing one's belief in non-natural properties is instead just to drop the earlier metaethical belief that ethical judgments are beliefs about non-natural properties, and look for a better theory while retaining one's first-order ethical judgments. There are several options here. The first, and least revisionary, would be to aim to retain not only our first-order ethical judgments but also the objectivity and categorical normative force we were after, but to seek now to capture all this somehow within a naturalistic framework (in the hope that some of the considerations that originally drove us to non-naturalism were mistaken). One possibility would be to try to develop a more *expansive naturalism* that might naturalistically accommodate the kinds of irreducibly evaluative or normative properties and facts that seem to be required for realist forms of objectivity and categoricity (FitzPatrick 2016). Another would be to attempt to capture objectivity and categoricity without positing irreducibly evaluative or normative properties and facts after all.

If such moves fail, then a more revisionary option – which still leaves our first-order ethical judgments intact – would be to dial back the initial ambitions concerning objectivity and categoricity. Those of us who are currently non-naturalists must face the fact that at the end of the day we *might* wind up having to settle for what we can get within a purely naturalistic metaphysics, if objections to non-naturalism ultimately prove decisive. We might then fall back on something along the lines of David Copp's (1995) society-centered, standard-based moral naturalism, for example, as the best we can do in the way of ethical realism.[11] While this may not give us everything we originally hoped for, it might still be far more attractive than embracing moral *nihilism* and denying the wrongness of tormenting cats, for example. (Indeed, even if one gave up on ethical *realism* altogether upon jettisoning belief in non-natural properties, there would still be the option of embracing expressivism, which would allow for retaining even a kind of objectivity and categoricity as well as allowing us to preserve our first-order ethical beliefs.[12])

The underlying point here is that belief in wrongness is ultimately not like belief in angels: we are not simply *changing the subject* or ceasing to speak literally if we drop our non-naturalist metaethics and continue to speak of wrongness without positing non-natural properties, as we would be changing the subject or ceasing to speak literally if we continued to speak of angels without positing supernatural entities, as by calling very nice people 'angels'. Angels are understood by believers to be supernatural entities if they exist at all, so that in believing in angels believers take themselves to be believing in supernatural entities, which explains why losing belief in the supernatural can be expected to result in dropping belief in angels. By contrast, it is not part of ordinary belief about wrongness to take oneself to be believing in a non-natural property, as already noted in connection with Amy. This means that even where someone did take himself to believe in a non-natural property, as Ben did, if he then loses that conviction he still has something to fall back on: he can still have beliefs about wrongness, though stripped of any non-naturalness – a move that is not available to the former believer in angels, who cannot go on (literally) believing in angels that are just stripped of their supernatural nature.

These points are reinforced by recalling the earlier reflections on what ethical belief is. I have emphasized that to have an ethical belief that something is good, say, is not simply to believe that it instantiates some property such as pleasantness. Such a model portrays evaluating something as good as being similar to any other property attribution, such as judging that a piece of metal is magnetic, which in turn encourages the thought that evaluation for the non-naturalist is akin to judging that a crystal has occult healing powers. This in turn encourages Bedke's idea that if the non-naturalist ceases to believe in non-natural properties he should drop his evaluative beliefs, just as one would drop beliefs about the occult healing powers of crystals if one ceased to believe in the existence of occult powers. But my earlier point was precisely that this is an inapt model of evaluation, and so of ethical belief and of the properties represented by it. While it is formally and trivially true (at least on cognitivist assumptions) that evaluation involves attributing a property to something (e.g. attributing goodness to it), this is *not* like attributing magnetism to a piece of metal, or pleasantness to an experience, or occult healing powers to a crystal. It is instead attributing an *evaluative status* to something *by virtue of* its having certain other features (in non-basic cases) together with background facts about how those features make the thing stack up with respect to appropriate *evaluative standards*; and the evaluative properties represented in evaluation, as instantiated by the evaluated object, are the sorts of properties described in G and R (and their negative correlates, B and W, for badness and wrongness, which we needn't spell out here).

With this model of evaluation and evaluative properties in place, we can better see how the non-naturalist should respond to a loss of metaphysical belief in non-natural properties. When we evaluate the boys' cruel behavior as wrong, we are attributing to it a certain normatively significant evaluative status, which it has by virtue of having various features we take to be wrong-making features, i.e. features that make it violate appropriate standards for human action. Now again, some of us are led to non-naturalism by the conviction that we cannot give a fully adequate account of these ethical properties and facts without appealing at some point to irreducibly evaluative or normative properties and facts. We therefore add such elements to the picture, which then counts as non-naturalist. But it is not as if we have thereby switched the *objects* of our ethical belief to obscure new non-natural properties like 'exnat' that have nothing to do with the commonsense understanding of what makes tormenting cats wrong. If that's what we were doing, on the model of attributing new occult healing powers to crystals, then we would indeed have to give up our ethical beliefs if we came to reject the existence of non-natural properties. But we haven't done anything like that. Everything in the commonsense evaluative picture remains intact: what we are attributing to the act is simply *wrongness*, and the tormenting is wrong for exactly the reasons common sense tells us: it is a deliberate infliction of pain for amusement. We have just added the claim that at the *foundation* of the picture lie certain irreducibly evaluative or normative – and therefore non-natural – properties and facts, such as the objective, intrinsic, reason-giving badness of suffering.

If we now come to believe that there are really no non-natural properties and facts in the world, and so no irreducibly evaluative or normative ones, nothing forces us to abandon the entire structure (as if wrongness were just an arbitrary posit, like exnat, proposed as a placeholder for some non-natural property). All that is affected is our understanding of its foundation: we would have to concede that it doesn't rest on irreducibly evaluative or normative properties and facts after all (unless these turn out to fit into an expansive naturalism after all), but has to be understood in a way that doesn't rely on such things. For example, perhaps the standards are defensible as the appropriate ones *given* certain very basic commitments and ends which are at least widely shared, or would be if people underwent improvements in empirical knowledge and deliberated in rich and procedurally rational ways. Again, this may not give us everything we had wanted when we turned to non-naturalism to try to account for more, but if non-naturalism were taken off the table then we would just have to accept that this is the best we can do. Such a view would remain fairly robust and needn't in any case lead us to dismiss the content of our first-order ethical beliefs as being false. What *would* lead us to regard the content of our ethical belief as false would be coming to accept that there is conclusive evidence that the features we took to be wrong-making *aren't after all wrong-making*, which is to say that we were mistaken about the standards for action and there is, for example, nothing wrong after all with deliberate infliction of suffering for amusement. But dropping the non-naturalist construal of the foundation of the standards doesn't in any way lead us to such a (morally implausible) conclusion.

Nothing in the non-naturalist's position, therefore, implies any problematic commitment to dropping plausible ethical judgments such as the condemnation of the boys' behavior, or to embracing moral nihilism, if it turns out that there are no non-natural properties. The claim is just that as long as non-natural properties remain on the table as possibilities, as we currently believe they do, the most attractive account of ethical properties and facts includes some appeal to such non-natural properties in the form of irreducibly evaluative or normative elements of reality. Obviously if some metaphysical argument convinces us that they are no longer on the table, then we will have to reassess our metaethical picture. But there is no expectation that this should also force a reassessment or abandonment of our first-order ethical views.

4.3. Bedke's argument from responses to direct discovery of non-natural properties

The second argument Bedke offers is also meant to show the irrelevance of beliefs about non-natural properties to our first-order ethical beliefs, in support of the conclusion that ethical judgments are not beliefs about non-natural properties. Return to the case of the boys tormenting the cat. Bedke takes the non-naturalist to hold that 'there is a possible non-natural property that is possibly exhibited by the boys' actions, and discovery that this property is so exhibited would dispose one to judge that tormenting the cat is right,' even 'while holding fixed one's beliefs about the natural properties of the case and one's non-cognitive attitudes' (Bedke 2014, 197). Yet, the argument goes, it is absurd to suppose that there is any such non-natural property you could 'discover' through 'direct cognition' that 'would convince you that an action that causes intense pain for fun, and toward which you have strong negative conative attitudes, is actually right.' To put it another way, Bedke asks: 'Is it because they are causing it pain that the action normatively matters in the way it does, or because there is some non-natural property or relation at play? Surely the former.' Again, 'the direct discovery of any non-natural property or relation (were this possible) would be as idle to the action's judged normative status as a man's height is to the judgment that he won the lottery' (Bedke 2014, 197).

There is, however, a straightforward response to this challenge. First, as we have seen in connection with Jackson's objection, the non-naturalist is not committed to the existence of any obscure non-natural property, such as Gibbard's 'exnat', conceived as a feature possessed by an action alongside its various natural features (such as causing pain, deliberately, for amusement), and capable somehow of canceling out their wrong-makingness. That is, we are in no way committed to a picture according to which it could be the case that if some such mysterious exnat were added to the act's list of features, holding the rest fixed, a hideous act would be made right and we could in principle come to see its rightness by peering at the act through 'magic spectacles that reveal all non-natural properties' (Bedke 2014, 198) and thus directly cognizing this exnat or the resulting rightness. Non-naturalists posit no such properties and no such intelligible possibility, metaphysical or epistemic. The only non-natural property we posit that is relevant to this case is *wrongness* itself (and any irreducibly evaluative or normative properties on which wrongness here depends, such as the intrinsic, reason-giving badness of suffering). And as we have seen, evaluative properties such as rightness and wrongness are not directly cognized, on the model of some direct cognition of occult healing powers, but are rather attributed as *resultant* properties *through an act of evaluation that applies relevant standards to an object in light of its natural features*.

There is, then, no possible *exnat* (to be directly cognized, even in principle) that could change the evaluative status of the action, for the latter status depends simply on the natural wrong-making features and their wrong-makingness. And there is no intelligible possibility of a direct cognition of (a surprising) rightness here, as if rightness were just some distinct occult quality that could be arbitrarily thrown on top of any set of natural properties and so could, for all we know, just show up anywhere. What we have is instead an act with an evaluative status of wrongness, by virtue of the wrong-makingness of its natural features (as implied by the appropriate set of standards for human action), together with the claim that a proper and full account of the ethical properties and facts here ultimately bottoms out in certain appeals to irreducibly evaluative or normative properties and facts, which are for that reason (and no other) best thought of as non-natural.

None of this implies or even suggests a commitment to the intelligible possibility that there is some non-natural property that, while holding everything else fixed, 'could dispose you to think that walking down the street is wrong, or that

... slavery is just' (Bedke 2014, 197). The non-naturalism I have described gives no such potential role to non-natural properties in evaluation, and so does not, as Bedke suggests, imply any implausible 'power to change our normative beliefs [while] holding fixed our beliefs about natural properties and holding fixed our conative attitudes' (Bedke 2014, 197). The only intelligible way for us appropriately to come to change our minds about ethical matters is by way of *ordinary ethical methodologies*, reflecting on the normative significance of relevant natural features of actions and on the related standards of action appropriate to human beings. And the non-naturalist is no more vulnerable to a surprising and implausible change of mind about the wrongness of tormenting cats, via such ethical reflection on appropriate ethical standards, than anyone else is.

4.3. Dreier on non-naturalist realism and motivational requirements

Finally, the above elucidations of non-naturalism and responses to Bedke's objections also provide a straightforward answer to worries raised by Dreier (2015) in connection with explaining the irrationality of failing to be motivated by one's own normative judgments. Dreier first of all characterizes non-naturalist realists as holding that 'ought judgments are simply beliefs about which things have a certain ineffable non-natural property' (Dreier 2015, 180). He then imagines beings who 'are disposed to be motivated by their judgments about which actions and states have some other non-natural property (the shmought property, perhaps).' What, he wonders, would make it the case that it is rational to be motivated by beliefs about one ineffable non-natural property (the ought property) rather than by beliefs about the other (the shmought property, or exnat, or whatever)? Realists, he claims, have nothing to say about this crucial matter, and so the view is 'unacceptably mysterian': for 'the idea that what we have had in mind all along when we talked about rationality was the disposition to be motivated by which actions we believe to have a certain ineffable property seems pretty strange' (Dreier 2015, 180).

Pretty strange indeed, but fortunately not an idea belonging to any sensible non-naturalist realism. First of all, it is worth emphasizing again that non-naturalists do not claim that ordinary ethical judgments are beliefs about non-natural properties in the sense that they are beliefs *that* certain actions 'have a certain ineffable property'; nor do we hold that what people have 'had in mind' in talk of rationality was something about an ineffable property. In fact, since the whole point of the move to non-naturalism is the insistence that ethical judgments are *irreducibly evaluative or normative*, non-naturalists are committed to *rejecting* any reduction of ethical beliefs to *de dicto* metaphysical beliefs about the instantiation of non-natural properties, such as the reduction of the belief that tormenting cats is wrong to the belief that tormenting cats 'has a certain ineffable property' (the latter plainly *not* being an evaluative or normative judgment). The belief that tormenting cats is wrong is the belief *that tormenting cats is wrong*, not a belief that some unnamed ineffable property is instantiated (which would be a non-evaluative, metaphysical belief). What the non-naturalist is claiming is just that it is true *of* wrongness that it is irreducibly evaluative and therefore a non-natural property – though not a particularly 'ineffable' one, it's worth noting.

To return to Dreier's objection, then: what the non-naturalist thinks about ought judgments is (1) that they are irreducibly normative judgments (not reducible to metaphysical judgments that some strange properties are instantiated), which play a certain role in practical deliberation about reasons, and (2) that normative truths about reasons or about what ought to be done can be fully accounted for only within a non-naturalistic framework, since the account will ultimately bottom out in some irreducibly evaluative or normative elements. Now one could obviously make the connection to rationality look mysterious by ignoring 1 above and just asking why rationality should be concerned with some non-natural property, X, rather than with another, Y, being told nothing more about the actual natures of X and Y – using a dummy term such as 'exnat' or 'shmought' merely to indicate some obscure non-natural property. Put that way there is of course nothing to say and it is indeed utterly mysterious why rationality should be concerned with such things. But none of this is a problem for non-naturalists because we do not simply posit generic, 'ineffable' non-natural properties and claim that rationality is concerned with them, as if it were the non-naturalness of the properties that does some magical ethical work by itself, regardless of the specific nature of the properties in question.

What rationality is concerned with is *essentially evaluative or normative properties* such as goodness, rightness, or the property of being a reason for acting, as such, and there is nothing mysterious about this connection when we understand these properties in the context of their role in ethical evaluation as described earlier – rather than just thinking of them as obscure non-natural properties on the model of occult healing powers, which are for some inexplicable reason supposed to be of interest to rational agents. It is no mystery why a rational agent occupying the deliberative perspective, trying to figure out how to live, should be concerned with what there is genuine reason to do (or ought to be done) and with what is good to pursue and what will constitute acting well (or rightly) for her in her circumstances: *this is precisely what rational deliberation is about*. In claiming that goodness, rightness and reasons are ultimately to be understood as non-natural we are not thereby positing some 'menagerie of curiosities' (as Bedke puts it, 2014, 190, 198–99) featuring 'exnat' or 'the shmought property' – properties it would indeed be bizarre to care about, since they are just meaningless posits divorced from any plausible role in agency and evaluation, thus lacking any intelligible claim to our attention.

Bedke is right, then, that learning that such curious and free-floating properties are instantiated would be as irrelevant 'to our first-order normative attitudes as learning about spiral nebulae or waterspouts' (Bedke 2014, 197). But this irrelevance in no way carries over to goodness, rightness, or 'oughtness'. The non-naturalist's claim about the metaphysical status of these latter properties comes in *only after their essential roles in agency and evaluation have been established*, simply insofar as it appears that their nature is irreducibly evaluative or normative, making them not purely natural aspects of the world (at least as 'the natural' is typically understood). Adding that last claim about irreducibility and therefore non-naturalness does nothing to obscure the relevance of these properties to practical rationality, understood as the virtue pertaining to the sphere of ethical deliberation and evaluation.[13]

Notes

1. This contrasts with 'quietist' or *non-metaphysical* cognitive non-naturalist views according to which non-natural ethics facts and properties stand outside of the world, on the model of logical or mathematical abstractions having no metaphysical grounding in or implications for what the world contains. Derek Parfit, for example, denies that normative properties and facts are part of (or are grounded in) reality or the fabric of the world, as they exist only in a 'non-ontological sense' (Parfit 2011). Cf. also T.M. Scanlon (2014) who, while not denying the ontological import of normative claims, restricts any such import to a domain-specific ontology such that the ontological commitments of normative claims have no more to do with what the world contains, in the usual sense, than do the commitments of mathematical or logical claims. In contrast, I defend a worldly, metaphysically committed non-naturalist view in FitzPatrick (2008) and something substantively similar to this but conceived as a form of expansive naturalism in FitzPatrick (2016).
2. For critical discussion of Moore's arguments see Brink (2001) and Sturgeon (2003). I explore some of the insights that are nonetheless to be found in Moore's discussion, and how they might be developed into more successful challenges to familiar forms of naturalism, in FitzPatrick (forthcoming).
3. The last three paragraphs and parts of what follows in this section draw from FitzPatrick (forthcoming).
4. This last part is meant to be neutral as between value-based accounts of reasons and buck-passing accounts of goodness in terms of reasons, though I favor the former. The crucial point here is that goodness in the ethical sphere is reason-involving in this way (cf. Parfit 2011).
5. Similarly, *contra* Gibbard (2006), the hedonist should *not* claim that the property of being pleasant is just identical to the property of being what one ought to do. These are distinct properties even if it is true that all and only pleasant things are things that ought to be done. See Dancy (2004, 2006) and FitzPatrick (2011, 16–27) for critique of this and related conflations of resultant normative properties with resultance base properties, by both Gibbard and Jackson.
6. We can, of course, *refer* to such properties without using evaluative or normative concepts, as by referring to goodness using the description 'Moore's favorite property'. The point is that we cannot provide any adequate characterization or account of the property except through employing such concepts.
7. There are of course natural facts about the various effects of living according to one set of standards or another, or about natural inclinations we may or may not have toward one set or another, either as we are or with certain (naturalistically specifiable) idealizations of our psychologies. But there are reasons to doubt that

any such plainly natural facts can succeed in capturing the robust *normative* facts in question, or so non-naturalists believe.
8. For present purposes I will just grant this assumption. In FitzPatrick (2016), however, I question whether naturalism should necessarily be understood to exclude irreducibly evaluative or normative properties and facts from the natural world. Perhaps there can be a more expansive form of ethical naturalism that accommodates irreducibly evaluative or normative properties and facts within an enriched naturalist ontology. If such a view is viable, everything the non-naturalist really wants can be captured within a naturalist picture after all and there would be no further reason to posit non-natural properties. I shall set this possibility aside here, however, and continue linking metaphysically irreducible value and normativity with non-naturalism.
9. 'Exnat' is Gibbard's (2003, 16) made-up term for a dummy non-natural property about which we are told nothing except that it is non-natural, which unsurprisingly then seems entirely superfluous when thinking about ethical evaluation: how could it possibly help, ethically speaking, to be told that an act has this obscure property on top of the familiar sorts of natural with which we are concerned in ethical evaluation? Gibbard (2006, 328–330) gives a caricature of non-naturalism very similar to Jackson's in imagining a non-naturalist hedonist claiming (implausibly) that the fact that eating chocolate is pleasant (and otherwise harmless) is not enough to justify it without adding some strange non-natural property (like exnat) to the mix.
10. Perhaps part of Jackson's point in the earlier quote is that such natural facts as that an action will kill many and save none can plausibly be taken *directly* to ground a *reason* to avoid the action, without an appeal to *wrongness* as an intermediary that really directly grounds the reason and is held by some to be non-natural. But that would still miss the point. Even if we allow that the natural facts directly ground the reason to avoid the action as well as the wrongness of the action (though on any plausible view the wrong-makingness and reason-groundingness of the facts in question here will still be intimately related), the non-naturalist's claim is just that *this normative metafact* – the fact that these natural facts do ground such a reason – cannot be cashed out in a purely naturalistic way. We are not positing some superfluous additional property. Thanks to Evan Tiffany for helpful discussion here.
11. I explain why I consider this 'settling' for less than we might have wanted in FitzPatrick (2008, 189, fn. 2; 2011, 26–27; and 2014, 575–578). That said, it would go too far to claim that having categorical reason-giving force is a conceptually 'non-negotiable' feature of morality, as Richard Joyce (2001) holds as part of an argument for error theory. While I agree that it is an important feature to try to preserve in our theorizing – which is precisely what leads some of us to embrace non-naturalism – and that it would be a significant loss to settle for something less, it is just not plausible to suppose that the many theorists who have embraced ethical realism *without* robust categoricity (holding instead neo-Humean, instrumentalist views of practical reasons, for example) have simply changed the subject and are failing literally to address *morality* at all – like someone who goes on talking of phlogiston after conceding that she is not speaking about any substance released during combustion (where we would say that she is not then really talking about phlogiston at all). Their accounts of morality may be somewhat deflationary (which is precisely why I resist them), but they are not simply about another topic. Thanks to Matt Bedke for helpful discussion on this topic.

12. See the contribution to this volume from Terry Horgan and Mark Timmons, 'Gripped by Authority' (forthcoming). I explain why I think it is important to try to hold out for a realist account of objectivity and categoricity, as against non-realist expressivist views, in FitzPatrick (2011). But again, if it were the only alternative to moral nihilism it might well be a preferable option for a metaphysically disillusioned non-naturalist.
13. I am grateful to Matt Bedke, Stefan Sciaraffa, Evan Tiffany, and participants in the *Representation and Evaluation* conference in Vancouver, 2017, for very helpful comments.

Disclosure statement

No potential conflict of interest was reported by the author.

References

Bedke, Matthew. 2014. "A Menagerie of Duties? Normative Judgments are not Beliefs about Non-Natural Properties." *American Philosophical Quarterly* 51 (3): 189–201.
Brink, David. 2001. "Realism, Naturalism and Moral Semantics." *Social Philosophy and Policy* 18 (2): 154–176.
Copp, David. 1995. *Morality, Normativity and Society*. Oxford: Oxford University Press.
Dancy, Jonathan. 2004. "On the Importance of Making Things Right." *Ratio* 17: 229–237.
Dancy, Jonathan. 2006. "Nonnaturalism." In *The Oxford Handbook of Ethical Theory*, edited by David Copp, 122–145. Oxford: Oxford University Press.
Darwall, Stephen. 2003. "Moore, Normativity, and Intrinsic Value." *Ethics* 113 (3): 468–489.
Dreier, Jamie. 2015. "Can Reasons Fundamentalism Answer the Normative Question?" In *Motivational Internalism*, edited by Gunnar Bjornsson, Caj Strandberg, Ragnar Francen Olinder, John Eriksson, and Fredrik Bjorklund. Oxford Scholarship Online. doi:10.1093/acprof:oso/9780199367955.003.0009.
FitzPatrick, William. 2008. "Robust Ethical Realism, Non-Naturalism and Normativity." In *Oxford Studies in Metaethics*. vol. 3, edited by Russ Shafer-Landau, 159–205. Oxford: Oxford University Press.
FitzPatrick, William. 2011. "Ethical Non-Naturalism and Normative Properties." In *New Waves in Metaethics*, edited by Michael Brady, 7–35. New York: Palgrave MacMillan.
FitzPatrick, William. 2014. "Skepticism about Naturalizing Normativity: In Defense of Ethical Non-naturalism." *Res Philosophica* 91 (4): 559–588.
FitzPatrick, William. 2016. "Ontology for an Uncompromising Ethical Realism." *Topoi*. http://rdcu.be/m3x3.
FitzPatrick, William. Forthcoming. "Open Question Arguments and the Irreducibility of Ethical Normativity." In *The Naturalistic Fallacy*, edited by Neil Sinclair. Cambridge: Cambridge University Press.

Gibbard, Allan. 2003. *Thinking How to Live*. Cambridge, MA: Harvard University Press.
Gibbard, Allan. 2006. "Normative Properties." In *Metaethics After Moore*, edited by Terence Horgan and Mark Timmons, 319–338. Oxford: Oxford University Press.
Horgan, Terry and Mark Timmons. Forthcoming. "Gripped by Authority." *Canadian Journal of Philosophy*.
Jackson, Frank. 1998. *From Metaphysics to Ethics*. Oxford: Oxford University Press.
Joyce, Richard. 2001. *The Myth of Morality*. Cambridge: Cambridge University Press.
Moore, G. E. (1903) 1994. *Principia Ethica*. Ed. and with an introduction by Thomas Baldwin. Revised ed. Cambridge: Cambridge University Press.
Parfit, D. 2011. *On What Matters*. 2 vols. Oxford: Oxford University Press.
Scanlon, Thomas. 2014. *Being Realistic about Reasons*. Oxford: Oxford University Press.
Sturgeon, Nicholas. 2003. "Moore on Ethical Naturalism." *Ethics* 113 (3): 528–556.

A semantic challenge to non-realist cognitivism

David Copp

ABSTRACT
Recently, some philosophers have attempted to escape familiar challenges to orthodox nonnaturalist normative realism by abandoning the robust metaphysical commitments of the orthodox view. One such view is the 'Non-Metaphysical Non-Naturalism' or 'Non-Realist Cognitivism' proposed by Derek Parfit and a few others. The trouble is that, as it stands, Non-Realist Cognitivism seems unable to provide a substantive non-trivial account of the meaning and truth conditions of moral claims. The paper considers various strategies one might use to address the challenge. There is a rich field of views that are cognitivist and non-realist. But the paper is skeptical of the prospects of Non-Realist Cognitivism.

In its familiar orthodox form, nonnaturalism is a kind of moral realism. It holds that there are true substantive moral claims, such as, perhaps, that lying is wrong. It holds that there are normative moral properties, such as wrongness, and that these properties are instantiated. Nonnaturalists typically would add that the normativity of these properties is a matter of their being a source of reasons. Perhaps most centrally, nonnaturalists reject the normative naturalist's thesis that moral and other normative properties are natural ones – properties that, roughly speaking, fit within the ontology of science. They hold that these properties are in a fundamentally different metaphysical category from natural properties, such as physical, psychological, or economic ones.

Orthodox nonnaturalism faces familiar challenges (e.g. Enoch 2011, ch 6–9). Recently, some who agree with orthodox nonnaturalists in rejecting normative naturalism have attempted to escape these challenges by abandoning the robust metaphysical commitments of the orthodox view while otherwise remaining orthodox to the extent possible. I will call views of this kind, 'avant-garde nonnaturalism.' In this paper, I address one such view.[1] It agrees with orthodox nonnaturalism that moral and other normative judgements are beliefs like any other beliefs, that moral assertions express such beliefs, and that some such beliefs are true. So it is a version of 'cognitivism.' It agrees as well that there are moral properties such as wrongness, that these properties are instantiated, and that they are not natural ones. But unlike the orthodox view, it contends that these claims have no 'robust' or 'heavy-weight' ontological implications. So it can be described as a version of 'non-realism.'

Avant-guard views of this kind have been proposed by Derek Parfit (2011, 2017) and John Skorupski (2010), among others, perhaps including Ronald Dworkin (1996), Thomas Nagel (2012) and T.M. Scanlon (2014). Parfit initially called his view 'Non-Metaphysical Non-Naturalism' (2011, II, 486) but more recently he has called it 'Non-Realist Cognitivism' (2017, 59). I will use this newer label.

Non-Realist Cognitivism might seem to give both moral naturalists and orthodox moral nonnaturalists all that they have reason to want in a metaethical view. It offers *naturalists* a view that is cognitivist and that allows there are moral truths. It claims to have no robust ontological implications, and if so, it presumably is compatible with metaphysical naturalism – the view that, roughly, reality is exhausted by the natural (see Railton 2017). It offers *nonnaturalists* a position according to which moral concepts are nonnatural and irreducible and moral properties are nonnatural even though not metaphysically robust. Accordingly, Non-Realist Cognitivism stakes out an interesting compromise position.

This paper investigates the intelligibility of the view. Section 1 sets out the basic idea and explains how Non-Realist Cognitivism seeks to avoid the standard objections to orthodox nonnaturalism. Section 2 explains a challenge to the view. As it stands, it seems unable to provide a substantive non-trivial account of the meaning and truth conditions of moral claims. There are various strategies Non-Realist Cognitivism might use to address the challenge, including 'quietist' strategies. I argue against quietist strategies in Section 2. Section 3 explains the 'Non-Referential' strategy taken up by Parfit, as I reconstruct his view, and Section 4 argues that Parfit does not have an adequate response to the challenge. In Section 5, I discuss expressivist versions of the Non-Referential strategy, exemplified by Simon Blackburn's quasi-realism (2006). Section 6 addresses the 'Meinongian strategy,' as found in the work of Skorupski (2010). Section 7 briefly discusses the option provided by approaches to semantic theory, such as conceptual role semantics, that are friendly to non-realism about a variety of non-normative discourses. The upshot is skeptical of the prospects for Parfit's version of Non-Realist Cognitivism but it shows there is a rich field of views that are cognitivist and non-realist.

1. Introducing and motivating non-realist cognitivism

To begin, I need to sketch and motivate the basic idea, as I understand it. Only later in the paper will I look in detail at what Parfit and others have said in developing their own versions of the view.

Non-Realist Cognitivism is 'cognitivist' and 'descriptivist.' It holds that moral judgments are beliefs, literally and strictly speaking, and that they at least purport to describe or represent something. The belief that lying is wrong represents lying as being wrong. Non-Realist Cognitivism holds in addition that some moral beliefs are true. Yet it denies that moral beliefs represent or describe *ontologically robust* facts or states of affairs that involve *ontologically robust* moral properties. And it denies that moral and other normative properties are natural ones. Moral truths have no robust ontological implications, says Parfit (2017, 60). At least, *pure* moral truths have no such implications.[2]

The view is accordingly committed to distinguishing between ontologically robust facts and ontologically non-robust facts and between ontologically robust properties and ontologically non-robust properties. It is obscure how these distinctions are meant to be understood, but I will propose a reading that I call *the base-line reading* and that, I believe, captures the basic idea.

Let metaphysical naturalism be the view that 'reality' is exhausted by the 'natural,' that all ontologically 'robust' properties and facts are natural ones. It would take me too far afield to have a thorough discussion of what is meant by 'natural' in this context. In what follows, I will assume an 'empirical characterization,' according to which, roughly, natural properties are those such that any substantive knowledge we can have of them is empirical or a posteriori.[3] This characterization is more ecumenical than familiar science-based characterizations since it allows us to say that some humdrum properties are natural even if they are not, and perhaps are not reducible to, properties of a kind that would ever be studied in any science. On the empirical characterization, for example, the properties of being a swimming pool and of having been born in September are natural properties. Russ Shafer-Landau opts in the end for an epistemological characterization (2003, 61) and Parfit in effect proposes a similar account (2011, II, 306–307).

Nonnaturalists would not deny that there are natural properties and facts so understood. And nothing in their view commits them to denying that natural properties and facts are metaphysically robust. On the base-line interpretation, Non-Realist Cognitivism agrees that natural properties and facts are metaphysically robust and it adds that moral truths have no implications that are incompatible with metaphysical naturalism.[4] That is, moral truths have no implications that are incompatible with the view that natural properties and facts are the *only* ontologically 'robust' ones.[5]

On the base-line interpretation, Non-Realist Cognitivism holds that there are moral truths, facts, and properties, but only in 'minimalist' senses of the relevant terms. Roughly speaking, in minimalist senses of 'there is' and 'fact,' there is a fact that p just in case it is true that p, and in a minimalist sense of 'true,' it is true that p just in case p. Further, in a minimalist sense of 'property,' there is a property F-ness just in case something is or could be F. On the base-line interpretation, Non-Realist Cognitivism holds that talk of moral 'truths,' 'facts,' and 'properties' is to be understood in minimalist senses of the terms, such that there is no robust ontological implication (see Beall and Glanzberg 2008).[6]

To summarize, on the base-line interpretation, Non-Realist Cognitivism holds that some moral beliefs are true, yet these beliefs do not have ontologically robust truth conditions. There are moral facts and moral properties, but only in 'minimalist' senses. Moral truths, facts, and properties are not natural properties nor are they ontologically robust ones. Their existence is compatible with metaphysical naturalism. In Parfit's words, if Non-Realist Cognitivism is correct, then 'normative truths ... do not raise any difficult ontological questions' (2017, 62).

Unlike Non-Realist Cognitivism, *orthodox* nonnaturalism claims that reality includes robust moral properties and facts that are 'over and above' those studied in the sciences, those of which we have empirical knowledge, and those that are reducible to properties and facts of the kind just specified.[7] That is, orthodox nonnaturalism views the existence of moral facts and properties as incompatible with metaphysical naturalism. This, I believe, is the basis of at least many of the familiar metaphysical and epistemological objections to orthodox nonnaturalism.

On the base-line reading, Non-Realist Cognitivism has a bold response to these objections. For, it denies that the existence of moral properties and facts is incompatible with metaphysical naturalism. It claims that 'there are' moral 'properties' in the minimalist sense. It claims that we can have knowledge of substantive moral truths about how to live our lives. But it holds that these claims are compatible with metaphysical naturalism. Clearly, then, Non-Realist Cognitivism is a striking approach. It sets out a cognitivist position that avoids the standard metaphysical objections to orthodox nonnaturalism, is compatible with metaphysical naturalism, but is neither a form of normative naturalism nor a form of fictionalism or error theory. Non-Realist Cognitivism therefore would appear to offer a promising way of understanding the relation between the moral truths and natural facts about the empirical world.

2. A semantic challenge

The most important worry about Non-Realist Cognitivism is one that I describe as *semantic*. Orthodox nonnaturalism explains what moral judgments are about, and explains their truth conditions, by postulating robust moral properties, such as wrongness. One cannot simply subtract this robust ontological commitment from the view and expect the result to be intelligible, any more than one can remove one of the legs of a three-legged stool and expect it to remain standing.

Some non-trivial adjustment must be made. Otherwise it will be mysterious what a moral judgment could be *about*, and it will be mysterious what the *truth conditions* of such a judgment could be. It will be unclear whether anything substantive distinguishes Non-Realist Cognitivism from moral fictionalism, or, indeed, from an error theory. Let me explain.

On a familiar, intuitive, referential or representational semantic view, typical predicates pick out and ascribe properties – their semantic value is, or determines, the property to which the predicate refers. As I will say, they 'refer' to properties.[8] On such a view, the meaning and truth conditions of the sentence, 'Lying is widespread,' is a function of the semantic values of the terms 'lying' and 'widespread,' and the predicate 'widespread' refers to a familiar property. Orthodox nonnaturalism and normative naturalism, as usually understood, assume such a semantics. They agree that moral predicates refer to moral properties. On the view they share, 'wrong' refers to the property of being wrong, and the sentence, 'Lying is wrong' is true just in case lying has the property referred to by 'wrong.' Naturalists and orthodox nonnaturalists would disagree of course as to whether 'wrong' refers to a natural property, but they would agree that its referent is a robust property that is suited to figure in a semantic theory as a relatum of the relation of reference.

What can Non-Realist Cognitivism say about this matter, on the base-line reading? It does not accept the claim, shared by naturalism and orthodox nonnaturalism, that 'wrong' refers to a robust property. On the base-line reading, Non-Realist Cognitivism says that wrongness is a property merely in the minimalist sense of 'property,' but to say this is just to say, in other words, that something is or could be wrong. This does not help to explain the semantics of 'wrong' since it *presupposes* that 'wrong' is a meaningful predicate. Non-Realist Cognitivism seems, then, to leave us with the mystery of what the semantic value of 'wrong' could be. It appears to deny that 'wrong' refers to anything that can serve as a relatum of the semantic relation of reference. In a nutshell, it seems to deny that moral predicates refer – except, perhaps, in a minimalist sense of 'refer,' as we will see. If this is right, then Non-Realist Cognitivism owes us some other account of their meaning.

Further, although, on the base line reading, Non-Realist Cognitivism allows that there are moral 'facts' in the minimalist sense, the 'minimalist fact' that p is not a candidate for something that might make it true that p. This is because, in the minimalist sense of 'fact,' to claim it is a fact that p is just to claim, in other words, that p. So the 'minimalist fact' that p is not something logically distinguishable from the claim that p, such that the claim could be about *it* or that the claim could be true in virtue of *its* obtaining. Non-Realist Cognitivism owes us an account of what moral claims are about, and of their truth conditions.

One way to appreciate the issue is to ask what distinguishes Non-Realist Cognitivism from an error theory, according to which there are no (pure) moral truths. The error theory and Non-Realist Cognitivism can agree about all the non-moral and non-normative facts. They agree that the moral predicates and moral concepts do not refer to robust properties of any kind. They agree that there are no robust moral facts – certainly there are none that consist in the instantiation of a robust moral property. So they agree that no (pure) moral belief is true in virtue of corresponding to such a robust moral fact. Hence, if we assume a robust account of the meaning of 'true,' the error theory would seem to follow. No pure moral claim is true. The Non-Realist Cognitivist rejects this inference, however, so she presumably must reject a robust account of the meaning of 'true.' Yet on a minimalist account, to assert that a moral claim is true is merely to affirm that claim. So, on a minimalist account, the assertion that some moral claims are true is nothing more than a signaling, by the Non-Realist Cognitivist, that she affirms some moral claims. It seems, then, that the key difference between the Non-Realist Cognitivist and the error theorist is that the former affirms certain (pure) moral claims whereas the latter does not.[9] What explains this disagreement? It does not turn merely on the adoption of a minimalist account of the meaning of the word 'true,' for nothing prevents the error theorist from adopting such an account. It seems that the disagreement must instead depend on a disagreement about the semantics of moral claims. And this disagreement must depend in turn on a disagreement about the semantics of the moral predicates and concepts.

The challenge to Non-Realist Cognitivism, then, is to explain what the moral predicates and moral concepts are about. Or better, it is to provide a semantics of the moral predicates and concepts. Is there a coherent and plausible way to understand their semantics on this view? Is there a coherent and plausible way to understand what moral judgements are about, or to understand their truth conditions? Several strategies are available to Non-Realist Cognitivism.

First is the 'Non-Referential Strategy.' This is the strategy of abandoning a robust referential or representational semantics for moral and other normative predicates and providing instead a special doctrine to account for their semantics, one that does not assign them (robust) referents but that nevertheless provides a non-trivial, substantive account of their semantics, while retaining a referential semantics for (most) other predicates. The Non-Referential strategy seems to be the obvious one to take, assuming I am correct to have characterized Non-Realist Cognitivism as committed to denying that moral predicates refer (in a robust sense). As I will explain, there are various ways to take up the Non-Referential strategy, including Parfit's approach, which I will address in sections three and four. Another Non-Referential approach is expressivist, as I will explain in section five.

Second is the 'Meinongian Strategy,' which I will discuss in section six. It proposes that there are special 'irreal entities' that serve as the referents of moral predicates but that do not exist in any robust sense. It is not clear whether postulating that there are these things is compatible with metaphysical naturalism.

Nevertheless, on a Meinongian reading, Non-Realist Cognitivism postulates ontologically non-robust truth conditions for moral judgments.

Third is the option of advocating or developing some semantic theory that is congenial to non-realist construals of a variety of *non-normative* constructions and truths, and then applying it to moral and other normative discourse. For want of a better term, I will call this the 'Wide Non-Realist Strategy.' There are indeed such theories, including, most importantly, conceptual role or inferential role semantics (Harman 1982; Wedgwood 2007; Chrisman 2016). An appraisal of theories of this kind is beyond the scope of this paper, but I will address them briefly in looking at the prospects for Non-Realist Cognitivism.

Finally, there is the strategy of denying that Non-Realist Cognitivism faces a semantic problem at all, perhaps on the basis of a general rejection of semantic theorizing. On the base-line reading, the Non-Realist Cognitivist has adopted a minimalist view regarding the terms 'true,' 'fact,' and 'property,' at least regarding moral truths. 'Semantic Quietism,' as I call the position, adopts a fully minimalist view about *all* semantic terms and holds that *this is all that needs to be said* about semantics, in effect denying that the semantic terms have more robust senses. Semantic Quietism might say that, in minimalist senses, the belief that S is 'about' whether S; a term 'N' 'refers' to N; and so on – where we can replace 'S' with any meaningful declarative sentence and we can replace 'N' with any noun or noun phrase. The belief that Harry Potter is short is 'about' whether Harry Potter is short, and 'Harry' 'refers' to Harry. Semantic Quietism accordingly replaces truth-conditional semantic theory with its minimalist shadow. Yet it does have a response to the semantic challenge. It says that the belief that lying is wrong is about whether lying is wrong; that it is true just in case lying is wrong; and that 'wrongness' refers to wrongness – where 'about,' 'true,' and 'refer,' are understood in minimalist senses.

Semantic Quietism renounces the need to provide a general theory of the relation between language and thought and the world. I maintain, however, that there are genuine philosophical puzzles and problems here, and that it is a mistake to ignore them. Obviously this is not the place to argue for this claim. But Semantic Quietism is a radical break with philosophical orthodoxy, and because of this, I think Non-Realist Cognitivism should avoid it. It would be a strike against Non-Realist Cognitivism if it needed to renounce semantic theorizing in order to avoid the semantic challenge.

Moreover, intuitively, it is a mistake to interpret all semantic claims in a minimalist fashion. Consider, for instance, claims in astronomy, such as that the sun is more massive than the moon. Claims of this kind have substantive, non-trivial truth conditions. They are about the stars, where, intuitively, this aboutness relation is a substantive, 'robust' relation that, here, takes the stars as one relatum. So, arguably, even if Non-Realist Cognitivism introduces minimalist senses of the semantic terms, it also needs to recognize robust senses of these terms in order to make sense of claims about robust semantic relations between language and the world.

It is important to distinguish Semantic Quietism from 'Moral Quietism,' which we can view as an example of the Non-Referential Strategy. Moral Quietism is, or is a relative of, the view advocated by Ronald Dworkin (1996; see Enoch 2011, 121).[10] It does not reject semantic theorizing in general, but it uses minimalist senses of the semantic terms in accounting for moral discourse and thought, and it marries its minimalist moral semantics to a robust semantics for naturalistic discourse and thought. It says there is not a substantive, non-trivial account of the meaning of any moral term or of the truth conditions of moral claims. It says that there is a property of wrongness (in the minimal sense), where this amounts to saying that some things are or could be wrong. It says that a claim to the effect that a kind of action is wrong is true (in the minimalist sense) just in case that kind of action instantiates wrongness (in the minimalist sense), which it does just in case that kind of action is wrong. Clearly, however, an account of this kind is not explanatory and it does not provide an adequate response to the semantic challenge.[11] Its claims about the semantics of moral discourse and thought are a sophisticated form of word salad. Moral Quietism does, however, provide a benchmark against which to measure other responses to the semantic challenge. An adequate response must go beyond Moral Quietism.

If I am correct, Non-Realist Cognitivism faces a problem. To account for the semantics of moral predicates – to provide a non-trivial, substantive account of their semantics – it must choose among the Non-Referential strategy, the Meinongian strategy and the Wide Non-Realist strategy. It could instead reject the very idea of semantic theorizing by taking up Semantic Quietism, but this would mean rejecting a whole field of philosophy, and one might hope to defend Non-Realist Cognitivism without having to go this far. The Non-Referential strategy is the most conservative of the approaches, for it seeks to combine an orthodox truth-conditional semantics for non-normative thought and talk with a substantive non-referential semantics for the normative. Moral Quietism is a version of this strategy, but it only gives the appearance of answering the semantic challenge. In what follows, therefore, I turn to other versions of the Non-Referential strategy, beginning with Parfit.

3. The non-referential strategy – Parfit

Parfit holds that normative truths (in the reason-implying sense) have no 'weighty ontological implications' (2017, 60). He acknowledges that the idea of *ontological weightiness* is unclear. But he claims he does not need to explain it since it is an idea of those who disagree with him and it is up to them to explain what it means (2017, 60–61). This, I think, is clearly a mistake. Parfit wants to deny that there are moral properties in some ontologically weighty sense. So he cannot plausibly claim that he can ignore questions about what this means.

Parfit tries to explain what he has in mind by reference to mathematics. He says that numbers do not exist in an ontologically weighty sense and he denies that logical and modal truths correctly describe or correspond to how things are in some 'ontologically weighty part of reality' (2017, 59). He says that 'there is' can be used in a 'non-ontological sense' as when we say there are prime numbers (2017, 61). But this does not help to explain his view since philosophers of mathematics worry about how to understand its metaphysics. For every metaethical position, except expressivist theories and, perhaps, the error theory, there is a similar position in the philosophy of mathematics. It is not clear that we can understand mathematical truth in a way that has no 'weighty ontological implications.'

It would help us to understand Parfit if we could assume that he accepts the base-line interpretation. For on this interpretation, Parfit would be saying that normative truths and mathematical truths have no ontological implications that are incompatible with metaphysical naturalism. Since he rejects *normative naturalism*, according to which moral and other normative predicates refer to natural properties, he would therefore to be committed, on the base-line interpretation, to accounting for the meaning of moral predicates without taking them to refer to properties – except in a minimalist sense of 'refer' and 'property.' On the base-line interpretation, recall, there are moral truths, moral facts, and moral properties, but only in 'minimalist' senses. Parfit would agree. But as we will see, after laying out some of Parfit's central theses and distinctions, he at one point makes a claim that seems incompatible with the base-line interpretation.

The first key to understanding Parfit's view, I believe, is his rejection of 'Alethic Realism,' the thesis that 'all true claims are made true by the way they correctly describe or correspond to how things are in some part of reality' (2017, 58) – that is, in some *ontologically weighty* part of reality (2017, 59). As we saw, Parfit thinks that mathematical truths are *not* made true by correctly describing or corresponding to how things are in an ontologically weighty part of reality, and he has the corresponding view about moral and other normative truths.[12] If the natural world is all of reality in an 'ontologically weighty' sense, he says, then moral claims are not made true by correctly describing how things are in some part of reality so understood (2017, 62). This is one key to understanding Parfit.

A second key to understanding Parfit is his account of properties in the 'pleonastic sense' (2017, 66). Parfit holds that any (simple, subject-predicate) claim about a thing can be restated as a claim about its 'properties' in the pleonastic sense (2017, 66). This is intended, I think, as a prosaic remark about the use of the term 'property' and as such it has no ontological significance in itself. In this sense, a claim about a thing's properties adds nothing to the content of a claim made by using ordinary predication (2017, 66). Anyone who agrees that lying is wrong should be able to agree that lying has the 'property' of being wrong (in this pleonastic sense) without being *thereby* committed to an ontology that includes wrongness. Accordingly, Parfit's pleonastic sense of 'property' is what

I earlier called the minimalist sense. Parfit says that he uses the term 'property' in this pleonastic sense (2017, 66). In the pleonastic sense, given that there are simple moral truths, such as that lying is wrong, it follows that there are moral properties, such as the property wrongness. There are also, I assume, normative relations in this sense, such as the relation that holds between a fact, a person, and a kind of action when the fact is a reason for the person to do an action of that kind.

This account leaves it open, for any given predicate, whether it refers to a property in an ontologically robust sense. The claim that the Sun is massive can be restated using the term 'property' in the pleonastic sense, but, despite this, the predicate 'massive' presumably refers to an ontologically robust property. Parfit agrees that there are ontologically robust properties. He thinks that all robust properties are causal, and he explains that causal properties are 'the features of concrete objects or events which can have causes and effects' (2017, 68). The property of being massive is an example. Parfit denies that moral properties are robust on the ground that they are not causal, but one could contest this claim, and also the conclusion Parfit draws from it that moral properties are not robust. His claim that all robust properties are causal is undefended as far as I can see.

The distinction between the pleonastic use of 'property' and its use to refer to ontologically robust qualities is sufficient to put Parfit's position into relief. Unfortunately, Parfit introduces two additional concepts, the concepts of a property in 'the description-fitting sense' and of a property in 'the necessarily co-extensive sense.' I believe we do best to understand these as two concepts of property *individuation* rather than as two new concepts of what kind of thing a property is. (Of course, an account of property individuation might have implications for what kind of thing a property is.) The distinction between these two concepts of property individuation seems to cut across the distinction between properties in the pleonastic sense and ontologically robust properties.

In the 'the necessarily co-extensive sense' (NCE sense), a property F is identical to a property F* just in case F and F* are necessarily co-extensive (2017, 68). The NCE notion of property individuation is of doubtful utility for our purposes. Naturalists and nonnaturalists alike, provided they are consequentialists, might agree that the property wrongness is necessarily co-extensive with the property of failing to maximize the general happiness. But the nonnaturalist would insist that these properties are nevertheless numerically distinct since they have different *natures*. The property wrongness is *normative* while the property of failing to maximize the general happiness is not normative, she would claim. Parfit would say that the latter is ontologically robust whereas the former is not. To make sense of these claims, Parfit introduces the idea of property individuation in 'the description-fitting sense' (DF sense).

In the DF sense, we do not say that a sufficient condition of F and F* being 'identical' is that they are necessarily coextensive. Parfit explains that properties 'fit' the phrases or terms by which we refer to them and different phrases or terms can refer to the same property (2017, 66–68). To be identical in the DF sense, F and F* must 'fit' exactly the same descriptions. That is, Parfit seems to mean, F and F* must themselves have exactly the same properties. Say that a description 'fits' a property just in case it 'accurately describes' the property. If so, then Parfit's idea seems to be that, in the DF sense, a property F is identical to a property F* just in case every expression that refers to F also refers to F*, and vice versa, and every expression that accurately describes F also accurately describes F*, and vice versa. For example, in the DF sense, the property of being luminous is identical to the property of radiating light (2017, 66). Every accurate description of luminosity is also an accurate description of the property of radiating light, and vice versa.

Parfit holds that properties in the pleonastic sense are *also*, at least often or typically, description-fitting (2017, 66). I take him to mean by this that properties in the pleonastic sense can often or typically be identified and distinguished using the DF concept of property individuation. How does this work? Note first, that to say that a property 'is pleonastic' is an abbreviated way of saying that there is this property in the pleonastic senses of 'there is' and 'property.' Parfit might claim, for instance, that the property of being an even number 'is pleonastic,' which would be to say that there is this property in the pleonastic senses of 'there is' and 'property.' And to say this would be to say, in plain terms, merely that something (a number) is or could be even. Now the property of being even is identical in the DF sense to the property of being exactly divisible by 2. That is, every expression that refers to the one property also refers to the other, and vice versa, and every expression that accurately describes the one also accurately describes the other, and vice versa. Since of course, for Parfit, there is the property of being even only in pleonastic senses of 'there is' and 'property,' the claim that this property can be 'referred to' and 'accurately described' presumably must also be understood in pleonastic or minimalist senses of 'refers' and 'accurately describes' (or 'fits'). In general, then, if F is a property in the pleonastic sense, then it is identical in the DF sense to a property F* just in case, in pleonastic senses of the quoted terms, every expression that 'refers to' F also 'refers to' F*, and vice versa, and every expression that 'accurately describes' F also 'accurately describes' F*, and vice versa.[13]

In denying normative naturalism, Parfit has in mind the DF sense of property individuation. Consider non-analytic naturalism, according to which our normative concepts refer to natural properties even though they cannot be reduced to or analyzed in terms of naturalistic non-normative concepts (2017, 57, 70). A non-analytic naturalist who is a consequentialist might claim that the concept of wrongness refers to the property of failing to maximize the general happiness. Parfit denies that such a view could be correct.[14] As we saw, he holds that the property of wrongness is not ontologically robust, so it is not identical (in the DF sense) to any robust naturalistic property (2017, 71–72).

I am now in a position to return to the question whether Parfit accepts the base-line reading of Non-Realist Cognitivism. There is evidence to the contrary. For Parfit wants to say that some moral claims are true in some more-than-minimal sense, a 'strong Cognitivist sense' that would explain how, in making a moral claim, we might be 'getting it right' (2017, 195). We could perhaps interpret 'getting it right' in a minimalist sense, but this would not give us a more-than-minimal sense in which moral claims would be true.

I do not see how a more-than-minimal notion of moral truth is compatible with the key features of Parfit's view: his rejection of Alethic Realism for the case of moral claims, his idea that moral properties exist only in a pleonastic sense, and his claim that the existence of moral truths has no robust ontological implications. What, then, might explain Parfit's idea that some moral claims are true in a more-than-minimal sense?

Parfit doesn't explain his remark but I speculate that it might reflect a confusion between the claim (1) that properties in the pleonastic sense are *also* description-fitting and the claim (2) that properties in the pleonastic sense exist in some more-than-minimal but less-than-robust sense. On Parfit's account, to say that a property F *in the pleonastic sense* is *description-fitting* does not add anything more-than-minimal to the claim that F is a property in the pleonastic sense. For, on his account, to say that a property F in the pleonastic sense is description-fitting is simply to say (a) that some things are or could be F – for this is what the existence of the property comes to, in the pleonastic sense – and (b) there are (or could be) expressions that 'refer to' or 'accurately describe' F, in pleonastic senses of the terms – for this is what it is for F to be description-fitting. In a case in which F is a property *merely* in the pleonastic sense, there is no ontological significance to this. So the idea that moral properties are pleonastic and also description fitting is compatible with supposing that Parfit accepts the base-line view.

Given all of this, I think we can conclude, albeit cautiously, that Parfit's view fits the base-line view. There are moral truths, moral facts and moral properties, but only in 'minimalist' or 'pleonastic' senses of the relevant terms. So understood, the claim that there are moral truths, moral facts, and moral properties, has no ontological implications, so it is compatible with metaphysical naturalism. Yet the moral truths, moral facts, and moral properties are not natural ones.

4. The semantic challenge revisited

Parfit is explicit in denying that a true moral claim is true in virtue of its referring to or correctly describing some (ontologically robust) aspect of reality. And he denies that there are ontologically robust moral properties to which moral predicates or concepts refer. They do 'refer' in the pleonastic sense to 'properties' in the pleonastic sense but this is verbal legerdemain. It amounts simply to saying that there are true moral claims such as that lying is wrong. It is of no help in explaining what the claim that lying is wrong is about or what could make it true. It is of no help in explaining the semantic value of moral predicates. The non-referential strategy was to abandon a robust referential or representational semantics for moral predicates but to offer instead a substantive, non-trivial account of their meaning and of the truth conditions of moral claims. Parfit does not seem to offer such an account. It is not clear that his account goes beyond Moral Minimalism.

Parfit is clearly committed to abandoning a (robustly) referential account of the semantics of moral predicates. He denies that moral predicates refer to natural properties, and, given his view that moral truths have no 'weighty ontological implications,' he is committed to denying that moral predicates refer to any robust properties. Indeed, on the base-line interpretation, he holds that the only robust properties are natural ones. Accordingly, he is committed to denying that moral predicates refer to ontologically robust properties. And moral properties in the pleonastic sense are not suited to figure as the semantic values or referents of moral predicates, for they are merely shadows of the moral predicates.

Parfit ought to accept the terms of this challenge, for at one point he recognizes that quasi-realist expressivism faces an analogous challenge. He says that expressivism lacks a non-trivial account of the truth conditions of moral claims. It lacks an answer to the question, What would it be for an action to be wrong? (Parfit 2017, 166). Parfit claims that his view *can* answer this question. In his view, he says, the claim that an act is 'wrong' means that everyone has 'morally decisive reasons not to act in this way' (2017, 166–167). But this account merely moves the goal posts without changing the nature of the game. Before we asked, What is it for an action to be wrong? Now we ask, What is it for there to be a morally decisive reason not to do something? In the pleonastic sense, there is a 'property' or 'relation' of being a morally decisive reason, but this is unhelpful, as we saw in discussing Moral Minimalism.

Parfit could perhaps try to answer the challenge by invoking the idea that a moral claim is 'non-causally made to be true' by certain relevant reason-giving natural facts. For an action to be wrong, he might say, is for relevant natural facts to non-causally make it to be true that the action is wrong, or that there are decisive reasons not to do it. For instance, the claim that lying is wrong is non-causally made to be true by the natural facts about lying in virtue of which it is wrong – according to the best moral theory (2017, 78–79). This non-causal making-true relation is primitive and undefined in Parfit's account, but this is not a problem. Every moral theory needs to postulate this relation. And the fact that it is primitive and undefined does not distinguish it from the relation of reference, which is deployed in truth-conditional semantic theories. It is typically left as primitive and undefined.

The problem, however, is that the non-causal making-true relation is supposed to relate natural facts to normative truths. The natural facts are robust facts or states of affairs such as the fact that hitting you over the head with a crowbar will cause you pain. According to Parfit, however, the normative truths are sentences or propositions that do not refer to or describe any ontologically robust facts, and that are true, if they are true, only in a minimalist sense of 'true.' Assuming Parfit is correct about this for the sake of argument, then in what sense could a natural fact make a normative sentence or proposition *be true*? On a minimalist account of the meaning of 'true,' there is no (robust) property a sentence or proposition can have of *being true*; to call something true is simply a way of expressing acceptance of it. Consider then the claim that the fact that hitting you over the head will cause you pain *makes it be true* that it would be wrong to hit you over the head. This claim can only be understood, it seems to me, as a way of expressing acceptance of a claim to the effect that it would be wrong to hit you over the head *because* doing so would cause you pain. And since this is a normative claim, if it is true, it is true only in a minimalist sense. It seems, then, that invoking the non-causal makes-true relation does not help address the semantic challenge. We can agree with Parfit that there are natural facts about crowbars and human heads that non-causally make it be true that it would be wrong to hit you over the head with a crowbar. What this comes to, on Parfit's account, is that, in light of these facts about crowbars and heads, we are prepared to affirm that it would be wrong to hit you over the head with a crowbar. This does not provide us with an account of what this claim is about. It does not explain *what we are affirming*.

In short, the non-causal making-true relation is not, and cannot serve as, a semantic relation. This is because the idea that there is this relation *presupposes* that moral predicates and sentences are meaningful, such that they are *candidates* for 'being true,' and, such that, when we think a moral sentence stands in the non-causal making-true relation to a natural fact, we can coherently think it is true.[15] To adequately address the semantic challenge, then, Parfit's story needs to be supplemented. I can see two ways of doing this that appear compatible with Non-Realist Cognitivism.

First, we can introduce a notion of licensing assertions. For instance, we might say, the facts about the crowbar together with the nature of the non-causal making-true relation *license asserting the sentence*, 'Hitting you with the crowbar would be wrong.' The trouble is that the kind of licensing we are looking for is a licensing to assert a sentence *in virtue of its truth*. There can be things I am licensed to assert in virtue of their being polite, such as 'I apologize.' There are things I might be licensed to assert in virtue of being an owner of a boat, such as 'This boat is now the Santa Maria.' But Parfit needs an account that elucidates the licensing of a person to assert a sentence *due to its truth*, not to anything else.

Second, we could perhaps try to use the idea of a concept to leverage an account. We could say that the non-causal making-true relation holds, when it does, in virtue of the nature of the relevant concepts.[16] On this view, for instance, given the concept of wrongness, and given that lying 'falls under' the concept, the sentence 'Lying is wrong' is true. The central problem with this move is that Non-Realist Cognitivism gives us no account of what this *concept* is about. We can say that lying 'falls under' the concept wrongness just in case lying is wrong, but this is trivial. That is, the semantic challenge simply reappears as a challenge to explain what the moral concepts are about.

Perhaps it will be useful at this point to compare Non-Realist Cognitivism – assuming the base-line interpretation, and assuming the non-relational strategy for addressing the semantic challenge – with non-analtyic normative naturalism. The non-analytic naturalist agrees with Non-Realist Cognitivism that the concept of wrongness is a concept with a nonnatural content. She holds, however, that this concept and the predicate 'wrong' refer to the property of wrongness, which is an ontologically robust natural property. Non-Realist Cognitivism, on the suggested interpretation, denies this. It says that the property of wrongness exists only in a pleonastic sense and it insists that this property is not a natural one. It may seem that Non-Realist Cognitivism is the simpler view since it does not postulate an ontologically robust property of wrongness. Yet, for the naturalist, the property of wrongness is identical to some natural property that Non-Realist Cognitivism would also acknowledge to exist. So there is no gain in simplicity. The advantage of the naturalist view is that it has is a substantive account of the semantics of moral predicates and concepts, of what moral beliefs are about, and of their truth conditions. Non-Realist Cognitivism, if it follows Parfit, has no such account.

5. The non-referential strategy – expressivism

Metaethical expressivism claims to provide exactly what the Non-Referential strategy calls for: a substantive, non-trivial doctrine that purports to account for the meaning of moral and other normative predicates without assigning them referents, except perhaps in a minimalist sense. One might therefore seek to combine Non-Realist Cognitivism with metaethical expressivism. Orthodox, old-fashioned metaethical expressivism is non-cognitivist, of course, but contemporary quasi-realist expressivism seeks to treat moral judgment as a kind of belief, so it is not merely Quixotic to combine quasi-realist expressivism with Non-Realist Cognitivism. Parfit objects at one point that quasi-realist expressivism lacks a non-trivial account of the truth conditions of moral claims (Parfit 2017, 170–171), but he suggests at another point that quasi-realist expressivism could be developed in such a way that the result would be a version of Non-Realist Cognitivism (Parfit 2017, 193).

Expressivism is a theory of both moral thought and discourse. In its account of moral discourse, it treats moral predicates as having the semantic role of expressing motivational states of mind, such as approval or disapproval or the acceptance of a plan, rather than the role of referring to properties (except perhaps in a minimal sense). It treats the meaning of a moral predicate as a function of the kind of state of mind that is its semantic role to express. In its account of moral thought, it holds that moral judgments are at least partly constituted by motivational states of mind. These states of mind might be characterized as beliefs, yet if so, they are beliefs that do not represent states of affairs (Gibbard 1990, 7–8; Blackburn 2006).

We can use Blackburn's 'quasi-realism' to illustrate the basic ideas. According to Blackburn, moral judgments are correctly described as beliefs, yet they do not 'represent' states of affairs. Since they are non-representational, they are different in nature from ordinary descriptive non-moral beliefs. For example, a moral belief, such as the belief that lying is wrong, does not represent lying as having a property that would be countenanced in a correct ontology. Yet, for Blackburn, there are moral properties in minimal senses of 'there are' and 'property' (Blackburn 2006). And of course anyone engaged in moral thought could properly affirm that there is such a thing as wrongness.

Expressivist theories such as Blackburn's do therefore echo the base-line reading of Non-Realist Cognitivism, but they are not congenial to the picture that seems to be shared by Non-Realist Cognitivists. Blackburn holds, for example, that the meaning of 'wrong' is a function of the 'stance' of disapproval – or something like disapproval – that is expressed by the assertion of subject-predicate sentences in which a kind of action is said 'to be wrong.' Furthermore, Blackburn takes it that moral judgment has a characteristic action-guiding role that ordinary cognitive states of mind do not have. So he sees moral belief as a different kind of belief from ordinary descriptive belief. Non-Realist Cognitivism does not share this picture. It takes from orthodox nonnaturalism an orthodox cognitivist view of moral judgment. It does not view moral belief as partly constituted by motivational states. The problem is that it is completely unclear how a moral judgment, such as the belief that lying is wrong, can be the kind of state that orthodox nonnaturalism takes it to be if there is no property 'in-the-world' to which 'wrong' refers, such that the belief could represent lying as having that property.

To summarize, quasi-realist expressivism could be developed, or viewed, as a version of Non-Realist Cognitivism. As such it would answer the semantic challenge to Non-Realist Cognitivism by proposing a substantive yet non-referential semantics for moral predicates. The resulting view would be a significant departure from orthodox nonnaturalism, however, one that would go well beyond a simple denial of orthodox nonnaturalism's view that there are ontologically robust, nonnatural moral properties. Because of this, I think it would be confusing to view quasi-realist expressivism as a version of Non-Realist Cognitivism.

6. The Meinongian strategy

The Meinongian strategy is to postulate 'Meinongian, non-existent' properties to serve as the referents of moral predicates (Reicher 2016). According to this strategy, these properties do not exist in any robust sense of 'exist,' but nevertheless *there are* these properties in some not-merely-minimal sense of the relevant terms. The Meinongian strategy represents a departure from Non-Realist Cognitivism, on the base-line interpretation. For, on the base-line interpretation, Non-Realist Cognitivism says that it is only in a minimal sense that there are moral properties. Meinongianism denies this. Further, on the base-line interpretation, Non-Realist Cognitivism is compatible with metaphysical naturalism. It is unclear whether Meinongianism is compatible with metaphysical naturalism, for it is unclear what it means for moral properties to *have being* in some not-merely-minimal sense even though they do not exist. Despite these issues, the strategy arguably remains true to the intent of Non-Realist Cognitivism, for it postulates ontologically non-robust truth conditions for moral judgments.

Parfit can perhaps be interpreted as a Meinongian. He wants to say that some moral claims are true in a more-than-minimal sense, such that a moral claim might be 'getting it right' (2017, 195). On a Meinongian reading, Non-Realist Cognitivism would hold that, although moral properties do not exist, *there are* these properties in some more-than-minimal sense. There is wrongness, available to be instantiated, even though it does not exist. This claim is undeniably mysterious, but it would apparently allow a Meinongian to hold that moral claims can be true in some more-than-minimal sense.

Skorupski contends that *there are* moral properties – or 'reason relations' – and *there are* moral truths – or truths about reason relations – but *there being* such things does not imply that they *exist* (2010, 428).[17] 'To exist is to have causal standing,' Skorupski says, but there is much in reality that does not exist in this sense (2010, 428). There are numbers, for example, and there are fictional people, such as Harry Potter, but neither numbers nor Harry exist. Skorupski insists that he is not merely stipulating that only entities with causal roles shall be said to 'exist' (2010, 439). Rather, he says, his claim is synthetic (2010, 428). *There are* the things that are referred to by true claims of any kind, but not all things so referred to *exist*. Fictional entities and numbers do not exist, although *there are* such things. They are 'irreal objects' (2010, 137, 423).

Skorupski's position seems to hover uneasily between a view that treats moral properties as having the same ontological status as fictional properties, and a view that treats them as having the same ontological status as (other) existing properties, although they lack a causal role. The former view is a kind of moral fictionalism. The latter view is merely a notational variant of orthodox nonnaturalism. Of course, Skorupski wants to reject both horns of this dilemma.

Metaphysicians and philosophers of language have developed Meinongian theories to address problems that face truth-conditional semantics, such as the problem of negative existence claims and the problem of fictional discourse (Reicher 2016). As such, Meinongian theories do not mesh well with the goals of Non-Realist Cognitivism, for Non-Realist Cognitivism does not want to treat wrongness as on a par with fictional properties. Skorupski thinks he can avoid fictionalism since, in his view, fictional truths, such as those having to do with the properties of Harry Potter's wizards, are 'mind-dependent,' whereas moral truths are 'mind-independent' (2010, 439). Unlike fictional properties, moral properties are '*objective* irreals' (2010, 420). Skorupski seeks to explain this on the basis that fundamental normative principles are synthetic a priori (2010, 428, 137). Yet even if we accept this epistemological thesis for the sake of argument, it is not clear how it enables Skorupski to avoid fictionalism, at least if we understand fictionalism as a metaphysical view. For it remains that, on his view, moral properties are *metaphysically* akin to fictional properties in that they are irreal objects.

Even if Skorupski can avoid fictionalism, it is not clear how he can avoid the charge that his view amounts to a reformulation of orthodox nonnaturalism. The main problem is that it is not clear what difference there is supposed to be between *objective irreality* and *existence*. Skorupski holds that only entities with causal roles exist, but he insists that this is neither a stipulation nor an analytic truth (2010, 428, 439), so there remains the question what difference there is between objective irreality and existence. Skorupski explains that propositions about objective irreals are not 'factual' whereas propositions about existing things are factual (2010, 8, 137). But even if the non-factuality of propositions about objective irreals follows from the latter's non-existence, this does not explain what it is for these things to be objectively irreal. Skorupski holds, as we saw, that propositions about objective irreals are synthetic a priori (2010, 137). But even if this explains the difference between *objective* irreals and *mind-dependent* irreals, it does not explain in what sense something that does not exist can *have being*. So it is not clear how Skorupski can avoid the charge that, if his view is not a form of fictionalism, it is merely a notational variant of orthodox nonnaturalism.

Even if we waive these worries, it is not clear how, on a Meinongian reading, Non-Realist Cognitivism avoids the familiar objections to orthodox nonnaturalism. These objections seem to have nothing to do with whether moral properties exist or instead are merely 'objectively irreal.'

The fundamental problem with the Meinongian strategy is that it is unclear what distinguishes things that *exist* from things that do not exist but *are*. If Non-Realist Cognitivism is going to help itself to the Meinongian strategy, it will need to explain this, and explain how it avoids fictionalism, while at the same time avoiding the familiar objections to orthodox nonnaturalism.[18]

7. Conclusion

Avant-garde nonnaturalism attempts to avoid the familiar challenges to orthodox nonnaturalism by eschewing robust metaphysical commitments. Non-Realist Cognitivism is one such position. It holds that there are moral truths, properties, and facts, but only in minimalist senses of the relevant terms. I contend that this view faces the challenge of explaining both what moral judgments are *about*, and what their *truth conditions* are. On a familiar intuitive referential or representational semantics, the semantic value of a predicate is, or determines, the property to which the predicate refers. According to Non-Realist Cognitivism on the base-line reading, however, moral predicates do not have robust referents. Non-Realist Cognitivism says that 'wrong' refers to a property in the minimalist sense, but this is just to say that some things are or might be wrong. It *presupposes* that 'wrong' is a meaningful predicate without telling us anything about its meaning.

I have considered a number of strategies that Non-Realist Cognitivism might pursue in an attempt to address this challenge. I focused mainly on Parfit's version of the Non-Referential Strategy and I argued that Parfit's view is unable to account for the meaning of moral predicates and moral sentences. I briefly considered an expressivist variant of the Non-Referential strategy, as illustrated by quasi-realist expressivism. The trouble is that expressivist accounts of moral judgment sit uneasily with Non-Realist Cognitivism. I also considered a Meinongian strategy, according to which there are special non-existent Meinongian entities that serve as the referents of moral predicates. The central weakness of this approach is the obscurity of its basic idea.

There remains one option that I identified early in the paper but have not yet discussed, the so-called Wide Non-Realist Strategy. This is the strategy of proposing or developing a semantic theory that is congenial to non-realist construals of a variety of *non-normative* constructions and truths, and then applying it to moral and other normative discourse. Consider, for example, conceptual role semantics (Harman 1982; Wedgwood 2007; Chrisman 2016). Obviously I cannot go into detail here, but the central idea, crudely, is that the 'role' of a concept in our thought and talk determines its semantic content as well as the semantic content of the term that expresses the concept. The import of such a view for metaethics depends crucially, of course, on what one takes to be the relevant conceptual roles. As Matthew Chrisman points out, conceptual role semantics is compatible with expressivism, but it is also compatible with moral naturalism as well as orthodox nonnaturalism (Chrisman 2017; see Loewer 1982; Wedgwood 2007). Further, it is compatible with the kind of hybrid moral naturalism that I have proposed. In my view, if it is read as a version of conceptual role theory, the fundamental characteristic role of moral and other normative concepts determines that these concepts, and the predicates that we use to express them, refer to robust natural properties while also figuring in judgments that characteristically motivate action (Copp 2017b). For present purposes, however, the important point is that conceptual role semantics might be able to support a non-realist view that is congenial to Non-Realist Cognitivism. For instance, Chrisman (2016) proposes that 'ought' plays the role of a sentential operator, as in the sentence, 'It ought to be that I tell the truth.' And he suggests that 'ought' in such contexts neither refers to a property of actions, nor to a relation between actions and agents, nor does it express a motivating attitude. So his approach seems to mesh nicely with a non-realist yet cognitivist view. As Chrisman concedes, however, it is unclear whether this approach can be extended to all moral terms (Chrisman 2017). I mention it as an example of a way in which the Wide Non-Realist Strategy could be pursued.

The fundamental problem is to explain the semantics of moral terms and concepts – what moral talk and thought are about – while denying that there are any robust moral properties, and without compromising the goal of avant-garde nonnaturalism, which is to retain an orthodox cognitivist position while rejecting orthodox nonnaturalism, normative naturalism, fictionalism, and the error theory. Non-Realist Cognitivism can explain what moral thought and talk are about in a minimalist sense of 'about'. It can say, for example, that the claim that lying is wrong is about whether lying is wrong. But this is trivial when understood in a minimalist sense. What we need, and what Non-Realist Cognitivism may be unable to deliver, is a substantive, non-trivial, and philosophically interesting account. The best chance of achieving this, in my view, is to pursue the Wide Non-Realist Strategy, yet it remains to be seen where this approach will lead.

Notes

1. A second species of avant-garde nonnaturalism is 'Conceptual Nonnaturalism' (Cuneo and Shafer-Landau 2014). I discuss this view in Copp (2018).
2. To simplify, I will usually write of moral beliefs and truths when, strictly speaking, I mean to refer to what we could call 'pure' moral beliefs and truths. An example is the belief that lying is wrong. Some logically complex moral beliefs clearly do have robust ontological implications. An example is the belief that lying is wrong because God commands that we not lie.
3. In earlier work, I offered a more cautious development of an epistemological characterization (Copp 2007).
4. I do not say that Non-Realist Cognitivism *accepts* metaphysical naturalism because it is compatible with postulating the existence of God and denying that we have empirical knowledge of God.
5. On the base-line reading, Non-Realist Cognitivism is not committed to any account of metaphysical robustness. It holds that there are (robust) natural properties and facts, and that, *whatever* metaphysical account one gives of this, there are not in this sense any *normative* properties or facts. It distinguishes 'robust' properties and facts from facts and properties in 'minimalist' senses, as I will explain (see Beall and Glanzberg 2008). Compare the 'metaphysically nonchalant' view taken by Enoch (2011, 5).

6. The base-line view thus replaces the idea of a distinction between ontologically robust and non-robust facts and properties with a distinction between senses of the relevant terms. One might take it to be committed to a thesis about the ambiguity of these terms in ordinary English. Or one might read it as drawing a distinction between ordinary senses of the terms and technical philosophical senses. I set this issue aside.
7. Enoch uses the 'over-and-above' locution (2011, 101–102).
8. Perhaps there are exceptions, such as the term 'true,' on a minimalist account of its meaning. As I understand it, the view that (most) predicates refer to properties is not committed to any specific metaphysical account of the nature of these properties, although it is committed to holding that properties are relata of the semantic relation of reference. As I will explain, this seems to rule out 'minimalist' views about these relata (See Beall and Glanzberg 2008).
9. There is room here for an epistemological challenge. What justifies these claims? But this challenge can be answered in familiar ways. It is not the fundamental issue.
10. I see Dworkin as a kind of Non-Realist Cognitivist (although he would perhaps reject this label) because he seems both to reject normative naturalism and to hold that pure moral truths have no ontological implications. He rejects the goals of metaethical inquiry, but I set aside this feature of his position.
11. For discussions of moral minimalism and issues it raises, see Dreier (2004) and Smith, Jackson, and Oppy (1994).
12. He concedes that there is a 'wide' sense of the term 'reality,' and perhaps a 'wide' sense of the term 'describe,' whereby every true claim describes some aspect of reality. In this sense, Alethic Realism is trivially true (2017, 61). Parfit indicates, however, that he understands Alethic Realism to be a thesis about 'ontologically weighty parts of reality.'
13. For future reference, note that if I write of a property (or a relation) 'being pleonastic,' I mean that there is this property (or relation) in merely the pleonastic senses of 'there is' and 'property' (or 'relation').
14. I discuss Parfit's arguments against the view in Copp (2012, 2017a).
15. Compare Smith, Jackson, and Oppy (1994).
16. See Cuneo and Shafer-Landau (2014) for a view of this kind.
17. Skorupski holds that normative propositions are propositions about reason relations (2010, 137). So, for him, the central issue is about reason relations, not about moral properties. This detail about his view does not matter for our purposes.
18. Scanlon's position can be viewed as a relative of Meinongianism even though Scanlon does not hold that there are things that do not exist. He holds that existence is relativized to a domain of enquiry (2014, 19). Things that exist relative to normative enquiry might not exist relative to scientific enquiry. It is not clear how this view avoids the standard, familiar worries about nonnaturalism, since these problems seem to have nothing to do with whether existence is relational to a domain of enquiry. Further, in relativizing existence to domains of enquiry, Scanlon seems to take existence to be fundamentally epistemic in nature. I am not confident that this is coherent.

Acknowledgement

A version of this paper was presented to the 2017 Vancouver conference on Representation and Evaluation, and I am grateful to all the participants for their helpful comments and suggestions. Mark van Roojen presented enormously helpful comments to the conference. I am also very grateful for extended conversations and, in some cases, written comments, with and from Matt Bedke, Matthew Chrisman, Jamie Dreier, Tyrus Fischer, Josh Gert, Anandi Hattiangati, Diego Machuca, Kian Mintz-Woo, Laura Schroeter, François Schroeter and Stefan Sciaraffa. I apologize to those I have forgotten to mention.

Disclosure statement

No potential conflict of interest was reported by the author.

References

Beall, J., and M. Glanzberg. 2008. "Where the Paths Meet: Remarks on Truth and Paradox." In *Truth and its Deformities, Midwest Studies in Philosophy*, edited by P. A. French and H. K. Wettstein, 32: 169–198.

Blackburn, Simon. 2006. "Anti-Realist Expressivism and Quasi-Realism." In *The Oxford Handbook of Ethical Theory*, edited by David Copp, 146–162. New York: Oxford University Press.

Chrisman, Matthew. 2016. *The Meaning of Ought: Beyond Descriptivism and Expressivism in Ethics*. New York: Oxford University Press.

Chrisman, Matthew. 2017. "Conceptual Role Accounts of Meaning in Metaethics." In *The Routledge Handbook of Metaethics*, edited by Tristram McPherson and David Plunkett, 260–274. London: Routledge.

Copp, David. 2007. "Why Naturalism?" In *Morality in a Natural World*, 33–54. Cambridge: Cambridge University Press.

Copp, David. 2012. "Normativity and Reasons: Five Arguments from Parfit Against Normative Naturalism." In *Ethical Naturalism: Current Debates*, edited by Susana Nuccetelli and Gary Seay, 24–57. Cambridge: Cambridge University Press.

Copp, David. 2017a. "Normative Naturalism and Normative Nihilism: Parfit's Dilemma for Naturalism." In *Reading Parfit On What Matters*, edited by Simon Kirchin, 28–53. London: Routledge.

Copp, David. 2017b. "Realist Expressivism and the Fundamental Role of Normative Belief" *Philosophical Studies*. On-line. https://link.springer.com/article/10.1007/s11098-017-0913-6.

Copp, David. 2018. "Are There Substantive Moral Conceptual Truths?" In *Moral Skepticism*, edited by Diego Machuca, 93–114. London: Routledge.
Cuneo, Terence, and Russ Shafer-Landau. 2014. "The Moral Fixed Points: New Directions for Moral Nonnaturalism." *Philosophical Studies* 171: 399–443.
Dreier, James. 2004. "Meta-Ethics and the Problem of Creeping Minimalism." *Philosophical Perspectives* 18: 23–44.
Dworkin, Ronald. 1996. "Objectivity and Truth: You'd Better Believe It." *Philosophy and Public Affairs* 25: 87–139.
Enoch, David. 2011. *Taking Morality Seriously: A Defense of Robust Realism*. Oxford: Oxford University Press.
Gibbard, Alan. 1990. *Wise Choices, Apt Feelings*. Cambridge: Harvard University Press.
Harman, Gilbert. 1982. "Conceptual Role Semantics." *Notre Dame Journal of Formal Logic* 23: 242–256.
Loewer, Barry. 1982. "The Role of Conceptual Role Semantics." *Notre Dame Journal of Formal Logic* 23: 305–315.
Nagel, Thomas. 2012. *Mind and Cosmos*. Oxford: Oxford University Press.
Parfit, Derek. 2011. *On What Matters*. In two volumes. Oxford: Oxford University Press.
Parfit, Derek. 2017. *On What Matters*, Vol. 3. Oxford: Oxford University Press.
Railton, Peter. 2017. "Two Sides of the Meta-Ethical Mountain?" In *Does Anything Really Matter: Essays on Parfit on Objectivity*, edited by Peter Singer, 35–60. Oxford: Oxford University Press.
Reicher, Maria. 2016. "Nonexistent Objects." In *The Stanford Encyclopedia of Philosophy*, edited by Edward N. Zalta (Winter 2016 Edition). https://plato.stanford.edu/archives/win2016/entries/nonexistent-objects/.
Scanlon, T. M. 2014. *Being Realistic about Reasons*. Oxford: Oxford University Press.
Shafer-Landau, Russell. 2003. *Moral Realism: A Defence*. Oxford: Clarendon Press.
Skorupski, John. 2010. *The Domain of Reasons*. Oxford: Oxford University Press.
Smith, Michael, Frank Jackson, and Graham Oppy. 1994. "Minimalism and Truth Aptness." *Mind* 103: 287–302.
Wedgwood, Ralph. 2007. *The Nature of Normativity*. Oxford: Oxford University Press.

∂ OPEN ACCESS

Moral supervenience

Anandi Hattiangadi

ABSTRACT
It is widely held, even among nonnaturalists, that the moral supervenes on the natural. This is to say that for any two metaphysically possible worlds *w* and *w'*, and for any entities *x* in *w* and *y* in *w'*, any isomorphism between *x* and *y* that preserves the natural properties preserves the moral properties. In this paper, I put forward a conceivability argument against moral supervenience, assuming non-naturalism. First, I argue that though utilitarianism may be true, and the trolley driver is permitted to kill the one to save the five, there is a conceivable scenario that is just like our world in all natural respects, yet at which deontology is true, and the trolly driver is not permitted to kill the one to save the five. I then argue that in the special case of morality, it is possible to infer from the conceivability of such a scenario to its possibility. It follows that supervenience is false.

1. Introduction

It is a dogma, almost universally accepted, that the moral supervenes on the natural.[1] This is roughly to say that there can be no moral difference between two entities without a corresponding natural difference between them; if any two entities are alike in all natural respects, then they are alike in moral respects. Given that Martin Luther King was a good person, if someone were exactly like King in all natural respects, he too would be a good person. After all, anyone just like King in all natural respects would have done exactly what King did in exactly the same kinds of circumstances, and would have had exactly the same intentions, evaluative attitudes, and moral views as King had. Any such person would likewise be a good person. Similarly, if act A is right, and act B is wrong, then A and B must differ in some natural respect: perhaps A maximizes

---

This is an Open Access article distributed under the terms of the Creative Commons Attribution-NonCommercial-NoDerivatives License (http://creativecommons.org/licenses/by-nc-nd/4.0/), which permits non-commercial re-use, distribution, and reproduction in any medium, provided the original work is properly cited, and is not altered, transformed, or built upon in any way.

happiness whereas B does not, or perhaps A is the keeping of a promise, whereas B is the breaking of one.

There are various ways to make this supervenience claim more precise. We will encounter some alternative supervenience theses in due course, but the formulation that will take center stage here is metaphysical, strong supervenience ('SUPERVENIENCE' for short):

SUPERVENIENCE. For any two metaphysically possible worlds w and w', and for any entities x in w and y in w', any isomorphism between x and y that preserves natural properties preserves moral properties.

Despite its widespread acceptance, SUPERVENIENCE has given some meta-ethicists no end of grief.[2] Nonnaturalists, who claim that at least some moral properties are *sui generis* and irreducible to natural properties seem unable to explain why moral and natural properties necessarily co-vary. If moral concepts are irreducible, then they cannot be reductively analyzed in naturalistic terms; if moral properties and facts are *sui generis*, then they are not identical to, constituted by, or continuous with natural properties or facts.[3] But if moral properties are in this sense wholly distinct from natural properties, it seems difficult to explain why they necessarily co-vary with natural properties – and this explanatory deficiency strikes some critics as a major theoretical cost (MacPherson 2012; Schroeder 2014, Väyrynen 2017). Still, most contemporary non-naturalists are reluctant to reject SUPERVENIENCE.[4] I will argue here that rejecting SUPERVENIENCE is exactly what nonnaturalists ought to do.

My case against SUPERVENIENCE is inspired by the analogy G.E. Moore drew between moral concepts, such as the concept 'good', and phenomenal concepts, such as the concept 'phenomenal yellow' (Moore 1903). It turns out that there is more to this analogy than met Moore's eye. As we shall see, there is a crucial similarity between moral and phenomenal concepts, making it possible to mount a conceivability argument against supervenience along the lines of David Chalmers' well-known conceivability argument against the supervenience of phenomenal consciousness on the physical (Chalmers 1996, 2012).[5]

The argument, in broad outline, goes as follows. Let's say that N is a sentence in a canonical language stating all positive natural facts about our world. I will assume that the natural facts include: all of the physical, biological and chemical facts; all of the non-moral, social, linguistic, and psychological facts, such as that uttering sentence s of L counts as making a promise in context C, or that a particular act caused suffering; and all of the facts that are relevantly similar to, or continuous with, the aforementioned facts.[6] N thus constitutes a complete, non-moral description of all of the positive facts about our world.[7] It is a *positive* fact that there is a rabbit at such and such a position in space-time; it is a negative fact that there are no vampires.

Let's say that T is a 'that's all' statement to the effect that nothing more exists than is needed to satisfy N, and that I is an indexical marker, specifying an agent, time and location, marking the 'center' of a world that satisfies NT.[8] Finally, let's say that *M* is an arbitrary normative, moral truth, such as that the holocaust was an atrocity, or that suffering is intrinsically bad. SUPERVENIENCE entails that □(*NT* ⊃ *M*), where □ is the metaphysical necessity operator and ⊃ is the material conditional.[9] In the next section, I will argue that instances of *NTI&~M* are conceivable,[10] and in §3, I will argue that that if *NTI&~M* is conceivable, then *NT&~M* is metaphysically possible. Clearly, if *NT&~M* is metaphysically possible, then SUPERVENIENCE is false.[11,12] Note that I will assume nonnaturalism throughout this argument – my central claim, after all, is that *nonnaturalists* ought to reject SUPERVENIENCE, though many of the considerations that I raise will have a wider appeal.

2. The conceivability of *NTI&~M*

For a sentence *S* to be prima facie conceivable is for it to be logically consistent and conceptually coherent, at least on the face of it. For a sentence *S* to be ideally conceivable is for it to remain coherent under ideal rational reflection. If *S* is ideally conceivable, then it is possible for an ideally rational being to maximally fill in the details of a scenario in which *S* is true without detecting any logical inconsistency or incoherence with anything knowable a priori.[13]

Some instances of *NTI&~M* are prima facie conceivable. For example, suppose that as a matter of fact, utilitarianism is true, and you ought to kill the one to save the five. Nevertheless, it is surely conceivable that deontology is true, and you are not permitted to kill the one to save the five. After all, deontologists might be mistaken, but they are not conceptually deficient. The conjunction of *NTI* and 'you are not permitted to kill the one to save the five' is neither logically inconsistent nor conceptually incoherent.[14] Or suppose that as a matter of fact, moral realism is true, and it is a robust, moral fact that you are permitted to kill the one to save the five. Nevertheless, it is surely conceivable that moral nihilism is true, and there are no robust, moral facts. After all, moral nihilists might be mistaken, but they are not conceptually deficient. The conjunction of *NTI* and 'it is not the case that it is morally permissible to kill the one to save the five' is neither logically inconsistent nor conceptually incoherent. Either way, we have good reason to think that *NTI&~M* is prima facie conceivable.

Despite the prima facie conceivability of *NTI&~M*, many friends of SUPERVENIENCE put it forward as a *conceptual* truth (Cf. Dreier 1992; MacPherson 2015; Ridge 2007). So, they clearly do not regard instances of *NTI&~M* as ideally conceivable. But why should we think that no instance of *NTI&~M* is ideally conceivable? One reason is that we find it difficult to imagine a situation in which, say, Hitler did all the things he actually did, yet did no wrong. However, as Allison Hills (2009) argues, our failure to imagine morally abhorrent scenarios might better be explained by the phenomenon of imaginative resistance: if we try to imagine a world that satisfies *NTI* but where Hitler did no wrong, we are prevented from doing so by a powerful feeling of moral disgust. If this is the best explanation of our failure of imagination here, then unimaginability does not in this case imply inconceivability. Similarly, many of us will experience imaginative resistance if we try to imagine taking pleasure in eating human flesh, though it is conceivable for someone to take pleasure in eating human flesh nonetheless. Nevertheless, though we may be unable to imagine a world where Hitler did all the things that he actually did yet did no wrong, we *can* imagine worlds that are just like ours but where deontology is true, utilitarianism is true, or virtue theory is true, regardless of which first order normative theory is in fact true at our world (Rosen forthcoming). Since we can imagine these innocuous violations of Supervenience, while we cannot imagine the more horrific sort, it seems that the best explanation of the limitations on our imagination in the horrific cases is not that Supervenience is a conceptual truth. At any rate, the falsity of Supervenience does not require that *every* instance of *NTI&~M* is possible. There may be some constraints, perhaps placed by our normative concepts or by the essences of normative properties, that rule out worlds that satisfy *NTI* but where Hitler's actions were morally permissible. It is enough to reject Supervenience that there are innocuous violations of *NTI&~M* that are ideally conceivable.

Since imagination is not a good guide to conceivability in this case, how can we establish whether or not violations of Supervenience are conceivable? One way to do so is to determine whether there is an a priori entailment from *NTI* to an arbitrary moral truth *M*. If there is such an a priori entailment, *NTI&~M* is not ideally conceivable, since it is incompatible with something that we know a priori.[15] As we shall see, however, none of the usual arguments for a priori entailments of this kind is satisfactory, particularly from a nonnaturalist point of view.

2.1. Conceptual entailments

One way to argue that there is an a priori entailment from *NTI* to *M* would involve showing that moral concepts are reductively analyzable. If moral concepts are reductively analyzable, then an ideal being who knows *NTI* and grasps our moral concepts is in a position to deduce *M* without recourse to any further empirical information. However, this strategy for defending the a priori entailment from *NTI* to *M* is not open to nonnaturalists, who follow Moore (1903) in denying that moral concepts are reductively analyzable. The central insight of Moore's infamous Open Question Argument can be glossed as follows: any statement of an analytic equivalence between an arbitrary normative concept and any naturalistic definition of it can be coherently questioned. Someone who is fully competent with the term 'good' and with relevant natural terms can sensibly raise the question: 'x is F, but is x good?', where 'F' can abbreviate any natural term that you like. The moral is that there is no reductive definition of any moral term that underwrites an a priori entailment from *NTI* to *M*: knowledge of *NTI* together with a full grasp of the meanings of the terms in *N* does not put one in a position to know *M* without recourse to any further information.

Now, Moore assumed that a reductive analysis of a normative concept takes the form of a definition. An alternative view is that normative concepts can be given a reductive *functional* analysis (Jackson 1998). A third view is that normative terms cannot be reductively analyzed in either way, though they nevertheless *designate* natural properties – just as 'water is H$_2$O' is not analytic, though 'water' picks out H$_2$O nonetheless (Boyd 1988). Though these theories are prominent forms of naturalism, and no more attractive to non-naturalists than analytic naturalism, it will be instructive to consider one central objection to all such theories: the disagreement problem.[16]

The disagreement problem arises with the attempt to assign a meaning or a content to moral judgments and moral concepts in such a way that can make sense of genuine, substantive moral disagreements. In order for there to be a genuine moral disagreement between, for instance, a utilitarian and a deontologist over whether it is right to kill the one to save the five, the utilitarian and the deontologist must be talking about the same thing – *rightness* – when they disagree about what is right. If they have distinct concepts of rightness, and if their concepts have different extensions, then they talk past one another; their disagreement is merely verbal. The problem is that any account of the principle that fixes the reference of a moral concept to a natural property renders some intuitively genuine moral disagreements merely verbal.

For instance, consider Jackson's moral functionalism, according to which moral terms and concepts can be functionally analyzed in terms of a network of platitudes of three broad types. First, the pure moral platitudes specify analytic relations between pure moral concepts, and include such platitudes as: 'if something is good, then it is not bad'. Second, moral psychological platitudes characterize the role moral concepts play in motivation, such as, 'if a rational agent judges that she ought all things considered to do A, then she is typically motivated to some degree to do A'. Third, mixed platitudes specify a priori entailments between the natural and the normative. The mixed platitudes are clearly where the action is, since they include natural-normative conditionals, such as 'if an experience is pleasant, then it is to some extent good,' or 'if S promises to do A, then S has a *pro tanto* reason to do A.' Jackson argues that these platitudes – or rather those that would be included in our mature moral theory – fix the reference of our moral concepts to the occupiers of the relevant functional roles. For instance, the concept 'good' picks out the property that occupies the goodness-role, that satisfies the platitudes that define the concept 'good'. The mixed platitudes ensure that if any property satisfies the goodness-role, it will be a natural property of some kind, albeit potentially one that is highly disjunctive.[17]

The disagreement problem arises when we imagine that we come across a community of people who are very much like us, who speak a language very much like English, and who use all of the natural predicates, such as 'pleasure', 'pain', 'torture', etc. in much the same way that we do. The only difference lies in their use of moral predicates, such as 'good' and 'right'. Though they accept the same analytic and psychological platitudes that we accept, they accept radically different mixed platitudes. For instance, whereas our mature moral theory contains the platitude 'if something is pleasant, then it is to some extent good', their mature moral theory contains the platitude, 'if something is painful, then it is to some extent good'. Let's call them the Evils, and their language Evil-English. (Of course, Evil-English may just be English, as spoken by Evil people.)[18]

Intuitively, we have a genuine disagreement with the Evils about whether pleasure is good. Yet, Moral Functionalism predicts that there is no genuine disagreement here at all. According to Moral Functionalism, the Evils' expression 'good' does not receive the same functional analysis as the English expression 'good', since the mixed platitudes are not shared between us. In addition, the Evil's term 'good' has a different extension from our term 'good', since different natural properties occupy the functional role of their term 'good' than occupy ours. If our moral terms have both different functional analyses and different extensions from the Evils' moral terms, there is no shared meaning or content that we accept and they reject; the dispute between us is merely verbal. We can all agree that 'pleasure is good' is true in English, but not in Evil-English. And we can all agree that pleasure is F, where F is the natural property picked out by 'good' in English, and that pleasure is not F^*, where F^* is the natural property picked out by 'good' in Evil-English. Though we *appear* to disagree with the Evils whether pleasure is good, there is no genuine disagreement between us.[19]

The problem with Moral Functionalism is that it treats the mixed platitudes, which are substantive moral judgments, as fixing the referents of our moral terms and concepts, and this entails that genuine disagreement over those substantive moral matters is impossible. This problem generalizes to other ways of fixing reference to natural properties. We can state the problem in general terms by focusing on the status of normative bridge principles of the form 'If x is F, then x is G' (where F is a natural property and G is a moral property). Now, consider some such normative bridge principle, B. If B is analytic of some moral concept of ours, then genuine disagreement over B is impossible, because a member of a linguistic community in which B is not accepted does not share our moral concepts. If B fixes the referent of some moral concept, then similarly, genuine disagreement over B is impossible, once again because a member of a community in which B does not play a reference-fixing role does not share our moral concepts.[20] However, some bridge principle must be either analytic or reference-fixing if there is to be an a priori entailment from the natural to the normative truths.

The disagreement problem is not the exclusive bugbear of naturalists (Eklund 2017). Cuneo and Shafer-Landau (2014) have argued for an a priori entailment from the natural to the moral truths, which is explicitly nonnaturalist in its meta-ethical commitments, yet which faces the disagreement problem nonetheless. Shafer-Landau and Cuneo argue that there is a set of what they call 'moral fixed points', which are a priori knowable moral truths, such as that it is wrong to torture others simply because they have inconvenienced you. According to Cuneo and Shafer-Landau, the moral fixed points do not directly constitute moral concepts, but constitute the moral domain – in order for a system of beliefs to count as a moral system, it must contain the moral fixed points. Nevertheless, the claim that the moral fixed points constitute the moral domain faces the disagreement problem.

Consider once again the Evils, who use the terms 'pleasure' and 'torture' as we do. Now suppose that they do not accept the moral fixed points; in particular, they judge that it is permissible to torture others just because they have inconvenienced you. Once again, despite the differences, we seem to have a genuine moral disagreement with the Evils about whether it is wrong to torture others just because they have inconvenienced you. However, Shafer-Landau and Cuneo's theory predicts that our disagreement is not genuine. On their view, since the Evils' system of beliefs does not contain the moral fixed points, it is not a moral system, however much it may seem like one. If the Evils' system of beliefs is not a moral system, then the concepts that figure in those beliefs are not moral concepts, and do not pick out the moral properties that our genuinely moral concepts pick out.[21] Let's say that the Evils' concept 'wrong' picks out the property of being wrong*, whereas our concept picks out the property of being wrong. We can all agree that torturing someone merely because they have inconvenienced you has the moral property of being wrong but not the non-moral property of being wrong*. So this cannot be what the disagreement between us and the Evils is about. Once again, we disagree with the Evils on fundamental moral principles. To treat these principles as constitutive of the moral domain is to misrepresent fundamental moral disagreement.

In general, any theory that postulates a conceptual or analytic a priori entailment from *NTI* to *M* will give rise to difficulties similar to those we have encountered above. If acceptance of some moral bridge principle is necessary for deployment of a particular moral concept, or the deployment of moral concepts in general, then any community that rejects a principle that we accept fails to deploy the same moral concepts that we do, no matter how much they resemble us in other respects. Yet when we consider disagreement cases, where some group of people resemble us in every respect, save that they reject some moral principle that we accept, we have the strong intuition that we have a genuine disagreement, and hence that their moral terms have the same meanings and extensions as ours.[22] This suggests that these fundamental moral principles – such as that if something is pleasant then it is to some extent good, or that it is wrong to torture others simply because they have inconvenienced you – are neither analytic nor reference-fixing.[23] And this undercuts one kind of argument for the claim that there is an a priori entailment from the natural truths to the moral truths.

2.2. Synthetic a priori entailments

Instead of arguing that the a priori entailment from *NTI* to *M* is analytic, perhaps it could be argued that the entailment is synthetic. If there is a synthetic a priori entailment from *NTI* to *M*, then an ideal being who knew the natural facts and this synthetic a priori entailment, would be in a position to deduce the normative facts without recourse to any further empirical investigation. It would follow that *NTI&~M* is not compatible with all we know a priori, and thus is not ideally conceivable.

For instance, there might be a synthetic a priori principle which states that a metaphysical relation holds between the natural and the moral. What could this relation be? We can at the outset set aside the suggestion that the relation is identity, since nonnaturalists explicitly deny that normative facts or properties are identical to natural facts or properties. Two alternatives immediately suggest themselves. The first is to say that the normative facts are grounded in the natural facts. The second is to say that normative properties have natural essences. As we shall see, neither suggestion proves to be compatible with nonnaturalism.

2.2.1. Grounding

There is a tempting picture of moral explanation according to which if any entity has a moral property, there must be some natural properties *in virtue of which* it has that moral property: if an act is right, there are some natural features of the act in virtue of which it is right; if something is good, there are some natural features of it in virtue of which it is good (Cf. Jackson 1998; Olson 2014). These natural features are the so-called 'right-making', and 'good-making' features. One of the central tasks of moral theory is to identify the most fundamental right-making and good-making features; to arrive at fundamental moral principles which state the natural properties in virtue of which something is right or good.

This picture suggests that moral explanation is a kind of metaphysical grounding explanation, which also concerns the facts in virtue of which some further fact obtains, or what makes it the case that some fact obtains (Cf. Rosen 2010). To say that what makes an action right is that it maximizes happiness, on this view, is to say that rightness is metaphysically grounded in happiness maximization. If moral explanation is a species of metaphysical grounding explanation, and if every moral fact can be explained in naturalistic terms, then the moral facts are fully grounded in natural facts. If this is true, then this gives friends of SUPERVENIENCE all they need. Though the concept of grounding is highly contested, it is widely agreed that there is a link between grounding and necessity (where [p] is the fact that p, Γ is a collection of facts, and [p] ← Γ says that [p] is fully grounded in Γ):[24]

Grounding – Necessity Link: If [p] ← Γ then $\Box((\Gamma \supset [p]))$

If the moral facts are fully grounded in natural facts, then SUPERVENIENCE follows. And if the basic moral principles that state these grounding relations are knowable a priori, then there is an a priori entailment from the natural facts to the moral facts.

However, we can put pressure on the claim that the moral facts are fully grounded in natural facts by appeal to the *Moral Relevance Argument* (Schroeder 2005; Väyrynen 2013). Suppose that we give an explanation of a moral fact, *M*, by appeal to some natural fact, *N*. Suppose we say, for instance, that act A is right in virtue of the fact that it maximizes happiness. The Moral Relevance Argument then goes as follows:

The Moral Relevance Argument

(P1) *N* explains *M* if and only if *N* is morally relevant to *M*.

(P2) A complete explanation of *M* by *N* must explain the fact that *N* is morally relevant to *M*.

(P3) The fact that *N* is morally relevant to *M* is a moral fact.

(P4) *N* cannot explain the fact that *N* is morally relevant to *M*.

(C1) The explanation of *M* by *N* is incomplete. To be completed, it must be supplemented with a moral fact.

(C2) Since *N* and *M* are schematic letters, there is no complete naturalistic explanation of a moral fact.

Each of the premises of the moral relevance argument is plausible. First, it is plausible that maximizing happiness makes an act A right iff maximizing happiness is morally relevant to A's rightness.[25] This is difficult to deny: many other natural facts, such as the fact that A was triggered by a particular pattern of neural activation in a particular agent's brain, are not morally relevant to the fact that A is right, and hence need not be included in the complete explanation of what makes A right. Second, it is plausible that part of the complete explanation of what makes A right ineliminably includes the fact that A's maximizing happiness is morally relevant to its rightness. Any explanation of the rightness of A that left this out would leave out a vital piece of information. Third, it is plausible that moral relevance facts are moral facts. After all, moral relevance facts relate natural properties to moral properties; they state that some natural fact *N* (that act A maximizes happiness) is morally relevant to some moral fact *M* (that A is right), just as basic moral principles do. If these are not moral facts, it is difficult to know what are.[26] Fourth, it is plausible that the fact that A maximizes happiness does not explain why its maximizing happiness is morally relevant to its rightness: explaining the relevance of maximizing happiness to rightness by appeal to the fact that A maximizes happiness seems to put the explanatory cart before the horse.[27] However, if the Moral Relevance Argument is accepted, then it is not the case that every moral fact has a complete metaphysical grounding explanation in terms of natural facts. Thus, there is no grounding relation between natural and moral facts that delivers an a priori entailment from *NTI* to an arbitrary moral fact *M*.

Clearly, a proponent of the view that the moral facts are wholly grounded in the natural facts needs to resist the Moral Relevance Argument. An obvious way to do so is to reject the view that the moral relevance of *N* to *M* cannot be explained by *N* itself. One might argue, for instance, that the intrinsic nature of the natural fact *N* both guarantees that *M* exists, and also guarantees that *M* has the intrinsic nature that it does (Cf. Bennett 2011; Väyrynen 2013). In guaranteeing that *M* exists, *N* explains its relevance to *M*, while in guaranteeing that *M* has the intrinsic nature that it does, *N* explains *M*. However, it is not clear that this move is open to the nonnaturalist. For, this way of resisting the normative relevance argument entails that, given the existence of the natural facts, and given their intrinsic natures, nothing more has to obtain for the moral facts to exist. And this seems to be incompatible with the claim that the moral facts are *sui generis* (Väyrynen 2013). To say that the moral facts are *sui generis* entails that the moral facts are not constituted by the natural facts. But it is hard to see how the moral facts could be *sui generis* in this sense if the existence of the natural facts guarantees the existence of the moral facts. Since constitution is generally understood to be distinct from merely necessary co-variation, it is plausible that a central part of what it is for Γ to constitute [p] is for it to be the case that the existence of Γ guarantees the existence of [p]. However, the claim that the moral facts are constituted by natural facts is a central doctrine of a familiar form of moral naturalism, which is obviously incompatible with non-naturalism.

2.3. Essentialism

Instead of postulating a grounding relation between the moral and the natural facts, it might be argued that it is in the essence of some collection of entities (objects, properties, relations, or whatever) that the moral supervenes on the natural. Essentialists about metaphysical modality hold that,

MODAL ESSENTIALISM: If it is metaphysically necessary that *p*, then there is some collection of entities X such that it is in the essence of X that *p*.

However, as Gideon Rosen has argued, MODAL ESSENTIALISM and SUPERVENIENCE are incompatible with nonnaturalism. His argument (simplified considerably) goes as follows.

First, the nonnaturalist's claim that moral properties are *sui generis* entails that there is some moral property *M* that does not admit of real definition in wholly non-normative, naturalistic terms. On a simple account of real definition, φ defines *F* iff,

(a) It is in the essence of *F* that $\forall x \, (Fx \leftrightarrow \varphi x)$.
(b) The essences of the constituents of φ make no non-trivial reference to *F*.

Second, SUPERVENIENCE entails that each normative property is necessarily equivalent to some (potentially infinite) disjunction of natural conditions. If we let $N_i(x)$ denote the fact that x instantiates some purely natural property, and let G denote an arbitrary normative property, then SUPERVENIENCE entails:

(1) $\Box \forall x (Gx \leftrightarrow (N_1(x) \lor N_2(x) \lor \ldots))$

Now, if (1) is an essential truth, then assuming MODAL ESSENTIALISM, there must be some collection of entities, such that it is in the essential natures of those entities that (1). One possibility is that it is in the essence of the moral property G that (1). But if so, then (1) constitutes a real definition of G, stated in naturalistic terms. If we make the simplifying assumption that G is the only moral property around, then this amounts to the claim that moral properties have natural essences, which is clearly incompatible with nonnaturalism. This simplifying assumption is not as outlandish as it might seem, since many hold that some normative property or other is fundamental in the sense that all other normative properties can be reduced to it. But even if this is not the case, the simplifying assumption can be lifted, and the argument goes through.[28]

Alternatively, one might try to argue that it is in the essence of some natural property or properties that (1) holds. Rosen rejects this 'pan-normativist' strategy since he claims the essences of natural properties make no non-trivial reference to moral properties – for instance, the essence of being a proton makes no non-trivial reference to goodness. To Rosen's considerations, we can add a further difficulty: the suggestion that (1) lies in the essence of some natural properties is incompatible with nonnaturalism, if we assume the plausible principle that essence requires existence:

ESSENCE REQUIRES EXISTENCE: The claim that it is essential to x that p logically entails the existence of x and of every entity mentioned in p.

ESSENCE REQUIRES EXISTENCE is hard to deny. It is hard to see how something could have an essence if there were no such thing to have the essence. And it is hard to see how something could figure in the essence of another thing, if there were no such thing to figure in its essence (Cf. Kment 2014:155). The trouble is that if it is essential to some natural property F that (1), then the existence of F guarantees the existence of G. Once again, this might be captured by the claim that the natural property F *constitutes* the moral property G, which conflicts with the nonnaturalist's claim that moral properties are *sui generis*.

Stephanie Leary (2017) has recently advanced a third suggestion. She claims that there are hybrid properties whose essences involve both natural and moral properties. For example, she claims that it is in the essence of being a pain that,

(c) If one's C-fibres fire, then one is in pain.
(d) If x is a painful experience, then x is bad.

Leary's suggestion is that the essence of pain both grounds the supervenience of the badness-facts on the pain facts, and grounds the supervenience of the pain facts on the purely natural facts. More generally, the suggestion is that the essences of hybrid properties ground both the supervenience of the moral on the hybrid, and the supervenience of the hybrid on the purely natural. Since the supervenience relation is transitive, it follows that the moral supervenes on the purely natural.

This proposal is not ultimately compatible with nonnaturalism, however. To see why, note that the supervenience of the moral on the hybrid entails that the moral facts necessarily co-vary with some conditions stated in hybrid terms. If we let $H_i(x)$ denote the fact that x instantiates some hybrid properties, the supervenience of the moral on the hybrid entails:

(2) Necessarily, $\forall x\,(Gx \leftrightarrow (H_1(x) \vee H_2(x) \vee,\ldots))$

And the supervenience of the hybrid on the natural entails (3):

(3) Necessarily, $\forall x\,(Hx \leftrightarrow (N_1(x) \vee N_2(x) \vee,\ldots))$

The claim that (2) and (3) are grounded in essential truths about some collection of hybrid properties, as Leary suggests, together with ESSENCE REQUIRES EXISTENCE, is incompatible with nonnaturalism. If (2) is an essential truth, then given ESSENCE REQUIRES EXISTENCE, the existence of the hybrid fact guarantees the existence of a moral fact. Once again, this claim is equivalent to the claim that moral facts are *constituted* by hybrid facts, which is incompatible with the non-naturalist's claim that moral properties and moral facts are *sui generis*. Moreover, if (3) is an essential truth, then the existence of a hybrid fact guarantees the existence of a purely natural fact, which amounts to an implausible pan-normativism, given that hybrid facts are partly normative.

These are some of the main options for supporting the view that there is a synthetic a priori entailment from the natural facts to the moral facts. No doubt there are others, but it is plausible that they will suffer similar difficulties. The trouble is that to postulate an a priori entailment from the natural to the moral, whether analytic or synthetic, involves postulating a more intimate connection between the moral and the natural than is compatible with nonnaturalism. The non-naturalist's distinctive claim that moral facts and properties are *sui generis* seems to be incompatible with there being *any* more intimate relation between the natural and the moral than metaphysically necessary co-variation. However, if there is no a priori entailment from the natural truths to the moral truths, then NTI&~M is ideally conceivable.

3. From conceivability to possibility

Nonnaturalists' good reason to think that instances of *NTI &~M* are ideally conceivable gives rise to good reason to think that instances of *NTI &~M* are metaphysically possible. It is widely agreed that conceivability is at least a good guide to metaphysical possibility, even if there are certain cases in which conceivability does not entail possibility (Cf. Yablo 2002). However, as we shall see, in the particular case of morality, the inference from conceivability to possibility seems to go through.

One way to resist the inference from conceivability to possibility here would be to appeal to familiar Kripkean a posteriori necessities, such as 'water is H_2O': since 'water is H_2O' is a posteriori, it is conceivable that water is not H_2O; but since 'water is H_2O' is necessary, it is not metaphysically possible that water is not H_2O. Assuming that our world is a utilitarian world, perhaps 'act A is right if and only if it maximizes happiness' is an a posteriori necessity. In that case, it is conceivable that deontology is true, but it is not metaphysically possible.

There are several points that can be made in response to this line of resistance to the inference from conceivability to possibility. First, if moral truths are Kripkean a posteriori necessities, and if this is modeled on 'water is H_2O', then moral concepts must designate natural properties, just as 'water' rigidly designates H_2O. If 'good' designates some natural property, such as pleasure, and this is an a posteriori necessity, then it might be conceivable that experience *E* is pleasant but not good, though it is not metaphysically possible that *E* is pleasant but not good. However, the claim that moral concepts designate natural properties is a central thesis of a familiar form of naturalism (Boyd 1988); this is obviously incompatible with the nonnaturalist's claim that moral concepts pick out *sui generis* moral properties. So, nonnaturalists cannot resist the inference from conceivability to possibility in this way.

Another way to resist the inference from conceivability to possibility appeals to nesessitarianism about basic moral principles:

NECESSITARIANISM: basic moral principles are metaphysically necessary.

If NECESSITARIANISM is true, then the basic moral principles trivially supervene on the natural facts. And if contingent moral facts are fully explained by natural facts together with basic moral principles, then the contingent moral facts likewise supervene on the natural facts. If utilitarianism is true, on this view, then it is a necessary truth, and deontology, though conceivable, is necessarily false. Compare: it is both conceivable that God exists and that God does not exist, but if God exists, then it is necessarily true that God exists, and necessarily false that God does not exist, in which case, you cannot infer from 'it is conceivable that God does not exist' to 'God does not exist'.[29]

However, this line of resistance faces exactly the same difficulties that have been raised against SUPERVENIENCE. As we have seen, nonnaturalists have good reason to deny that there is any more intimate connection between the natural and the moral truths than metaphysically necessary covariation, such as conceptual entailment, identity, grounding, or constitution. But this seems to eliminate in one stroke all of the ways in which one might argue that NECESSITARIANISM is true. So, though NECESSITARIANISM entails SUPERVENIENCE, it is unclear how NECESSITARIANISM might be defended, at least if the foregoing arguments are on the right track.

Finally, we can provide positive support for the inference from conceivability to possibility by noting that just like phenomenal concepts, moral concepts are 'super-rigid'.[30] Let's say that an epistemically possible scenario is a maximal and consistent description of a way things could actually have turned out to be that cannot be ruled out a priori. Super-rigidity can then be characterized as follows.

SUPER-RIGIDITY. A concept is super-rigid if it has the same extension in all metaphysically possible worlds, and in all epistemically possible scenarios.

If an arbitrary sentence S contains only logical vocabulary and super-rigid terms, then it is super-rigid, and 'it is conceivable that S' entails 'it is metaphysically possible that S'. It is easy to see why this is so: to say that S is conceivable is to say that there is some epistemically possible scenario at which it is true. Epistemically possible scenarios can be seen as descriptions of centered worlds, $\langle w, a, t \rangle$ consisting of a metaphysically possible world marked with a 'center', indicating an agent a and a time t. To say that S is metaphysically possible is to say that there is a metaphysically possible world at which S is true. If the terms in S have the same extension in all metaphysical and epistemic possibilities, then if S is true at an epistemically possible scenario, there must be a corresponding metaphysically possible world w in $\langle w, a, t \rangle$ at which S is true.

A strong case can be made for the super-rigidity of moral terms, at least from a non-naturalistic point of view. First of all, according to the non-naturalist, 'good' picks out a *sui generis* moral property. Though this does not entail that 'good' picks out the same *sui generis* moral property in all metaphysically possible worlds, this is a plausible further assumption for a non-naturalist to make. Furthermore, it is plausible that our moral terms are epistemically rigid. This is supported by the intuitions that are involved in the disagreement problem. If genuine disagreement on all substantive moral matters is possible, then no bridge principle B is either analytic or reference-fixing. This shows that the extensions of our moral terms at epistemically possible scenarios do not depend on the natural descriptions of those scenarios: *however* the actual world might turn out to be in natural respects, moral terms such as 'good' and 'right' pick out the same non-natural properties. Since it is plausible that our moral terms are both metaphysically and epistemically rigid, it is plausible that they are super-rigid.

Of course, if we want to know whether we can infer from the conceivability of $NT\&\sim M$ to its possibility, it is not enough that M is super-rigid; we need to know whether NT is super-rigid as well. If it is, then there is a straightforward inference from the conceivability of $NT\&\sim M$ to the metaphysical possibility of $NT\&\sim M$, and hence to the failure of SUPERVENIENCE. Moreover, it is plausible that at least some of the morally relevant terms in N are super-rigid, such as the terms for pleasure and pain, which are phenomenal terms, and hence super-rigid.[31]

However, if NT is not super-rigid, then the failure of SUPERVENIENCE does not immediately follow. For instance, suppose that 'mass' is not super-rigid, and picks out different intrinsic properties at different epistemically possible scenarios: if it turns out that some property mass* actually plays the mass-role, 'mass' picks out mass* not mass. If *NT* is not super-rigid, then the inference from the conceivability of *NTI&~M* to the metaphysical possibility of *NT&~M* fails, because we have to acknowledge that a possible world at which *NTI&~M* is true might be one that differs from our world in some of its intrinsic natural properties. However, the result is a view that is decidedly odd. According to this view, the fact that some act A is right does not supervene on such facts as that it maximizes happiness, but on some facts about intrinsic natural properties, such as that mass occupies the mass-role, as opposed to mass*. Yet, it is implausible that rightness supervenes on such intrinsic natural properties, because these properties seem not to be morally relevant at all. For the foregoing reasons, we are justified in accepting the inference from the conceivability of *NTI &~M* to the possibility of *NT&~M*.

4. Primitivist moral realism

In the remainder of this paper, I would like to make a case for primitivist moral realism. The primitivist agrees with the nonnaturalist that the moral is irreducible and *sui generis*, but departs from traditional nonnaturalism in rejecting SUPERVENIENCE. Rather, according to primitivism, all moral facts are metaphysically contingent, both particular moral facts, such as that a particular act A is right, and universal moral facts, such as that, for all acts *x*, *x* is right iff *x* maximizes happiness. The particular fact that A is right is fully explained by the natural facts together with this basic moral principle. Basic moral principles are universal generalizations, and support counterfactuals: if it is a basic moral principle that an act is right iff it maximizes happiness, then if some act A* *were* to maximize happiness, it *would* be right. Moreover, basic moral principles hold with their own, *sui generis* kind of normative necessity, understood as a kind of 'fact-independence'. Following Rosen (forthcoming), we can say:

> FACT-INDEPENDENCE: for a proposition *p* to be fact-independent at *w* is for *p* to be a proposition true at *w* such that for any wholly non-normative proposition *q*, the counterfactual "if *q* had been the case, *p* would still have been the case" is true at *w*'.[32]

And, still following Rosen, we can define normative necessity and normative possibility as follows:

> NORMATIVE NECESSITY: for a proposition *p* to be normatively necessary at *w* is for *p* to be either fact-independent at *w*, or for *p* to be true at every possible world *w*' such that every fact-independent moral principle true at *w* is true at *w*'.

> NORMATIVE POSSIBILITY: for a proposition *p* to be normatively possible at *w* is for *p* to be true at some possible world *w*' such that every fact-independent moral principle true at *w* is true at *w*'.

With this in place, we can see how the primitivist can capture many of the pre-theoretic intuitions with which we began. For instance, take the intuition that if anyone were exactly like King in natural respects, he would be a good person. According to the primitivist, this intuition is to be taken at face value – as a *counterfactual*. And the truth of this counterfactual is compatible with the rejection of SUPERVENIENCE. When we evaluate the truth of counterfactuals, we need only look at the closest possible worlds at which their antecedents are true (Cf. Lewis 1973). In this context, the closest possible worlds are those that are just like our world in every respect, save those respects that are incompatible with the existence of someone distinct from King, but exactly like King in all natural respects. Crucially, among the facts we hold fixed when considering the truth of this counterfactual are the basic moral principles that are true at our world. Since these basic moral principles, together with the natural facts, fully explain King's goodness, they will, together with the natural facts at w, fully explain the goodness of someone just like King in all natural respects.

Or consider the intuition that there can be no moral difference without a corresponding natural difference. The primitivist takes this to be an intuition involving *normative* as opposed to metaphysical possibility. What it says is that it is not *normatively* possible that w and w' differ in moral respects without differing in some natural respects. Once again, to evaluate this claim, we look at worlds w and w' that share the same basic moral principles, and consider whether there can be a moral difference between w and w' without a corresponding natural difference. According to the primitivist, any particular moral fact is fully explained by the natural facts and basic moral principles, so if w and w' are alike in all of their basic moral principles, as we have assumed, then any moral difference between w and w' must be explained by a difference in natural facts. The primitivist can readily capture the intuitions typically invoked in support of SUPERVENIENCE.

Furthermore, there are several supervenience theses, weaker than SUPERVENIENCE, that are compatible with and can be explained by primitivist moral realism, such as for instance the following:

> WEAK SUPERVENIENCE: For any metaphysically possible world w, and any individuals, x and y in w, if x and y are alike in natural respects, then they are alike in moral respects.

Some have argued that non-naturalists, or cognitivists more generally, cannot explain WEAK SUPERVENEINCE (Cf. Blackburn 1993, Hare 1984). Yet, this is not the case. Cognitivists in general, and primitivists in particular, can easily explain WEAK SUPERVENIENCE, so long as it is assumed that moral principles are universal laws:[33] if it is a universal moral law at w that an act is right iff it maximizes happiness, then this holds everywhere in w. It follows that if acts A and B in w both maximize happiness, then A and B are both right in w.

Indeed, the primitivist can accept that the moral strongly supervenes on the natural, albeit with normative as opposed to metaphysical necessity:

> NORMATIVE SUPERVENIENCE: For any two possible worlds w and w' that share basic moral principles, if w and w' are alike in natural respects, then they are alike in moral respects.

Thus, primitivism seems to do well at capturing our intuitions. However, there are two objections to primitivism, which many will no doubt find pressing. The first, I have touched on already: I have argued that traditional nonnaturalists have good reason to reject the view that moral principles are a priori. But this threatens to undermine our capacity to know moral principles at all, since many hold that knowledge of fundamental moral principles is a priori.

The solution to this difficulty is to recognize a grey area between a priori and a posteriori knowledge: our knowledge of moral principles is 'armchair', continuous with our knowledge of counterfactuals in scientific and mundane contexts. As Williamson (2005) has argued, knowledge of counterfactuals is neither strictly a posteriori nor strictly a priori, since it can involve varying degrees of sensitivity to evidence. Empirical background beliefs constrain our imagination of how things would be under the conditions stated in the antecedent of the counterfactual under consideration.[34] When we consider moral counterfactuals, empirical evidence together with moral background beliefs constrain our imagination of how things would be under the stated conditions. Though Williamson rejects the traditional view of a priori knowledge, there is no need for us to go this far. We can accept Williamson's model of our knowledge of counterfactuals without subscribing to the view that this exhausts the methods by which we can come to know modal truths.

The second objection to primitivism is that it leaves the basic moral principles unexplained (Cf. Väyrynen 2017). Why is it that utilitarianism is true at w, while deontology is true at' w'? If utilitarianism is a contingent truth, there seems to be no deeper explanation available of why it is true at one world but not another. Of course, primitivism can explain non-basic, contingent moral truths, such as that a particular act is right. But it cannot explain why the basic moral laws hold here but not elsewhere.

Even so, it is not immediately clear why this is a problem. Notice that a similar objection could be raised against the widespread view that the laws of nature are metaphysically contingent. If the laws of nature are contingent, then there are some worlds at which they do not hold, and there is no deep metaphysical explanation as to why these laws hold at some worlds and not at others. If this worry is not pressing with regard to contingent laws of nature, there is no reason why it should be pressing with regard to contingent laws of morality either.

Moreover, traditional nonnaturalists, who accept NECESSITARIANISM and SUPERVENIENCE do not have a lighter explanatory burden. If there are necessary connections between natural properties and moral properties, then this stands in need of explanation. As we have seen, since traditional nonnaturalists hold that moral properties are irreducible and *sui generis*, they cannot explain these necessary connections by appeal to a priori entailments, be they analytic or synthetic.[35]

Notes

1. Though I discuss moral supervenience here, everything that I say here extends to normative supervenience more generally.
2. There are several different versions of the supervenience argument against non-naturalism. For a historical overview, see MacPherson 2015. Blackburn 1971, 1984, 1985 (whose target is cognitivism more generally) appears to assume WEAK SUPERVENIENCE: For any metaphysically possible world *w*, and any entities *x*, *y* in *w*, if *x* and *y* are exactly alike in all natural respects, then they are exactly alike in all moral respects. And as I argue in §4, nonnaturalists can explain WEAK SUPERVENIENCE. A more pressing worry for nonnaturalists, relying on the assumption of SUPERVENIENCE, has been put forward by MacPherson 2012; Schroeder 2014; and Jackson 2003. See Väyrynen (2017) for an excellent overview.
3. One might quibble with this characterization of nonnaturalism; some might characterize nonnaturalism as the narrow thesis that the moral facts are not identical to the natural facts. But that would lead us to classify as a nonnaturalist someone who denies that moral properties are identical to natural properties, but maintains that all moral properties have natural essences. Yet this view is really just a familiar form of naturalism, according to which the moral terms 'good', 'right' and so on, pick out essentially natural properties.
4. Contemporary non-naturalists include Cuneo 2007; Enoch 2011; Fitzpatrick 2012; Huemer 2005; Shafer-Landau 2003, Wedgwood 2009; Parfit 2011;. Some non-naturalists who reject SUPERVENIENCE include Allison Hills (2009), Debbie Roberts (forthcoming), Kit Fine (2002) and Gideon Rosen (forthcoming), and Ralph Wedgwood (2000). Fine and Rosen reject supervenience on broadly essentialist grounds. Wedgwood (2000) suggests that we can accept SUPERVENIENCE together with a weaker modal logic than S5. However, I take it that S5 is widely assumed to be the logic of metaphysical modality. So, insofar as Wedgwood rejects SUPERVENIENCE together with S5, he rejects the most common form of the moral supervenience thesis. (See Schmitt and Schroeder 2011 for discussion.) Moore is generally taken to assume SUPERVENIENCE, though Fine (2002) claims that Moore (1922) can be read as rejecting the metaphysical supervenience of the ethical on the natural.
5. Rosen (forthcoming) has recently argued that nonnaturalism is incompatible with SUPERVENIENCE, assuming an essentialist account of metaphysical modality (see also Fine 2002). The argument presented here is more general, since it does not assume essentialism throughout. I discuss Rosen's argument against SUPERVENIENCE in Section 3, and his account of normative necessity in §4.
6. This characterisation of the natural facts, as including those facts that are 'continuous' with the paradigmatic natural facts (MacPherson 2012) does not beg the question against Sturgeon (1988), who holds that moral properties are natural properties, but that they are not identical to any other natural properties. If Sturgeon is right, then the canonical language contains some natural predicates that pick out moral properties, though *N* does not contain any moral predicates.
7. What about the supernatural facts, such as facts about what God favours? I will simply set aside the supernatural facts here for simplicity. Nothing much hinges on this simplification.
8. In this framework, if the moral truths supervene on the natural truths, then it is possible for an ideal being, who is omniscient of the natural truths and the a priori truths to deduce the moral truths without recourse to any further empirical information. The indexical marker *I* is needed because it is arguably not possible

to know the indexical truths on the basis of knowledge of natural truths and a priori principles (Cf. Lewis 1979; Perry 1979). If there are any agent-relative moral truths, for instance, then knowledge of these will require knowledge of some indexical information. Notice, however, that the claim is not that the moral truths supervene on the indexical truths. These figure in the 'scrutability' base, which is epistemic, not in the supervenience base, which is metaphysical (Cf. Chalmers 2012).

9. Notice that $\Box(NT \supset M)$ is a *minimal* supervenience thesis, much weaker than SUPERVENIENCE, since SUPERVENIENCE entails $\Box(NT \supset M)$, but $\Box(NT \supset M)$ does not entail SUPERVENIENCE. Whereas SUPERVENIENCE describes a relation that holds across all metaphysically possible worlds, $\Box(NT \supset M)$ only states that necessarily, if any world is like *our* world in all natural respects (and that is all), then it is like our world in all moral respects.

10. It is worth noting that Chalmers himself seems to be inclined to favour the view that there is an a priori entailment from the natural truths to the moral truths, and hence that *NT&~M* is not ideally conceivable (Cf. Chalmers 2013). However, Chalmers' arguments assume some form of normative anti-realism, which is obviously incompatible with nonnaturalism. As a result, his arguments for an a priori entailment from the natural truths to the moral truths are not strictly relevant here. Moreover, it is not clear that Chalmers' normative anti-realism is compatible with other parts of his doctrine, such as his account of the determination of semantic and intentional content, which is achieved at least in part by a subject's *ideally rational* dispositions: what you mean by 'bachelor' is determined in part by your ideally rational dispositions to assign an extension to 'bachelor' when presented with various logically possible scenarios (See Chalmers 2011). Crucially, Chalmers takes rationality to be normative – what an ideally rational agent does in a given situation corresponds to what an ordinary agent ought rationally to do in that situation. But if there is a determinate fact of the matter what 'bachelor' means, and if this is determined in part by which extension an ordinary agent rationally ought to assign to 'bachelor' at a scenario, then there must be a normative fact of the matter what extension the agent rationally ought to assign to 'bachelor' at that scenario. This is incompatible with normative anti-realism.

11. The formulation follows Chalmers (2012).

12. The argument assumes that there are some moral truths. But since this is entailed by nonnaturalism, it is uncontroversial in the present context.

13. The notion of ideal conceivability that I will be working with here is what Chalmers (2002) calls *negative* ideal conceivability. In contrast, a sentence S is *positively* ideally conceivable just in case it is possible to imagine clearly and distinctly a scenario in which S true. The problem with appealing to positive conceivability in this context has to do with the imaginative resistance we encounter when we attempt to positively conceive of morally abhorrent scenarios (Hills 2009). In this special case, our inability to imagine these scenarios does not entail that those scenarios are not positively, ideally conceivable. Fortunately, negative ideal conceivability is sufficient for my purposes here. As I have suggested, a sentence S is ideally negatively conceivable just in case it remains coherent under ideal rational reflection. What this means is that an ideally rational being can arbitrarily fill in the details of a scenario in which S is true without detecting any logical inconsistency or incoherence. As I discuss in §3, a sentence S is epistemically possible just in case there is some epistemically possible scenario at which S is

true, where an epistemically possible scenario is a maximal and consistent set of sentences describing a way the world could have turned out to be that is compatible with everything we know a priori. If S is negatively ideally conceivable, then it is possible for an ideally rational being to fill in the details to yield a maximal and complete description of a way the world could have turned out to be without detecting any incoherence; in short, if S is negatively conceivable, then S is epistemically possible. And it is the epistemic possibility of S that is crucial for the argument from conceivability to possibility that I sketch in §3. One worry about working with a notion of merely negative conceivability arises from cases of unprovable mathematical statements, where both the statement and its negation are negatively ideally conceivable, but only one of them is true. I will set this issue aside here, since moral truths do not seem relevantly similar to mathematical truths, where it can be proven that some truths are unprovable. Moreover, negative ideal conceivability can at least been seen as good evidence for positive ideal conceivability.

14. The example is due to Yablo (ms).
15. Thus, the burden of proof shifts onto the friend of SUPERVENIENCE. Another way to motivate this shift in the burden of proof appeals to the Lewisian *Principle of Recombination* according to which 'patching parts of different possible worlds yields another possible world...anything can exist with anything else, at least provided they occupy distinct spatiotemporal regions. Likewise, anything can fail to exist with anything else.' (Lewis 1986, 87–88) Of course, the Principle of Recombination must be restricted. For instance, if consciousness is essentially a physical process of the brain, then a conscious brain is possible, though a brain without consciousness is impossible. Nevertheless, the Principle of Recombination acts as the *default* assumption that the space of metaphysical possibility has no gaps. Any violation of the Principle of Recombination must be *established*. I am grateful to discussion with Tristram MacPherson on this point.
16. This is similar to what Mark Schroeder (presentation) calls the 'common subject matter problem'.
17. Jackson (1998) assumes that the class of natural properties is closed under disjunction and conjunction.
18. This case is reminiscent of Moral Twin Earth cases, where the relevant community is on Moral Twin Earth, modelled on Putnam's famous Twin Earth. Though there are versions of such cases in Hare (1952); as well as Smith (1994); the most prominent recent versions were put forward by Horgan and Timmons in 1991. In the Horgan and Timmons (1991) characterisation, on Moral Twin Earth there is a different property occupying the goodness role, whereas in my characterization, certain aspects of the role (the mixed moral platitudes) differ. Moral Twin Earth cases have been extensively discussed, and details of the formulation of these cases has been called into question (Cf. Dowell 2016). The disagreement problem can be seen as the central issue at the heart of Moral Twin Earth arguments (Cf. Eklund 2017).
19. It might be tempting to respond to such a case by claiming that we have a practical disagreement about what to do, or a clash of attitudes, rather than a disagreement in belief (Stevenson 1944). However, one of the signal virtues of cognitivism – the view that moral judgments are belief-like – is that it can give a straightforward account of moral disagreement, whereas non-cognitivists must resort to treating moral disagreements as practical disagreements about what to do, or clashes of attitude. These strategies are thus not congenial to nonnaturalism. Moreover, as I have argued elsewhere, non-cognitivists have

more trouble than they typically acknowledge in making sense of normative disagreement (Hattiangadi forthcoming).
20. One attempt to sidestep this issue involves appealing to external use facts to determine a common subject matter (Recanati 1997; Schroeter 2014). However, the problem in cases of substantive moral disagreement is that the use facts do not determine a unique subject matter. Given the unresolved dispute between utilitarians and deontologists, and given the complex array of moral intuitions in the face of various iterations of the trolley problem and other test cases, it is not clear whether our collective use of the term 'right' picks out the property of maximizing happiness or not. Moreover, even if it did turn out the use facts determine that 'right' picks out the property of maximizing happiness, this would not suffice to settle the dispute. Deontologists would not advocate a revised use of 'right'; rather, they would claim that their view captured rightness all along.
21. I make the plausible assumption that non-moral concepts do not pick out moral properties.
22. Could fundamental moral principles be both substantive and analytic? Perhaps, but this would not solve the problem, since *genuine disagreement* is lost so long as the principles are thought to be analytic, whether or not they are also thought to be substantive. I am grategul to Gurpreet Rattan for discussion on this point.
23. For further discussion of this point, see Bedke (2012).
24. Cf. Rosen (2010) and Fine (1994). However, note that Leuenberger (2013) questions this.
25. I take this to mean not that maximizing happiness is relevant to *some moral fact or other*, but that it is specifically relevant to the *fact that A is right*.
26. I will later consider the possibility that the principles that link the natural and the moral are *both* metaphysical and moral facts. The point here is that it is implausible that these facts are metaphysical but not moral.
27. This loosely follows Väyrynen's formulation of the normative relevance argument which, as the title suggests, in Väyrynen's case is couched in terms of normative explanation, rather than moral explanation.
28. See Rosen (forthcoming) for details.
29. I am grateful to Jonas Olson for the analogy.
30. The terminology is due to Chalmers (2013).
31. For an argument to the effect that phenomenal terms and phenomenal concepts are super-rigid, see Chalmers (2013).
32. Rosen ms. Note that Rosen calls this principle 'normative necessity'. See also Danielsson (2001), who puts forward a notion similar to Rosen's notion of fact-independence.
33. It can also arguably be explained by analytic naturalists (Cf. Jackson 2003) and traditional nonnaturalists (Cf. MacPherson 2012).
34. Does this offer a way out for the traditional nonnaturalist? After all, Williamson defines metaphysical necessity and possibility in terms of counterfactuals, and argues that we have armchair knowledge of metaphysical modality. However, no armchair argument for SUPERVENIENCE is forthcoming. On the face of it, even if our world is a utilitarian world, we can imagine a world that is just like our world in all natural respects at which deontology is true. The natural facts do not constrain the imagination in such a way as to rule out the truth of deontology. At best, we might hope that we will discover that the natural facts will do so in the long run. Nevertheless, at present, there is no argument for SUPERVENIENCE.
35. Early versions of this paper have been presented at the Normativity Workshop, Uppsala University, the Higher Seminar in Theoretical Philosophy at the University

of Gothenburg, and at the Representation & Evaluation conference at the University of British Columbia. I am grateful to the audiences at each of these venues for comments and discussion. I am particularly grateful to Matt Bedke, Krister Bykvist, Tristram MacPherson, Jonas Olson, Stefan Sciaraffa and Teemu Toppinen for comments on earlier drafts of the paper. The paper has improved immeasurably as a result of their input, though any errors that remain are mine. The research for this paper was generously supported by the Riksbanken's Jubileumsfond.

Disclosure statement

No potential conflict of interest was reported by the author.

References

Bedke, M. 2012. "Against Normative Naturalism." *Australasian Journal of Philosophy* 90 (1): 111–129.
Bennett, K. 2011. "Construction Area (No Hard Hat Required)." *Philosophical Studies* 154: 79–104.
Blackburn, S. 1971. "Moral Realism." In *Morality and Moral Reasoning*, edited by J. Casey, 101–124. London: Methuen.
Blackburn, S. 1984. *Spreading the Word*. Oxford: Oxford University Press.
Blackburn, S. 1985. "Supervenience Revisited." In *Exercises in Analysis*, edited by I. Hacking, 47–68. Cambridge: Cambridge University Press.
Blackburn, S. 1993. *Essays in Quasi-Realism*. Oxford: Oxford University Press.
Boyd, R. 1988. "How to Be a Moral Realist." In *Essays on Moral Realism*, edited by G. Sayre-McCord, 181–228. Cornell University Press.
Chalmers, D. 1996. *The Conscious Mind. In Search of a Fundamental Theory*. Oxford: Oxford University Press.
Chalmers, D. 2002. "Does Conceivability Entail Possibility?" In *Conceivability and Possibility*, edited by T. S. Gendler and J. Hawthorne, 145–200. Oxford: Oxford University Press.
Chalmers, D. 2011. "Revisability and Conceptual Change." *Journal of Philosophy* 108 (8): 387–415.
Chalmers, D. 2012. *Constructing the World*. Oxford: Oxford University Press.
Cuneo, T. 2007. *The Normative Web: An Argument for Moral Realism*. Oxford: Oxford University Press.
Cuneo, T., and R. Shafer-Landau. 2014. "The Moral Fixed Points: New Directions for Moral Nonnaturalism." *Philosophical Studies* 171 (3): 399–443.

Danielsson, S. 2001. "Moorean Possible World Semantics for Supervenience." In *Omnium-Gatherum: Philosophical Essays Dedicated to Jan Österberg on the Occasion of His Sixtieth Birthday*, edited by Erik Carlson and Rysiek Sliwinski, 93–103. Uppsala: Uppsala University Press.

Dowell, J. 2016. "The Metaethical Insignificance of Moral Twin Earth." In *Oxford Studies in Metaethics 11*, edited by Russ Shafer-Landau, 1–27. Oxford: Oxford University Press.

Dreier, J. 1992. "The Supervenience Argument against Moral Realism." *The Southern Journal of Philosophy* 30 (3): 13–38.

Eklund, M. 2017. *Choosing Normative Concepts*. Oxford: Oxford University Press.

Enoch, D. 2011. *Taking Morality Seriously*. Oxford: Oxford University Press.

Fine, K. 1994. "Essence and Modality: The Second Philosophical Perspectives Lecture." *Philosophical Perspectives* 8: 1–16.

Fine, K. 2002. "The Varieties of Necessity." In *Conceivability and Possibility*, edited by T. S. Gendler and J. Hawthorne, 253–281. Oxford: Oxford University Press.

Fitzpatrick, W. 2012. "Ethical Non-Naturalism and Normative Properties." In *New Waves in Metaethics*, edited by M. Grady, 7–35. Basingstoke: Palgrave MacMillan.

Hare, R. M. 1952. *The Language of Morals*. Oxford: Oxford University Press.

Hare, R. M. 1984. "Supervenience." *Aristotelian Society Supplementary* 58 (1): 1–16.

Hattiangadi, A. Forthcoming. "Logical Disagreement." In Daniel Whiting and Conor McHugh, edited by *Meta-Epistemology*. Oxford: Oxford University Press.

Hills, A. 2009. "Supervenience and Moral Realism." In *Reduction, Abstraction, Analysis, 151–163*, edited by H. Alexander and H. Leitgeb. Ontos Verlag.

Horgan, T., and M. Timmons. 1991. "New Wave Moral Realism Meets Moral Twin Earth." *Journal of Philosophical Research* 16: 447–465.

Horgan, T., and M. Timmons. 2009. "Analytic Moral Functionalism Meets Moral Twin Earth." *Essays on the Philosophy of Frank Jackson*, edited by I. Ravenscroft, 221–230. Oxford: Blackwell.

Huemer, M. 2005. *Ethical Intuitionism*. Basingstoke: Palgrave Macmillan.

Jackson, F. 1998. *From Metaphysics to Ethics*. Oxford: Oxford University Press.

Jackson, F. 2003. "Cognitivism, a Priori Deduction, and Moore." *Ethics* 113 (3): 557–575.

Kment, B. 2014. *Modality and Explanatory Reasoning*. Oxford: Oxford University Press.

Leary, S. 2017. "Non-Naturalism and Normative Necessities." *Oxford Studies in Metaethics* 12: 76–105.

Leuenberger, S. 2013. "From Grounding to Supervenience?" *Erkenntnis* 79 (1): 227–240.

Lewis, D. 1973. *Counterfactuals*. Oxford: Blackwell.

Lewis, D. 1979. "Attitudes De Dicto and De Se." *The Philosophical Review* 88 (4): 513–543.

Lewis, D. 1986. *On the Plurality of Worlds*. Oxford: Blackwell.

MacPherson, T. 2012. "Ethical Non-Naturalism and the Metaphysics of Supervenience." In *Oxford Studies in Metaethics*, edited by R. Shafer Landau, Vol 7, 151–163. Oxford: Oxford University Press.

MacPherson, T. 2015. "Supervenience in Ethics." In *The Stanford Encyclopedia of Philosophy*, (Winter 2015 Edition), edited by Edward N. Zalta. https:77plato.stanford.edu/archives/win2015/entries/supervenience-ethics/

Moore, G. E. (1903/1993). *Principia Ethica*. edited by T. Baldwin. Cambridge: Cambridge University Press.

Moore, G. E. 1922. *Philosophical Studies*. edited by K. Paul. London: Trench, Trubner & Co.

Olson, J. 2014. *Moral Error Theory: History, Critique, Defence*. Oxford: Oxford University Press.

Parfit, D. 2011. *On What Matters*. Vol. 2. Oxford: Oxford University Press.

Perry, J. 1979. "The Problem of the Essential Indexical." *Noûs* 13: 3–21.

Recanati, F. 1997. "Can We Believe What We Do Not Underastand?" *Mind and Language* 12 (1): 84–100.

Ridge, M. 2007. "Anti-Reductionism and Supervenience." *Journal of Moral Philosophy* 4 (3): 330–348.

Roberts, D. Forthcoming. "Why Believe in Normative Supervenience?" In *Oxford Studies in Metaethics*, edited by R. Shafer-Landau. Oxford: Oxford University Press.

Rosen, G. 2010. "Metaphysical Dependence: Grounding and Reduction." In *Modality: Metaphysics, Logic, and Epistemology*, edited by B. Hale and A. Hoffman, 109–136. Oxford: Oxford Univrsity Press.

Rosen, G. (Forthcoming). "Normative Necessity." In *Metaphysics, Meaning and Modality: Themes from Kit Fine* edited by M. Dumitru. Oxford: Oxford University Press.

Schmitt, J., and M. Schroeder. 2011. "Supervenience Arguments under Relaxed Assumptions." *Philosophical Studies* 155 (1): 133–160.

Schroeder, M. 2014. "The Price of Supervenience." In *Explaining the Reasons We Share*, edited by M. Schroeder, 124–144. Oxford: Oxford University Press.

Schroeder, M. 2005. "Cudworth and Normative Explanation." *Journal of Ethics & Social Philosophy* 1.3. www.jsp.org.

Schroeder, M. presentation. "A Common Subject for Ethics." Presented at the Fourth Normativity Workshop at Uppsala University, Sweden.

Schroeter, L. 2014. "Normative Concepts: A Connectedness Model." *Philosopher's Imprint* 14: 1–26.

Shafer-Landau, R. 2003. *Moral Realism: A Defence*. Oxford: Oxford University Press.

Smith, M. 1994. *The Moral Problem*. Oxford: Blackwell.

Stevenson, C. L. 1944. *Ethics and Langauge*. New Haven, CT: Yale University Press.

Sturgeon, N. 1988. "Moral Explanations." In *Essays on Moral Realism*, edited by Geoffrey Sayre-McCord, 229–255. Ithaca and London: Cornell University Press.

Väyrynen, P. 2013. "Grounding and Normative Explanation." *Aristotelian Society Supplementary* 87 (1): 155–178.

Väyrynen, P. 2017. "The Supervenience Challenge to Non-Naturalism." In *The Routledge Handbook of Metaethics*, edited by T. MacPherson and D. Plunkett, 170–184. London: Routledge

Wedgwood, R. 2000. "The Price of Non-Reductive Physicalism." *Nous* 34 (3): 400–421.

Wedgwood, R. 2009. *The Nature of Normativity*. Oxford: Oxford University Press.

Williamson, Timothy. 2005. "I *-Armchair Philosophy, Metaphysical Modality and Counterfactual Thinking." *Proceedings of the Aristotelian Society (Hardback)*. 105 (1): 1–23.

Yablo, S. 2002. "Coulda, Woulda, Shoulda." In *Conceivability and Possibility*, edited by T. S. Gendler and J. Hawthorne, 441–492. Oxford: Oxford University Press.

Why conceptual competence won't help the non-naturalist epistemologist

Preston J. Werner

ABSTRACT
Non-naturalist normative realists face an epistemological objection: They must explain how their preferred route of justification ensures a non-accidental connection between justified moral beliefs and the normative truths. One strategy for meeting this challenge begins by pointing out that we are semantically or conceptually competent in our use of the normative terms, and then argues that this competence guarantees the non-accidental truth of some of our first-order normative beliefs. In this paper, I argue against this strategy by illustrating that this competence based strategy undermines the non-naturalist's ability to capture the robustly normative content of our moral beliefs.

1. Introduction

An adequate non-skeptical moral epistemology must not only tell us how we have justification for moral beliefs. It must also explain how the preferred route(s) of justification ensures, in at least some cases, a non-accidental connection between justified moral beliefs and the moral truths. Call this *Non-Accidentality*.

Although Non-Accidentality is a general epistemic requirement, it is widely accepted that meeting it is particularly difficult for the non-naturalist.[1] But there is a wrinkle in this challenge that is not widely recognized: Non-naturalists must explain not just how our moral beliefs are non-accidentally connected to some facts or other, but how our moral beliefs are connected to the robustly normative facts – that is, those facts that have genuine normative authority. Non-naturalists, or at least those I will be concerned with here, believe that there is a unique (or nearly unique) set of robustly normative properties that ground the robustly normative facts. So non-naturalists must not only ensure that we have non-accidentally true moral beliefs; they also must ensure that the content of these beliefs are robustly normative. This wrinkle is non-trivial. As I argue below, at least three recent attempts to meet Non-Accidentality fail because they overlook this fact. As a result, these three moral epistemologies are inadequate, because they provide no explanation of how the epistemic relations that they propose hold between moral beliefs and facts connect us to the robustly normative properties. The lesson is clear. Non-naturalists must keep in mind their commitment to a unique set of robustly normative facts when providing an explanation of how Non-Accidentality is met. They must do this not only to ensure that their account of the epistemic relation between moral beliefs and moral facts is of the right kind, but also to ensure that the relation features the right kind of relata: robustly normative facts.

I begin in Section 2 by reviewing a distinction between robust and formal normativity originally found in Copp (2005) and McPherson (2011).[2] In Section 3, I explain why this distinction is of importance to all non-naturalists worried about moral epistemology, regardless of the robustness of their metaphysics. In particular, they must ensure that the concepts or properties that figure in our beliefs are the robustly normative ones. In Section 4, I briefly explain the conceptual competence strategy and why it falls afoul of this requirement. In Sections 5–7, I argue that three recent attempts to meet Non-Accidentality fail because they overlook the considerations adduced in Sections 3 and 4.

2. Robust and formal normativity: a distinction

An increasingly recognized distinction within the metaethical literature is that between robust, or authoritative, normativity and merely formal normativity.[3] Formal normativity involves the existence of some standards, rules, or conditions, such as the rules of chess, etiquette, or legal procedures. Formal normativity is cheap in the sense that, for all it says, we may have no practice independent reason to care about its guidelines. If we're not interested in following the rules of chess, for example, then it doesn't matter if we move our pawns backwards. The mere existence of a standard is not in itself authoritatively binding.

Within a formally normative activity, we can make mistakes. But what is crucial about formal normativity is that such activities exhibit *normative symmetry* amongst each other. Though chess players and players of some nearly identical game, 'schmess', may run into practical difficulties when they play each other, there shouldn't be any serious concerns about who is playing the 'right' game and who is failing. It is in an important sense arbitrary whether people decide to play chess or schmess. There is nothing intrinsically authoritative about formally normative properties.

Robust, or authoritative normativity, on the other hand, involves those normative facts or properties that '*really* tell you what to do', that have 'normative force', are 'significant'.[4] If someone claimed that there was no sense obeying the rules of morality when we could just as easily obey the rules of 'schmorality', we would see her as making some kind of serious mistake, or at least as engaging in a non-terminological disagreement. Morality is, for the non-naturalist, intrinsically binding in a way that merely formally normative activities are not. There is what we might call a normative asymmetry between morality and schmorality. This normative asymmetry illustrates that morality exhibits something more than merely formally normative activities: It is robustly normative.[5]

We can make use of the robust/formal normativity distinction with respect to different kinds of entities. Robustly normative properties are those properties (such as *being-morally-wrong*) which are intrinsically binding and authoritative in the way that merely formally normative properties (such as *being-a-legal-chess-move*) are not. Robustly normative concepts are those concepts that are either intrinsically binding or those that refer to robustly normative properties.[6] In short, we might say that

> An entity is *robustly normative* iff it is either fundamentally intrinsically binding (in the way that formally normative entities are not), or not fully explicable without reference to some fundamentally intrinsically binding entity.[7]

In what follows, I won't assume a particular view of which non-natural entity is fundamental.

3. Robust and Formal normativity: a lesson

I now illustrate the significance of the distinction for non-naturalists attempts to meet Non-Accidentality. Suppose that the following two claims are true:

> *Metaphysical Non-Naturalism.* There are irreducible robustly normative truths.
>
> *Formal Realism.* There are formally normative truths.

Metaphysical Non-Naturalism is a core commitment of non-naturalism. Furthermore, setting perhaps some unorthodox views aside, most everyone accepts Formal Realism. So Metaphysical Non-Naturalism and Formal Realism are relatively safe assumptions to make at present.

As it's been traditionally understood, the epistemological objection to non-naturalism requires that the non-naturalist explain how the following can be true:

> *Non-Accidentality:* At least some of our justified, first-order, and paradigmatically normative beliefs are non-accidentally true.

If non-naturalists can explain how Non-Accidentality is true, they have made important epistemological progress. However, the robust/formal normativity distinction can help to illustrate how Non-Accidentality must connect the non-accidentally true normative beliefs with the right normative content. Even if Metaphysical Non-Naturalism and Non-Accidentality are both established, it remains an open question whether our paradigmatically normative beliefs contain robustly normative contents. In order to vindicate an anti-skeptical non-naturalism, our normative beliefs must pick out robustly normative propositions. An epistemological story that only shows us how we can have non-accidentally true beliefs of formally normative propositions would show that Non-Accidentality is true, but it would not vindicate non-naturalist moral knowledge. This illustrates that Non-Accidentality isn't the full story.

Instead, in order to defuse epistemological objections, non-naturalists must also meet:

> *Content Success* At least some of our justified, first-order, and paradigmatically normative beliefs contain robustly normative contents.

Explaining how some of our first order normative beliefs could be non-accidentally true involves illustrating some positive epistemic relation between our normative beliefs and some stance-independent facts.[8] But for all that's been said, Non-Accidentality can be met even while a subject's normative beliefs contain merely formally normative concepts or properties. Non-accidentally true normative beliefs are a necessary component of a non-skeptical non-naturalist epistemology, but they are not sufficient.

Non-Accidentality and Content Success are distinct conditions on an adequate moral epistemology. But it is important to keep in mind that the non-naturalist must explain how both can be met with respect to many of the very same beliefs. Showing how some paradigmatically normative beliefs of type *A* are non-accidentally true and showing how some paradigmatically normative beliefs of type *B* are of robustly normative propositions is not enough. It must further be shown that there is some overlap between *A* and *B*. In other words:

> *Overlap.* At least some of our justified, first-order, and paradigmatically normative beliefs are *both* non-accidentally true and contain robustly normative contents.

Content Success, and its relationship to Non-Accidentality, have been overlooked.[9] Both are crucial to a proper understanding of how non-naturalists must respond to the epistemological objection. This interplay between Non-Accidentality and Content Success is an important one.

The robust/formal distinction, then, is important for non-naturalist epistemologists to keep in mind, regardless of their other metaphysical commitments. Content Success must be met by anyone committed to Metaphysical Non-Naturalism, a core commitment of all non-naturalists. I turn now to illustrating how one recently popular strategy for meeting Non-Accidentality, the Conceptual Competence Strategy, fails. I then discuss how the objection applies to three particular versions of the Conceptual Competence view.

4. Conceptual competence and *Content Success*

Appealing to the epistemic conditions on conceptual or semantic competence has been one recently popular strategy for explaining *Non-Accidentality*.[10] The very rough idea is this: It's overwhelmingly plausible that we are competent users of our normative language, as well as the concepts that figure in our normative beliefs. Conceptual and semantic competence entails that certain epistemic conditions are met. These epistemic conditions ensure that some of our normative beliefs are justified and non-accidentally true. Further information and reasoning can help us to gain more justified and non-accidentally true normative beliefs. *Non-Accidentality* is met in virtue of our conceptual and semantic competence in the normative terms. To see how this is supposed to work in practice, let's consider an example from Foot:

> *Hedgehog*. It is wrong to look at hedgehogs in the light of the moon.[11] *Hedgehog* is clearly false. But, the thought is, it isn't just false, but it couldn't be true (barring some radical change in the laws of nature). As Foot says, 'there is some content restriction on what can intelligibly be said to be a system of morality.'[12] Interpreted in one way, this comes to the claim that the denial of Hedgehog is something of a conceptual truth. (I take no stand on whether Foot herself is committed to this.) And we can know this merely in virtue of our conceptual competence of WRONG.

The proponent of competence based epistemology, as I'll call it, wants to extend the structure of Foot's case to a variety of first order normative propositions. The details, both about the extent of substantive conceptual normative truths, as well as our ease or difficulty in grasping them, vary widely between different competence based epistemologists. I will discuss whether these details make a difference for the success of my objection in the following sections. For now, I present the objection in outline, before considering its application to a few prominent competence based epistemologists.

Non-naturalists, as we've seen, believe that moral properties are both robustly normative and stance-independent. That means that, for all that's been said, the normative concepts that we've developed may not have latched onto the robustly normative properties. Unless we have some assurance that our concepts have latched onto the robustly normative, rather than some merely formally normative properties, showing that we have knowledge grounded in normative conceptual competence does not make any genuine epistemic progress.

The normative concepts we have developed are, for all that the conceptual competence theorists have said, contingent. Those in a different evolutionary, social, or cultural niche may have had importantly different normative concepts, and with them, importantly different conceptual truths that could be grasped on the basis of their own conceptual competence.[13] At most one of these distinct conceptual frameworks latches onto the robustly normative. And, for all that conceptual competence theorists have said, we have no reason to believe that it is us, and some reason to think that it isn't. The three case studies also illustrate and reject a few potential ways to avoid the objection.

5. Huemer's *A Priori* moral epistemology

Michael Huemer has attempted to explain our epistemic access to non-natural moral facts via a general theory of a priori knowledge. Huemer identifies properties with universals.[14] Furthermore, as with most non-naturalists, he accepts that 'the moral realm is causally inert.'[15] And though he admits that moral properties, if they exist, would be metaphysically strange, he doesn't see this as evidence against their existence.[16] Finally, he accepts the received view that moral properties supervene on natural properties, though they do so in a non-reductive way.[17] An evaluative belief that *p*, on Huemer's view, has some initial positive epistemic status so long as it is grounded in an intellectual seeming that *p*.[18]

Huemer's explanation of a priori knowledge involves four important claims:

(U) (Mind-independent) universals exist necessarily.

(C) Having an adequate (consistent, clear, determinate) concept *constitutes* the grasping of a (mind-independent) universal.

(R) 'Having an adequate grasp of a universal puts one in a position to see that it has certain properties and/or relationships to other universals that you adequately grasp.'[19]

(A) 'All a priori knowledge is, or derives from, knowledge of the properties and relations of universals.'[20]

Taken together, these claims can explain how moral beliefs meet *Non-Accidentality*. Here is how Huemer explains it:

> Notice ... that the defining characteristics of an adequate grasp are *intrinsic* – consistency, clarity, and determinacy belong to the nature of the concept in itself, as opposed to depending on the relationships between the concept and something else. So the intrinsic characteristics of a concept sometimes are sufficient for its constituting an adequate understanding of the nature of a universal ... Therefore, in some cases – namely, when one's intuitions are caused (only) by clear, consistent, and determinate understanding – the internal process by which one forms beliefs guarantees their truth.[21]

Since forming an adequate[22] concept involves meeting purely *intrinsic* criteria, and meeting those very criteria *constitutes* adequately grasping a (mind-independent, causally inert) universal, Huemer has given us an explanation for how we can form non-accidentally true beliefs about universals without standing in some causal or quasi-perceptual relation to them: All that matters is whether the concepts which constitute the belief in question meet the (reflectively accessible) conditions, and we've got non-accidental truth.

An immediate question arises with respect to (C). Even if my concept *C* is consistent, clear, and determinate, that doesn't yet explain how *C* is guaranteed to have a corresponding (mind-independent) universal. As it turns out, for Huemer, this can't happen, because '[t]here is no possibility of one's [concept] failing to refer to anything (universals are plentiful in this sense, and their existence is necessary).'[23] As long as our concept is adequate, we can be sure that it refers to a real mind-independent universal. Huemer's way of meeting the Non-Accidentality, then, relies on a fifth important claim, which I'll call *Plenitude*:

Plenitude: For every possible *adequate* (consistent, clear, and determinate) concept, there is a corresponding mind-independent universal.

With this explicit statement of *Plenitude,* we have a complete story about how a priori moral beliefs can explain *Non-Accidentality*.[24] Since we are capable of reflecting on our moral concepts, adjusting them to become more adequate, and since we know that these moral concepts have corresponding mind-independent universals (of which our adequate concepts *constitute* the grasping of them), we can have non-accidental a priori beliefs about at least some of the truths in which our moral concepts feature.[25]

We've seen Huemer's general story about how *Non-Accidentality* will be met. With an eye to *Content Success*, let's turn to a particular case of how epistemic access to moral facts works on Huemer's account. Consider a straightforwardly 'good' case of how a particular ethical intuition can guarantee the truth of its contents. Suppose Lucy is reflecting on her concepts of BADNESS and LYING, and on that basis it seems to her that:

(L) LYING is intrinsically BAD.

Furthermore, let's assume that her concepts of LYING and BADNESS are consistent, clear, and determinate,[26] and that BADNESS for Lucy plays the sort of roles we traditionally associate with normativity. Then, by *Plenitude*, they both refer to mind-independent universals. Let's call the universals they refer to *being-a-lie* and *badness*, respectively. Since Lucy's concepts are consistent, clear, and determinate, and she formed an intuition based on reflecting on those concepts, the following is guaranteed to be true:

(L*) *Lying* is intrinsically *bad*.

So we have gone from a claim about Lucy's mind-dependent concepts to a mind-independent fact about universals. And presumably, since she has met the conditions that guarantee the truth of my belief that (L*), she *knows* it, or at least is justified in believing it.

So far, so good. But now consider Carol. Carol is also engaged in ethical inquiry, and also reflects on her concepts of BADNESS and LYING. Carol's concepts are *also* clear, consistent, and determinate. But reflecting on these concepts, she has the intuition that:

(-L) LYING is not intrinsically BAD.

By *Plenitude*, then, for similar reasons, the following is guaranteed to be true:

(-L*) *Lying* is not intrinsically *bad*.

Since (-L*) is guaranteed to be true, and Carol has formed her belief in a way that guarantees it to be true, she also *knows* it, or at least is justified in believing it.

It should be obvious at this point that something has gone wrong. (L*) and (-L*) are incompatible with each other, so they can't both be 'guaranteed' to be true – at least one of them has to be false. And I certainly don't mean to suggest that Huemer is unwittingly committed to contradictory ethical claims both being true. Rather, there is a subtle but informative mistake in the reasoning given above. Lucy and Carol both grasp their respective concepts clearly, consistently, and determinately. This means that, so long as they are being careful, they won't misapply those concepts. Their concepts have a clear and determinate extension, and they will both be able to classify things as picked out by their concepts or not. But, by *Plenitude*, so long as their concepts have clear and determinate extensions, there will be properties that their concepts track. So they do both form true beliefs about the extension of their concepts. However, as the difference between (L) and (-L) shows, the extension of their concepts of LYING and BADNESS differ. And this doesn't show us that one of them is mistaken – after all, their respective concepts are all fully adequate – rather, it shows us that they *have different concepts altogether*.

The right way to classify the case, then, is to distinguish Lucy's concepts from Carol's concepts. Call Lucy's concept $BADNESS_L$ and Carol's concept $BADNESS_C$.[27] With this distinction in mind, we can more precisely characterize their respective ethical intuitions:

(L_L) LYING is intrinsically BAD_L.

($-L_C$) LYING is not intrinsically BAD_C.

Given *Plenitude*, both Lucy's and Carol's concepts correspond to mind-independent properties. And since their concepts are adequately grasped, they will both have knowledge of the corresponding mind-independent facts. However, since their concepts differ, the corresponding properties will differ as well. The knowledge that Lucy has gained from her ethical intuition is not best characterized as (L*), but as:

(L_L*) *Lying is intrinsically bad_L*.

Furthermore, the knowledge that Carol has gained from her ethical intuition is not best characterized as (-L*), but as:

($-L_C$*) *Lying is not intrinsically bad_C*.

Once we get clear about what Lucy and Carol believe based on their intuitions, then, we see that they do not contradict each other after all. This is analogous to the merely formally normative chess case discussed above. The schmess players truly believe that knights can move diagonally, while chess players do not. But this is because the schmess players have beliefs about *being-forbidden-in-schmess*, while chess players have beliefs about *being-forbidden-in-chess*. If the schmess players and the chess players were in an argument about this, they would be merely talking past each other.[28]

We can multiply cases like Lucy and Carol's indefinitely. There are many different fully adequate possible 'moral' concepts, each of which differs about the extension of 'bad'. Huemer can't deny the multiplicity of adequate 'moral' concepts, since adequacy is merely about internal consistency. These concepts are all compatible with one another, so long as we are clear about whether we are talking about bad_1, bad_2, etc. However, unlike in the chess case, or the case of any formally normative concept, there is a further question in the moral case: Which concepts adequately characterize the robustly normative properties? By *Plenitude*, any adequate moral concept will correspond to some mind-independent property or other. Huemer has shown that (e.g.) Lucy's beliefs meet *Non-Accidentality*. Her belief (L_L*) is a non-accidentally true first order normative belief. But he has provided no reason to accept that Lucy's normative concepts actually refer to the robustly normative properties, and thus no reason to accept that her normative beliefs were of the robustly normative facts. In other words, though Huemer has shown how *Non-Accidentality* can be met, he has not shown how *Content Success* can be explained, and so has not provided a wholly adequate non-naturalist epistemology. To paraphrase Street, so long as it hasn't been shown that there is a relation between the moral concepts we happen to have and the normative facts, the appeal to conceptual competency offers no way, in the absence of an incredible coincidence, of showing how our moral beliefs could meet *Content Success*.[29]

However, there is a disanalogy here between the moral case and the *chess/schmess* case. Moral properties, unlike the rules of chess, are robustly normative—indeed, that is where our problem arises. But why couldn't Lucy pack into her concept that it refers to the robustly normative *badness*, if it refers at all? This would ensure that she can meet Content Success—it's a condition on her concept that it refers to the robustly normative *badness*, after all. And since this addition doesn't render her concept incompatible with the other conditions on conceptual adequacy, it looks like the explanation of Non-Accidentality is still met as well.[30] Problem solved?

Not quite. As we saw above, Huemer's strategy for meeting Non-Accidentality essentially relies on *Plenitude*. An adequate concept can't fail to refer to a property, because there is a property for any extension that a given concept might fix. Any adequate concept is sure to hit a target property, because there are an abundance of targets. If we give up *Plenitude*, there becomes a non-trivial chance that an adequate concept will fail to target any property, and so won't ensure non-accidentally true beliefs, at least about mind-independent properties.

In order for Huemer's strategy to work, then, the proponent needs to ensure that the conditions she places on the adequacy of a concept leave open the abundance of possible referents. Consider a toy example. Polly the Pythagorean has the concept TEN_P. Her concept is extremely similar to our concept TEN. She takes it to refer to the successor of nine, the thing that results from five added to five, etc. In fact, Polly and us agree about all of the first-order mathematical facts. However, Polly has a further view about the nature of the referent of TEN_P. Unlike our own concept, it is internal to Polly's concept that TEN_P refers to a sacred and holy property, if it refers at all. If she were to become convinced that Pythagoreanism is false, she would see her TEN concept as defective.

There is certainly no in principle problem with the existence of concepts like TEN_p. However, insofar as there are such concepts, they are incompatible with *Plenitude*. Suppose Polly's TEN_p concept is completely adequate in Huemer's sense. This would not be enough to guarantee true beliefs, since it must also be the case that the concept's extension latches onto a property that is holy and sacred. And nothing about the internal conditions on Polly's concept can guarantee that such a property exists. *Plenitude* says that there is a property for every extension. But it doesn't say that there is a holy and sacred property for every extension. So Polly's concept will not ensure Content Success, if holiness is a non-negotiable internal feature of her TEN_p concept.

For similar reasons, moral concepts like Lucy's BADNESS cannot contain, as an internal condition, that it refers to robustly normative *badness* if it refers at all. If this can be an internal condition on Lucy's concept, it can on Carol's as well. But, either one of them is mistaken about the extension of their concept, or one of their concepts fails to refer (because, for example, there is no robustly normative property of *badness* that applies to lying). If the former, Non-Accidentality is not met.[31] If the latter, Content Success is not met. So adding this further condition on our normative concepts will not solve the problem after all.

Notice that the success of the objection does not rest on the possibility of divergence between two agents such as Lucy and Carol. The case of Lucy and Carol is merely meant to help illustrate the problem. The problem is that a wholly adequate non-naturalist epistemology requires more than the mere having of normative beliefs that track some facts non-accidentally. It must be that those beliefs track the robustly normative facts non-accidentally. Even convergence amongst agents would not be enough to explain how our normative beliefs are responsive to the robustly normative facts. For all that's been said, and for all we know, our beliefs in such a situation would be converging on some merely formally normative facts.

6. Schroeter & Schroeter's metasemantic solution

Schroeter and Schroeter (2017) suggest that the moral realist can meet Non-Accidentality by appeal to Chalmersian metasemantics. Although their view is strictly incompatible with non-naturalism,[32] a slight variation on the view to be discussed below allows the non-naturalist to make use of the same general strategy. Even though Schroeter & Schroeter are not themselves non-naturalists, their view is important to discuss because it is perhaps the most developed version of what I'm calling the conceptual competence strategy.

The crucial principle that they appeal to in their epistemological story involves an idea originally found in Chalmers and Jackson (2001):

Ideal Accessibility (IA) The correct semantic interpretation of the referential concept expressed by a term 'X' must make the subject's ideal, empirically-informed beliefs about what it takes to be X in any possible world come out true.[33]

The empirical information must be given in an 'ideal base-level descriptive vocabulary', rather than in natural language, on pain of circularity. An ideal base-level descriptive vocabulary is 'an exhaustive microphysical description of the actual world, together with a 'that's all' clause and an 'I am here' clause.'[34] I'll grant for the purposes of this paper that such a vocabulary is in principle possible.[35] The basic idea behind (IA) is that the reference of a subject's concepts 'respect[s] the subject's own ideal, fully informed verdicts about the reference of her words and concepts.'[36]

In order to resolve epistemological objections to non-naturalism, IA only needs to be true of *normative* terms. Suppose, as Schroeter & Schroeter argue, it is. Recall that Non-Accidentality requires some explanation as to how our actual normative beliefs can track the moral properties, given that those properties are causally inert. IA tells us that a subject's moral beliefs under ideal conditions are guaranteed to be true, given that those beliefs themselves determine the referent properties of the moral concepts that figure in them. So our ideal selves' moral beliefs can straightforwardly explain Non-Accidentality. However, this also means that some subset of our actual moral beliefs are non-accidentally true as well. This is because

> [I]deal beliefs about X must be justifiable on the basis of the subject's actual beliefs about X on pain of changing the topic. So Ideal Accessibility constrains the subject's actual understanding of 'X' indirectly: all of the subject's actual attitudes and dispositions that would ultimately figure in justifying her ideal, fully-informed verdicts about what it takes to be X must be roughly true or truth-preserving.[37]

Some of our actual moral beliefs must survive the idealization process, lest those beliefs not be *our* ideal moral beliefs. This means that some of our actual moral beliefs are non-accidentally *guaranteed* to be true, though we don't know which ones.[38] We also have reason to believe, given IA, that further reflection and information will help weed out more and more false beliefs. Our giving beliefs upon receiving more information is very good evidence that they wouldn't survive ideal reflection, and thus are not true. IA helps establish that some of our actual moral beliefs must be true, and also that further reflection and information is likely to result in more true moral beliefs.[39] These results are enough to meet any reasonable epistemological demand on the non-naturalist, and thus the non-naturalist who endorses IA can meet Non-Accidentality.

Schroeter & Schroeter see IA as best fitting with a naturalist realism. This is because they endorse the identity of necessarily coextensive properties.[40] Given that there will be some set of natural property instances across all possible worlds that is extensionally equivalent to the normative properties, there will be a straightforward identification between any normative property and a natural property. Of course, as Schroeter & Schroeter themselves admit, non-naturalists (as well as others) have rejected this claim, lest their views collapse into naturalism.[41] Schroeter & Schroeter are worried that rejecting the identity of extensionally equivalent properties will cause problems for IA, since the procedure of IA only seems to generate an extensional set of property instances across worlds. So it is too coarse grained of a procedure to fit with the rejection of an extensional equivalence theory of property identity.

I think the non-naturalist that is otherwise attracted to something like IA should push back on this claim. For the non-naturalist *does* think there is an important and graspable difference between the normative properties and the natural properties that are extensionally equivalent–namely, the normative properties exhibit *robust normativity*, whereas the natural properties do not (and perhaps *cannot*). So long as competent users of normative terms take robustness to be crucial to what it takes to be, for example, *wrong*, they can make a more fine-grained distinction between normative and natural properties than extensional equivalence will allow. There may be reasons to think competent users of normative terms don't have a grip on robust normativity in this way. But it seems plausible that non-naturalists would think that they do, and Schroeter & Schroeter have not given an argument to think that this is not so. The non-naturalist should be able to help themselves to IA after all, contra Schroeter & Schroeter.

With all that in mind, let's return to the distinction between formal and robust normativity. Schroeter & Schroeter's view faces a dilemma, each horn of which is incompatible with the truth of either Non-Accidentality or Content Success. It must turn out that (a) at least some of our substantive first-order normative beliefs are true, and (b) the properties picked out by our moral terms are the robustly normative properties. We've seen above how IA could ensure that (a) is met: Since our ideal beliefs are a result of some function on our actual beliefs coupled with empirical information, there is a quasi-constitutive connection between our first order normative beliefs and the properties that figure in them.

Return to Lucy's judgment that:

(L) Lying is intrinsically bad.

Suppose for the sake of argument that (L) is one of Lucy's beliefs that *would* survive idealization. Call the property that figures in Lucy's 'bad' thoughts *badness*$_L$. Recall that Carol believes that:

(-L) Lying is not intrinsically bad.

And suppose for the sake of argument that (-L) is one of Carol's beliefs that would survive her own idealization.[42] Call the property that figures in Carol's 'bad' thoughts *badness*$_C$.

As with Huemer, Schroeter & Schroeter ascribe to something like Plenitude, so there is no worry about Lucy or Carol's terms failing to refer.[43] However, the same problem arises for Schroeter & Schroeter's view that arose for Huemer's view. They have given a metasemantic story which can explain how to avoid a skeptical moral epistemology, but it makes meeting Content Success extremely difficult. Lucy and Carol both meet Non-Accidentality. Some set of Lucy's actual normative beliefs S figures in (partially) determining her idealized normative beliefs. By IA, the members of S are non-accidentally true. However, if the normative beliefs that make up S don't match the first order *robust* normative truths, Lucy's normative beliefs won't meet Content Success. While some of Lucy's normative beliefs would be non-accidentally true, it would be extremely unlikely for those beliefs to be of the robustly normative facts. But Carol's epistemic situation is identical to Lucy's. Schroeter & Schroeter have provided an epistemology that can explain Non-Accidentality but not Content Success.

6.1. Internal Conceptual Robustness to the Rescue?[44]

The argument provided so far against Schroeter & Schroeter's view is incomplete. This is because their metasemantics provides a way for our normative terms to pick out the robustly normative properties (thus meeting Content Success). Moral terms may contain, as part of their metasemantics, an implicit reference-fixing description that they pick out the robustly normative properties. If I stipulate that my term 'wrong' picks out a robustly normative 'not-to-be-doneness' property if it refers at all, then, so long as there is some such property, 'wrong' will refer to it (Compare stipulating that 'Julius' refers to the inventor of the zip, if it refers at all).[45]

Normative terms do not have explicitly stipulated reference-fixing descriptions, but the metasemantics of normative terms may nevertheless contain implicit reference-fixing descriptions which do similar work. Whether this is so depends on whether a subject would consider robust normativity an essential feature of 'what it takes to be', e.g. 'wrong', after the idealization procedure given in IA.[46] And it's at least plausible that such a judgment would survive the idealization procedure. Non-naturalists motivated by 'just too different' and 'where's the normativity?' intuitions against naturalist metaethics presumably think so.[47] This would ensure that our normative terms did pick out the robustly normative properties. All the conceptual competence theorist needs is a story about how robustness of referent is internal to the normative concepts themselves.

So far, so good. However, as we saw above, a response that is similar in spirit to this one was given above when discussing Huemer. We saw there that it would not work, but it is worth seeing why this variation on the strategy won't work either. Recall that Non-Accidentality and Content Success must be met with respect to the very same set of beliefs (Overlap). I claim that the explanation just given of how to meet Content Success undermines the account's ability to explain Non-Accidentality. The conceptual competence theorist who plumps for robust normativity as internal to the normative concepts themselves faces a dilemma in trying to meet Non-Accidentality and Content Success simultaneously. Return to Lucy and Carol. 'Badness' refers to different properties for Lucy and Carol, as their idealized divergence about lying shows.[48] Suppose that Lucy and Carol realize this. There are two ways they might react:

> *Relativity*: Lucy and Carol accept that 'badness' is not univocal, that they refer to different properties, and that this is an acceptable end to normative inquiry.
>
> *Univocal Robustness:* Lucy and Carol both take 'badness' to refer to a robustly normative property. Since they accept that there is only one robustly normative 'not-to-be-doneness'-type property (if any), they take their dispute about lying to be a genuine disagreement not settled by empirical information alone (otherwise idealization would have resolved the dispute).

Suppose that Relativity occurs. In that case, Non-Accidentality is met, since Lucy and Carol both have beliefs which are non-accidentally true. However, it is met at the cost of giving up on Content Success. By the non-naturalist's lights, there is a unique robustly normative property of *badness*. But since we could multiply cases like Lucy and Carol's indefinitely, if we accept Relativity then we can't preserve this fundamental commitment of non-naturalists.[49] So Relativity would result in an explanation of how our normative beliefs could be non-accidentally true, but it would fail to explain how our moral beliefs were of robustly normative facts – in fact, it would give us positive reason to believe that most of our moral terms do not refer to the robustly normative properties, since the possibility that our terms picked them out would be no better than chance, for all the conceptual competence theorist has said.

Alternatively, suppose Univocal Robustness occurs. Then moral terms, at least for Lucy and Carol, operate more like Kaplan's 'Newman1', picking out the robustly normative properties via something like an implicit reference-fixing description. Unique Robustness, then, is a situation in which Content Success is clearly met. However, this comes at the cost of undermining any reason to accept Non-Accidentality. If picking out the robustly normative properties is a non-negotiable feature of the semantics of our moral terms, then we'd need some independent reason for accepting that our first-order normative beliefs – idealized or not – are true, just as Kaplan would need some further evidence before accepting any first-order beliefs about Newman1. Kaplan might believe that Newman1 will become a philosopher, that he will have black hair, and that he will be an excellent knitter. These beliefs do no work toward fixing the content of 'Newman1', and none of them could be non-accidentally correct. They may, for all that we know, all be false and thus rejected under idealization. Now these rejected beliefs will, in the case of Newman1, be replaced by true beliefs under idealization, because part of the idealization process will involve giving Kaplan all the base level descriptive information about the world he needs to deduce all the facts about Newman1. However, in the normative case, base level descriptive information will not correct for fundamentally mistaken normative beliefs. By the non-naturalist's lights, non-normative information alone won't entail robustly normative facts (in any non-trivial way). Non-normative information alone won't help correct an agent's wildly mistaken first order normative beliefs.

As above, although instances of idealized disagreement help to illustrate the problem, the objection is not an argument from disagreement, nor does it require any disagreement, actual or possible, to succeed. The problem is that if our actual normative beliefs don't latch onto the robustly normative facts, then no amount of non-normative idealization will help to meet Content Success. Alternatively, if Content Success is met via building robust normativity into the semantics of normative terms, then no amount of non-normative idealization will help to meet Non-Accidentality. The lesson, then, is that no metasemantic view alone can tell us what actions, states of affairs, or persons to which the robustly normative properties apply.

7. Cuneo and Shafer-Landau on 'moral fixed points'

In an ambitious recent paper, Terence Cuneo and Russ Shafer-Landau's crucial claim is that 'there is a battery of substantive moral propositions ... that are also nonnaturalistic conceptual truths.'[50] They go on to argue that if this claim is accepted, it does a wide-ranging amount of metaphysical and epistemological work for the non-naturalist. (Here I am only worried about the alleged epistemological work that can be done.) For example, the following claims are, they argue, excellent candidates for being non-naturalistic conceptual truths:

It is pro tanto wrong to engage in the recreational slaughter of a fellow person.
It is pro tanto wrong to humiliate others simply for pleasure.
If acting justly is costless, then, *ceteris paribus*, one should act justly.[51]

First-order non-naturalistic conceptual truths such as these they call the *moral fixed points*. Any normative system which fails to endorse the moral fixed points would thereby not count as morality. Cuneo & Shafer-Landau argue that the moral concepts provide substantive constraints on moral theorizing.

A natural question arises: What reason do we have to believe that our moral concepts pick out anything stance-independent? Cuneo & Shafer-Landau's answer to this question appeals to what they call the 'traditional view' of concepts.[52] On the traditional view, concepts have three important features. First, concepts are the constituents of propositions.[53] Second, concepts are referential devices that 'enable thinkers to refer to things such as objects and properties.'[54] Finally, concepts are 'abstract, sharable, mind-independent ways of thinking about objects and their properties. As such, they are very much objective, 'out there' sorts of things, extra-mental items whose existence does not depend on our employing them in thought or language.'[55] As mind-independent entities, concepts have essences which underlie conceptual truths such as the moral fixed points.[56] This last feature of the traditional view is crucial for answering the above question. Our question was how individual moral representations can pick out anything mind-independent. The answer, once the traditional view is granted, is simple: Concepts themselves are mind-independent, so once we have a competent grasp of one, we already have a competent grasp of the essence of a mind independent entity.

We are now in a position to see how Cuneo & Shafer-Landau can use the traditional view along with the moral fixed points to explain Non-Accidentality.[57] Take some moral fixed point *m*. Now suppose I am conceptually competent with respect to the concepts (normative and otherwise) that figure in *m*. Suppose, furthermore, that upon reflection I accept *m*. My belief will be non-accidentally true: I formed it in light of my conceptual competence, and my conceptual competence ensures that, if I don't make some mistake, my belief is true. So my belief that *m* is not just true, but is true non-accidentally. And such an explanation will extend to the beliefs of all conceptually competent agents when their beliefs are of moral fixed points.

Cuneo & Shafer-Landau's view explains Non-Accidentality, at least with respect to the moral fixed points. But can these beliefs simultaneously explain Content Success? As we've seen, on Cuneo & Shafer-Landau's view, the truth-makers for a moral fixed point are just the concepts that make it up. No further 'worldly fact' is needed to ground its truth. This is what constitutes the fact that moral fixed points are conceptual truths. But neither are conceptual truths merely analytic truths. Analytic truths are sentences which are true in virtue of the meaning of the words that compose them. Analyticity, as Cuneo & Shafer-Landau understand it, is a linguistic, not metaphysical, phenomenon. Conceptual truths, on the other hand, are metaphysically robust in that they involve mind-independent essences. Since concepts have essences, and, as in the moral fixed points, concepts' essences bear relations to each other, it seems like a genuine possibility that moral concepts could themselves be robustly normative, on Cuneo & Shafer-Landau's view. If this were correct, then no further relation between the moral concepts and any non-natural properties would need to hold for robust normativity to get in the picture. The moral concepts would just have robust normativity built into their essences.

Grant that the traditional view of concepts is correct and that moral fixed points are true in virtue of the essences of the concepts that constitute them. Furthermore, grant that there are concepts which have robust normativity built into their conceptual essence. These three assumptions can clearly support an explanation of Non-Accidentality, but what about Content Success? It might seem as though Content Success can be explained, once we've granted that robust normativity is built into a concept's essence. By now the problem is a familiar one. Showing that we have substantive conceptual moral knowledge and that some concepts are robustly normative is not enough: We need to show that *our* moral concepts are the robustly normative ones. For again, there could be any number of alternative sets of broadly speaking normative concepts which deny some or all of the moral fixed points while affirming others. There are, for example, the *schmoral* concepts, and with them, the *schmoral* fixed points, which are conceptual truths grounded in the essences of the schmoral concepts.[58] We could enumerate such non-moral but broadly speaking normative sets of concepts, fixed points, and essences indefinitely. What we need is some reason to believe that our moral concepts, as opposed to any of these other sets, are the robustly normative ones. This is what explaining Content Success requires, and it is difficult to see how it would fall out of Cuneo & Shafer-Landau's view.

Interestingly, Cuneo & Shafer-Landau acknowledge a related point, asking 'Why think that we have reason to pledge our allegiance to *this* normative system, rather than another – call it *schmorality* – that fails to incorporate ... the moral fixed points?'[59] (I take it that they mean 'reason' here in the robustly normative sense.) In response to this question, they concede:

> It's an excellent question, but one that we don't propose to answer here ... this question is a perennial worry for *all* forms of moral realism ... And while regarding some substantive moral norms as a species of conceptual truth might not specifically aid us in explaining the reason-giving power of moral facts-, neither does it make our version of realism any less apt to offer such an explanation, whatever it may be.[60]

In itself, this is a fair enough concession: A single paper can't defend every controversial piece of non-naturalist metaphysics. However, this concession has a crucial epistemological upshot. We have no explanation – by Cuneo & Shafer-Landau's own lights – as to why we should think our moral concepts are robustly normative. There are any number of alternative systems of normative concepts, each from our epistemic standpoint equally likely to be the robustly normative concepts. For all that's been shown so far, we have more reason than not, probabilistically speaking, to think that our moral concepts are not robustly normative. This would mean that without further argument, Cuneo & Shafer-Landau have shown that (many of) our beliefs in the moral fixed points are non-accidentally true, but of no more normative interest than our beliefs about the rules guiding how one can move one's pawn in chess.[61]

8. Conclusion

A core commitment of non-naturalist moral realism is that there is some unique or nearly unique set of robustly normative facts. Moral norms, along with rational norms, share a distinctively binding normative authority that other conventional norms – such as the norms of chess – do not. Non-naturalists also separately acknowledge that, given the irreducible and non-causal nature of normative facts, some explanation must be given as to how our first-order justified moral beliefs could be non-accidentally true. This requirement is traditionally considered independent from the robustly normative nature and uniqueness of the normative facts. The arguments above have demonstrated that this is a mistake. Establishing *Non-Accidentality* does not establish that the robustly normative properties or concepts feature in those beliefs – that is, *Content Success*. Without further argument, we have no reason to believe that our normative beliefs, even if justified, pick out the robustly normative rather than some merely formally normative properties or concepts.

I have tried to defend the importance of integrating *Non-Accidentality* and *Content Success* by way of three case studies: Huemer (2005), Schroeter (ms), and Cuneo and Shafer-Landau (2014). Each of these approaches to meeting Non-Accidentality, while importantly distinct from each other, appeal to conceptual or semantic competence to attempt to resolve the epistemological worries. Each is subject to the same concerns related to the connection between *Non-Accidentality* and *Content Success*. At best, these views do not explain *Content Success*. At worst, the explanations given for *Non-Accidentality* undermine any chance at also explaining *Content Success*. The lesson here is not that we should give up on non-naturalist epistemology (though that is a possible response). Rather, the lesson is that non-naturalist epistemologists must pay close attention to the relationship between their explanation as to how our moral beliefs can be non-accidentally true and their explanation as to how our moral beliefs refer to the robustly normative. An adequate non-naturalist epistemology must show substantial overlap between the set of justified moral beliefs and the set of moral beliefs that pick out the robustly normative. For the non-naturalist, *Non-Accidentality* and *Content Success* need to stand or fall together. And while this may not be an impossible task, it is certainly non-trivial.

Notes

1. For arguments that it can't be met, see e.g. Street (2006), Fraser (2014), and Bedke (2014a). For attempts to meet it, see e.g. Enoch (2011, Ch.7), Parfit (2011), and Vavova (2014).
2. McPherson uses the distinction en route to a metaphysical argument against quietist non-naturalism. My argument differs in being (a) epistemological, and (b) intended to be of relevance to all non-naturalists, quietist or not.
3. See, for example, Copp (2005), McPherson (2011), Baker (2017).
4. Baker (2017), Section 2.
5. *Robustness* is not synonymous with *categoricity* on at least some understandings of the latter, as the case of etiquette (see Foot 1972) shows. Etiquette, for Foot, is categorical in the sense that agents are criticizable from the standpoint of etiquette regardless of their desires. This is compatible with the criticism in question's being merely formal criticism. However, on a more Kantian understanding of categoricity, where a fact is categorically binding just in case it applies to rational agents as such, is even more difficult to tease apart from robustness. I stick to the language of robustness throughout as to not assume any particular understanding of categoricity is correct.

   (Thanks to Nicole Dular and Hille Paakkunainen for discussion here.)
6. Similar distinctions could be made between robustly normative and formally normative propositions, standards, and rules.
7. This conception of robust normativity is meant to be compatible with the error theoretic claim that our moral concepts aim at picking out robustly normative properties but universally fail to do so. Such error theoretic concepts would not

be explicable without appeal to the idea of some fundamentally instrinsically binding entity – it just turns out that no such entity exists.
8. Shafer-Landau (2005, 15).
9. Authors who have considered claims related to Content Success for non-naturalists generally do not connect the issue with Non-Accidentality (see Schroeter (2014), Suikkanen (2017)). But see Bedke (2014b) for a related discussion concerning the relationship between the epistemic properties of normative beliefs and the (would-be) non-natural facts.
10. Audi (2008, 2015), Huemer (2005), Schroeter and Schroeter (2017), Shafer-Landau (2005), Cuneo and Shafer-Landau (2014), and Wedgwood (2007).
11. Foot (1995, 2).
12. Foot (1995, 2–3).
13. Conceptual role semanticists, such as Peacocke (1993) and Wedgwood (2001, 2007), may balk at this claim: Rival normative 'concepts' are defective, and thus not concepts at all, much like Prior's (1960) 'tonk'. But this response only moves the problem, rather than solving it. For now we have no reason to believe that it is us that have the genuine normative concepts, rather than defective 'concepts'. See Lenman (2010) on this point.
14. Huemer (2005, 124–125) contains an argument for realism about universals.
15. Huemer (2005, 122).
16. Huemer (2005, 200–201).
17. Huemer (2005, Ch. 8).
18. Huemer has defended this claim at length (Huemer 2001, 2007).
19. Huemer (2005, 125).
20. Huemer (2005, 126).
21. Huemer (2005, 126).
22. Note that 'adequacy' here is a technical term in Huemer's system.
23. Huemer (2005, 126).
24. Assuming, at least, that some of these beliefs based on an adequate understanding are first order normative beliefs. I grant Huemer this point in what follows. (Thanks to Hille Paakkunainen for pointing this out to me.).
25. Interestingly, a similar *Plenitude*-based strategy has been advanced as a way for the mathematical Platonist to meet Non-Accidentality, developed independently by Balaguer (1998) and Linsky and Zalta (1995).
26. It should be noted that the conditions on an adequate grasp of a universal are pretty difficult to meet. But I aim to grant Huemer as much as possible here.
27. It may also turn out that Carol and Lucy have subtly different concepts of LYING, as well. I set this aside for simplicity.
28. What if the chess and schmess players had some higher-order agreement that there is a unique fact about the single right way to play a chess-like game? Analogously, what if Lucy and Carol has some higher-order agreement that, whatever the case may be, their concepts aimed at the robustly normative, and thus their disagreement is not merely terminological? Because Schroeter (ms) clearly has machinery available to her to make this move, I address this kind of response below, in Section 6.1. But I think what I say there would apply, *mutadis mutandis* to a similar response made in Huemer's defense.
29. Paraphrasing Street (2006, 124–125).
30. I thank Matt Bedke for pointing out this possible response.
31. Could it be claimed that at least one of them has a concept that is not clear, consistent, and determinate, if they continue to have differing intuitions about whether lying is bad? It is hard to see that this *must* be the case, given that there

doesn't appear to be any internal incoherence in the claim that lying is [not] intrinsically bad.
32. Schroeter and Schroeter (2017, 14).
33. The wording is Schroeter and Schroeter (2017), 10. She credits Chalmers (2004) with the revision of Chalmers and Jackson's (2001) original proposal. A further minor complication is whether or not to include phenomenal information – the question turns on whether or not one thinks the phenomenal facts are reducible to the empirical – but settling this dispute is not important for present purposes.
34. Schroeter and Schroeter (2017, 9).
35. For much more discussion on such a vocabulary, see Chalmers (2012).
36. Schroeter and Schroeter (2017, 9), emphasis mine.
37. Schroeter and Schroeter (2017, 10).
38. Or at least, the true moral beliefs are a function of our actual moral beliefs, so our fundamental moral beliefs cannot be radically off track. I set this complication aside in what follows.
39. Schroeter & Schroeter call this 'Improvement' (see their 2017, 16).
40. They call this Property Identity. See Schroeter and Schroeter (2017, 11).
41. See, e.g. Shafer-Landau (2005, 93–95), Enoch (2011, 137–140). For Schroeter & Schroeter's discussion of this point, see their p.14.
42. They may deny that this divergence under idealization between Lucy and Carol can occur, as least so long as they are members of the same community. I return to this point shortly.
43. Schroeter and Schroeter (2017, 11).
44. I thank Matt Bedke for pressing me to clarify the objection of this section as well as my response to it.
45. Evans (1982, 25).
46. Recall from the previous section that it may turn out that non-naturalists must be committed to this if they are to avoid collapsing into naturalism.
47. See, for example, Enoch (2011, 104–109), Parfit (2011, Chs. 25–26), and Paakkunainen (2017). Thanks to Matt Bedke for pointing out the relationship between this motivation for non-naturalism and the argument of the text.
48. Of course it is also possible that the divergence is a result of their notions of 'lying', but I set this possibility aside for simplicity.
49. See Schroeter and Schroeter (2017, 22) for related discussion.
50. Cuneo and Shafer-Landau (2014, 2).
51. Cuneo and Shafer-Landau (2014, 7). They are explicit that, while these are excellent candidates for being conceptual truths, the specific examples they choose are irrelevant to the more general claim that some substantive first order normative claims are conceptual truths.
52. Cuneo and Shafer-Landau (2014, 11). As they freely admit, the traditional view is heavily indebted to Frege.
53. Cuneo and Shafer-Landau (2014, 11).
54. Cuneo and Shafer-Landau (2014, 12).
55. Cuneo and Shafer-Landau (2014, 11).
56. Cuneo and Shafer-Landau (2014, 13).
57. I should be clear that this is my best reconstruction of what I think they would say. They don't directly address *Non-Accidentality* in their paper, but they address enough related epistemic issues that I am confident that something like this is what they would say (See Cuneo and Shafer-Landau (2014), esp. Sections 4 and 5).

58. Some conceptual role semanticists, such as Peacocke (1993) and Wedgwood (2001, 2007), will balk at this claim, arguing that the schmoral 'concepts' are defective. This does not solve the problem – see n13.
59. Cuneo and Shafer-Landau (2014, 8–9).
60. Cuneo and Shafer-Landau (2014, 9).
61. Interestingly, Cuneo & Shafer-Landau reference an earlier Shafer-Landau article (2009) for a defense of the claim that there are categorical reasons. As noted above, categoricity is not the same as robust normativity, but they do seem to be closely related. However, whatever strengths Shafer-Landau's argument has in the categoricity case, it won't solve the present problem, because it relies on substantive first order judgments of the very sort which are in question.

Acknowledgments

For extremely helpful comments on earlier drafts of this paper, I am thankful to Matt Bedke, Ben Bradley, Teresa Bruno, Terence Cuneo, Nicole Dular, David Enoch, Nikki Fortier, Bar Luzon, Hille Paakkunainen, Russ Shafer-Landau, Byron Simmons, David Sobel, two anonymous referees, and an audience at the Central European University summer workshop in moral epistemology.

Funding

This work was supported by the Israel Science Foundation [grant number 1972/17].

References

Audi, Robert. 2008. "Intuition, Inference, and Rational Disagreement in Ethics." *Ethical Theory and Moral Practice* 11 (5): 475–492.
Audi, Robert. 2015. "Intuition and Its Place in Ethics." *Journal of the American Philosophical Association* 1 (1): 57–77.
Balaguer, Mark. 1998. *Platonism and Anti-Platonism in Mathematics*. Oxford: Oxford University Press.
Baker, Derek. (2017). "The Varieties of Normativity." *The Routledge Handbook of Metaethics*.
Bedke, Matthew. 2014a. "No Coincidence?" *Oxford Studies in Metaethics* 9: 76–101.
Bedke, Matthew. 2014b. "A Menagerie of Duties? Normative Judgments Are Not Beliefs about Non-Natural Properties." *American Philosophical Quarterly* 51 (3): 189–201.
Chalmers, David. 2004. "Epistemic Two-Dimensional Semantics." *Philosophical Studies* 118 (1/2): 153–226.
Chalmers, David. 2012. *Constructing the World*. Oxford: Oxford University Press.
Chalmers, David, and Frank Jackson. 2001. "Conceptual Analysis and Reductive Explanation." *Philosophical Review* 110 (3): 315–360.

Copp, David. 2005. "Moral Naturalism and Three Grades of Normativity." In *Normativity and Naturalism*, edited by Peter Schaber, 249–283. Frankfurt: Ontos-Verlag.

Cuneo, Terence, and Russ Shafer-Landau. 2014. "The Moral Fixed Points: New Directions for Moral Nonnaturalism." *Philosophical Studies* 171: 1–45.

Enoch, David. 2011. *Taking Morality Seriously*. Oxford: Oxford University Press.

Evans, Gareth. 1982. *The Varieties of Reference*. Oxford: Oxford University Press.

Foot, Philippa. 1972. "Morality as a System of Hypothetical Imperatives." *The Philosophical Review* 81 (3): 305–316.

Foot, Philippa. 1995. "Does Moral Subjectivism Rest on a Mistake?" *Oxford Journal of Legal Studies* 15 (1): 1–14.

Fraser, Benjamin James. 2014. "Evolutionary Debunking Arguments and the Reliability of Moral Cognition." *Philosophical Studies* 168 (2): 457–473.

Huemer, Michael. 2001. *Skepticism and the Veil of Perception*. Lanham: Rowman & Littlefield.

Huemer, Michael. 2005. *Ethical Intuitionism*. Basingstoke: Palgrave Macmillan.

Huemer, Michael. 2007. "Compassionate Phenomenal Conservatism." *Philosophy and Phenomenological Research* 74 (1): 30–55.

Lenman, James. 2010. "Uggles and Muggles: Wedgwood on Normative Thought and Justification." *Philosophical Studies* 151 (3): 469–477.

Linsky, Bernard, and Edward N. Zalta. 1995. "Naturalized Platonism versus Platonized Naturalism." *Journal of Philosophy* 92 (10): 525–555.

McPherson, Tristram. 2011. "Against Quietist Normative Realism." *Philosophical Studies* 154 (2): 223–240.

Paakkunainen, Hille. forthcoming. "The 'Just Too Different' Objection to Normative Naturalism." *Philosophy Compass*.

Parfit, Derek. 2011. *On What Matters*. Oxford: Oxford University Press.

Peacocke, Christopher. 1993. "How Are a Priori Truths Possible?" *European Journal of Philosophy* 1 (2): 175–199.

Prior, A. N. 1960. "The Runabout Inference Ticket." *Analysis* 21: 38–39.

Schroeter, Laura. 2014. "Normative Concepts: A Connectedness Model." *Philosopher's Imprint* 14 (25): 1–26.

Schroeter, Laura, and François Schroeter. 2017. "The Generalized Integration Challenge in Metaethics." *Nous*: 1–32.

Shafer-Landau, Russ. 2005. *Moral Realism: A Defence*. Oxford: Clarendon Press.

Shafer-Landau, Russ. 2009. "X-a Defence of Categorical Reasons." *Proceedings of the Aristotelian Society* 109(1pt2): 189–206.

Street, Sharon. 2006. "A Darwinian Dilemma for Realist Theories of Value." *Philosophical Studies* 127 (1): 109–166.

Suikkanen, Jussi. 2017. "Non-Naturalism and Reference." *Journal of Ethics and Social Philosophy* 11 (2): 1–24.

Vavova, Katia. 2014. "Debunking Evolutionary Debunking." *Oxford Studies in Metaethics* 9: 76–101.

Wedgwood, Ralph. 2001. "Conceptual Role Semantics for Moral Terms." *Philosophical Review* 110 (1): 1–30.

Wedgwood, Ralph. 2007. *The Nature of Normativity*. Oxford: Oxford University Press.

Index

Page numbers followed by "n" denote endnotes.

accommodation 19, 56
acknowledgement 9–12, 14, 21n11
Alethic Realism 268
Amsterdam 2
anti-representationalism 45, 63n12
assertoric disagreements 60
assertoric discourse 51, 57, 61
assertoric speech 51, 57, 58, 60–2
attitudes 180, 183–4, 189, 195n3; conative 39, 157, 158, 250; derivative moral 114; distinctive 145; full-fledged moral 126; non-cognitive 86, 94, 139, 249; non-judgment 129; propositional 39, 42n12, 116, 118, 128; self-directed reactive 18
attribute badness 80
authoritative normativity 12
authority: *Amsterdam* 2; cognitivist expressivism 1–2; experienced authority 1–2; metaethical expressivism 1, 4; moral judgments 1; moral realism 1; motivational dimension 2; normative justificatory dimension 2; reasons 2 (*see also* moral reasons experience); self-justification 3
The Authority of Reason 4
avant-garde nonnaturalism 258, 275, 276
Ayer, A. J. 81, 95–6, 99, 105, 108

Bedke, Matthew 237, 244–52
behavioral dispositional states 138
bifurcation thesis 47, 53–4, 57, 61
binding mechanism 180, 194
Björnsson, Gunnar 135–6, 141–8, 152–3
Blackburn, Simon 81, 200, 202, 228–9, 272
blaming 81
Block, N. 166

Boyd, Richard 200, 227
Boyd-style naturalist realism 6
Brandomian model 51
Brandom, Robert 50–1, 54, 57, 162–3, 223

categorical-authoritativeness phenomenology 7–8, 14
Chalmers, D. 281, 313
Chalmersian metasemantics 313
Chrisman, Matthew 53–5, 198–9, 202–8, 215–216, 222–5
chromatic illumination 20n6, 21n7
claims: distinct 13; expressivist 77–8; modal 54; moral 145, 157, 159–160, 162, 262; moral objectivist 7; normative 53; semantic 26, 169
cognitive dispositions 180, 183, 184, 189, 195n3
cognitive judgements 76
cognitive mechanisms 179
cognitive phenomenology 194
cognitivist expressivism 1–2, 15, 20, 22n20
communicative rules 101, 107
community-wide inferential norms 167
compelling rightness 5, 8, 11, 13
compositional account 81
compositional representations 117
compositional semantics 100
conative attitudes 39, 157, 158, 250
concepts *vs* Fregean senses 181–3
conceptual competence: BADNESS concepts 310–1; Chalmersian metasemantics 313; claims 309; coextensive properties 314; *Content Success* 307–8; Ideal Accessibility 314; internal conceptual robustness

316–318; intrinsic characteristics 309; LYING concepts 310–1; moral fixed points 318–20; non-accidental connection 304; normative properties 304–5; *Plenitude* statement 310, 312; robust and formal normativity 305–7; robust normativity 315
conceptual non-naturalism 22n15
conceptual role semantics 40, 232–3
consequentialism 241
content-determining semantic features 80
Content Success 307–8, 312
conversational dynamics 96
conversational score 50–1, 103
conversational state 52, 55–6
cooperative social behavior 164
Copp, D. 247, 305
correctness-conducive methods 86
creeping minimalism: EMU 208–9; e-representation 199, 209–11; ethical language 199; incompatibility 213–214; inferentialism 207–8; metaethical expressivism 198; minimalist views 199; moral realism 200; non-representational theories 199; representationalism 199; 'that'-clause 200; Tiefensee's arguments 211–2; unintelligibility 214–215; *see also* 'explanation' explanation
cultural-evolutionary explanations 138
culture-dependent norms 6
Cuneo, T. 285–6, 318–320

Davidsonian theory 231
daydreams 120
declarative sentences 26, 28–9, 45, 55, 78, 84
de dicto beliefs 245
deflationary accounts 25–6, 30, 33, 42n13, 43n17, 151
deflationism, *that*-clauses 42n11, 174, 228; ethical univocity, inferential account 157–9; meaning-attributions 31–4; meta-semantic expressivism 31, 38–41; non-representational fashion 31, 34–8; normativism 168–73
de jure sameness 149–150, 152–3
deontic modals 229
derivative moral attitudes 114
description-fitting sense (DF sense) 266–7
descriptive assertoric speech 62
descriptive content 96, 99–105
descriptive discourse 61

descriptive judgements 26
descriptive sentences 53, 84
descriptive speech 47, 50
distinct claims 13
distinctive attitude 145
Dreier, James 198, 200–6, 208, 212, 215–216, 237, 251–3
Dworkin, Ronald 258
dynamic semantics 50

Eleatic explanationism 225–6
emotivism 74, 96
EMU *see* Explanation of Meaning (EMU)
Enoch, D. 10
epistemic modal statements 102
e-representation 199, 209–11
error theory 13, 14, 114, 254n11
ethical judgments 244–6, 249
ethical naturalism 239, 254n8
ethical non-naturalism 10–1
ethical reality 247; adequacy condition 239–40; consequentialism 241; ethical naturalism 239; Evaluation-Based Condition 237–8; evaluative/normative properties 236; genuine evaluation 240; good-making properties 238, 240; motivational requirements 251–253; non-natural properties 237, 242–51; 'open-question' 238–9; pleasantness 239–41; right-making property 241; water concept 239
ethical univocity, inferential account: behavior-guiding aspects 165; cooperative social behavior 164; deflationism 157–9; dispositional forms 166; genuine disagreement 159–62; MAP 165; moral assertions 162–3; moral claims 157, 162; moral discourse 164; non-cognitive states 157; normativism 168–73; regulatory account 167–8; rules 165; socially-embedded practice 163
Evaluation-Based Condition 237–8
evaluative discourse 50, 56
evaluative sentences 51–2
evaluative speech 47
exaptation 127–9
expansive naturalism 246
experienced authority 1–2; Janus-faced 2, 8–11
'explanation' explanation: causal tracking 206; distinctive advantage 202; ethical facts and properties 202; ethical language 201, 205;

false beliefs 204; minimalism threat 205; moral judgement 201; nonrepresentational mental states 203; normative statements 201; ontology, representational accounts 203; representationalism 203; representational mental states 203
Explanationism 221–3
Explanationist criteria 229, 233
Explanation of Meaning (EMU) 208–9, 211–2, 225–6
expressivism 1–2, 74, 76–7, 212, 225, 229; anti-representationalist stance 47; bifurcation thesis 47; cognitivist 1; core concepts 29; declarative discourse 49; declarative sentences 26, 28–9; deflationary account 25–6, 30; deflationism 30 (see also deflationism, that-clauses); descriptive judgements 26; descriptive speech 47; evaluative speech 47; Frege-Geach Problem 28; functional pluralism 30; legitimacy 29; meaning-attributions 31; meaning-constituting properties 29; metaethical 1; 'meta-language' 27; meta-normative commitments 28; meta-normative expressivism 25; metasemantic proposals 46; meta-semantics 29; motivational dimension 47; non-descriptive speech 48; non-representational function 30, 47; normative judgements 26; normative speech 47; object-language 26; propositional contents 27, 31; psychologistic semantics 27–9; realism 209; representationalist metasemantics 46; representationalist theories 46; representational minimalism 48; representational states 26, 29; semantic claim 26; 'The Specification Problem' 135, 141–152; truth-conditional semantics 27–30
expressivist claims 77–8
expressivist models 61
external source 8
External Source 22n22

fallacies, metaethics: attribute badness 80; blaming 81; compositional account 81; conceptual framework 73; content-determining semantic features 80; expressivism 74, 76–7; fallacious reasoning 74; Frege-Geach point 74, 77–9; gambling 80–1;

logical consequence 83–4; moral judgements 74, 82–3; non-cognitivism 74–6; perspectival conception 83; perspectival contents 85–8; Schroeder's fallacy 84–5; semantic assignments 82; truth-values 82; Unwin's negation problem 79; valid argument form 82
fallacious reasoning 74
false assertion 57–8
fecund research program 93
fictionalism 42n16
Fine, Kit 202, 221, 223
fittingness-experience, phenomenological elements 8–9
Fodor, Jerry 126
force-indicator approach 89n15
Fregean sense model 182
Frege-Geach point 74, 77–9, 84
Frege-Geach problem 28, 113, 124
Frege, Gottlob 69, 94, 105, 149
full-fledged moral attitudes 126
functionalism 40, 284; moral 284, 285
functional pluralism 30
functional role 39–40

gambling 78–81, 80–1
Geach, P. T. 77–81, 106, 115
genuine disagreement 159–62, 169
Gibbard, Allan 6, 202, 220, 223–4, 228–9, 232, 237, 243–4, 250
global pragmatism: assertoric discourse 51; Brandomian model 51; Brandom's inferentialism 50; characteristic functions 49; conversational score 50–1; descriptive speech 50; dynamic semantics 50; evaluative discourse 50; mental states 49; metasemantic thesis 49; non-representationalist account 51; non-representational pragmatism 49; semantic features 49; Stalnakerian model 50; static semantic theory 50; use-based theory 49
Golub, Camil 213, 222, 228–31
good-making properties 238, 240
good-statements 108, 110n14
grip 8, 17, 20n6
grounding relations 287–9
guiding conception 188, 191–2, 195n5

Hampton, J. 2, 4, 8, 10–1, 13, 15, 17–18
Hare, R. M. 81, 96, 99
Hills, A. 282
hope 86, 121, 159

Horgan, T. 141
Horwich, Paul 213, 223, 230–1
Huemer, Michael 309–313, 315–316
Hume 75, 76, 86, 87
Humean intuition 53–4
hybrid expressivism 125–6

Ideal Accessibility (IA) 314
immigration restrictions 122
'inconsistency-transmitting' attitude 140
independence 8, 18
inescapable-authoritativeness phenomenology 14
inescapable necessity 8, 18
inferentialism 43n18, 207–8, 223–5
inferentialist program 224
inflationary metaethics 158, 164
information-bundling system 184
information-carrying states 180
information-management system 179
intellectual intuition 87
intensional operators 97, 99, 105
i-representation 209, 211

Jackson, F. 237, 243–4, 250, 284, 313
James, LeBron 106

Kant, Immanuel 94, 105
Kaplan 179, 317
Khan, Genghis 149

Levitical community 168
Lewis, David 35, 51, 72
licensing assertion 270
linguistic community 144–5, 150, 152, 231
looming trilemma: acknowledgement 9–12; authoritative normativity 12; 'compelling rightness' 11; ethical non-naturalism 10–1; metaethical theory 9; metaphysics 9, 11–2; moral-authority phenomenology 12; moral error theory 10–2; moral judgments 10–2; motivational dimension 12; preservation 9, 11–2; reductive ethical naturalism 10–1; reductive expressivism 10

MacFarlane, John 58, 60
Mackie, J. L. 2, 4, 6–7, 13, 222
'make-true' operator 96
MAP *see* Moral Attitude Problem (MAP)
McEwan, I. 2–3
McPherson, Tristram 135–6, 141–8, 152–3, 305

meaning-attributions 31; meta-semantic expressivism 38; non-representationalism 35–8; *that*-clauses 31–4
meaning-constituting properties 29, 38, 40
meaning-explananda 32–3
Meinongian Strategy 262–3, 273–4
mental filing system 179–81; representational purport 183–91
Merli, D. 160–1, 166, 168, 171, 173
metaethical non-cognitivism: cognitive judgements 76; emotivism 74; empirical justification 76; epistemological 75; expressivism 74; The Formula 75; metaphysical 75; moral judgements 74; moral statement 74; psychological 75
metaethics 94; commitments 41; descriptivism 106; expressivism 1, 4; fallacies (*see* fallacies, metaethics); inferentialism 173; perspectival representational contents (*see* perspectival representational contents); project 109; spectrum 161; theory 2, 4, 9
meta-language 27, 31–2
meta-level reflection 178
meta-normative expressivism 25
metaphysical commitments 37
'metaphysical discovery' 237, 246
metaphysical naturalism 258–60, 273
metaphysics 9, 11–2, 14, 19, 21n11
meta-semantics 29, 231; expressivism 31, 38–41
metasemantic thesis 49
'mind-entry' conditions 40
minimalism's revenge: incompatibility 213–214; unintelligibility 214–215
mixed normative judgments 116
modal claims 54
modal judgments 94
modal-operator account 94
modus tollens 78
Moore, G. E. 105, 222–3, 238–9, 281, 283–4
moral assertions 14, 161, 162–3, 172, 258
Moral Attitude Problem (MAP) 160–1, 165–6, 174, 175n20
Moral attitudes: cognitive structure 116; cognitivists and noncognitivists 114; compositional representations 117; derivative moral attitudes 114; diversity and unity 130; error theory

114; exaptation 127–9; Frege-Geach problem 113; logical complication 115, 130n2; mixed normative judgments 116; moral judgments 113–114; negation 115; non-semantic properties 116; normative noncognitivism 113; orthographic identities 117–118, 131n6; predicative forms 115; propositional attitudes 116; quantification 115; 'recipe semantics' 114 (*see also* recipe semantics); representational properties 116, 130n4; RTM 116–117; social expectations coordination 126–7; spandrel contexts 118, 126, 131n8; truth-functional interpretations 115; utilitarianism 116

moral-authority phenomenology 12–13, 16, 22n18
moral claims 145, 157, 159–160, 162, 262
moral disagreement 142, 156; *see also* genuine disagreement
moral discourse 143, 164, 170–1
moral error theory 1, 10–2
moral fixed points 318–20
moral functionalism 284–5
moral judgements 1, 9–12, 14, 74–5, 82–3, 113–114
moral normative authority 5; 'outsideness' 7
moral objectivist claims 7
Moral Quietism 264
moral realism 1, 10
moral reasons experience: first stage 4–5; metaethical theory 4; non-naturalist moral realism 4; normativity 4; second stage 5–9
moral supervenience: conceivability to possibility 291–4; evaluative attitudes 280; moral truths 297n8; Moral Twin Earth 299n18; NTI&M conceivability (*see* NTI&M conceivability); 'phenomenal yellow' concept 281; primitivist moral realism 294–6
Moral Twin Earth 141, 145, 299n18
motivation 8–9; commitment 4; dimension 2, 9, 12, 47

Nagel, Thomas 258
natural language sentences 117
necessarily co-extensive sense (NCE sense) 266
NECESSITARIANISM 292, 296
negational moral judgments 122, 131n10

neo-pragmatism 135, 153; assertoric form 140; behavioural dispositional states 138; biological-evolutionary explanations 137; causal/historical theory 139; cultural-evolutionary explanations 138; first-order phenomena 136; 'inconsistency-transmitting' attitude 140; metaphysical methods 138; non-cognitive attitude 139; non-linguistic primates 137; reference relations 136; 'The Specification Problem' (*see* 'The Specification Problem,' expressivism); truth-assessments 139–141; truth-talk account 138; uniformity 137; verbal descriptions 140

neutrality thesis 13–14, 16
Newman1 317
non-cognitive attitudes 84, 86, 94, 139, 249
'non-cognitive' judgements 90n21
non-cognitivism 68, 74–6, 88; 'The Specification Problem,' expressivism 142–8
non-descriptive assertoric speech 62
non-descriptive discourse 61
non-descriptive sentences 53
non-descriptive speech 46, 48, 53, 56
nondescriptivist views: communicative rules 107; fecund research program 93; good-statements 108, 110n14; intensional operators 105; measurement functions 106; metaethical descriptivism 106; metaethics 94; modal judgments 94; modal-operator account 94; non-cognitive attitudes 94; nonrepresentationalism 107; normative and evaluative statements 94–6; ought-statements 93–4 (*see also* ought-statements); planning states 94; prescriptions 94; representationalism 106; scalar rules 106
non-judgment attitudes 129
non-linguistic primates 137
non-motivating moral judgment 147
'non-naturalistic' fallacy 14, 19
non-naturalist moral realism 4, 14
non-natural properties 237, 242–3; belief loss 244–9; direct discovery 249–51; motivational requirements 251–3; superfluousness 243–4
non-normative belief 39

Non-Realist Cognitivism: avant-garde nonnaturalism 258; licensing assertion 270; Meinongian Strategy 262–3, 273–4; moral assertions 258; moral claims 257, 262; moral facts 262; motivation 259–60; non-causal making-true relation 270; Non-Referential Strategy 262, 264–8, 271–2; normative naturalism 261; orthodox nonnaturalism 257, 260; pleonastic sense 268; quasi-realist expressivism 269; Semantic Quietism 263–4; semantic theory 263; weighty ontological implications 269; Wide Non-Realist Strategy 263
nonreductive expressivism: action-guidance 16; 'cognitivist expressivism' 15; moral assertions 14; non-descriptive beliefs 16; non-reductive metaethical expressivism 15; ought-commitment 15; psychological commitment state 15
non-reductive metaethical expressivism 15
Non-Referential Strategy: Alethic Realism 268; description-fitting sense (DF sense) 266–7; expressivism 271–2; licensing assertion 270; necessarily co-extensive sense (NCE sense) 266; non-causal making-true relation 270; ontological weightiness 264; pleonastic sense 265, 268; quasi-realist expressivism 269; weighty ontological implications 269
non-relativistic assertion 46, 63n14
non-representational account 42n11
non-representational function 30, 47
non-representationalism 107, 224
nonrepresentational mental states 203
non-representational pragmatism 49
non-representational theories 199
normative authority 4, 5, 170, 304
normative belief 39, 251, 306–8, 312, 313, 315–18
normative claims 53, 141, 160, 242, 253n1
normative concepts 177, 193–5, 242, 253n6, 267, 283, 284, 306–8, 312, 313, 316, 319, 320
normative dimension 9
normative discourse 45; bifurcation thesis 53; conversational state 52; descriptive sentences 53; evaluative sentences 51–2; Humean intuition 53–4; inferentialist model 52; justification 54; modal claims 54; motivation 54; non-descriptive sentences 53; normative claims 53; ought-claims 54
normative ethical symbols 95
normative judgements 26, 39–40
normative justificatory dimension 2
normative noncognitivism 113
normative speech 46, 47, 51, 54
normativist inferentialism 173
NTI&M conceivability: conceptual entailments 283–6; conceptual truth 282; essentialism 289–91; normative theory 283; synthetic a priori entailments 287–9

'objectivist' thesis 6
object-language 26, 31–2
Ogden, C. K. 81
O'Leary-Hawthorne, J. 202, 221
Olson, J. 12, 13
Olson-style error theory 19
ontological commitments 13, 211, 253n1
ontological weightiness 264
Ortcutt, Bernard J. 178
orthodox nonnaturalism 257, 260, 274
orthographic identities 117–118, 131n6
ought-claims 54
ought-statements 223; descriptive content 99–105; embedded uses 110n10; modal operator 96–9

paradigmatic moral judgments 146–8
Parfit, Derek 258–9, 264–71, 273
person-level phenomenon 186–7
perspectival conception 70–2, 83
perspectival representational contents 85–8, 88n2; classic conception 69–70; correctness status 71; explanatory uniformity 73; judgement and claim 71; objectivity requirement 70; perspectival conception 71; representation 67–9; truth-values 70, 72; uncontroversial representations 71; unstructured contents 72
Plato 222–3
pleasantness 239–41
pleonastic sense 265, 268
prescriptivism 96, 102
preservation 9, 11–2, 14, 19, 21n11
Price, Huw 30, 45, 138–40, 199, 202, 207, 209, 216, 221, 223
primitivist moral realism 294–6
propositional attitudes 39, 42n12, 116, 118, 128

propositional contents 27, 31, 37, 78–9, 97
psychological motivation 86
psychologistic semantics 27–9
Psychologized Semantics 34, 41n3
psycho-social thesis 6–7
pull 8, 9, 17, 18
Pylyshyn, Zenon 186

quasi-realism 22n16
quasi-realist expressivism 269
Quine, Willard V. O. 117

real and quasi-real: conceptual role semantics 232–3; Davidsonian theory 231; deflationism 228; deontic modals 229; Eleatic explanationism 225–6; error theory 222–3; Explanationism 221–3; Explanationist criteria 229, 233; expressivism 229; inferentialism 223–5; linguistic community 231; meta-semantics 231; moral beliefs 221; non-naturalist realism 221; non-representationalism 222; representationalism 222; self-described Pragmatists 220; Simpson's explanationism 226–8; tautological conception 230; truth conditions 230
recipe semantics: attribute representational contents 123; daydreams 120; hope 121; hybrid expressivism 125–6; moral attitudes 120–1; negation 122–3; non-mental representations 118; non-representational presentations 119; orthographic class 119; orthographic properties 124; predicative moral judgments 124; presentational theory of mind 119–120; propositional attitudes 118; resemble error theory 124; traditional expressivism 124–5
reductionist approach 34
reductive ethical naturalism 10–1
reductive expressivism 10, 19
reductive functional analysis 284
reductive naturalism 19
reference-fixing criteria 149, 182
reference-points 35–6
'regions of modal space' 99–100
relativism: assertoric discourse 61; bifurcation thesis 61; correctness-standards 57; descriptive discourse 61; expressivism 59–61; false assertion 57–8; non-defective conversational state 57; non-descriptive discourse 61; non-relativistic assertoric speech 62; relativistic disagreements 59; relativistic discourse 58; semantic features 58
relativistic assertion 46, 59, 63n14, 64n15
relativistic discourse 58
representational account 159, 203
representational concepts 119–20, 123, 131n8, 177, 191
representationalism 26, 32, 101, 105, 106, 199, 203, 212, 217n13, 224
representationalist metasemantics 46
representationalist theories 46
representational mental states 68, 203
representational minimalism 46, 48
representational purport: 'bad manners' 188; biological characteristics 190; coherence requirement 187; coherent instantiation conditions 190; core features 189; epistemic oversight 184, 186; features tracking 192; guiding conception 188, 191–2, 195n5; long-term binding and storage 183–6; mental filing system, features 183, 185; 'morally right' 191, 196n8; *Mutatis mutandis* 193; natural and artifact 183; non-normative descriptive properties 192; normative concepts 194; open-ended learning 190; ordinary physical objects 183; outward-directed engagement 187; person-level phenomenon 186–7; reflective equilibrium 193; reflective moral epistemology 192; reinterpretation 184–6; self-regulation 189; shared filing tradition 191; 'Trump' judgments 189; visual indices 186
Representational Theory of Mind (RTM) 116–117, 119, 121
Richards, I. A. 81
Ridge, Michael 39
right-making property 241
Rosen, G. 27, 289–90, 294

scalar rules 106
Scanlon, T.M. 258
Schroeder, Mark 27, 74, 81, 84–5, 140
Schroeter, François 135–6, 142, 149–52, 153, 313–318
Schroeter, Laura 135–6, 142, 149–52, 153, 313–318
self-directed reactive attitudes 18
self-regulation 189
Sellarsian account 34–8, 40, 42n16

INDEX

Sellars, Wilfrid 26, 33–4, 54, 223
semantic assignments 82
semantic claims 26, 169
Semantic Quietism 263–4
semantic values 62n2, 143
Shafer-Landau, R. 259, 285–6, 318–320
Simpson, Matthew 222–3, 226–8
Skorupski, John 258, 273–4
social flexibility 127
spandrel contexts 118, 126, 131n8
'The Specification Problem,' expressivism: community-referential account 149–52; Earthlings 141–2; moral disagreement 141; Moral Twin Earth arguments 141; non-cognitivism 142–8; normative claims 141; Twin Earthlings 141–2
Stalnakerian model 50
static semantic theory 50
Stevenson, C. L. 15, 81, 160
structural flexibility 128
subpersonal cognitive mechanisms 177, 179, 181

test dynamics: assertoric discourse 57; bifurcation thesis 54, 57; conversational state 55–6; declarative sentences 55; evaluative discourse 56; metaconceptual operations 54; modal claims 54; modal sentences 56; non-modal sentence 56
theoretical modelling exercise 37
Tiefensee, Christine 199, 206–12
Timmons, M. 141
translation 31–2
Trump, Donald J. 178–9, 184–5, 188
truth-assessments 139–141
truth-conditional semantic model 27–30, 34, 41n2, 110n10
truthmakers 158, 168
truth-talk account 138, 139
truth-values 69–70, 72, 82

Unwin, Nicholas 79–81
utilitarianism 116, 282, 283, 292, 296

Wedgwood, Ralph 27, 232
Wide Non-Realist Strategy 263
Williams, M. 164, 171, 199, 202, 207–9, 211, 216, 223, 225–6, 231
Williamson, Timothy 296
Wittgenstein, Ludwig 139
wrong-makingness account 243–4, 250